The Epistle to the Hebrews

The Epistle to the Hebrews

David J. Garrard

RESOURCE *Publications* · Eugene, Oregon

THE EPISTLE TO THE HEBREWS

Resource Publications
An Imprint of Wipf and Stock Publishers
199 W. 8th Ave., Suite 3
Eugene, OR 97401

www.wipfandstock.com

PAPERBACK ISBN: 978-1-6667-7593-8
HARDCOVER ISBN: 978-1-6667-7594-5
EBOOK ISBN: 978-1-6667-7595-2

08/28/23

Unless otherwise indicated, the verses in this commentary are translated from Barbara Aland et al., eds., *The Greek New Testament*, 5th rev. ed. (Stuttgart: Deutsche Bibelgesellschaft, 2014).

Contents

Abbreviations	*vii*
The Epistle to the Hebrews	*xi*
1.	1
2.	26
3.	49
4.	67
5.	81
6.	90
7.	105
8.	124
9.	139
10.	166
11.	195
12.	229
13.	256
Appendix A	279
Appendix B	282
Appendix C	283
Appendix D	287
Appendix E	289
Appendix F	291
Appendix G	293
Bibliography	295

Abbreviations

11Q	Qumran cave number 11.
AD	Anno Domini–In the year of our Lord
aor.	aorist
Arndt & Gingrich	Arndt, W.F and Gingrich, F.W. *A Greek English Lexicon of the New Testament and other Early Christian Literature*, (an English translation of W. Bauer's, *Griechisch-deutsches Wörterbuch zu den Scriften des Neuen Testaments und der übrigen urchristlichen Literature* (4th Ed.) 1949–52),
BC	Before Christ
C.	Century
c.	circa/about
ch.	chapter
chs.	chapters
cms.	centimeters
Coverdale	*The Coverdale Bible*
Darby	*The Darby Bible*
DRCongo	Democratic Republic of Congo
ed.	edition
ERV	Easy to Read Version
ESV	*English Standard Version*
cms.	centimeters
et al.	Latin *et alia* which means: and others when referring to references.
fut.	future
GNT	Good News Translation

Hist. Eccl.	Eusebius Pamphilus' *Historia Ecclesisastica*. English: *Ecclesiastical History*
HNT	*Handbuch zum Neuen Testament*. Mohr Siebeck, Tübingen.
ICC	International Critical Commentary
ins.	inches
ind.	indicative
JGRChJ	Journal of Greco-Roman Christianity and Judaism. McMaster Divinity College. Hamilton ONT. Canada.
Leg. Alleg.	*Legum allegoriae.On the Allegorical Interpretation of the laws*, Philo.
LXX	The Septuagint version of the Old Testament in Greek.
Macc.	Maccabees
masc.	masculine
MEV	*Modern English Version*
MS	Manuscript
MSS	Manuscripts
NASB	*New American Standard Bible*
NASC	*New American Standard Version*
NIB	*New International Bible*
NIV	*New International Version*
NLT	*New Living Translation*
n. pl.	No place (Publication)
NRSV	*New Revised Standard Version*, Anglicized version, Oxford, Oxford University Press, 1989, 1995.
NT	New Testament
OT	Old Testament
p.	person
perf.	perfect
Phillips	*New Testament in Modern English*
pl.	plural
pres.	present
REB	*Revised English Bible*

rev.	Revised
RSV	*Revised Standard Bible*
sing.	singular
SPCK	Society for Promoting Christian Knowledge
subj.	subjunctive
TLV	*Living Bible*
TWNT	*Theologische Wörterbuch zum Neuen Testament.* 10 vols. Edited by Gerhard Kittel and Gerhard Friedrich. Stuttgart: Kohlhammer, 1932–79.
TDNT	*Theological Dictionary of the New Testament.* 10 vols. Edited by Gerhard Kittel and Gerhard Friedrich. Translated by Geoffrey W. Bromiley. Grand Rapids: Eerdmans, 1964–76.
Wycliffe	*The Wycliffe Bible*
ZNTWT	*Zeitschrift für die Neutestamentliche Wissenschaft und die Kunde des Urchristentums*, Walter de Gruyter, Berlin.
v.	verse
vv.	verses

Textual sources

{A}	the text is certain	
{B}	the text is almost certain	
{C}	a high degree of difficulty deciding the text.	
א 01	[Aleph] Sinaiticus	4th C.
A 02	Alexandrinus	4th C.
B 03	Vaticanus	4th C.
C 04	Epraemi Rescriptus	5th C.
D 05	Canatbrigiensis	5th C.
K	Moscow	9th C.
L	Paris	8th C.
P	Paris	8th C.
Ψ 044	Athos	9–10th C.

𝔓13   Papyrus   3–4th C.

𝔓46   Papyrus including Pauline literature from 3rd C.

The Epistle to the Hebrews

General Introduction

The Epistle to the Hebrews is one of the books of the New Testament concerning which there are many questions that are, up to the present, the subject of scholarly debate. This commentary does not pretend to enter into the depths of the scholarly and critical debate which preoccupies much of New Testament scholarship at present. Its purpose is to present a clear interpretation of the themes that are present by means of an explanation of the material at hand. For those who are familiar with *Koinē* Greek (the Common Greek of the first Century AD) some words and phrases are transliterated to help in understanding the nuances which the language presents but this does not mean that if the reader is not familiar with Greek that this should limit their grasp of what is written. I have undertaken my own translation of the Greek Text (*The Greek New Testament*, 5th Rev. ed.) as an aid to all who follow through the exposition of each verse. This translation tends to be quite literal in order to facilitate the purpose of the interpretation but there are times when for the sake of understanding some adverbs, adjectives, prepositions, nouns and even verbs, extra words have been added because they are most certainly part of the thinking of the original grammatical construction. Some of the additions are included between brackets. All verses are recorded in italics but italics with the inclusion of quotation marks. Italics are also used for emphasis in the comments.

The nature of the communication

Unlike the other letters of the New Testament, Hebrews does not start like a letter at all. It has none of the marks of the other New Testament letters where authors introduce themselves and give some indication as to who it is to whom they write. Has the opening paragraph been lost at some point? It seems unlikely, since there is no indication in any manuscript found, that this is a possibility and there is no difficulty either with style or grammar when it comes to the first sentence as it stands at present. The opening words are perfectly logical and flowing in their presentation so, it is highly unlikely that any part of the original introduction is missing. The ending certainly shows all signs of a personal letter with its request for prayer, some personal information, plans to visit together with Timothy and the mention that this is to be viewed as *a few words* that the author has addressed to this specific, yet unnamed community (13:22, 23).

The Title, the Recipients & the Purpose of the Epistle

The title: *Pros Ebraious,* is literally: *to Hebrews.* There is no clarity as to the origin of the title, if indeed it was the original name afforded to the writing by its author. Bruce points out that this letter was known by Clement of Rome about 96 AD[1] but it was, according to Bruce, only later in the second century that the name by which we know it now is found appended to the writing.[2] The earliest manuscript found, containing the present letter's title, is included in the papyrus $\mathfrak{P}46$ on a page, of what is entitled as the Pauline body of literature. It was for this reason that it was for many, included as one of the writings of Paul.[3]

Was it addressed only to Jews? From the content of the letter and the heavy dependence upon the Old Testament, as well as the way in which the arguments are presented, it appears that those who were its intended recipients were Jewish Christians and not Hellenistic Jews. This is because they are encouraged to go on with their faith and not to go back to the shadows of the figures portrayed in the past. All that was pictured by the faith of the past is now fulfilled in Jesus.

Some authors, including, Käsemann, Moffatt and Windisch[4] held views that the letter was written to Christians from a Gentile context who were considering renouncing completely their faith in the living God (3:12) but that does not seem to be the center of the thought presented by the author in this work because the argument, in their view, is about going back to

1. Bruce, *Hebrews*, xxiiin3.

2. Bruce, *Hebrews*, xxiiin4.

3. Bruce, *Hebrews*, xxiiin4. However, later he states that this does not tie in with the comment made by the author regarding their not having shed blood. *Hebrews*, 267.

4. Käsemann, *Das wandernde Gottesvolk.* [1938]; Moffatt, *Hebrews*, xvi; Windisch, *Der Hebräerbrief,* 31.

THE EPISTLE TO THE HEBREWS

dead works and trusting in external religious acts and not abandoning God altogether. There are more than a few portions of the letter which make it very clear that those to whom the instruction was addressed were considering going back to what was their previous practice of outward observances (see 6:1–8), so it is unlikely that these were non-Jews taking up some form of rule keeping.

The emphasis upon the Old Covenant as the system to which the readers wanted to adhere as their authority, makes it very clear that the recipients would have been familiar with the writings which dominate the letter from start to finish. Matters such as the Jewish priesthood, and individuals like Melchizedek, together with the list of people of faith, would be relatively obscure to non-Jews, who would have been unfamiliar with the details of the Old Testament. If that were the case, then the force of the argumentation throughout would have not meant anything to them. They must have been Jews, so whatever the original title may or may not have been, the present is certainly pertinent.

What then can be said of the people to whom the letter was addressed? It is not possible to be dogmatic since there is no clear indication given in the text. However, Bruce believes that, "One of the most persuasive views of its purpose regards it as written to a 'house church' or synagogue of Jewish Christian in Rome who found themselves out of sympathy with the prevalent trend of Roman Christianity" and as a consequence they were thinking about withdrawing and going back to Judaism.[5] However, since as is stated later in this commentary that the author says none of them has spilled blood during the maintenance of their faith in Christ (12:4) and as early as AD 64 there were martyrs at Rome, this is unlikely (see notes on 10:32). Consequently, the truth is that this suggestion regarding the addressees is only conjecture. Certainly, the addressees would have been known by the author (as is clear from the conclusion of the letter), who also knew their circumstances and their present tendencies to abandon their following after Christ. The way in which the contents are presented are such that two factors are central: on the one hand the Old Testament and on the other Christ.[6] What is known to us as 'The Old Testament' or Hebrew Bible, was the source of authority, the unequivocal word of God himself, for the author. However, he is also making it very clear that Christ is the one who introduces this New Covenant, which does away with and replaces the Old. The latter could never satisfy God's demands through the Levitical system.

---

5. Bruce, *New Testament History*, 378. who points to a reference by W. Manson, *Hebrews*.

6. See Ellingworth, *Hebrews*, (Epworth Commentaries), ix.

He is writing as someone who knows the Jewish Scriptures well and who is basing his reckoning totally upon what those scriptures have to say as through them, one is pointed to the coming of the Messiah or for the Greek speaker: the Christ. He wants his readers to recognize that the Christ, over whom they appear to hesitate, is at the heart of all that the Old Testament has to say about the future. Indeed, the background in the Levitical legal system, was fading away long ago because it pointed to the one who would supersede everything promised under that covenant. So, the author carefully draws upon a number of texts which demonstrate the specific points which he wishes to make in this letter. All of these are intended to highlight the superiority and design of God to replace what was in the past and imperfect, with an entirely new way of doing things through Christ, who was and is God's Son; he is the person through whom all things were created (1:2).

There is no doubt but that the author was most familiar with the Septuagint (LXX),[7] the Greek translation of the Hebrew Bible. It is for this reason that it is widely held by scholars that the LXX is the Greek text which stands behind the sections drawn from the Old Testament in the letter to the Hebrews, or at least that there must have been a Greek text upon which the arguments are based. There is no evidence that the author spoke or wrote any Hebrew. The texts from the LXX, which he uses are carefully expanded and even interpreted, to emphasize every point where there are comparisons.

Even if the original of this letter was addressed to Christians from a Jewish background and we need to understand what that meant for them, the task of the modern reader is to understand how the past and the present in each person's life, no matter what their language or culture, has to be grasped in the light of varying circumstances and how in everything, Christ has to have first place. He has to be the overarching theme of every individual's hope or all else will be in vain. The same warnings given to the Hebrews are presented to each person, in every age so that the outcome of all choices is absolutely vital in determining one's status for eternity.

---

7. The Septuagint (LXX) was the Greek translation of the Hebrew Bible or what we know as the Old Testament. It was supposedly translated by seventy scholars located at Alexandria in Egypt.

The Date

Raymond Brown says that the persecution mentioned in 10:32–34 would appear to refer to that which occurred at the time of Nero in 64 AD.[8] However the nature of the persecution mentioned in those verses is too general to be able to link it specifically to Nero. It could be any persecution which, as we know, became more pronounced as time went on. Bruce thinks that this persecution could more likely indicate the period when Jewish believers were forced to leave Rome in 49 AD.[9] If this is correct then it depends upon his theory that the Hebrews were part of a house group in Rome who were not necessarily representative of all believers who lived in Rome and that is yet to be demonstrated.[10] Again, because the author is unknown and there is no clear indication within the letter itself regarding historical factors such as the destruction of the temple in Jerusalem, which could help pin down the date, it is difficult to be precise as to the date of the Epistle. We do know that Clement of Rome refers to material from Hebrews in his letter to the Corinthians, known as 1 Clement.[11] That letter was written about 96 AD. There have been many scholarly assertions as to the date of writing from 63 to 95 AD. Much is speculative but it is most likely that the Hebrews was written sometime between the year 50–95 AD.

The Author

From the earliest of years, the identity of the author has been unclear. There have been numerous attempts on the part of scholarship to determine its origins and authorship. The assumed association with Paul by the Alexandrians, influenced views held by those in the East and later those in the West and has held sway periodically for large portions of time throughout its history. Most likely this was due, in part, to the link between its appearance in the manuscript associated with the Pauline corpus. But even at Alexandria not all the members of that school of thought were convinced of its Pauline authorship. Eusebius writing in the fourth century said that some in the Roman church disputed Hebrews' place in the canon because they did not accept its Pauline authorship.[12]

---

8. Brown, *Hebrews*, 17.

9. Bruce, *New Testament History*, 281 & 378.

10. Bruce, *New Testament History*, 378.

11. Clement of Rome, 1 *Clement to the Corinthians*, see as in 17:1, 5 et al.

12. Eusebius, *Historia Ecclesiastica*, iii.3.5.

Clement of Alexandria said it was written in Hebrew by Paul and translated into Greek by Luke. Origen who came later and who was versed in both Greek and Hebrew, said that it had not been translated from Hebrew because the author uses the Septuagint (LXX) translation of the Greek when he cites from the Old Testament and his style shows this very clearly. He writes of the superiority of the Greek expression in Hebrews being far better than anything in the Pauline writings. He felt that it may have had Paul's thoughts and influence behind it but as to who it was that actually wrote it was another matter and no one really knew who the author was. Consequently, he could say as quoted by Eusebius: "But who wrote the epistle, in truth, God knows."[13] Eusebius suggests that Clement of Rome may well have been the author.[14] Others who did not ascribe the letter to Paul included Irenaeus,[15] Hippolytus[16] and Gaius of Rome.[17]

Tertullian thought that the author must have been Barnabas.[18] Scholars reckon that this preference of his was due to the fact that it was the most commonly held view at that time and logically followed Barnabas' association with Paul and the other apostles. Some like Hughes, citing Weiss and Salmon, indicate that Barnabas' standing in the apostolic community, his association with Paul and his Jewish training together with his ability to teach and engage in missionary service are important factors in favor of his consideration.[19] Since the Reformation there have been those like Luther who rejected the Pauline authorship[20] and a number of more recent scholars who considered Hebrews to be Apollos' work because of his Jewish roots and links with Alexandria.[21] However, it is considered that this is most

13. This categorical declaration of Origen's is quoted by Eusebius in his *Hist. Eccl.* vi.25.14.

14. Eusebius, *Hist. Eccl.* iii.38.

15. See Turner, *Novum Testmentum Sancti Irenaei*, 226–27.

16. See Photius, *Bibliotheca*, 121.

17. See Eusebius, *Hist. Eccl.* vi.20.3.

18. See Spicq, *Hébreux*, I, 199–202. One of the more recent to look at this whole question of authorship is Dyer in an article entitled: "The Epistle to the Hebrews," 104–31.

19. See Hughes, *Hebrews*, 24–25; Weiss, *Brief an der Hebräer*,18; Salmon, *Introduction to the New Testament*, 425.

20. Luther, in the preface to his "Lectures on Hebrews" (1522 edition).

21. Luther wrote: "This Apollos . . . is a man of high intelligence. The Epistle to the Hebrews is certainly from him." in a sermon on 1 Cor. 3:4 et al. in 1537, Weimar Edition xlv, 389 and also in his *Commentary on Genesis*, 48:20, 1545, Wiemar ed. xliv, 709; T.W. Manson, *Studies in the Gospels and Epistles*, Manchester, MUP. 254–5 although even he wonders why Clement did not mention Apollos in his writing to the

unlikely, since there should have been some record of the fact in historical writings from Alexandria, if such a famous member of their community had indeed been its author. Clement of Alexandria says nothing in this regard and opts for Paul as its source and Luke as its translator into Greek.[22] Other proposals are Peter,[23] and even Priscilla, together with her husband Aquilla.[24]

In spite of ongoing research on the part of many scholars, unless there is a document to be discovered in some archaeological dig yet future, which reveals absolute and compelling information related to this question of the authorship of the letter, we are going to have to be satisfied with the knowledge that no one really knows who the author was. At the same time there is little question that this work should be maintained as part of the New Testament canon because it is unique in its presentation, widely acclaimed by all Christians because of its high Christology and the style used to present its arguments from start to finish. There is nothing within its pages which could cast doubt upon the value of its teaching and there is every evidence that, even if it is not from one of the known apostles, there is nothing which places it at variance with the apostolic writings.

The preference for the text of the Septuagint (LXX) and the author's methodology in using the Old Testament

There has been considerable interest of late in the way in which the author to the Hebrews applies the Old Testament in his letter.[25] As the author draws heavily upon the Old Testament texts for his argument, it is essential to grasp that he uses the LXX Greek as his source, rather than the Hebrew of the Massoretic text. From the very start of his comparative section, where the quotation from Psalm 2:7 mentions the angels, it is evident that the Hebrew "sons of God" is translated from the LXX which is rendered "angels." This procedure is continued throughout the epistle.

Some commentators believe that the author has manipulated the LXX text in numerous places in order to force his points but Docherty disagrees. She believes that the author was faithful to the texts used at that time but

---

Corinthians, considering he had played a significant role in their history. See also W. Manson, *Hebrews*, 171 et al.; and Spiq, *Hébreux*, I, 209–219.

22. Clement of Alexandria, *Hypostyposes*, cited in Eusebius, *Hist. Eccl.* vi.14.2.

23. Welch, "*The Authorship of the Epistle to the Hebrews*," 1–33.

24. von Harnack "Verfasser des Hebräerbriefs," 16–41.

25. See. Docherty, *Old Testament in Hebrew,* for a thorough critique of the methodology but see especially chapters 4 & 5.

that there were a number of variants within the texts available. This meant that even when some of the statements appear to have been truncated, the background and context of the entire passage is part of the thinking of the author and this is in evidence overall.[26]

This last point regarding context, needs to be emphasized in all the places where the author may appear to use isolated texts from the Old Testament in his development of the themes in the letter. It is evident that the texts which he uses are not to be read without consideration of the entire context from which they are drawn. For example, this procedure is apparent in the section from 2:12, where the question is a matter of Jesus' suffering and death. At that point Psalm 22:22 is quoted but the entire Psalm and especially the first part, is key to the whole citation. This is because it is Messianic and underlines the terrible suffering and death of the follower of God who consequently seems to be forgotten by him only to find that ultimately, he is included in the number of the holy congregation as a beloved brother. Therefore, when the snippets, which appear as quotes, are found in the letter, the entirety of the original setting needs to be fully appreciated in order to grasp the fulness of all that the brief quotation represents (see notes on chapter 2:12).[27] Where this methodology is missed, failure to grasp the significance of the individual Old Testament quotations, will lead to a lack of the full meaning of what the author intends in the entire passage which is under review.

The use of "one off" words in the New Testament

One of the notable things about this letter is the number of times words which are only found here in the New Testament (*hapaxlegomena*–once only words) are used. Obviously, subject matter in any discussion, will influence the choice of words in any piece of literature but what we find in this epistle is that the author chooses words throughout, which could easily have fitted into other New Testament discussions just as well, but are used exclusively in this work. Although they are *once only words* in the New Testament, they are however used by other authors in the literature of the day and consequently their meanings are not generally difficult to discover. Their presence however, does tend to demonstrate that the author is not one who is already represented in other canonical books.

26. This comes out especially in Docherty ch. 5.

27. Dodd, wrote a book entitled, *According to the Scriptures*, in which he examines this methodology in the use of Old Testament scriptures and their significance in New Testament quotes.

Partial Conclusion

This introductory material is a necessary background to the understanding of the content which is to follow, especially when there are assumptions made which do not appear to be based on any immediate understanding of a given text. It is not meant to be comprehensive but the unique nature of the letter requires that this background and the factors which it represents be grasped from the onset of the study.

$$1.$$

Hebrews 1:1–3 The Prologue

God's Revelation through the Son

The introduction to this letter is an introduction to the Son of God who is the revelation of the person of God himself, presented in such a manner that there is no room for any doubt about what his coming to earth meant. The coming of Christ to earth enables a knowledge of God which surpasses anything and everything which was known about God and his will in the past. The emphasis is upon him from the beginning to the end of the Epistle. Now that his work of redemption is complete, he is once more upon the throne, at the right hand of God with all power at his disposal.

vv. 1–2 "*Long ago, God spoke to the fathers at many times and in many ways by the prophets, but at the end of these days he spoke to us by his Son* [by a son], *whom he has appointed as heir of everything, by whom he created the universe* (the ages)," This communication begins very abruptly, in a manner similar to that of John's first Epistle, so the style, though unusual as compared with the majority of the Epistles in the New Testament, is not unique (for the questions of style see above in the introduction). The author does not waste any time getting to the heart of his theme. *God has spoken.* God has not been silent; as in the past, he spoke to his creatures through the mouths of the prophets. He has not left the creature on its own to get by as the Deists claim because he has consistently interacted with those who he created. This declaration makes it clear that this is what is generally understood as special and not general revelation, as through the creation itself, which is referred to, as in Paul's letter to the Romans 1:19, 20. Here God gave specific direction through the prophets but it was not given in any systematic or consistent manner. It was nevertheless given over many years as the occasion arose and as God saw fit to inform, warn or exhort his people. The phrase "this is what the Lord says" (Greek: LXX–*tade legō Kurios*; Hebrew: *ko amer yahwh*) is a common declaration, made by the prophets throughout the Old Testament when they made known what Yahweh had told them to declare to the people (see for example: Exod 4:22; 8:1, 20; 2 Sam 7:5; 1 Kgs 11:31; Isa 7:7; 30:15; 48:17 et al.).

The word *prophets*, should be understood in a broader manner than merely those whom one would normally class as falling within the "prophetic" in the Old Testament books. This descriptor has to encompass all who God used, like Moses and David, to bring his word to the people. Their word was God's word and, in this way, God spoke, whether it was recognized by all or not.[1] Since the author goes on to especially highlight the Levitical code, within the Pentateuch and along with all the other portions in the Psalms and elsewhere, which are used in this letter, the whole of the Hebrew Scripture must be included in what the prophets had to say. In reality, this means that the entire Old Covenant is part of this revelation and bears record of what God has spoken. The many times and ways would include specific words given to prophets, visions as well as God's acts among men such as the plagues of Egypt and the crossing of the Red Sea, together with all that is recorded.[2] Nevertheless, the past and what was said, was partial at best and it was always God speaking through intermediaries. So, it was not perfect and it was not always clear.

God Spoke by the Prophets

The prophets here are clearly those of the Old Testament who were the vehicle of God's promises and commands to his people. What they said they declared on the part of God so that their words were fully divine and authoritative. They spoke and what they said was recorded for the benefit not only of the people who lived at that time but for all of the following generations. To ignore what they said is the same as ignoring the very utterance of God himself. That is why the author to the Hebrews can say unequivocally that God spoke by means of the prophets. This also means that the Old Testament

1. In the Greek of the original of this verse there is a clear play on alliteration on the use of words beginning with the letter "P"–Π–pi (*polumerōs, polutropōs, palai, patrasin and prophētas*) for emphasis in the declaration.

2. See Guthrie, *Hebrews*, 66.

authors were prophetic and to reject the divinely inspired nature of Scripture is equivalent to rejecting what God has said and who he is.

When it comes to the divinely inspired writings recorded in the New Testament there is a change in the way the messengers of God's will, are perceived. It is no longer the prophets during the New Testament epoch who are the infallible spokesmen of God's purposes but the Apostles who God chose to put pen to paper and explain his laws, as well as the law of the Spirit. Included in their writings we find the way in which members of his Kingdom are to conduct themselves and the criteria necessary for all who wish to participate in God's Kingdom. The latter is offered to all men and women through the propitiatory work of the one and only Savior–Jesus Christ–who is the Son who has spoken during these last days.[3]

What God said was important and that is the reason why the past is continually referred to in this literature. It is the center of what was but not of what has to be in the future because it was not complete and that is why it is necessary to understand it together with its imperfections. It becomes the basis of all that needs developing in the future, through what is yet to come under the New Covenant.

Note that the author apparently identifies himself with those who received the prophetic instruction when he writes about "*the fathers.*" If the suggestion that the author was indeed a Hebrew (see the introduction) is correct, then this reinforces the fact that he identifies not only with the fathers as one of their descendants but with the people to whom he writes, when he uses this term. However, even if he were not a Jew, he could have used this term if he merely intended to underline the general family of humanity to which all belong. Yet it is less likely that he would have written in this way if the people he was addressing were not Jews, as they would have been less likely to have acknowledged their descendancy from this same source.

The next verse takes the reader from dependency upon the partial in the prophetic to a new and complete word from the Son. There is a progression in the nature of the revelation God gave at first under the Old Covenant through the prophets, in the sense that more truth is explained and to

---

3. For a fuller explanation of the question regarding the nature of prophetic input during the Old and New Testament periods see Grudem's treatment of the subject in his book entitled *The Gift of Prophecy in the New Testament and Today,* 21–34 & 49.

a greater degree. There is no thought that what was previously in place was not truth but that it was partial. The transition is spoken of in terms of "*at the end of these days.*"[4] This expression indicates the fulfilment of prophetic promise which awaited the coming of the Son and shows that this time is now here. The end of the days, spoken of previously by the prophets is in place.[5] The reader is no longer in the age dependent upon what is incomplete and awaiting the promise of what was partial and prophetic yet spoken by God, given through human intermediaries but has been fast forwarded to the direct revelation, given through the Son himself, in direct speech and presence. This means that the Son is immediately the bridge between the Old Covenant and the New.

The end of the days or the end of Time

Students of Eschatology divide the work of God into different dispensations or eras. Jewish scholars saw the time prior to the coming of the Messiah as "the present age," which was evil and they looked forward to the "day of the Messiah" when all would be perfect and when they would be delivered from their enemies. However, Christians saw things differently. The period of the Old Covenant, up until the coming of Christ, was a time when much of God's working was presented through types and images of the perfect that was to come. In this way the Levitical system, with its priesthood, was part of this former age, which the author to the Hebrews contrasts with the New Covenant. This New Covenant is totally dependent upon Christ: The Son. He alone is the means of this New Covenant because of his death upon the cross and his victory over sin and death at his resurrection. His Person and his Work usher in this new Age, which is at the present, only in its infancy. This is because, although all that is

4. This expression: *ep' eschatou tōn hēmerōn toutōn,* and its variants, as Bruce points out in *Hebrews,* 3n14 is taken directly from the Greek of the LXX as in numbers of OT texts: see Jer 23:20; Ezek 38:16; Dan 10:14; Hos 3:5; Mic 4:1 et al.

5. This expression does not mean that the *eschaton* or the last of the last days, is now here, as that awaits the second coming of Christ but it does mean that the end time is seen as a protracted period and not a single event. Again, although the Son has now come and introduced the perfect covenant, this does not mean that his followers now know everything they will eventually know and experience because, even though the perfection promised by the Old Covenant is now possible because of the Son, the total outworking of God's plan, through the Son, is not yet complete; it awaits his return to subdue all opposition to his rule. This is evident in the Revelation of John with the New Heavens, the New Earth and the New Jerusalem (Rev chapters 21—22).

necessary to make God's overall plans for the future take place, there is still the total fulfilment of the plan to be enacted after Christ comes at his *Parousia*–his Second Coming. Therefore, students of Scripture discuss the "end times," usually with the Second Coming of Christ in mind, and what is properly called in Greek: the *Eschaton*. This name is attributed to the to *the end* of "the end times," as it includes all the events described. These include the wrath of God poured out upon the ungodly prior to that day, the reaction of Satan and his henchmen, the Beast and the False Prophet, then the coming of Christ with the settling of all scores. There is also Christ's granting of rewards to the faithful, then the final transition to the New Creation with the combination of the New Heavens and the New Earth. With the introduction of all these things, all hostility toward God's rule is set aside; only perfection, as it was perceived by God at the first creation, is established finally when all these elements are completed.

With this understanding in mind, it is necessary to grasp that any perfection declared in this present letter has to be understood as proleptic[6] for those who live upon the earth. God sees the entire plan as fulfilled and in place but the participants in God's plan, have not yet arrived at the final point of all that pertains to the end times.

Now God has spoken to us (literally) *by* or "in" a son. It appears intentional that the author left out the definite article "the" here. For some this construction may create a difficulty but if the significance of the statement and the meaning, as it is developed in the following verses is understood, it should not prove a problem. God's Son is no mere human son. His nature will be revealed as the narrative progresses. In verse 5 God calls him "*my Son*" and in verse 8 he is called the *God–ho theos*. Therefore, there is no doubt about his identity. The title here is meant to show intimacy and clear responsibility accorded to him by the Father. It is also associated with Christ's incarnation. There are seven significant factors related to the Son which are declared in the following two verses.[7] Each one of them is devel-

6. The term proleptic can be understood as anticipatory. In Scripture it is used in a sense as prophetic, to speak of what God sees as complete and perfect even when those who are living through the events of time do not experience them yet. Certainly, the New Covenant is perfect and Christ is the fulfilment of all the Old Covenant types and images but until Christ finally returns to complete his entire plan, imperfection is still present.

7. See Bruce, *Hebrews*, 3.

oped further in the rest of the letter, in a manner somewhat similar to that found in the prologue to the Gospel of John.

i) Initially the Son is described as *"the designated heir of all things."* It is necessary to understand that the One responsible for designating here is Yahweh. There is undoubtedly a reference here to the Messianic Psalm 2, where in verse 8, God says of the Son, *"Ask of me and I will give you the nations as your inheritance and the ends of the earth as your possession."* In the original context of the Psalm, the *ethnē-the nations-* are seen as the non-Jewish opponents of God but this verse promises victory over them by the Son, who is at the same time the promised Messiah. This is because, as the one who now rules in this Psalm, he has overcome all his enemies; they are totally submitted to him and to his command. Again, in this original context, the promise is made that the ends of the earth will be under his hand. It is necessary to see the author, is speaking of more than an earthly kingdom in this instance, in the light of what he adds in chapter 2:5 about the world to come; that world is to be totally subject to him.

There is no possibility of claiming any fulfilment of this scripture, either here in Hebrews or in Psalm 2. Therefore, although we do not see the Son, as yet, being heir of all things, that day will come, when he will be fully seen as heir of all. This is a proleptic declaration of what is yet to come because all is properly his. Usually, inheritance is something passed on to descendants at the death of a parent but here it is what is already Christ's by right, as Creator, as well as by redemption. The significance of inheritance or heirship is an important theme in the letter (1:2, 4; 9:15; 11:8).

The Son

The title "Son" is used in a variety of ways in biblical literature.[8] Adam was the first of the human race and therefore the first man (Gen 1:26, 27). In the Hebrew writings the expression: *ben Adam-*"Son of man" (See Ezek 33:2)–means nothing more than *man* or *the son of Adam.* However, by the time Daniel receives his prophetic vision in chapter 7:13, when he saw, *"One like a Son of Man coming with the clouds of heaven and coming before the Ancient of Days to be presented to him,"* this Son suddenly takes on divine character, which is immediately elevated above and beyond anything at the human level. The narrative says concerning this Son, that, *"To him was given dominion and glory and kingship, that all peoples, nations, and languages should serve him. His dominion is an everlasting dominion that shall not pass*

8. For more on "Sonship" see Martin, in *New Dictionary of Theology,* 651–53.

away, and his kingship is one that shall never be destroyed" (Dan 7:14 NRSV). This passage refers to the end of time when God restores everything and when, once more, his kingdom is the one and only that is in place. This Son of Man, is to take on an everlasting reign and kingdom and is certainly going to participate in the fullness of this role together with the Ancient of Days for all eternity. "The Ancient of Days" is another title of honor given to the Father God.

In Matthew 2:15, Israel is called God's son, in the sense that God has adopted him and made the nation his own. Also, John and Paul used the term "sons of God" to depict all who belong to Christ (John 1:12; Rom 8:14). Yet to return to the particular emphasis given to the name when it associated with Christ, when Jesus was being interrogated by the High Priest as to his identity, he was asked if he was the Messiah, the Son of God (Matt 26:63); then he responded: "*But I tell you that from now on you will see the Son of Man seated at the right hand of Power and coming on the clouds of heaven*" (Matt 26:64 NRSV). The High Priest immediately associated Jesus' words with the passage in Daniel. For Jesus was making himself equal with God and was therefore, in his view, most certainly guilty of blasphemy. This indicates that the Jews of Jesus' day, read the title "Son of Man," used in this context, to speak of this divine Son of God, who was the promised Messiah. In John's Gospel, Jesus used the title in a special way to refer to himself as having a unique relationship with the Father (John 1:14, 18, 34). When the Jews of the same period used the title, it spoke to them of the one who was their coming Messiah (See the affirmations of Nathanael, John 1:49; Peter, John 6:69; Martha, John 11:27 and John himself, John 20:31). In Hebrews 2:6 the title "Son of Man" is used in a special way so that it refers both to mankind[9] as a whole, as well as to this primary sense described above, as the title of the perfect man: Christ (see notes on 2:6). In the light of this background when the author to the Hebrews writes, as he does about the Son, or simply a Son, this is the unique Son, who is this promised Messiah and none other. The text itself explains his unique character and person in its entirety. The Son or the Son of God, is

9. This study does not cater to the most recent cultural gender views, which influence present day English literature. For this reason, there is no inherent bias intended in the use of words such as "humanity" or "human kind," both of which refer to men and women collectively without any emphasis or priority given to one or the other.

the favorite name given to Jesus throughout this letter while Jesus is mentioned 15 times. So, the theme of the letter is the Son.

ii) *"through whom he made the ages* (universe)." In the Greek text, the word *aiōnes* properly means: ages. However, from its appearance in 11:3 where it has a similar meaning and from parallel passages such as in John 1:3 where the Word–*Logos*–is responsible for the creation of everything, it is properly rendered "the universe" or "worlds" by most translators. This statement makes it evident that the creation of the universe is undertaken by God the Father, together with the Son. The significance of the Creation being God's work–the Father together with that of the Son, is primary in other New Testament writings, as it shows the origin of all things and hence, the legitimate ownership of the Father and the Son over everything (see Rev 4:11; Col 1:15–17); in Revelation 3:14 Christ is called the head or chief of God's creation (*hē archē tēs kitseōs tou Theou*). Consequently, the teaching of evolution is an attempt to deny the rightful claims of the architect and maker of this creation. If, as was stated in the previous phrase, Christ is the heir of all things, then this merely underlines the logic of why it is that he should be so. He made them and they are his, so he will eventually take them all back, since not only did he make them, he has also redeemed them.[10] This point is made clear in the next verse where the author writes about *"the cleansing of our sins"* which took place through Christ's redeeming act.

v. 3 "who is the radiance of his glory and the exact stamp of his being and he holds everything together by his powerful word. After he provided cleansing for sins, he sat down at the right hand of the Majesty on high,"

iii) *"He is the radiance of his glory,"* The author continues to describe the nature of the Son until the end of the introduction in this verse. The Greek word *apaugasma* is translated by a number of words in English: radiance, effulgence and in the passive form: reflection.[11] The deuterocanonical book of Wisdom of Solomon points out that Wisdom "is the radiance of the eternal light . . . of God" (Wisdom 7:22—8:1 and especially 7:26) and Philo the Jew, uses this word when he wrote about the relationship between the *Logos* and God. It is not possible to separate between the Son and the Father.[12] Christ is the exact representation of the person of God the Father,

10. See Guthrie, *Hebrews*, 69.

11. Arndt and Gingrich, 81.

12. Philo in *De Opficio Mundi* (Loeb ed.) 136, 114–115; See Paul Ellingworth,

in every way. When it comes to the interpretation of human terms in any attempt to indicate divine reality (*hypostasis*), there is often room for mis-understanding and the loss of the intended force conveyed by the author.

The Son is the perfect radiance of the glory of the Father. Glory in the Old Testament was the visible expression of the presence of God. It was associated with him from the earliest times but particularly when the Law was given by Yahweh at Sinai. The glory of the Lord came down upon the mountain.[13] It settled as a cloud for six days and is described as being: "*like a devouring fire*" (Exod 24:16–17; for more on God being like a devouring fire see notes on chapter 12:28). All Israel saw it and knew that God was there. When the tabernacle was first set in place Moses could not enter it because the glory of God filled the place (Exod 40:34–35); similarly, when the temple of Solomon was first dedicated, the cloud of this glory was so powerfully present that when the priests came out of the holy place they could not stand; this was once more due to God's glory which filled the house (1 Kgs 8:10–11). The glory is therefore equivalent to God himself, in all his fulness and power, manifesting himself in such a manner as to reveal his Person to those who are his own followers. It reassures them of the reality of who he is.

Here in this third verse of Hebrews, it is the same glory of the same God that is represented with the same significance but through the Son. Christ is thereby the direct and perfect representation of the Father. This should not be surprising to any reader of John's Gospel who will recall that when Thomas requested of Jesus that he show him the Father, he replied that, "*the one who has seen me has seen the Father*" (John 14:9 see also John 1:18). Again, in his prologue to the Gospel John writes, "*And the Word (ho Logos) became flesh and lived among us and we beheld his glory the glory as of the only born from the Father full of grace and truth.*" This Son, who is the *Logos*, and this glory, which radiates the person of the Father in every way possible, are the very same as that which is described here by the author to the Hebrews. This is reinforced in the next descriptor of the sentence related to his character, which will be examined shortly.

It needs to be remembered that not only does the Son reflect the glory of the Father, he has his own glory, as part of his own divine being. He is, after all, as is shortly demonstrated, named God (v.8); this is just as in John's Gospel, where he is "the only born God" (John 1:18).[14] His being

Hebrews, 2.

13. See Brown, *Hebrews*, 30–31.

14. It needs to be emphasized that the Johannine text of John 1:18 reads *monogenēs Theos* (only born God) and not *monogenēs huios* (only born Son), even if the majority

born relates to his incarnation, as does his Sonship in this introduction to the Hebrews.

iv) *"and the exact stamp of his being."* The word stamp (*charactēr*), is the word from which we get character and is found only here in the New Testament. It is used in the process of making an imprint such as would be used to stamp an image upon a coin.[15] The thought here is that Christ the Son, is in every way exactly representative of God, although he is his own distinct person. He has the same being or nature (*hypostaseōs*) as God the Father because he is God the Son. The same is taught by Paul in 2 Corinthians 4:4, where the apostle calls Christ the image of God (*hos estin eikon tou theou*). This backs up all that has already been said in the previous phrase. Once more, if there is a question as to the nature and person of God the Father, one long and hard look at the Son makes everything very clear.[16]

v) *"and he holds everything together by his powerful word."* The Son is the active agent in keeping everything in its rightful place. The verb, "to hold together" or "to bear up" is *pherō*. Here it is a participle indicating ongoing action. It shows that whatever is being held up, is actively being maintained and that without this sustenance it would fall apart or cease to exist. The thought is parallel to Paul's where he says of Christ: *"that in him all things hold together"* (*ta panta en autō sunestēken*) (Col 1:17). The Son not only brought the universe into being by his creative word but he also maintains it and is carrying it on to its final destination. He made it out of nothing and if he did not continue to carry it towards its final goal, then it could just as easily return to nothingness.[17] That is why it is a simple matter to change its essence when in the book of Revelation God does away with the old creation and brings about a totally new one, which is completely different from the first (Rev 21:1-2). This fits with what this epistle develops to some degree, in chapter 12:26-7. Here the structure of the phrase may be that which Bruce calls, an "Hebraic adjectival genitive."[18] Consequently, "by the word of his power" has the overall sense of Christ's powerful and or enabling command. When he speaks, whatever he wills happens, whether it be creative, sustaining or destructive.

---

of translations unfortunately maintain the traditional reading "only begotten Son."

15. See *charactēr* in Arndt and Gingrich, 884.

16. For more on this see Bruce, *Hebrews*, 5–6; Hughes, *Hebrews*, 43–45; Guthrie, *Hebrews*, 70–1.

17. See Hughes' discussion of this matter. *Hebrews*, 45–6.

18. Bruce, *Hebrews*, 6.

The Word–Logos and Rhēma–What is the difference?

In both Hebrews 1:3 and 11:3 the Greek *rhēma,* is translated as Christ's word. Some Theologians of the so called *"Rhēma* school of positive confession," make much of the difference between the significance related to the two terms: *logos* (word) and *rhēma* (word). They claim that the latter is a creative word while the former is more factual and less significant when it comes to revelation. It is not possible to attempt a thorough treatment of the subject here. A quick glance at the ways in which *rhēma* is used shows that it can be a creative word but it can also be a teaching (Matt 4:4; John 5:47). The sword of the Spirit is also the word (*rhēma*) of God (Eph 6:17). There is a word of faith but that is, in the context of Romans 10:8–10, the preaching of the Gospel message, which when it is proclaimed, results in the salvation of the hearers who place their faith in Christ. It is not as the *Rhēma* school maintain, a specific proclamation by faith for what one desires (for more on faith and outcomes see 11:35b). It can also be used in other ways such as an accusation against someone (Acts 6:13) or a mere word of witness in a law court (Matt 18:16). The meaning of each particular occurrence depends, as in all grammatical expression, upon the immediate context of its appearance.

The same can be said of the use of the Greek word *logos.* One of the well-known ways in which it is known is as a descriptor of Christ himself, who is the *Logos* of God in the prologue of John's Gospel (John 1:1–18), where he is the creator of all things. Even in the Old Testament in Psalm 107:20 (LXX 106:20), God sends his *logos* to heal and deliver; there it shows its active and creative nature. In Acts 6:7–8 the *logos* is preached, disciples are added and in the context signs and wonders are performed. Likewise in Acts 8:4, when the *logos* was preached, believers went everywhere evangelizing. One example is given of the consequences of this is given when Philip preached; the people obeyed (gave heed to) the message, demons were cast out people were healed and signs and wonders performed (Acts 8:5–8; see also Acts 14:3; 18:10–11). *Logos* is used of Paul's speech in 2 Cor 11:6, which in that context, resulted in the conversion of the Corinthians themselves. In John 2:22 it refers to Jesus' prophetic words regarding his resurrection. In Luke 4:36 it refers to a word Jesus commanded to cast out a demonic spirit and is recognized as being authoritative and powerful. In Matthew 5:37 it is what you say. In 1 Corinthians 12:8 it is a word of wisdom which is a gift of the Spirit. In Matthew 15:6 it is

God's word which is being broken because of human traditions. In 1 Timothy it is in the context of prayer and the word which sanctifies whatever one is requesting. There are many distinct ways in which the *logos* can be understood in a variety of contexts.

What then is the conclusion? The terms are generally synonymous but take on a variety of meanings and nuances depending upon each context and the purpose of the author at each and every instance. It cannot be maintained that one form has greater distinctives compared to the other, as some maintain. To do this is to force a certain interpretation of Theology upon a word, which is something that can never be done with honesty and goes against all principles of correct interpretation.

Those who adhere to the *Rhēma* school of doctrine, advance what they call the teaching of "positive confession" which maintains that by proclaiming something verbally, what you want, brings about its existence. For this reason, they would say that when an individual who is a Christian goes through negative experiences and times of trial and persecution, it is because they have not made the right kind of declarations and this has meant that the faith factor linked to the words, has not enabled the right outcomes. For them, "What you say is what you get." This is more in line with the thinking of magic and parallel to what happens in African Traditional religion, rather than the teaching of scripture, although scripture is very clear that faith and words do go together in matters such as blessing and curses. But the teaching of Scripture also shows very clearly that faith is linked to the will and purpose of God. The teaching of the epistle to the Hebrews and especially chapter 12, shows for example that discipline by the Lord, of his own people, is part of the love and care he has for them. This aspect would be against the understanding of the Rhēma school of thought.

vi) *He has made cleansing for sins.* The nature of what was involved in the provision of this purification is not mentioned here but it does appear that the link with the previous upholding of everything by his word is not by chance. The provision of the purification is part of steering God's entire plan toward his designed end, one which can only take place when the rebellion brought about by sin has been totally terminated. This is in order that whatever must happen afterwards has been made possible by what has already been set in place. The nature of the purification of the sin will nevertheless, become prominent as the letter is developed. The construction with, "*having made (poiēsamenos) cleansing for sin*" is an aorist participle, showing that the action was complete in the past. It refers to the Son's provision, as the High Priest of humanity, to lay down his own life as the supreme and only sufficient sacrifice; it is the only sacrifice able to satisfy God's righteous demands concerning mankind's rebellion. The Latin Vulgate translates this action as a present and so incorrectly gives the thought that Christ is now in the heavens continually offering sacrifices for sin.[19]

With this declaration regarding the Son making purification for sin, there is a change in the participation of the Son; it goes from being associated with God, engaged in his continued role throughout the universe and within the order of the divine and cosmic in the previous section, to that of becoming the one to take upon himself the personal role of the redeemer of all who put their trust in him. He had to become the all sufficient and once for all sacrifice (10:10). This theme of his sacrifice is one of the central subjects of the epistle (see 2:9, 17; 7:27; 9:12, 14, 26; 10:10, 19, 20). In order for this sacrificial task to be fulfilled and because he is God (see verse 8), he had to take upon himself the nature of man. The cleansing for sins could never have happened without the incarnation and the cross.

vii) The Son "*sat down on the right hand of the Majesty on High.*" The significance of each phrase in the prologue, builds to this final declaration, where the Son who has participated in an absolute and essential manner in all that precedes, has now completed his task of the cleansing of sin and resumes his rightful role with the Almighty in heaven. Without settling the matter of mankind's rebellion, this would not have been possible because the future of all God's plans depended upon all creation being in perfect harmony with the Son and the Father. Only now that all has been made possible for this plan to be fulfilled, can the Son take up his place at the right hand of the Majesty on High. The *right hand* is the traditional place of honor. Here "the Majesty on High" is another way of representing the person of Yahweh. Majesty, apart from here and in 8:1, is only used in Scripture in Jude v.25.[20] This means that the Son now shares with full title the role of God, together with the Father.[21] He is not just seated but he has the same

19. See Bruce 6n31. who makes it clear that the absence of the appropriate active perfect in Latin, has led to this difficulty.

20. The Greek word *megalōsunē*–Majesty–in biblical writings, is a periphrasis for God. See Arndt & Gingrich, 498.

21. This teaching is in full accord with what John writes in Revelation 22:3 where there is only one throne shared by both God and the Lamb.

authority being seated together with God upon the throne, which is the very center of all rule.[22]

There is little doubt but that the expression the author uses here to describe the Son seated at the right hand of God, recalls the teaching of the messianic Psalm 110:1, "*The Lord says to my lord, 'Sit at my right hand until I make your enemies your footstool.'*" (NRSV). The author uses quotations from this psalm a number of times in the Epistle (see 8:1; 10:12) and the Melchizedek passage is also found embedded in it. The earthly priests stand because, as the author states in 10:11, their work is never done but not so with this Son who has fulfilled his mission and no other sacrifice of this nature is ever going to be necessary because the task is now complete. To sit down, is to show that the work has been fully accomplished.[23] Later in the epistle, we see that Christ has an ongoing priesthood and he presently continues to make intercession during the present age, for all who come to God through him (7:24). The aspect of the nature of his sacrifice is further developed in chapter eight. Another interesting factor is that even the angel Gabriel stands in the presence of God but this Son sits upon the throne in the presence of God (see Luke 1:19) reinforcing the matter of his full right to be there and that after his reincarnation he is back in full control of all things.[24] This does not mean that during his incarnation he was not in full control.

The prologue to this epistle is emphatic that this Son is unique in every way possible. It incorporates his person and in his work. Consequently, any thought of abandoning faith related to serving him and his message, would be complete folly.[25]

1:4–14 Christ is so much better than the Angels

v. 4 "*Having become* (aor. part.) *so much better than the angels he has inherited a more excellent name than theirs.*" This verse serves as a transition and takes the reader immediately to the matter of the Son's superiority to the

22. See Hughes, *Hebrews*, 47.

23. The fact that the Son is seated does not mean that he is inactive but that he has full authority on a par with that of the Father and that his work of redemption is complete.

24. This does not mean that he was not in charge prior to his incarnation but it means that he had work to carry out, which was of an essential nature and upon which the entire future of heaven and earth depended.

25. See Brown, *Hebrews*, 33.

angels. It should be noted that grammatically, this verse still belongs to the previous sentence.

Those living in the western world may wonder how the subject of angels is suddenly the center of focus, since for many today, they would be mythical and non-existent beings. This is not however, the view of many living in areas of the majority world today, where the unseen does not signify the absence of spirits and other beings. It is necessary to place oneself in the position of the Jews to whom the letter was addressed. The whole Bible has more than 280 references to angels. The place of angels was also developed considerably during the intertestamental period so that there are statements made regarding their activities after that time which are not necessarily clear from the earlier canonical writings. For example, the role of the angels in the giving of the Law (2:2) and that they worked for God's people (1:14). Scripture shows that they are beings who are at the command of God who also serve as his agents and his messengers. The Jews most certainly saw them as significant and the book of Revelation attributes to them a very important role at the end of time.

It seems that there was a temptation for people to offer them worship and a role greater than what was permissible in God's eyes. In Colossians 2:18, Paul warns the church that the worship of angels was out of the question, showing that it was an issue during his day, even in the Hellenistic world. This indicates therefore, that the matter of angels was of great importance to those being addressed by the present letter. In the majority world there is still a tendency for some Christians to give angels a greater role than that afforded them by Scripture so the subject matter is not just one of historical significance but one which is real in our time. The fact that the superiority of the Son takes such an important place means that there must have been a significant problem among the addressees related to the way in which they saw angels and the powers which they attributed to them. They were according angels a superior position to that of the Son, something that could not and must still not be tolerated.

The superiority of the Son has already been presented in the previous verses as a consequence of his very nature, his work and his inheritance of all things. Therefore, it is only logical that he has inherited a name which is far better than that of the angels. There are several important issues in this verse. First, the term "better" or "superior" (Greek *kreittōn*[26]) is introduced for the first of 13 times in the letter. It is an introduction to a dominant

---

26. That is, in either of the variant forms of the Greek *kreissōn* or *kreittōn*, both giving the sense of the comparative "better" or "superior." See Arndt and Gingrich, 450–51.

theme where the author wishes to underline the superiority of all that pertains to Christ and his role in this new covenant. The Son has not just become better than the angels, he always was better, since he is their creator. However, the aorist participle *genomenos*–having become–is concerned, as Spicq indicates, with the "superiority which was achieved and clearly indicates that the theme here is not the Son in his eternal existence but Christ with his glorified human nature elevated to the rank of divinity"[my translation] after his humiliation and the completion of his earthly mission.[27] The matter of the exaltation of Christ to the right hand of God is another significant theme in the letter and one which is developed considerably (see 8:1; 10:12; 12:2). In the following section an attempt will be made to demonstrate further what this means.

When the matter of the *name* is raised, it is more than a label. It is the intrinsic character of a person indicating who they really are. It has already been noted that the name *Christ*, is not common in this letter (see above at the end of the parenthesis on the Son verse 2). The author uses the *name* more as a title or as an indicator of the Son's full status. He is the Son of God and with that, goes all that this means in terms of rights, powers and status. It is his intrinsic being, which will shortly be expanded upon in the coming verses and chapters. If one recalls that Christ is to have a new name, according to Revelation 3:12 and 19:12, those verses indicate he will have a new title, which although as yet unknown, will reveal his attributes even further. The thought here in this passage is similar to that expressed in Ephesians 1:19–23 and Philippians 2:9–11, where in both passages Paul links this exaltation to the death and resurrection of Christ. He is exalted by God and seated at his right hand in the heavenlies (*en tois epouraniois*) and has already received a name that is above every name, not only associated with this present age but the one which is to come.[28] He may not yet be acknowledged as such by all but the Philippian passage emphasizes the fact that there will be a day when that does happen (Phil 2:10–11).

The emphasis here is that the Son's name is far superior to that of any angels and to contemplate granting them worship, makes no sense at all. If the name of angels is examined it meant messengers or agents (see v. 14 and notes) and no more and they would never be more than that, however individuals may regard them.[29] For a reason which may not be apparent to today's readers, this point is vital at that time or it never would have been addressed in the way it has been. Today, the closest parallel would be

27. Spicq, *Hébreux*, 2. 12. Compare with Delitzsch, *Hebrews*, 58–9.
28. See Hughes, *Hebrews*, 51.
29. On the significance of the name of the angels see Brown, *Hebrews*, 39–40.

the elevation of some supposed prophetic or apostolic individual, who by their behavior and teaching, has attempted to usurp the role of Christ and whose position has resulted in the surrender of people's trust in the one and only Savior, to a futile and vain hope in an individual. I am aware of such individuals in the Majority world today.

v. 5 "For to which of the angels did he ever say 'You are my Son. Today I have begotten you?' or 'I will be a father to him, and he will be a son to me'?" Starting with this verse, the author employs seven Old Testament texts which relate to the person and work of the Son; this is done to uphold his thesis that the Son is superior to all the angels. It needs to be remembered that the way in which the scriptures from the Old Testament were interpreted by the New Testament authors is very fluid. It does not always fit what would nowadays be considered a safe hermeneutical model. For this reason, not only the author to the Hebrews but others like Matthew, who in his gospel 2:15, uses a quotation from Hosea 11:1, a passage which would not have previously been considered messianic. Nevertheless, this illustrates the way in which it was considered legitimate by the early Christians to find numerous messianic confirmations in the Old Testament.[30] The entire procedure followed here is significant because it shows that the readers would have been open to the authority upon which the arguments are made and would therefore, have been convinced of the validity of the divine stamp on the scriptures cited. This alone would tend to indicate that they must have been Christians who had a Jewish background and who would have accepted the methodology used.[31]

i) The first of the quotations comes from Psalm 2:7: *"You are my son; today I have begotten you."*(NRSV)[32] First, it can be stated categorically that this statement was never made of any angel by God, even if collectively "sons of God" in the Hebrew text, are translated "angels" especially in the LXX (Gen 6:2; Job 1:6; 2:1 et al.).[33] In the original text, the passage refers to David, the divinely appointed king and his coronation day. However, the fulfilment there can only be applied to him partially and Christians have always seen this as a Messianic declaration, as Paul in his long discourse

30. See Guthrie, *Hebrews*, 76; Deilitzsch, *Hebrews*, says that the way the author pens his argument makes it very clear that he believes God is the only one responsible for the origin of Scripture. 61.

31. See Hughes, *Hebrews*, 53.

32. It should be noted that this quotation is directly taken from the LXX rather than from the Hebrew text of the Psalm. The Hebrew text says: "You are my son; today I have become your father."

33. The Hebrew *beney ha Elohim*–sons of God is rendered: *hoi angeloi*–the angels–in Greek.

in Acts 13:33–41 makes clear when he applies this passage to Jesus. Bruce says that the way in which the words are used in this declaration, follows a well-known format used when kings were enthroned throughout the region of the Ancient Near East.[34] In the Markan narrative of the baptism of Jesus by John the Baptist, we have the voice from heaven (*bath qol*) where God himself states almost the same words: "*You are my beloved Son*" with the additional descriptor: "*in you I am well pleased*" (Mark 1:11).[35]

However, there is considerable discussion on the part of scholars as to the meaning of "*today I have begotten you.*" When Augustine wrote about the "*today*" he added: "Although that day may also seem to be prophetically spoken of, on which Jesus Christ was born according to the flesh; and in eternity there is nothing past as if it had ceased to be, nor future as if it were not yet, but present only, since whatever is eternal, always is."[36] Bruce sees this day as the day of Christ's exultation after the completion of his earthly mission and his enthronement while awaiting the defeat of all his enemies.[37] Paul In Acts 13:33 applies this verse to Christ's resurrection as the day when his entire earthly mission is shown to have succeeded and all his claims are vindicated; this is the line to which Hughes holds with regards to the timing of the "today."[38] However he goes on to state that in reality this is also a combination of the resurrection and the ascension.[39]

Could "today" not be the entire mission of Christ's including his incarnation, ministry, death and resurrection, followed by his exaltation to the father's right hand? Rather than see it as any one part of the whole, why not see the "today" as inclusive of all that was required to fulfil every part of God's plan in its entirety? Christ's sonship incorporates all that is part of this divine design and there never was a time when he did not fulfil the criteria necessary. Certainly, there was a point when he entered the time he had created, to bring about the desired completion and there was a point when it was completed, even if its total fulfilment awaits the *Parousia*.[40] That is the point when the final overthrow of all God's enemies at the end of all things

---

34. Bruce, *Hebrews*, 11n57.

35. Note that the Western text of Luke 3:22 (D, it, Latin MSS to Augustine) include the words from Ps 2:7: *Hyios mou ei su, egō sēmeron yeyennēka se.* "You are my son today I have begotten you."

36 Augustine, *Enarrationes in Psalmos* on Psalm 2:7. https://www.newadvent.org/fathers/1801002.htm

37. Bruce, *Hebrews*, 13:23–24.

38. Hughes, *Hebrews*, 54–55.

39. Hughes, Hebrews, 55.

40. This term is used here to indicate Christ's second coming and all that is included in that event.

occurs. However, that event is not part of this present narrative. Therefore, for the sake of this letter and its argument regarding the superior nature of the Son, the exultation appears to be the terminus or the now which is called *today*. The main thrust is the superiority of the Son. The other factors are subsidiary to that.

The next issue of importance is: How is the phrase: "*I have begotten you*" to be understood? It is certainly linked to what has proceeded. The term "I have begotten you" (Greek *gegennēka* is a perfect) demonstrates an unquestionable link with God. As Ellingworth points out, this does not have a satisfactory English equivalent but it has to be understood that in both the original, in Psalm 2 and here in Hebrews, it cannot be understood in a literal sense.[41] Delitzsch explains that the Greek *gegennēka*–I have begotten you– translates the Hebrew root *yld* (ילד) in the original, which here means "*begetting* (not *giving birth to*)," even if it is not common.[42] It cannot therefore refer to giving birth. Therefore, the language in its entirety in this context is related to that of a coronation and the context of Psalm 2 would have referred to David and his installation as king or his adoption as the leader of all Israel and a "begetting" of his role as *the anointed* one involved in royal service.[43] However, in the context of the greater Son of David, now the center of this discussion, it must be related to the total mission and exultation already mentioned. If the discussion related to the subject of "today" is taken into consideration, it has to be understood as the declared authority the Son receives upon the completion of his earthly mission at his exultation.

ii) The second quotation upon which the author draws is 2 Samuel 7:14 or the parallel passage in 1 Chronicles 17:13. The entire context of that passage is one of a promise from the mouth of the prophet Nathan, given to David when he had overcome his enemies. The prophet tells him that he would not build a temple but that his son would. God promises the king that his kingdom will be established for ever and of his offspring: "*I will be a father to him, and he shall be a son to me.*" Once more the special relationship between the Father and the Son are at the center of this text.

Ellingworth points out that "nowhere else in Hebrews is God called 'father' without qualification."[44] It seems that the specific purpose here is to enhance the relationship that is key to this Son, in these first verses of the chapter. Another parallel passage in Psalm 89:18–37, which highlights this

41. Ellingwortth, *Hebrews*, 7.
42. Delitzsch, *Hebrews*, 64.
43. See Guthrie, *Hebrews*, 77; Delitzsch, *Hebrews*, 64.
44. Ellingworth, *Hebrews*, 8; see also Montefiore, *Hebrews*, 45.

fatherhood of God, accords the promised Son the title of the "first born" (Greek–*prōtotokos*–see notes on 12:23)[45] and states that "his throne is to endure as long as the heavens" (Ps 89:29). If the thought that Solomon was going to be the fulfilment of this prophecy is maintained, all know that he was a less than perfect example, especially with his multitudinous wives and concubines who led him to open the doors to laxity when it came to faithfulness to God. Therefore, although Solomon built the first permanent temple, it will be up to the Greater Son of David to inherit this throne and kingdom. That is the way the early Christians understood the passage and this is the way in which the author to the Hebrews views it; this would have been reinforced for them by quotations such as that in Micah 5:2, "*but you O Bethlehem of Ephrathah, who are one of the little clans of Judah, from you shall come forth for me one who is to rule in Israel, whose origin is from of old, from ancient days.*" Again, the declaration of the angel bringing the news of God's plan to Mary regarding her offspring was grounds enough to satisfy the Early Church that this son was the successor to David's throne: "*He will be great, and will be called the Son of the Most High, and the Lord God will give to him the throne of his ancestor David. He will reign over the house of Jacob forever, and of his kingdom there will be no end*" (Luke 1:32–33).

v. 6

iii) This quotation is introduced by the words, "*And again when he brings his firstborn into the world he says: Let all God's angels worship him.*" The text used here is a quotation of Deut 32:43 in the Greek (LXX) text but it is missing from the Massoretic text. Hughes believes that the original Hebrew, which reflects the LXX, was most likely available at the time the Greek translation was made and indicates that discoveries of a fragment in Cave 4 at Qumran validate this view. The only difference is that in the Hebrew fragment, the appropriate phrase is rendered by the Greek, "Sons of God." Hughes says that is not a difficulty because that phrase, as has already been noted above (v.5, i) is a common synonym for angels in the LXX.[46] Another similar text dealing with this same subject is found in the LXX for Psalm 96:7 (97:7) where again the text differs from the Hebrew (Masoretic text) and states "worship him all his angels." Anyway, either one or the other of these two passages is the text the author follows here.

There are several issues here. The first is how "*again*" is to be understood? Is it to be linked to the fact that there is another quotation and this identifies that fact? If so, we should read this verse: "He says again . . ." highlighting the biblical source. Or is "again" associated with the verb "bring"? if

45. On *prōtotokos* see Arndt and Gingrich, 734.
46. See Hughes, *Hebrews*, 59.

the latter, the phrase should be read: "When he brings again . . ." and refers to Christ's second coming. Since "again" is used in the previous verse as well as in a number of others in this letter, to introduce a quotation (2:13; 4:5, 7; 10:30), it is logical that this is the way in which it is to be understood here. If it did relate to the bringing his firstborn again, indicating a second coming of Christ, that thought does not fit the context here. The bringing of the firstborn into the world, therefore refers to the Son's first coming, which is his incarnation. This certainly fits the context, as has been indicated, since it is an essential part of what was necessary for his coming to deal with sin (v.3).

The next matter is the use of the term "firstborn." The link in the previous verse with Ps 89:27 and the use of this title has already been demonstrated. The title is a well-known Pauline descriptor of Christ in the New Testament (Rom 8:29; Col 1:15, 18) as well as here in the letter to the Hebrews, where it appears three times (1:6; 11:28; 12:23). There are nuances which may differ in each occurrence but it is clear that it is an honorific title not linked to mere human birth (which it is in Matt 1:25 and Luke 2:7). In Revelation 1:5, it is a clear affirmation of Christ's position as the firstborn after his resurrection, making him the first in the order of the new creation, of which he is the head (see the parallel in 1 Cor 15:20). Here the title is one of superiority and authority over all creation, including angels.

The third factor is that of the inhabited world (*oikoumenē*) into which the Son is brought. It is the universe of which even the angels are a part. Therefore, the firstborn son has preeminence, even over all angelic beings and mankind. Consequently, if God orders the angels to worship him then certainly, he must be superior to them.

v. 7 "And about the angels he says: 'The one who makes his angels winds and his servants a flame of fire.'" The second part of the verse is the fourth quotation from Psalm 104:4. The next three quotations go together and each depends upon the other.

iv) *"Who makes his angels winds and his servants flames of fire."* There is some difficulty over the translation of this verse, since angels can equally be translated by *messengers* and winds (*pneumata*) can also be translated by *spirits*. The Hebrew text emphasizes the fact that God uses the natural elements to fulfil his purposes but here angels are the subject at hand and their inferiority as compared to the person of the Son. For this reason, logically the translation of the Greek–*tous anglelous* (in the accusative)–should therefore be "the angels" and not messengers. Winds, in the context, is the required translation of the Greek *pneumata*–spiritual things or matters–because the angels are already spiritual beings and do not have to be transformed into such.[47] Another difficulty with the translation is that "the ministers," in the plural (*tous leitourgous*), are qualified by the singular flame of fire (*puros phloga*) and not "flames of fire." Once more the quotation is drawn from the LXX and not the Hebrew text of the Psalm; however, even then, we find an anomaly since the Greek phrase ending *pur phlegon* (flame of fire) has been changed slightly here in Hebrews.[48]

What then is the significance of the verse? The author is saying that angels can be transformed into nothing more than winds and fire, showing that as marvelous as they may appear to be to mankind, under the command of God, angelic beings have no fixed function and can become nothing more than natural elements when God so desires but in the light of the following verses this is not the case with the Son. It has already been shown from verses 2 and 3 that the Son made the universe and is the one who keeps everything together in its proper place.

vv. 8–9

v) This quotation, which is the fifth in the catena, starts out with the comparative: "*But with regard to the son.*" It depends upon what has just been said regarding the angels in the previous verse. There the quotation was introduced by "He said (*legei*)," which is not repeated here but is certainly understood when the following words are quoted from Psalm 45:6–7, "*Your throne O God is for ever and ever and the scepter of justice is the scepter of his kingdom. You loved righteousness and hated lawlessness; therefore, O God, your God anointed you with the oil of gladness above your fellows.*"[49] With very slight variations the words are, once more, taken from the Greek text of the LXX, where the context is that of a royal wedding. In Israel kings were, unlike those of the pagan nations,[50] never viewed as divine and it is for this reason that the Psalm, with its elevated language, has been viewed as indicative of the messianic king who was to come. It needs to be remembered that the Hebrew word "*Messiach*" like the Greek "*Christos*" meant "the anointed one," so that the oil of anointing here reinforces this aspect of his identity. It is not simple to associate the anointing and the oil of gladness with any single event in the life of Christ but rather should be understood of the overall favor of God with all that he accomplished, similar to what

47. The translation "spirits" as in the KJV relies upon the word *spiritus* in the Latin Vulgate.

48. For more on this discussion see Hughes, *Hebrews*, 61–62.

49. For the nature of the word "fellows" or "companions," see notes below and note 71 above.

50. There are people groups in Central Africa which viewed up until recent times, their kings as becoming divine when they had passed through all the necessary sacred initiation ceremonies. The Luba of the Katanga were one of them.

we see Psalm 23:5. The author is declaring that that this promised One, of whom the passage spoke, is now here and needs to be recognized as such. Another factor related to the anointing, is that in a letter which is highlighting the priesthood of the Son, the matter of his anointing is certainly important as far as the Jewish readers would be concerned.[51]

There are only seven places in the entire New Testament where Christ is called God (John 1:1, 18; 20:28; Rom 9:5; Tit 2:13; 1 John 5:20) and this is one of them here in Hebrews.[52] The language should not be considered extravagant in the light of what was said about the Son in verse 3, where he is "*the radiance of God's glory and the exact stamp of God's being.*" In that passage he also does the work of God in that "*he holds everything together by his powerful word.*" His throne or his rule and kingdom, which are eternal (see the parallelism in both 2 Sam 7:16 and Ps 89:14), are aimed at upholding justice; they must necessarily be directed vigorously at destroying lawlessness and sin. Only the God/Man who came to earth to do away with all sin by his "once for all" offering of himself, could qualify for what was necessary to implement all that was necessary to make this happen.

Finally, in this verse is the question related to the identity of the Son's "fellows" or "companions." It is likely that Bruce's suggestion is correct, that it should be those who are the "many sons" (2:10, 11), brought into the kingdom by his work and who now are called brethren and in 3:14 are those who "have become sharers of Christ," meaning, all who are a consequence of his work.[53] In both this verse and in the latter, the same Greek word for fellows, companions or sharers of Christ–*metochoi*–[54]is used.

vv. 10–12

vi) The longer quotation here is from Psalm 102:25–27, "*And 'You O Lord, at the beginning founded; the earth and the heavens are the works of your hands. They will be destroyed but you remain; and all like a garment will become old and like a cloak you will roll them up; like a garment they will also be changed; but you are the same and your years will not come to an end.*'" This quotation is linked to the former by the use of the conjunction "and" so that when the author calls the Son *God* in the psalm, here he calls him *Lord*. This is significant because the Greek *Kurios* or Lord, is the

---

51. See Guthrie, *Hebrews*, 82. It needs to be remembered that all priests had to be anointed before they could qualify for ministry.

52. Montefiore, *Hebrews*, 47 points out that this is the only place in the NT where Christ is called *ho theos* (O God!), where at least once it is used as a vocative.

53. Bruce, *Hebrews*, 20–21.

54. The only difference is that the first occurrence is in the plural of the accusative case *metochous* while in the second it is in the nominative *metochoi*.

normal translation of the Hebrew *Yahweh* (see Ps 102:1 and Heb 1:10). Here it designates Christ the Son, who is the creator of heaven and earth.

Once more the verses reflect the Greek texts of the LXX, rather than those of the Hebrew which omits the significant words, "You O Lord." The author takes these verses by the psalmist, originally addressed to God at a time of destruction and distress (Ps 102:1–2), to outline the transient and uncertain nature of the creation as compared to God who never changes. These words are then applied to the Son. This is, once more, in line with what has already been said in verse 2 where the Son has made the universe (*aiōnas*). There is also the hint here of what is to come in chapter 12:27–29 where the universe is to be changed (shaken) before the coming of the final unshakable kingdom (12:28). In that context, as here because he is "*the same*," "*Jesus Christ is the same yesterday, and today and forever*" (13:8). As the unchanging creator of all who never grows old, he is superior in every way to the angels.

v. 13

vii) The final quotation in the chain presented here is from Psalm 110:1. It is introduced by the words, "*But to which of the angels has he ever said:*" Once more reference is made to the words from God as expressed in the Psalm. "*Sit at my right hand until I make your enemies your footstool?*" Numerous times in the New Testament, with reference to Christ and drawing upon this Psalm, the phrase: "*Sit at my right hand*" is used. The thought of Christ's enthronement has already been expressed in verse 3 where he "*sat down at the right hand of the Majesty on High.*" However, here the fact that the Son is enthroned, is without doubt the pinnacle of all possibilities, as no angel would or could ever be invited to share the throne with the Almighty. When Paul writes of the resurrection, he includes Christ's work of having to abolish all wickedness, in terms of what is called "*all rule and authority and power*" (1 Cor 15:24); he says that "*he must reign until he has put all his enemies under his feet*" (1 Cor 15:25). So, although he is seated at the right hand of the Majesty on High, he is by no means passive as he reigns. The nature of what this entails is not elaborated upon.

Jesus himself, when confronted by the priests the scribes and the elders regarding his identity, used the words of this psalm to ask them how it was that Christ was the son of David (Mark 12:35–37). It is very clear that they, together with all Jews at the time, believed that the psalmist spoke of David's greater son. Not only is the Son's reign established here but the fact that his enemies are all totally subdued before him, is emphasized.

v. 14 "*Are they not all ministering spirits sent out to serve, for the sake of those who are about to inherit salvation?*" The question is rhetorical and more of a statement declaring the real role of the angels than anything else.

The angels do not sit in the throne room. They are sent ones or messengers. That means they are under the command of God, always ready to do his will. Their purpose is clearly given here as that of participating in the help of those who are the redeemed. Throughout Scripture angels encourage the people of God. To name but a few incidents where they appear in the Bible: they are revealed to Elisha and his servant when surrounded by the Arameans who are then struck with blindness (2 Kings 6:15–18); Peter is set free from prison by an angel on two occasions (Acts 5:19; 12:7); Philip is directed where to go by an angel and Cornelius, in a vision, was told by an angel to call Peter. In the same incident an angel also showed Peter he had to go to Cornelius's house (Acts 8:26; 10:3, 22) and one encouraged Paul, showing him what would happen in the future (Acts 27:23–24). In the book of Revelation angels are involved in the unleashing of the plagues (Rev 7:1, 2 et al.) and when Jesus comes again, they will accompany him and be involved in the fulfilment of his judgments (2 Thess 1:7–8). Therefore, once more there is no doubt that the Son, as the one seated upon the throne, is most certainly superior to the servants whom he commands.

All the verses drawn upon from the Old Testament texts examined, assert unequivocally the superiority of the Son over the angels. Since he is indeed the creator and the architect of the universe who holds everything together, to ignore his person and his role in favor of the servants who are at his command would be an act of total folly. Anyone who was contemplating reneging on any decision to follow this Sovereign of the universe, must immediately come to grips with what the consequences of such an action would be.

2.

The first chapter highlights the superiority of Christ, the Son, over all angelic beings. This second chapter starts out with the focus upon the nature of the message that this Son, who is the Lord, brought. This is because there is no room for indifference or drifting away from it. The presentation of the message here in Hebrews, unlike so many other New Testament epistles, which have large blocks of doctrinal teaching followed by shorter sections of practical application (For an example of this see Romans 1—11 with the practical being introduced in 12), moves back and forth easily from the doctrinal to the practical and exhortative because these factors are intricately linked in Christian life and can never be separated; theory alone is never the goal of true Theology but all practice has to be based upon sound biblical teaching.

2:1–4 Do not neglect the Salvation message

v. 1 "Therefore, we must give the closest attention to the things which were heard so that we do not drift away from them." The link with chapter one is the *therefore* here. It points to the fact that what is now to be stated depends upon the superiority of the Son in all things and that, what is to come must not be regarded in any manner as unimportant. To minimize the place of the Son, who is the one upholding all things and the God who put all things in place, can never occur. Is the author presenting a comparative here when he tells his readers to pay "more careful attention" as most translate this first clause or is he using a superlative? If the latter, rather than saying "pay more careful attention" to the Gospel than to the Law, he is saying pay "the closest attention" to what is involved in this message of Jesus. Westcott believes that the first phrase is relative to the degree of care which is to be given in observing what the message was all about and sees this as a superlative rather than a comparative; he would translate the phrase in the sense of having to pay "the most particular attention"[1]to what the contents of the message proclaim. In this way there is no immediate comparison with the value of the Law against the Gospel here, even if comparisons are made later in the narrative.

What then are the things which were heard? In the first chapter and second verse, the Son was the one who spoke. His words and his truth are what is depicted as the gospel message and what he said is recorded in the Gospels. Therefore, what was said is the Word of God, since chapter one and verse 8 calls him by that title (God) and includes what he declared and did. What was heard, as is further elaborated upon in the third verse, includes all that was reported by those apostolic individuals who were with him during the Son's earthly ministry, as well as what was handed down from the apostles by reliable witnesses (more is said on this matter in verse 3). The emphasis here then, is on the content of all the teaching of Christ.

There is, according to the author, a danger looming in the lives of the readers who had become followers of the Son but are now tempted to give up because they need to act speedily, for fear of drifting away. The expression translated "to drift away"[2] gives the impression that there is carelessness and a lack of focus on their part, so that rather than purposeful intent or apostasy, which is aimed at vehement antagonism, there is laxity and indifference. What we have here then, is a stern warning, that things cannot remain as they are at present. Christian belief requires constant active and practical engagement. This is a danger for Christians today who have lost their passion for Christ and put themselves first when it comes to life's choices.

v. 2 "Because if the word spoken through angels was steadfast and every act of transgression and disobedience received a just retribution." In a manner similar to that expressed by Paul in his letter to the Galatians in 3:19, the author includes the angels in the transmission of the Law. Likewise, Stephen in his speech condemning the laxity and unbelief of the leaders of the Jews in Acts 7:38 and 53, mentions the role of the angels in the granting of the Law. No mention is made anywhere in Exodus relating to the role of the angels but in Deuteronomy 33:2–4 the passage does speak of the Lord coming from Sinai and that, *"With him were myriads of holy ones; at his right a host of his own . . . all his holy ones were in your charge"* after which the text continues by stating that *"Moses charged us with the law, as a possession for*

1. Westcott, *Hebrews*, 36; see also Hughes, *Hebrews*, 73.

2. The Greek *pararuōmen* from *parappeō* gives the thought of letting something slip away, or flow by, as with a current of water. See Arndt and Gingrich, 627.

the assembly of Jacob." The Jews clearly believed that these saints were the angels that were active in the giving of the Law to Moses, who therefore participated in the mediation and transmission of the same.[3]

It is the purpose of the author, to point out some very severe consequence related to law breaking (transgression) and disobedience. This is because the Son, as the Creator and commander of all life, is also the author of the same covenant in which the end of law-breaking is clearly defined. Any infringement, whether carried out innocently or otherwise, had the severest of consequences. There is provision for sins of ignorance but disobedience is seen as flagrant disregard of God and his purposes; when this occurs, the death penalty is the price (Numbers 15:27–28, 30). The author wants them to understand that if neglect and law-breaking were punishable under the regime mediated by Moses and angels, the severity and the retribution to be expected under the New Covenant of the Son, would never be any more lenient. Later in this letter and on a number of occasions, much more about this New Covenant of the "word of the Son" or the "Gospel" will be developed (8:6; 9:15; 12:24); this is a warning and a prelude to all of those sections. It depends upon the logic of the link with the following verse.

v. 3 "How shall we escape if we neglect such a great salvation? It was at first declared by the Lord and was confirmed to us by those who heard (him)." There is no direct indication of what were the actual beliefs and practices of the people who were being addressed but there is sufficient to show that they were in danger of indifference (of drifting) and here it is stated that they were on the verge of neglecting all that is involved in this *great salvation* as it is only available through the Son who is the center of the entire discussion. This great salvation is all that is included in God's plan and is dependent upon the person and work of the Son in his incarnation and now in his exultation. The latter speaks of his government, described in terms of his being seated at the right hand of the Majesty on High. In fact, this entire gift of salvation is embodied, not only in what the Son had to say when he was upon the earth but upon he himself, his person and his work. He is its central message. Therefore, any minimalization of the Son, results in a watered-down version of what is contained within this great salvation.

The nature of the great salvation is such that if it is rejected or ignored, it results in the retribution or *pay day*, spoken of in the previous verse. This verse commences with mention made of escape. The escape is from the consequences of punishment following the rejection of a message and

---

3. There are mentions of this in the extra canonical works as well as those by other Jewish writers. See *Jubilees,* 1:27, 29; *Sifre* on Numbers 102 & Numbers 12:5; *Pesiqta rabati,* 21. *Mekhilta* on Exodus 20:18. Also in Josephus, *Antiquities* XV.v.3 and Philo, *De Somniis* i.143.

a provision that had far greater significance than any warnings made in the Law of Moses; all warnings were relative to punishment following failure to adhere to God's will. In addition, if there was failure here, it was not the result of ignorance or innocence. It would be blatant disobedience for which there is no mercy as already noted in verse two. The entire argument here in these two verses is the first of several in this letter to be presented in such a manner as to show that from the stronger point of view to the lesser, it is only logical that whatever is presented in the case of the covenant of the Son has to be accepted (what philosophers call an: *a fortiori* presentation). In other words, there is no escape and the outcome is absolutely disastrous for any who do not take heed of the warning.

The Great Salvation

The word "Gospel" is not found in this letter as such, but it is most certainly included here under the phrase "so great a salvation" (*tēlikautēs sōtērias*) because all that the Gospel includes is contained within the entirety of what that phrase indicates. The nature of the salvation is qualified in Greek by a demonstrative pronoun and in English by two adjectives in tandem: *such* and *great,* which amplify the nature of the wonder attached to this salvation; it means that it is difficult to describe its true nature in a satisfactory manner. It includes the entire plan of God to redeem, not only fallen humanity but the world itself; this is accomplished through the price paid by the Son and only possible through his incarnation and self-sacrifice at the cross. It was proven, as Paul says, by his resurrection from the dead (Rom 1:3–4). This salvation is equivalent to what Paul writes about in his letter to the Galatians. In fact, the Galatians seem to have had a similar difficulty in terms of abandoning the message of hope but they were guilty of attempting to replace salvation by faith for salvation by works (see Gal 1:6; 2:16). Here these individuals had become guilty of indifference and neglect. The danger for both groups was the same in terms of the outcome.

This great salvation is not just something that appertains to the present age but something that has eternal consequences; it means that retribution for mankind's sin has been dealt with by the Son so that those who embrace him can be forgiven and enter into the promises of God which have to do with the present as well as the future. This means that all of God's plans for his own, become a reality for those who submit to the Son. Elsewhere, this submission is spoken of in terms of placing one's faith in him and obeying his words and will. Through this great salvation, sinners are accepted as God's own family, together with all that this means in terms of his eternal design for a New Heaven and a New Earth where righteousness reigns; that will be in a future state of perfection under the rule of the Father the Son, and the Holy Spirit. Therefore, any neglect of this great salvation, is in effect, the spurning of the one who makes it all possible and it comes with all the penalties attached to such a rejection.

This message of such a great salvation, was first spoken by the Lord. The opening verse of the letter reminds the readers that in the past the prophets spoke the word of God. Then the word of God, in terms of the Law, involved the intermediaries who included, as already seen, Moses and the angels but now, the Lord himself is the one who brings the word. Note here, as already mentioned above, that the author uses the word "Lord" or the Greek *Kurios* which, as has already been indicated, is the equivalent in the LXX for *Yahweh* in Hebrew. This means that *Yahweh* himself has spoken as has the Son. There is therefore, no excuse for failure to listen and to obey. The Son spoke but over the entire period of his ministry so that his entire message concerns this salvation which has just been mentioned. Not only was the message one of words but it was his very life that speaks volumes as the author clarifies in the subsequent verses and specifically in verse four. Neither the author nor his readers had heard these words from the Son in person because he states that what was spoken was confirmed to himself and others by those who heard the Lord.

This factor indicates that the author was not one of the disciples of Jesus and had not been one of his followers during Christ's earthly ministry; neither could it have been Paul who had seen the Lord and heard from him directly (Gal 1:12 and see the introduction). Although the author was not an eye witness, he nevertheless, stands behind the reliability of the message as being that of the Lord himself and therefore that it is totally dependable.

v. 4 "God also bore witness by both signs and wonders and various powerful works and by gifts of the Holy Spirit given according to his will." God himself has born witness to the veracity of the message shared by these people who heard Christ, by backing up their passing on of his message with supernatural signs. These are described in terms of signs, wonders and powerful works as well as the apportioning of gifts of the Holy Spirit following his will. These three terms: signs, wonders and powerful works (*semeia, terata, dunameis* (Note that in 2 Cor 12:12, the same triplet is given by Paul) seem to be a collective grouping to show the same sorts of things that were part of Jesus' ministry during his lifetime but in the gospels, they were normally expressed in terms of signs and wonders, as in Matthew 24:24.)[4]

These supernatural events were a demonstration from God, vindicating the message that was spoken. A sign is an indicator that points to God who stands behind the miracle. Here the miracles were of various kinds which show that God is not limited to any single area of action. In spite of the teaching of the cessationists, there is nothing in Scripture that indicates that signs and wonders ever came to an end or that they were intended to do so.[5] My own experiences in Ethiopia and elsewhere, show that these signs and wonders still endure. Most of them occur in a context where the evangelism of non-Christians is taking place and the word preached is confirmed for the same reasons as at the beginning of the Church Age.[6] In the context of this letter the words would have impressed the reality of the message upon those individuals who were in doubt, since they must have also experienced the same among themselves in the past.

The way in which the author speaks of "distributions of the Holy Spirit" (*pneumatos hagiou merismois*) appears to distinguish between the witness coming from "the signs and wonders" and this category related to the "distributions." It appears to be referring to what is classified under the gifts or the *charismata* and *pneumatikōn,* which Paul elaborates upon in 1 Corinthians 12 but under a different term. Most certainly, the miracles are also identified elsewhere in the New Testament as being consequent to the preaching of the Gospel and the confirmation of God's word by the powerful works of the Holy Spirit which took place in the lives of Christ's followers.[7] Paul reminds the Galatians that the Spirit was responsible for

4. There are ten times that the couplet is used in the Gospels and Acts: Matt 24:24; Mark 13:22; John 4:48; Acts 2:43; 4:30; 5:12; 6:8; 7:36; 14:3; 15:12 once in Romans 15:19 while in Acts 8:13 there is a slight variation with "signs and great and powerful works."

5. There are conservative scholars today who cast doubt upon the reality of the continuation of the presence of these gifts at the present time. They are called cessationists because in their mind the gifts have ceased since the formation of the canon of Scripture. See Guthrie, *Hebrews,* 87, who emphasizes their presence "during the first Christian era."

6. Many converts to Christ in the mission fields of the world and especially those in lands where the Gospel has not previously been proclaimed, have been and still are being convinced by these miracles and powers, of the reality of Christ and his message. They are therefore included under what missiologists calls *power encounters.* These are occasions when signs and wonders bring about a change in mind of those who were previously unbelievers.

7. An abundance of references related to the work of the Holy Spirit in the New

the powerful works which took place among them (Gal 3:5). The qualifica-tion of the "distributions of the Holy Spirit according to his (the Spirit's) will" is significant. It demonstrates the fact that when there are miracles it has nothing to do with the people through whom the healings and miracles are operated but it depends totally upon the will of the Holy Spirit (1 Cor 12:11). He is, after all, sovereign and therefore, the signs and wonders are not in any way the result of the human instruments who are nothing more than that: The Spirit's instruments. This is important in a day when in some circles much ado is made about those who view themselves as the healers, prophets and apostles.[8]

v. 5 *"Because it was not to angels that God subjected the world to come, about which we are speaking."* It has already been pointed out that angels are servants doing God's will (1:14) but it is also true that as such they have been apportioned their activities among the present world's nations accord-ing to the LXX text of Deut 32:8, upon which this author depends. That text reads: *"When the Most High divided the nations, when he separated the sons of Adam, he set the bounds of the nations according to the number of angels."* In this way, their duties were related to the number of people upon the earth as well as this world's order.[9] However, the author of Hebrews wants to underline the fact that when it comes to the future status of the angels, the situation is very different. It is no longer the angels who will be in charge of running the governance God will put in place. The term translated "world to come" is *oikoumenē* which means the inhabited world. It is concerned with people and not just a cosmos–*kosmos* or age–*aiōnos* or "forever," which is more of a system, even if an endless one.[10] That world to come, is *subjected* to the Son of Man, who is to be named in the following verse. The word used for *subjection* is a strong one, indicating that there will be total authority wielded by him and there will be absolutely no room for any other. This aspect will be expanded upon in the following verses.

Testament are found from the day of Pentecost onward in Acts and the Epistles. Acts 2:4; 4:31; 8:17; 10:44; 15:8, 12; 19:6; 1 Cor 12:4–10; 14:1–40 et al.

8. There may be some in Western nations who boast about their healing or pro-phetic powers but in the Majority world there are many more who portray themselves in terms of God's special agents and who make claims which not only go against Scriptural teaching but pretend that their revelations have greater authority than God's word.

9. See Bruce, *Hebrews*, 32–33.

10. See Guthrie, *Hebrews*, 88. In this context *oikoumenē* is used to indicate the inhabited earth, while *kosmos* has the sense of the planet itself and *aiōnos* speaks of an indefinite age or period of time.

The author makes all this very clear when he says that it is this coming world order, which is the focus of the letter. This is the new world order, which has already been launched by the Son, through his redemptive act during the incarnation (referred to by the *cleansing* in 1:3) and followed by his resurrection. This means that, although the world to come is yet future, in terms of its finality, for all who now identify with the Son and his redemptive plan, it has already started. As is indicated in Hebrews 6:5, those who have given their allegiance to the Son have already "*tasted . . . the powerful works of the world* (age) *to come*" in the present.[11] They have not entered into it completely because there is yet work to be done on God's part, in the mopping up operation which will take place at the *Parousia*, but they have most certainly "tasted" of it.[12]

vv. 6–8a "*But someone solemnly testified somewhere saying: 'What is man that you should remember him? Or a son of man that you should watch out for him?'*" The author is not too concerned with the source of the original quotation, although we know that it is attributed to David, from Psalm 8:4–6, a psalm that is considered messianic in the New Testament. This is because Jesus himself cites from it when in confrontation with the priests and scribes after the cleansing of the temple and the reception of praise from the children (Matt 21:16 and see how Paul uses the Psalm in 1 Cor 15:27; Eph 1:22). This verse demonstrates, importantly, that the author regarded the entire Old Testament as God's word and therefore, no matter who the author or the location, it was as far as he was concerned, God speaking and therefore authoritative.

The question raised here is: "*What is man that you should remember him?*" The second strophe repeats the thought of the first since, "to remember" in the Biblical sense, is not just a mental recall; it is to take care of someone and this is what God does when he watches out on their behalf. The background of this whole quotation is most certainly related to the creation in Genesis from 1:26–28, where mankind is made in God's image and given dominion over the rest of the creation. God in all his glory bends to bestow that gift upon mankind made in His own image, just as he shares this with all through the entirety of all he has created, even if mankind lost it at the fall (Romans 3:23). The psalm introduces God's work in man, who he then goes on to call "the son of man," in the sense of being humankind. In the light of the psalm, man is the center of the declaration.

11. The thought here is much like that of Paul's in Eph 1:3 when he writes of already being blessed by God with all spiritual blessings in the heavenlies (heavenly places) in Christ. The potential is there but the not yet the finality.

12. See Hughes, *Hebrews*, 82.

However, in this context in Hebrews, as Guthrie points out, "the son of man" is more than any man but the one who portrays the perfect man who is to come or the representative and ideal man.[13] This title, which was used frequently of Jesus of himself during his earthly ministry, is the equivalent of the Last Adam (1 Cor 15:45),[14] who contrary to the first man Adam, failed and brought about the degradation of the human race. This "son of man" is the redeemer and restorer of all that was intended prior to that fateful event. Any Hebrew who knew his Scriptures would have been aware that this title referred to the *Son of Man* in Daniel 7:13 who is the Messianic figure who was to come. This perfect man therefore, anticipates all that is to come, and the author of the epistle identifies him in verse 9 as Jesus. It is to this ultimate Man to whom the phrase draws attention throughout the letter.[15]

There is, as the pattern emerges, a shifting back and forth from Adam/man, his race and its imperfections to the perfect man: Christ, in the weave of this narrative. It is vital that this is grasped early on, if the reader is to come to grips with the way in which the author intends that what is essential, should be understood.

v. 7 "*You made him a little less than the angels and you crowned him with glory and honor; you have subjected everything under his feet . . .*" The difference between the Hebrew text and that of the LXX is significant here because in the first it states: "*You made him a little lower than God*" while in the latter, "*You made him a little less than angels.*" The initial reference here is to the man who was created by God to rule over the creation which he had made. Mankind was intended to be superior to the entire creation apart from the angels. Note that the status of mankind is "*a little less than that of the angels.*" Scholars debate the significance of the Greek phrase *brachu ti*, which most translate "a little less" or "a little lower" but could also have a temporal value and would then mean "for a little time."[16] He is superior due to God's specific purpose in the creation. This declaration underlines the fact that man did not evolve from animals but that he was immediately distinguished from them and from all creatures including the angels. Therefore, apart from the angels all creatures were subjected to him.

Initially, man had glory and authority over all these creatures, as well as the planet upon which he lived but as already noted, the fall and the loss

---

13. Guthrie, *Hebrews*, 89.

14. For Paul's Adam theology see Rom 5:14–21; 1 Cor 15:22, 45.

15. See Wright, *Hebrews*, 15.

16. See Bruce, *Hebrews*, 34n22; Hughes, *Hebrews*, 85; Guthrie, *Hebrews*, 89. Who prefer "for a little while."

of the glory and honor, which were part of the original creation, meant that this subjection of the creation to him was surrendered.

It can be said that the creation, including man, is now in a state of rebellion against its Creator so that everything has changed. When this phrase is applied however, to the Son of Man (see the notes in chapter one on the "Son" and the "Son of Man") it needs to be remembered that the author is looking at two distinct levels: one related to mankind and his superiority over the creation and secondly, that of Christ, the Son at the time of his incarnation. In this second, the emphasis is upon the Son's humiliation and is parallel to the overall idea presented in Philippians 2:6–11 where Paul describes the voluntary humiliation of Christ, his incarnation and the work of the cross. This humiliation was necessary for the sacrifice required to deal with the sin question, mentioned in the prologue of this epistle (1:3) where sin was cleansed (or purged). This "Son of Man" was superior to the angels because, as already seen, he is the Creator of all and the one who upholds everything; yet for a time he becomes less than the angels when he took on humanity, in order to redeem the creation from the consequences of mankind's sin. This Son has already overcome and as stated in 1:3–4, is the inheritor of all things. For this reason, he is already crowned with glory and honor, despite the fact that this is not, as the following verse indicates, yet visible to all. In real terms it is proleptically complete.

v. 8 "You subjected all things under his feet. In the subjection nothing remains which is not subject to him. But now we do not see everything subject to him." Of mankind it is evident that originally everything was subjected to his governance. The practice of waring kings and leaders, when they overcame their enemies, was to place their foot upon the neck of the vanquished to demonstrate their absolute power over them (see Josh 10:24).[17] The picture painted here is one of absolute subjection of all and everything to mankind. The construction emphasizes the fact by means of the Hebrew style of repetition in the following phrase. But this subjection is not yet apparent to all. Man's rule however, unlike that of the Son of Man's, can never be sovereign as it is dependent upon their one and only representative who is to be named in the next verse.

If the same procedure is followed, as was indicated above and the application of these words are made at two levels, then the following needs to be understood here: First, when it comes to mankind and God's plan for the creature, everything was initially subject to him within the created sphere (except, as already noted: the angels); however, this was then lost. So, at the

---

17. See Nacht, "The Symbolism of the Show with Special Reference to Jewish Sources," 2.

next level, in the future, once more this will become a reality in the new creation, what was lost will be regained but of course under the headship of the Son of Man. As far as the Son of Man is concerned, it is not yet the fact that everything is seen to be under his jurisdiction since the evil in the world is not yet subdued as it will be in the world to come. Nevertheless, again proleptically and from God's perspective, everything has been done that needed to be put in place by the Son with his death and resurrection. The outcome is certain and in the Kingdom that is to come all will be totally under his command. This command and authority have, of course, to be seen as already in place since the One who will always be sovereign is the unchangeable God.

v. 9 *"But we see Jesus, who was made a little less than the angels, who was crowned with glory and honor because of the suffering of death so that by the grace of God he might taste death for everyone."* It is at this point that for the first time in the letter and after a long and most unusual order of words in Greek, the name of Jesus appears. It is the human name of the Son to whom the reader has been introduced from the second verse of chapter one. The significance of the paucity of Jesus' name has already been mentioned (see the section on the Son in chapter one). In this verse the fact that Jesus was made a little lower than the angels is specifically aligned with his incarnation and his redemptive plan.

To introduce this representative Man, it has to be understood that enigmas abound. He is superior to the angels but became less than them when he took on humanity. This verse speaks on the one hand of being crowned (*ēlattōmenon* a perfect participle, showing that he was and still is, crowned and will always be so) with glory and honor and then in the next breath, the author talks about the suffering of death, the fact that is central to the purpose of his incarnation. This suffering is expanded upon in the following verse. This is also the first time that the subject of Jesus' suffering of death and is introduced, although it has been referred to implicitly in 1:3, when cleansing for sin was mentioned.[18]

The theme of suffering is dominant throughout the letter (this under different headings such as diligence and endurance: 6:11; 10:32, 36; 12:7; 13:12, 13; willingness to shed blood: 12:4; following Jesus' example: 6:20; 12:2; and his sacrifice: 9:26). Here the crowning with honor and glory are linked to the suffering. The suffering of death was necessary so that Jesus should "taste death for everyone." This phrase is introduced with the construction showing that it was by the grace of God[19] that this provision was

18. See Guthrie, *Hebrews*, 90.

19. *chariti theou.* This reading is present in the majority of the major and oldest

made. This is the first of a limited number of mentions related to the grace of God in the letter (4:16; 10:29; 12:15, 28; 13:9, 12–13). The emphasis here is in the fact that without this provision of God in Christ's sacrifice, there would be no hope of escape for anyone from the consequences of mankind's rebellion.

The meaning of the "tasting" is discussed at length by scholars but without spending much unnecessary time on the subject, here it means that he died for everyone. The experience was all that death meant and it was complete; it was substitutional or on behalf of all who accept him, which means that those who then submit to his person do not have to die.[20] The significance of this substitution is another matter that is developed considerably in the rest of the letter (for the Subject of Christ's substitutionary death see *Appendix A*). It is also because of Christ's suffering of death and his subsequent victory over it, that he is then crowned with glory and honor. In the prologue (1:3) this crowning and honor is associated with the Son being seated "on the right hand of the Majesty on High," showing that the crowning is part of but consequential to, the suffering of death. The crowning would never have happened had not the former been part of the narrative.

The letter as a whole is concerned with the subject of faith and the theme fades in and out throughout because it is related to this matter of willingness to suffer, even when it seems to be inappropriate for the One who is God himself.[21] There are things which are seen and things which are not. The subjugation of all things to Jesus are not yet seen but they are certain.

v. 10 "*For it was fitting that he* (God), *for whom and by whom all things exist, in leading many sons to glory, should make the author of their salvation perfect through suffering.*" The introduction of this verse is linked to the previous by the word "For." But what is unusual is the statement that is linked to: what "*was fitting that God.*" What individual is in the position to be able to say what was fitting for God to carry out? It seems a rather audacious statement to be able to judge what was right or otherwise when

MSS but there is an alternative *chōris theou*–without God–in several minor MSS and a number of the Early Church Fathers.

20. In recent years there has been a vigorous debate regarding the whole question of the logic of substitutionary death of Christ.

21. Sometimes in this epistle the word *faith* indicates the belief manifested by the individual in the person or work of God and on other occasions it is the entirety of what being a follower of Christ stands for in terms of overall doctrine. For the first, the clearest section is in chapter 11 while in the second the verse dealing with Christ as the pioneer and finisher of our faith would be a clear representation (12:2).

it comes to God the Father's behavior. Jews could never contemplate their Messiah suffering, even if such is depicted in Isaiah 53:3–12. However, from God's perspective it was part of his entire plan and for that reason alone, it was fitting, even if it appeared to go against everything humanity could contemplate that the Father could ask of his Son. The phrase *"for whom and by whom all things"* exist, most certainly speaks of God the Father here because, the Father is the one who sent Jesus to undertake this earthly mission in order that the provision be made possible. However, without the subject of the sentence being the Father, it could have referred to Christ. This is because in the light of the Prologue (1:2–3), he is the one who is perfector and author or founder (*archēgos* see 12:2) of mankind's salvation. In terms which parallel what is mentioned in John 3:16, regarding how much God the Father cared for and loved the creation, here he put the plan for the reconciliation of mankind in place. This is why the Father provided the very means of the reconciliation of errant mankind to himself, through the Son. For that reason alone, doing what he did was fitting. Not only was it fitting but it was also essential for mankind's salvation.

This salvation is concerned with the redeemed of the earth, who become "sons of God." These are from among the sinners who are sons of Adam and who were previously totally lost but who now, because of the work of Christ are integrated into the family of God. The word "sons" here, is inclusive of all the offspring of Adam, whether male or female, who embrace Christ as redeemer.[22] The concept of family is again to be expanded upon in the next verse where the word brethren is central.

The second question which is raised here is related to the fact of perfecting the one who is the founder or the author of mankind's salvation. How could he be in any way imperfect, since it was he who was the creator of all things and the brightness of God's glory? (1: 3). There is no thought of any imperfection in the humanity of Christ or in any of his acts. Perfection has to be understood in a number of ways and the one that is at the center of the writer's thought here is that of being complete or finishing off a task (*teleioō* to bring to a completion or to accomplish something).[23] This verb is a favorite of our author's, as he uses it nine times in the letter. Perfection or completion only comes through Christ, his sacrifice and his covenant. Christ had to be made complete as the representative of humanity and in his incarnate state he had to experience everything which identifies with mankind, including the

22. The question of gender suitable language in English is relatively recent (mostly since its introduction by feminists since the 1970s). It would not have even been considered an issue at the time the New Testament was written. Sons of God would have been understood to include all who were followers of God without exception.

23. Arndt and Gingrich, 817.

suffering of death. The sin of the first Adam led to the death of all humanity, as Paul so clearly explains but the death and victory of the Last Adam leads to eternal life (Rom 5:12–19; 1 Cor 15:12, 15–22). This is the completion or the finishing off all that was necessary to bring about the fulfilment of the entire plan of God's redemption. Therefore, the plan of Christ's work and the only way of accomplishing the total identity with mankind was for him to be born as a man, live the life of a man but without sin. Then he had to die and be raised to life, to show that he was not held by the curse of sin and death. To return to the first part of the verse; this was the reason why the whole plan of God was fitting and absolutely necessary. It was the only way that the salvation, which is now available, could be made available. Christ, as the author or co-designer of the plan, together with the Father, was the only one who could make it happen.

The author of their salvation, means that Jesus was the initiator or founder and the very means of the salvation, which, as already seen, is the entire plan of God, not just of the initial step of saving or redeeming his people but the fulfilment of all that it includes subsequently as mentioned in v. 3 above.

v. 11 "Because both the one sanctifying and the one being sanctified are of one source. That is why he is not ashamed to call them brothers." The concept of sanctification or of setting oneself apart for the service of God is an important theme in this letter (10:10, 14, 29; 13:12), which has much to say about sacrifice and priesthood where Jesus is both the sacrifice and the priest. However, what is the main thought behind sanctifying or consecrating in this instance? The main thought is that of making something or someone holy but even that has a variety of implications which can be related to purification; negatively it conveys separation from what is either evil or wrong while positively it indicates making oneself totally available for the service of God.

Who is it that brings about the sanctification here? It is true that in the New Testament Paul tells believers that they are sanctified by the Spirit (Rom 15:16; 1 Cor 6:11) and in Jude it is God the Father who sanctifies his followers (Jude v.1) but here it is without question Jesus who is the subject of the entire discussion. All three members of the godhead are involved in bringing about this sanctification. More is said about this consecration/ sanctification brought about by Christ, especially in chapter 9:12–14; 10:10, 29 and 13:12. Christ was and is holy, as the one who brings about the consecration of these sons, but commitment to him and to his purposes enables those who are being sanctified to enter into the fulness of the salvation, which is not yet fully in place. Here it is also as a process because those who are participants with Christ are "being sanctified," which indicates that this separation, continues throughout one's life.

The author writes that both Christ as the sanctifier and the redeemed, who are being sanctified, are of one; this means that they both share one source or origin. What is this source? The phrase "of one" (*ex henos*) has a pronoun which could be masculine or neuter. This raises the question as to the source. Most scholars agree that if it is taken as a masculine pronoun it must refer to "one person" either God, Adam or Abraham[24] or "one thing" meaning a common humanity.[25] If it is God, it is because he is the source of all that is spiritual and physical. If it refers to something which common here, that would be their humanity, as Christ, since his incarnation, shares that with the redeemed. In whichever way it is understood, the outcome is the same; it is most likely God, because he has the final word in everything.

Christ is not ashamed to call them brothers because those who are being set apart (sanctified), are now sons; this is the reason why the Son of God is not ashamed to identify with them. After all, he is the means by which they have become part of the divine family, as they no longer identify uniquely with the human race of Adam.

v. 12 "Saying: I will proclaim your name to my brothers; in the middle of the assembly, I will sing your praise." There are now three Old Testament quotations to follow, all of which have the single intent of demonstrating Christ's filial rapport with those who are the redeemed.

i) The first is Ps 22:22, which comes from a psalm quoted several times in the New Testament (Mark 15:34 of Ps 22:1; John 19:24 quoting Ps 22:18). It was certainly recognized as Messianic by believers at the time. Bruce says, "Practically the whole of the lament to which the first part of the psalm is devoted was used in the Church from very early times as a *testimonium* of the crucifixion of Christ."[26] The quotation includes a slight variation of the LXX text.[27] In the original context the lament highlighting his suffering in the first part of the psalm, turns to public praise given among his fellows who he calls brethren in the congregation of the Jews. But here it is directed at the redeemed who are now *brothers*[28] and who gather in the congregation which by this time is known as the church (*ekklēsia*).

24. Referring to God: Guthrie, *Hebrews*, 94; Bruce, *Hebrews*, 44n64.

25. Ellingworth, *Hebrews*, 20; Hughes, Hebrews, 104–105. See that the same phrase in Acts 17:26 refers to Adam as the head of the human race.

26.. Bruce, *Hebrews*, 45.

27. The LXX opens with *diēgēsomai* I will relate, which becomes *apangelō*–I will announce, in this instance.

28. Note that brothers (*adelphoi*) here are inclusive of all, no matter what their gender.

The construction indicates that the brethren are therefore also one and the same as his Church; just as Christ passed through the deep waters of suffering and death to which all mankind is destined, he now identifies fully with his brethren in suffering, but also with them in this song of praise. It shows that the suffering has turned to victory that embraces all that is part of the new salvation of God's people. The name of brother and brethren takes on great significance, not only through the incarnation of Christ but also through suffering of his death on the cross and his resurrection; this makes him the firstborn among many brethren (Rom. 8:29). The term *brothers*, is importantly, one which, once more, indicates a level of identity with the redeemed, which would have otherwise been previously considered unthinkable. It demonstrates the complete change in status of those who were previously enemies and far from the household of God.

v. 13 The second quotation comes from Isaiah 8:17 and the third from verse 18 of the same chapter.

ii) "*And again, 'I will trust in Him.'*" At first glance, the link with the present quotation does not appear as convincing as the previous one but when it is recognized that there are considerable similarities between the prophet, his circumstances and those of Jesus, there is more to be said. For example, the name Isaiah means: Yahweh is Salvation (from a combination of *yasha*–to save–and *yah*–the abbreviated form of YHWH), which is exactly what the name Jesus means. In the same way that Christ was rejected by his own people and nation, so too the prophet during his day. Again, the Son trusted only in the Father God for all he said and did during his earthly ministry as an act of total obedience to him in all things (see John 8:28, 42; 10:25; 12:49, 50; 14:31 et al.). Even in his darkest hour, Christ looked to the Father alone when he committed his spirit to him at his death. For this reason, Isaiah could say, "*I will wait for God who has turned away his face from the house of Jacob and I will trust in Him*" (Isa 8:17 LXX). There is also the parallel statement from the psalm just quoted (22:24) which reads, "*he did not hide his face from me but heard when I cried to him.*" This bears a remarkable similarity to the words which precede the quotation here "*I will wait for the Lord, who is hiding his face from the house of Jacob*" (Isa 8:17a). These all tie the immediate thoughts together which show Christ's complete solidarity with the human race.

iii) "*And again, 'Look, I and the children God gave to me.'*" The filial language has already been mentioned (v.12). Consequently, through his suffering and death, as well as his resurrection, all of the human race who now trust in him become all of the following: sons (2.10), brothers (2.11) and children (2.13).[29] With regard to the latter these are the children born of his suffering. Isaiah had sons who were given to him to be signs to the disobedient nation concerning God's faithfulness. One was *Shearjashub* whose name meant "a remnant shall return" (Isa 7:3) and the other was *Maher-shalal-hashbaz* meaning "quick to the plunder, swift to the spoil" (Isa 8:3). Both were names indicating what God was about to do in bringing about certain judgement upon the disobedient and rebellious. Isaiah placed his complete trust in God in the midst of his circumstances.

Likewise, the Son, the one who was the Messiah, follows the Father and completes his earthly task. If the simile is followed, the brethren of Christ (the Church) are also a sign to the disobedient world of a similar judgment yet to come, if indeed they live their lives in such a way as to replicate that of their master. However, in this text the central thought is that of Christ in his humility, sharing the same humanity with all its sufferings as that of his brethren.

vv. 14–15 "*Therefore, since the children share[30] flesh and blood, Jesus also shared the same things with them so that through death, he might nullify the one having the power of death, that is the Devil and set free all those, who by fear of death were enslaved throughout their lives.*" Flesh and blood are the constituents of humanity. This seems a strange way of describing mankind in our day but it gets the point across clearly enough and that is what is intended here. It speaks of frailty and insecurity, as well as what is transient and quickly terminated by death. In his humility and in his willingness to identify with mankind, it was necessary that Christ became like man in every way. As Paul wrote, "*he emptied himself taking on the likeness of a slave he became the likeness of men*" (Phil 2:7). This is what is meant here by Christ sharing in the same things with mankind. When the author says that through death, he means the death of Christ. The purpose was so that he might destroy the one having the power of death, that means the Devil. The Greek *katargeō*, has the sense of totally abolishing or nullifying something or someone, in the sense of making it completely ineffective. In this instance the one being nullified is Satan.

---

29. Note that there are nuances attached to terms: sons–*huioi* and children–*paidia*. Moffatt sees *paidia* as the redeemed who belong to God. *Hebrews*, 33.

30. The Greek here is *kekoinōnēken*, a perfect of *koinōneō*, to share or have in common. This is similar to the idea of the verb *meteschen* (here the 3rd p. aor. of *metechō*– to share or partake in something) which shows that Christ shared this human nature but there is an important distinction. The verb relative to mankind in the perfect, shows what they were by nature from the very beginning and always were. However, with Christ, he took on this same nature of man at a point in time but was not always of that nature; he only shared it from his incarnation.

This declaration goes right to the heart of the reason for and the fact of the incarnation of Christ and his entire ministry. His earthly mission was for the sole purpose of bringing about the total downfall of Satan, including his power over death, which is necessary for the ultimate redemption of mankind. Christ had to become fully man in order to vanquish sin and the Devil on mankind's behalf. So, what appeared at first to be a defeat, when Christ died upon the cross, was in fact a declaration of victory when he rose from the dead. He had first to die but death could not hold him because he was without sin. His resurrection was a declaration that Satan was no longer a threat to the children of God because the question of sin and all its consequences had been dealt the final blow.

The question may be asked: How it is that Satan holds the power of death? Ultimately, all things lie in the hand of God as sovereign, including life and death. However, because of sin, which entered due to Satan, it is in that sense that he is the cause of death which is the result of sin and held it in his power. Now that the sin question has been resolved by Christ's sacrifice, so too is the question of the consequences of sin, which means that Satan has been stripped of the instruments he held, which led to this death. Consequently, sin and death no longer have the final word. Death is, after all, nothing more than a state of judgment or punishment and now that a way of escape has been provided for all the children of God, Satan no longer holds any power in that domain. More will be said about the subject of Christ's death and suffering as the letter progresses (5:7; 9:26; 13:12) as it is a recurring theme.

The setting free of those in bondage to the slavery of sin was the purpose of the entire mission of Christ. This slavery included all and every part of the life of any and all who have not submitted to the mastery of Christ. In the background of everything that occurs, the threat of death rules for all who are not Christ's followers. This bondage holds the whip over the life of all and tempers everything that occurs because it is spurred on by the fear of death. The fear of this death is not just a matter of the uncertainty of the physical cessation of life but the pressure of eternal judgment so that the fear is in every way real and limiting for the ungodly. This liberation now allows the full enjoyment of a life that is filled with the assurance of being in perfect accord with one's maker and the knowledge that the physical death which awaits all mankind, does not have the final say. This is because the same resurrection which brought Jesus back from the dead, awaits all who have been emancipated by his victory. Instead of the fear of death and its consequences, now there is the hope for the *now* as well as for the future (1 Cor 15:42–49, 52–55; 1 Thess 4:16–17).

It is for the above reasons that there should be no fear of death in the life of any believer in Jesus. There is no sting in death (1 Cor 15:56) now that sin has been conquered by Christ so that all children of God, indeed all those who are Christ's brethren, need have no fear, even when they stare death in the face.[31]

v. 16 *"Because, of course, it is not angels that he comes to help but he helps the offspring of Abraham."* The focus of this verse is once more to give assurance to those who need reminding that the Son who is Jesus, had a mission directed at humanity and not angels. The former are described here as Abraham's offspring. This does not limit the outcomes because Abraham is known as the Father of faith (Rom 4:12, 16–17). Jesus had no thought of coming to help fallen angels but humanity. The verb translated "to help" (*epilambanomai*),[32] has the sense of taking hold of something or someone either to help or to hinder. It is a certain action and elsewhere in this letter (8:9) is used to depict God's certain action when he took his people by the hand to lead them out of Egypt. Here it shows Christ's work of taking on human nature rather than an angelic one, in order to bring about a positive outcome with regard to mankind's salvation.

v. 17 *"For that reason he had to be made like his brothers in every way so that he might become a merciful and faithful high priest in matters related to God, to make propitiation* [see below] *for the sins of the people."* In order to help mankind, Jesus had to be human or like his brothers, in every way. This emphasizes his human nature, which is the same as that of all mankind. There is no way in which those who teach that Jesus was not a real man but some sort of elevated spirit, can get around what is stated so clearly in these verses. In this verse the reason is, furthermore related to his office as High Priest, where this title is introduced for the first time. He needed to be a merciful and faithful high priest. It becomes evident that his high priestly role is more than merely officiating, since he also becomes the sacrifice which is offered as the propitiation which covers all sin.

This High Priest's attributes are qualified by the words *"merciful and faithful,"* something which is not identified in other passages associated with Levitical priests other than in the promised faithful priest to come (1 Sam 2:35); they include Shelemiah, together with his colleagues, who are called faithful in the fulfilment of their duties (Neh 13:13). Christ was faithful in his fulfilment of the design of the Father who sent him (3:2, 5–6)

---

31. This has considerable consequences for all followers of Christ, especially when they face persecution and any physical pain associated with the event of the physical cessation of life.

32. See, Arndt and Gingrich, 295.

but also to the task to which he was committed in the giving of himself to the people, who were previously his enemies (10:23). In addition, he was merciful in his willingness to die for all sinners when he offered himself as their propitiation (8:12).

This title of "High Priest" is repeated (at least 18 times) in the letter and is a major theme, demonstrating the superior High Priesthood of Christ's in thirteen of them. In this matter, the title is unique in New Testament literature in pointing to Christ.[33] During his earthy ministry he was not qualified to be a priest. This was because he was not of the Levitical line; as the author points out when he gets to chapter 5:6, he was not from one of the tribes which qualified but his superior priesthood is like that of the order of Melchizedek. He predates the Levitical system and elevates the priesthood to an altogether different level from that of anything that follows Moses and the Law. Christ's offering of himself means that his propitiatory offering of himself can never be matched by any other high priestly sacrifice.

Propitiation or Expiation

The word from which *propitiation* or *expiation*[34] is translated in the Greek of this verse, is the verb *hilaskomai*. It is only used as a verb twice in the New Testament (Luke 18:13 and here in Heb 2:17). However, in its substantive forms, it appears twice as *hilasmos* (1 John 2:2; 4:10) and twice as *hilastērion* (Rom 3:25; Heb 9:5).

How are we to understand the sense of *hilastērion* (propitiation)? The Romans and the Greeks had the custom of giving propitiatory offerings when they had offended any particular god or gods. The reason behind this was the following: When someone has offended another, they will separate; the result will be that there is no communion between them. However, if the person responsible for the offence presents a votive or propitiatory offering to the offended one, then the latter will forget about what was done and communion will be re-established. In this case, God could not pardon the offenders for their wrong without contravening his own standards of what is right and what is wrong. But, instead of waiting for the offender to

---

33. See Ellingworth, *Hebrews*, 23.

34. Several scholars favor the concept of expiation or covering, over propitiation; see Dodd, *Romans*, 54–55; Morris, *Apostolic Preaching*, 144–147 is adamant that the major thought in the spilling of blood in *hilastērion*, is that of sacrificial death on behalf of another; therefore, it indicates substitution, a theme which many find hard to grasp in our day.

provide a satisfactory propitiation, which would never have been possible, it is God who takes the initiative by providing a propitiatory offering in the person of his Son. Christ becomes the *hilastērion* provided by the offended God.

A similar sense is found in the Old Testament when God provides the propitiatory offering (also called atonement or an expiatory offering) as in Leviticus 17:11 where we read that "the life of a creature is in the blood and I have given it to you to make atonement (כפר *Kipper,* in Hebrew, and in the Greek of the LXX: *exilaskomai*) for yourselves on the altar; it is the blood that makes atonement for one's life." In Romans 3:25, where Paul he adds to the fact that Christ is our propitiation "in his blood" and here in Hebrews 2:17, this is Christ's own offering of himself on behalf of the sins of all who would embrace his person and work. In this act, he fulfils in person and perfectly, what all the previous occasions when propitiation was carried out through the sacrifices, could only be portrayed figuratively and imperfectly. This sacrificial nature of the work of Christ cannot be misconstrued to mean anything else. In Romans 1:18, it is by faith in the expiatory offering of Christ, that the wrath of God, is turned away. This wrath has already been poured out upon the person of Christ, who died, the innocent for the guilty. This means that his sacrifice is the perfect substitution for mankind's sin.

Now God is able to forgive the sinner who accepts the sacrifice of Christ on the grounds that his sacrifice has satisfied the punishment due to the sinner, who is now covered by this atoning blood. In the LXX, *hilastērion* is also used to refer to the "mercy seat," or the cover of the ark upon which the sacrificial blood was poured out once a year on the day of atonement (Lev. 16:2, 15–34); that is how it is portrayed later in Hebrews 9:5. It was linked with the annual Day of Atonement. Therefore, in Romans It is very likely that Paul was portraying Christ as the fulfilment or the antitype of the "mercy seat" as does the author to the Hebrews. As Moo states:

> This interpretation, which has an ancient and respectable heritage, has been gaining strength in recent years. It is attractive because it gives to *hilastērion* a meaning that is derived from its "customary" biblical usage, and creates an analogy between

a central OT ritual and Christ's death that is both theologically sound and hermeneutically striking.[35]

Dodd, sees *hilastērion* in the LXX as "the means of expiation" but does not see the concept of turning away wrath as a biblical concept.[36] However, this interpretation of Dodd's is questionable because the connotation of propitiation has led the translators of the LXX to use the Greek root *hilask*–and although the primary thought with *kpr* may be that of wiping away of sin, the idea of turning away of wrath is not absent. Garnet points out that passages in the Old Testament, as well as those in the Qumran Scrolls, make it evident that *kipper* can, in certain usage, be understood to convey the idea of propitiation and that expiation and propitiation both imply the presence of the other. Having looked at Morris he says: "With the exception of Isa 28:18, *kipper* always retains overtones of the putting away of wrath, both in the Old Testament and in the Qumran literature."[37]

Nevertheless, if one comes back to the way in which *hilaskomai* is used here and in the other NT texts, God is always the one who makes the provision because his overriding goal is to bring back a fallen generation to himself, driven by his love (Rom 5:8) and that overrules wrath in this provision.

v. 18 "Because in the same way he suffered, when he was tempted, he is able to help those being tempted." This last verse may at first appear to be out of place in the discussion which has been taking place but this is not so at all. The central thought here is that because of his humanity and total identification with mankind, Christ is the ideal person to be on one's side. From the beginning of his ministry and throughout, until the very end, he was subjected to all kinds of temptations. It is not only the testing in the wilderness (Matt 4:1–11) that comes to mind but Christ's prayer to the Father, that if it be possible that he should avoid having to drink the cup of suffering represented by the cross (Luke 22:42). His suffering of every kind, was associated with his incarnation, which was entirely due to the redemptive plan. The fact that he was tempted, is part of that association and consequently, he is not some remote divine power who is unaware of mankind's

35. Moo, *Romans*, 232–33.

36. Dodd, *Romans*, 78–79.

37. Garnet, "Atonement Constructions in the Old Testament and the Qumran Scrolls," 161–163.

real struggles and temptations. As mankind's High Priest, who has walked the same path and overcome, he is able to intercede on man's behalf, at the right hand of the Majesty on High and provide the help that is required (see 4:16). This declaration makes it very clear that Christ is available and waiting to grant the help each believer needs in the vicissitudes of daily life.

3.

Jesus is superior to Moses 3:1-6

Moses was most highly regarded by the Jewish people as a whole because of his remarkable ministry, as well as his role in the granting of the Law. Perhaps some of the readers would have regarded Moses as having a ministry more significant than that of the angels because of their high regard for the Law. This section demonstrates the fact that in spite of his place in history, his person and his role, he was only a servant of God and therefore, inferior to the Son who was and is, over all God's household. Jesus outshines Moses by far and has to be given the first place.

v. 1 "*Consequently, holy brothers, you who share in a heavenly calling, consider Jesus, the apostle and high priest of our confession,*" The opening adverb of the verse "therefore" or "consequently," (*hothen*), shows its logical dependence upon what has gone before in the previous chapter, even if it does not appear at first glance to have anything to do with what follows. But it does because the author takes up once more, the concept of belonging to the divine family by linking the reality of holiness and being brothers. Any understanding of holiness has to include the consequence of being set apart or sanctified and that of being made brothers of the One who sanctifies all the redeemed (2:11-12). The word "holy" has already been included as the qualifier of the name of the Holy Spirit (2:4) and the same title is given to the Spirit of God five times in the letter. It is also used when associated with holy places[1] (8:2; 9:1, 2, 3, 8, 12, 24-25; 10:19; 13:11). Here the author uses it to qualify the brethren in a manner similar to that used by Paul who

---

1. Note that some form of the Greek word *hagios*–holy–is present in the original MSS of all these verses but sometimes is omitted in the translations.

addresses the believers as "saints and faithful brethren" (Col 1:2). The use of the name "saint" or "holy one" cannot be taken lightly when what it signifies reminds us of the only way of being designated such, is through the death and resurrection of Christ.[2]

The calling here is a *heavenly* one. The word "call" (*klēsis*) itself, which the author links to the heavenlies, is therefore divine. It comes from God and is brought about through the Son and the Holy Spirit. This term, in its various forms, is a favorite of Paul's (see Rom 8:28, 30; 9:11, 24 et al.[3]) and as in all these instances, always indicates that it originates from God. Those who respond to this call become, as already indicated, brethren of Christ and sons of God. Since the call is heavenly and it originates from there, its purposes are likewise distinct from those associated with mankind's temporary dwelling place. This means that the ultimate purpose of this calling is not to any earthly destiny, even if that is not completely absent in Scripture as a whole.

This is the first time that this term "heavenly" is introduced in the letter. It is the first of 6 occurrences related to what is to come (6:4; 8:5; 9:23; 11:16; 12:22). But it is not the first time the concept has been introduced, as the question of the subjection of the world to come, which was part of the earlier discussion, has already been raised (2:5).[4] The heavenly calling immediately differentiates between what is of the world to come and what is of the earth or of what is present and what belongs to the future.

The readers are ordered to consider with great care. The word *consider* is an imperative (*katanoēsate*), which has the force of taking hold of something mentally in such a way that you reflect deeply upon the subject. Here the subject is called "*the Apostle and High Priest of our confession: Jesus.*"[5] This means that much thought needs to be given to all that is relative to each

2. The way in which the Catholic Church classifies certain individuals as saints due to the supposed attainment of certain criteria, is not what the New Testament understands concerning this word. However, it should never be thought that the abundance of the grace of God means that being holy does not have any links to the necessity to live a lifestyle consequent with the name.

3. In Pauline usage it mostly has a technical sense of its own indicating an effective call. For more on the way in which "heavenly" is to be understood see Garrard, *Ephesians*, 7–8 and n11.

4. The concept of the heavenlies or heavenly dimension is not unique to Hebrews, as it is a common expression used by Paul in his letters and especially in Ephesians where, as here, it is used to differentiate between the heavens and the earth (see Eph 1:3 et al.).

5. Note that in some of the older translations such as the KJV, Christ is added to his name so that is becomes, Jesus-Christ. There is no justification for its inclusion according to the Greek Manuscripts.

individual's rapport with this Apostle and High Priest. This would include: his person, his work, his sovereign rule and the wonder of what the relationship means, not just in the present but for eternity in the world to come. The terms may not be spelled out as such but the author is calling each follower (brother) to have a full understanding of who Christ really is; this is absolutely incumbent upon each believer in Jesus.[6]

Jesus is called both the Apostle and High Priest in this verse. This is the only place in the New Testament that gives him this title of Apostle. The apostles elsewhere are representatives of Christ, commissioned and sent out by him but here he is the One sent out from the Father on an earthly mission as the Father's appointee. Elsewhere, especially in John's Gospel, Jesus does emphasize the fact that he was sent by the Father (John 3:17, 34; 5:36; 6:29 et al.), which indeed makes him the first and greatest of all the apostles. Similarly, he is the High Priest representing God on the one hand and man on the other. Jesus has already been called High Priest in the last chapter (2:17), a title which is frequently employed by the author of the letter, to identify him. If parallels here with Moses are the focus, then although Moses is nowhere called an apostle or a high priest, he was both, in the sense that he was chosen and appointed by God in both areas. He was certainly the bearer of God's word with all that meant in terms of God's full authority, as were the later apostles of the New Testament who established God's authoritative truth for all time in the period after the Old Testament. Jesus, as God in the flesh is the supreme model of what an Apostle should be. The rest of the narrative will demonstrate why Jesus is superior to Moses in all these functions.

Christ is both Apostle and High Priest of *our confession*. Paul uses the word "faith" or our common faith (see Titus 1:4) and Jude our "common salvation" (Jude v.3) when he refers to the whole body of belief and what this means to be a follower of Jesus but here the author speaks of "our confession." Certainly, part of the confession is an ongoing conviction on the part of each believer in Christ, which is more than a verbal declaration but the consequence of this consideration that leads to a healthy and vibrant relationship with him.

v. 2 "who was faithful to the one appointing him, as also Moses was (faithful) *in all his* [God's] *house."* This verse continues to expand upon the faithfulness of Christ to his Father in his earthly mission. He has already

6. In today's terms this means each believer should have some coherent understanding of a biblical Christology in order that, as Peter says in his first epistle 3:15, each person should be in a position to be able to give a defense (*apologia*) of the reason for the hope within them. More than that, they should know who Christ really is, so that they may render him his due in every way.

been qualified as faithful in the previous chapter (2:17). This reinforces that factor as he is sent by the Father, as both his apostle and high priest. The theme of faithfulness is central here to both Christ and Moses.

An Apostle does not represent himself but another (here it is God the Father) and it is the will of the one who sends him that is of foremost importance in their mission. The word translated *"to the one who made"* or *"appointed"* (*poiēsanti*) *"him,"* has nothing to do with Jesus being created, as some groups have misinterpreted the sense of this declaration but to the specific appointment and commission as Apostle and High Priest. Although, Athanasius[7] links the participle ("the one making him") to Christ's incarnation and redemptive task and not his origins in his arguments with Arius, it is simpler to understand the phrase as meaning "the one who *appointed* him." This is the way the same verb is used by Mark in 3:14 when Jesus appointed his apostles. Jesus carried out this mission faithfully and exactly, as it was designed, despite its severity and what it cost him. The fact of his service in the will of God is brought up again in chapter 10:7, 9 where it states *"Look, I have come . . . O God to do your will."* Yet Moses is in no way demeaned in this mention, because to have done so would have immediately antagonized the Jewish Christian readers.

When Aaron and Miriam contested Moses' behavior in his taking of a non-Jewish wife, God spoke to them together with Moses. He said of the latter: *"in my house*[8] *he is faithful"* (Num 12:7b. LXX). Interestingly, in the same passage, Moses is compared with the other prophets as being far superior, since his conversations with God were *"mouth to mouth . . . and not in dark speeches"* (Num 12:8 LXX). So, not only was he an ambassador but he was also a prophet. Further, although he was not an official priest, as was his brother Aaron, when it came to being a mediator on behalf of the people, there was no other like him, apart from Christ (see Num 11:2; 21:7).

The additional sphere of these prophets' faithfulness *"in my house,"* is significant because it not only means in the *house,* as in the temple of God but the *household* and the family of God's people. So, the activities are not limited to any one sphere but to the entirety of God's community and includes all those who are within that community. Similarly, Christ's service had no limits and was to the entire human community, even if not all that community appreciated who he was and the consequences of his service.

7. Athanasius, *Oariones contra Arianos*, ii. 9.

8. There is a variant reading in the MSS here where some well-known and early MSS add: *holō*–the whole (א, A, C, D, Ψ, the Old Latin, Vulgate, Syriac, Armenian and others). The reading: *"en tō oikō autou"* is present in 𝔓46, 𝔓13, B, the Sahidic, Boharic *et al.* and by Ambrose and Cyril. However, *holō* does occur in verse 5 and it is thought that most likely for that reason it was added here to facilitate agreement.

vv. 3–4 "For he (Jesus) was counted worthy of more glory than Moses, in the same way, the one who builds a house has more honor than the house itself. For every house is built by someone but the one who has built everything is God." Both Jesus and Moses were faithful in the tasks appointed to them but this does not mean that overall, they were equal and this is what the author wishes to underline here. The connection with what has preceded is indicated by the use of the conjunction "For" *(gar)* at the beginning of the verse. The name of Jesus is not used here but the demonstrative pronoun "this one" or "he" *(houtos* masc.) refers to Jesus in verse 1. The purpose is to show that the glory Jesus possessed, is greater than that of Moses, in the same way that the architect and constructor of any house is obviously more significant than the house itself.

Moses was a servant in the household but he was not its originator. Christ, the Son, is the one who brought everything into existence and who similarly maintains everything (1:2, 3) so he is the builder, while Moses is just a servant entrusted with God's house (Num 12:7). The concept of God being the builder of a house here, could have its origin in a number of Old Testament texts[9] but one of the clearest may be in 2 Sam 7:13 where the context is the establishment of David's eternal kingdom. Because of what has already been stated at the commencement of the letter regarding the Person of the Son and the fact that he was the one who brought everything into existence, as Bruce states, it could be that the statement related to God building everything. It could certainly apply to Jesus' divinity here but the thrust is rather that God is the maker of all things and the comparison with Moses is that he does not have that role and is therefore automatically inferior to Jesus.[10] There is no distinction made between the Father and Christ in this verse in terms of the outcomes of the finality of God building the house. They both work in perfect harmony in everything related to the creation; specifically, the Son as redeemer and the head of the new creation, is as Peter says, the "chosen cornerstone" of the spiritual house being built by Jesus (1 Pet 2:4–6).

v. 5 "And Moses, on the one hand, was faithful in all his household as a servant to bear witness to the things that were to be spoken later." The faithfulness of Moses to speak to what was known at that time concerning God's will, is beyond doubt. He was part of the household of Israel, which was God's people during the Old Covenant and he carried out his duties as God required in every way. In this verse the word for "a servant" *(therapōn)* is

---

9. Among other possible source texts are: 1 Sam 2:3, 5; 2 Sam 7:13, 27; 1 Kings 11:38; 1 Chron 17:10.

10. Bruce, *Hebrews*, 57 especially n14.

unique in this form in the New Testament. It does not have the same force as "slave" (*doulos*), the normal word used as the equivalent elsewhere in the epistles. In this form in Biblical literature, it is only used to qualify Moses (Exod 14:31; Num 11:11; 12:7, 8; Deut 3:24), so may be intended to show a special relationship between himself and God in this service. However, what Moses had to say was not the final word and with regard to the future there was much that was still obscure. This was not due to any fault or failing on his part but it was due to the fact that in the economy of God there was a plan which had to be progressively fulfilled. Everything at that time was the equivalent of what the author goes on to call "*a shadow of things to come*" (10:1) because all awaited the coming of Christ at his incarnation. That later time is now here, as was indicated in the prologue to the letter, when the author says that in these last days God has spoken to us through the Son. Immediately, whatever may have been spoken of by Moses, is surpassed and now put in place by Christ.

v. 6 "*But on the other hand, Christ, as a son over his household, whose household we are if we hold fast to our confidence and boasting in our hope.*"[11] Christ was everything Moses had been to Israel in God's house and more. He was not just a servant but a son. The nature of this sonship has already been discussed in the first chapter (v.2). This son is The Son who is Jesus the Creator of all and the one who upholds everything (1:2–3). The household is no longer limited to Israel but to all who accept the conditions which depend upon the Son. Today the equivalent of Israel has now become the new people of God–the Church–which has come under the jurisdiction of the Redeemer and is inclusive of all, not because of ancestral ties but because of the subjection of each individual's hope to the Son. There are a number of important issues in this verse.

First the Mosaic system has been overtaken by that of the Son. It becomes clear in the following chapters that this means that what was in place previously under Moses, has been replaced by the new order of Jesus. Certainly, Jesus the Son, has replaced Moses the servant, as head of the house. Secondly, the boundaries of the house have been extended to include non-Jews (Gentiles) and the Son is responsible for the conditions for each one to be included. This household now includes all followers of Jesus and we know them collectively as the members who constitute the Church. This verse underlines the fact that all followers of Jesus the Messiah (Christ), belong to this new household of God which no longer operates under the same Mosaic or Levitical rules. But any belonging to the household is conditional. The Greek construction of the phrase "*if we hold*

---

11. Some manuscripts add "firm to the end" probably transposed from 3:14.

fast to the confidence and boast in our hope . . ." (*ean tēn parrēsian kai to kauchēma tēs elpidos kataschōmen*) shows that to belong to the household requires an ongoing adherence to our hope demonstrated by being willing to boast about it. The sentence is very similar to what is stated in 10:23. The word translated *confidence* here is from the Greek *parrēsia;* primarily it has the sense of boldness and openness. Things are not hidden but out in the open. It elevates all one's hopes because uncertainty no longer has a place. This is important when it comes to faith because this boldness leads to the believer's strong conviction and complete assurance.

There has to be a taking hold of all that it means to be part of the household. In other words, there are *inhouse rules,* even if those rules are no longer based upon what they used to be (no longer those of the Old Covenant). The word translated "To take hold of" (*kataschōmen.* aor. *of katechō*), means to possess or adhere firmly to something. This exhortation to hold fast or cling onto something with all one's strength, appears here and three other times in the letter (3:14; 4:14; 10:23); it is used by the author to encourage passionate perseverance in one's faith. The hope here is not hope as it is understood in most circles today, as some whimsical desire or happenstance. It is equivalent to the focal point of all that being a follower of Christ means. The word hope itself (*elpidos*) comes from the same root as "faith" (*pis* from *pistis*) where that word means total trust in the person and work of Christ as Lord and Master.

It needs to be remembered that the people to whom the letter is addressed are contemplating going back to their former faith in Judaism, with its trust in forms and rituals wrapped up in the Levitical code. They are thinking that perhaps they will be able to escape the persecution associated with being Christians and thereby settle down to live a life acceptable to what was seen as the status quo in the Roman Empire. The author is showing them that if that happens there is great danger ahead, as far as their eternal lives are concerned. This is not the time for being in a freewheeling mode but the need is to hold fast to one's hope in Christ and all he represents and to do so with total conviction. This thought here is repeated several times in the letter. The author is underlining the fact that to continue to belong to this household, requires unflinching devotion, without which the danger of exclusion becomes a reality.

3:7–19 The rejection of God's offer under Moses had severe consequences

This section is a combination of thoughts related to what has just been said about holding fast to the Christian's hope. This matter requires immediate action in order to avoid the example of Israel in the wilderness (3:7–11) which develops Psalm 95:7–11 and the dangers of failing to enter into the rest which God promises his people for faithfulness and obedience. Here, it is especially the recalling of the people's rebellion in Numbers 14:1–35 that is brought to mind.

v. 7 *"Wherefore, as the Holy Spirit says 'Today if you hear his voice . . .'"* Again, the "wherefore" links this section with what has just been said regarding the importance of each individual holding fast with confidence to their hope in Christ. This same theme is reinforced here. It is significant that the author specifically attributes Psalm 95:7–11 to the inspiration of the Holy Spirit and thereby the words of the Old Testament in like manner (see 9:8). This is again an affirmation of the divine origin of the Old Testament. The thought is similar to the declaration of Paul to Timothy in his second epistle (3:16) where he affirms that all Scripture is breathed by God (see also 2 Pet 1:21b). The first part of the verse is an assurance that it is the Holy Spirit who is the one behind the declaration of this specific word related to the putting into practice of God's plans. In the instance of the Psalm 95, the section that is quoted is from the second part of the same, which bears upon his present theme: the need for obedience.

The children of Israel were delivered from Egypt by the hand of God when he divided the waters of the Red Sea and took his people to safety, although he destroyed their enemies in the flood as the waters covered them. The whole episode was miraculous and an object lesson that nothing was too hard for God. However, despite that, it was not long before these same people were quarrelling and testing God.[12] It was that which caused God's judgment upon the nation.

Here, *hearing* is not merely recognizing an audible message. The way in which the Hebrews understood the word was linked to the practical application of what the message implied. Therefore, it is not enough to hear something. It has to be followed up with action on the part of the hearer. This is the message of the Holy Spirit in this verse.

The word *"today"* is of great importance to the author, as he uses it three times in the context (here in vv. 7–8; then 15 and again in 4:7). What

---

12. The Hebrew words *Meribah*–strife, quarrelling, provocation or complaining and *Massah*–temptation or testing (see Exod 17:7).

he is doing is making what happened in Exodus applicable to his readers. If that same methodology is applied to readers now, then the present practice is the same for each generation. *Today* is just as meaningful for those who live in the twenty first century as for those who lived at the time of Moses, the Psalmist who wrote the words originally penned, or the first readers of the letter to the Hebrews.

v. 8 "do not harden your hearts as in the rebellion in the day of the testing in the desert" Do not harden your hearts, as was the case of the nation at that time. The actions of the people resulted in the names which testify to strife– *Meribah*–and testing or provocation and temptation–*Massah*–being given to the places where the events happened. That was when the people's rebellion occurred; that was because they were calling out for water and blamed God at Rephidim (Exod 17:1–3). The people themselves did not realize that they were the ones who needed to trust in the same God who had delivered them from Egypt. Moses became the object of their grumbling but they also were complaining against God when they asked the question: "Is the Lord amongst us or not" (Exod 17:7).[13] The author calls this the day of provocation or rebellion, as a consequence of the people's action. It became a notable and notorious event in terms of being remembered as a marker which brought about their eventual downfall. In addition to the rebellion, the fact of the people's spiritual state was central to what occurred. They had hard hearts. This was the real reason for their disobedience and their failure to trust in the God who should have been their hope. It took place when the nation was in the desert which the author goes on to elaborate upon in the following verse.

v. 9 " when your fathers tempted me in testing me and saw my works for forty years." This took place when the Jews' forefathers, saw the hand of God at work in all the miracles and participated in the provision of the quail, as well as the benefits of the daily manna (Exod 16:13–18). Nevertheless, unbelief and disobedience prevailed. In a manner similar to that in which Jesus identified the leadership of the Jews in the Gospels with the unbelievers who worked against the will of God, so too here the author of the letter identifies the readers with those of Moses' day (Matt 23:30–32; Luke 6:23; 11:47–48.; John 6:49) and of being in danger of a similar outcome. Not only was this disobedience true on this single occasion; it was a characteristic of the people that they continually behaved in the same faithless and disobedient manner. In Numbers 14:22–23. Yahweh made a very clear declaration that none of the people who had seen his acts from the time

---

13. Note that this rebellion is all the more striking in the light of the fact that it was just prior to the granting of the ten commandments in Exod 20.

of their deliverance from Egypt and participated in the provision but who nevertheless "*tested me these ten times and have not obeyed my voice shall see the land that I swore to give to their fathers.*"

This indicates that the disobedience was not just a single error but an ongoing series of actions over a protracted period of time (forty years) and all sprang from hardened hearts. Alford says that the *works* referred to here, do not include the miracles as a whole, in terms of provision and help but God's judgments which follow the disobedience of the people.[14] However, although the provocations were at the start of the forty years, the miracles, such as the provision of the manna, continued past that period, to the first harvest in the promised land (Josh 5:12). Therefore, in whichever way the forty years of seeing God's works, is to be viewed, whether in terms of years of punishment or in terms of miraculous provision, it would be a time during which all understood that it could have been avoided had the people been obedient. Consequently, they had all that time to contemplate the folly of their testing God (see the discussion on the subject in 6:4).

v. 10 "*Therefore, I was angry with that generation and I said 'They always go astray in their heart: they have not known my ways.*'" Because of this continued unwillingness to submit to God displayed in their disobedience, God was angry with that generation. The word which is translated variously: grieved, provoked or angry (*prosochthizō*)[15] is only found here and in verse 17 in the New Testament. Obviously, when human emotions are attributed to God it should be understood that we are speaking as humans and this is clearly an anthropomorphism, identified with him here. From the context of that generation testing God over a protracted time, the passage demonstrates an antagonistic spirit on their behalf. Consequently, there is great disappointment on the part of God (again an anthropomorphism), as he looks for a willing and obedient response from the people he has loved and sought to help over the entirety of that time. So, if there is anger here, it is mixed with hurt and that is why some translations have used the word "*grieved*" here. That generation, refers specifically to the one which rebelled in the desert. It included all the adults who had been taken out of Egypt and had seen all the miraculous works of God. The only two who were spared were Joshua and Caleb.

14.. Alford, "*Pros Ebraious.*" iv, 66, writes concerning the phrase "and saw my works . . . i.e. my penal judgements." He continues that to understand the "works" here in terms of "miracles of deliverance . . . is not so likely seeing that these provocations happened at the beginning of the forty years."

15. See Ardnt & Gingrich, 725. The sentiment is one which results from continual spurning of direction and help when the one making the request is doing their utmost to assure the best outcome for those involved.

The source of the disobedience which results in them "going astray" is given as a problem of mankind's heart. This dates back to Adam's desire to be independent, which was followed by his sin. Therefore, if there is a heart problem, it is firstly a sin problem. In verse 8, hard hearts were clearly behind the testing of God. This state is due to an unwillingness to subject oneself to God and his will. When this occurs, the consequence is errant behavior because the individual's conduct is instantly at odds with God's purposes. Conflict between God and the individual became the immediate issue. Following on from this war with their maker, is a state of ignorance. This ignorance is not because God does not wish to communicate or transmit the appropriate information but because the heart of the person is unable to perceive the information which only follows when obedience and trust is placed in him. For this reason, one leads to the other; hard heartedness to ignorance and ignorance to greater hard heartedness. It is a vicious circle. It needs to be remembered that in the example of Israel and what happened to them in the desert, God was doing everything necessary to reveal his will and ways to the people through his actions; these manifestations were not only visible but tangible. They had no excuse at all for their rejection of his continuous offer which would have led to trust. That is why God complains that they did not know his ways or plans, even if they had been the benefactors of his works and provision. This demonstrates that experience of the latter does not guarantee understanding of the former.

v. 11 "*As I swore in my wrath, 'They shall not enter into my rest.'*" Once more, emotions are expressed and attributed to the person of God. They are, as already stated, anthropomorphic expressions because wrath, when used to describe God, is associated immediately with the concept of rightness or righteousness, justice and correct behavior. Consequently, wrath is an action of God, which restores what he sees as necessary for what he requires as equilibrium in the rule of his creation. The swearing of an oath by God may appear out of place because usually an oath is only seen as binding where a divinity stands behind the words where an individual is avowing something before another. However, here and later in the letter, we see that God swears by himself (6:13) because there is no one greater. Therefore, when he does swear, as here, he is affirming that there is no alternative to what he has said. It is absolute. In this instance it is the matter that this disobedient generation would never enter into his rest. The Greek phrase: *ei eiseleusontai eis ten katapausin mou* ("if they shall enter into my rest") forms a construction in which the *ei*/if, forms a strong Hebraic idiom, meaning: it is never going to happen.[16] That this is the correct translation is verified in the repetition in a slightly different construction in verse 18 below.

How is the last phrase to be understood? To what does this *rest (katapausis)* refer? More will be seen in the treatment of the subject in chapter four. But in the context of Exodus, it was the promised land, to which the people were headed (Deut 12:9). They would not get there and would die in the desert. Even Moses was prevented from entering the promised land because of his disobedience when he struck the stone from which the water flowed, instead of speaking to it, as commanded (Num 20:11–12). Nevertheless, by the time Psalm 95:11 is written, there is already another meaning attached to this *rest*. This would have to be seen as a rest, in their entire relationship with God. Yet Bruce points out that Rabbi Aqiba, commenting on Ps 95 and Num 14:35, concluded that the rebellious generation which was sanctioned, would not have any "part in the age to come."[17] This shows that the thinking of Jewish scholars at approximately the same time as this letter, saw more to the *rest* than making it into the promised land.[18] When it comes to the present letter and its readers, the rest is a heavenly or, other than this worldly rest, which chapter 11:14–16 describes as, a country and a city prepared by God. Therefore, it is an eschatological and final rest.

v. 12 "*Watch out brothers, lest there should be in any of you, an evil unbelieving heart causing you to depart from the Living God.*" Since this is a strong warning, it is most likely the phrase is a command and as such, a present continuous injunction to keep on the lookout.[19] The author clearly has strong feelings toward his readers when he calls them *brothers*, which means they are still seen to be belonging to the household of Christ at that time. He has not yet condemned them all or classified them globally as associated with those described above. This is a call to action on the part of those who have been steadfast to take care of those who are on the brink of losing their faith in Christ and abandoning any hope in the only source of any hope. This is a call to the faithful, similar to the action called for by Paul when he writes to the Thessalonians (1 Thess 5:14) to warn the quitters, console those who literally, have small souls (are faint-hearted), and cling onto the weak. Here the thought is that the cause of their doubt is this

16. See a similar construction in the Hebrew of 2 Sam 3:35 where the *ki im* "if indeed" has the same force as *never*. In the case that "if" is followed by "then" in a sentence, it becomes a conditional but as it stands, it is a strong negative.

17. Bruce, *Hebrews*, 66n59 quoting Rabi Aqiba from the *Babylonian Talmud, Sanhedrin,* 110b.

18. His dates were from 50–135 AD. His name is also spelled Akiva.

19. *Blepete*–watch out–can be an indicative or an imperative. In the present context it is most likely an imperative because it is included in a strong warning.

unbelieving and hard heart. He gives them the benefit of the doubt when he qualifies what he writes when he uses the word "lest." From the earliest, man is described as having evil intentions (Gen 6:5; 8:21 see also Eccl 8:11; 9:3). The immediate danger is the evil heart because it is unbelieving. It is this unbelieving heart which then is the root of all the other actions which follow. The unbelieving heart becomes the cause which leads the individual to depart from the Living God. The Greek phrase "to depart" (*en to apostēnai*) should be understood as meaning to become apostate. The word indicates more than some disinterest and passive falling away. It shows a clear separation from but also rebellion and even antagonism toward God.[20] It is the result of reflection and a certain decision to cut oneself off from what was previously the center of hope mentioned in verse 6. Therefore, it is much more than a cessation of faith and results in the individual becoming an open rebel. This is very important in understanding what is said later about the impossibility of such a person being restored. The fate of these apostates is described further in chapter 6:4–8 and 10:26–29.

Their separation and apostasy result in a distance forming between them and the *Living God*. This title for God seems particularly favorite among the Jews and is part of the statement made by Peter when he gave his poignant declaration in Matthew 16:16 as to Jesus' identity, "*You are the Christ the Son of the Living God.*" It is used several times elsewhere in Hebrews (9:14; 10:31; 12:22). He is not a God to be compared with the idols of the pagan who are in fact no gods. The author is saying that this means that you cannot be a Christian convert from Judaism, abandon Christ the Son, who is the source of everything and the one who upholds all that is created (1:2–3), then think that you will go back to the Judaism of the past and be safe. There you considered yourself to be a member of the household and under the jurisdiction of Law of Moses; so, you think that somehow you will merely switch tracks, back up and still be considered to be a follower of the same God you served in the past. It does not work that way. To become apostate is the same as separating oneself from God for ever as well as life, forever.

v. 13 "*But encourage one another daily, as long as it is called today, for fear that any of you should be hardened by the deceit of sin.*" Encouragement of one another is vital as the activity of those who belong to God's house. The word is a present plural imperative, indicating that all in the Christian community are to be involved in this activity of mutual encouragement and that it is also to be something that never ceases. Not only is it a command but it is reinforced by the word "daily" as well as the phrase "*as long as it*

20. See Bruce, *Hebrews*, 66.

is called 'today' (kath hekastēn hēmeran)." In other words, as long as time exists for each and everyone in the community of faith and hope, this encouragement and challenge must continue. This then, also introduces the thought that "today" is an epoch during which there is the opportunity to work and serve the Living God. It is the equivalent of this present Church age where grace still prevails and during which repentance and forgiveness are still possible.

Later in chapter 10:24, 25 the author adds provocation to love and good works, to what must be part of this encouragement and places the significance of the believers' gathering together regularly as a community as the means of doing what is necessary for this to happen. It means that living in isolation is out of the question and being a follower of Jesus on one's own is not a tenable choice. The thought behind the exhortation to do what is correct and necessary in the community of believers on a continual and consistent basis, is that when this communal encouragement is present, it is less likely that individuals will have the opportunity to have their hearts hardened by the deceitfulness of sin. When people live in a community it is more likely that as they share their doubts, others will be in a position to show them from Scripture and by acts of love, that they are wrong and bring them back into line with the truth. For this reason, as the author underlines in 10:24–25, the necessity of being part of a group of believers on a consistent basis is emphasized. If they are on their own and solitary, the sin factor tends to dominate and convince them even more that their views are correct and should be adhered to. Here at the end of the verse, the way in which sin is presented, it appears to be personified and could stand for Satan.

v. 14 "For we have become sharers of Christ, if indeed we hold fast to our original assurance until the end." This verse largely replicates what was already stated in verse 6 above. There the emphasis was on being part of the household of Christ; the condition here however, is if steadfastness prevailed in the individual's life in terms of their hope and confidence in all things pertaining to what it meant to be a follower of Christ. It is a matter of sharing with Christ regarding the same and to the very end. Those who have a hard heart and who have been beguiled by the deceitfulness of sin, will miss out on such promises for the future. What does it mean to be a sharer with or of Christ? In chapter 1:9 (see notes) it was mentioned that Christ was anointed with the oil of gladness above his fellows (*metochoi*). Here the same word in the Greek text is used to describe those who are *sharers* with and in Christ. In other words, sharers and fellows are the same. Nothing is written here which clarifies the exact role of the sharers. Alford sees the grammatical construction as emphasizing "sharers of" rather than as "sharing with."[21] In Luke 5:7 the same word is used to describe the fishermen being co-workers. The concept of being co-workers with God is not new but the term used in 1 Cor 3:9 (*sun ergoi*–workers together with) is different. Most scholars think that the emphasis here is upon sharing with Christ in the eternal kingdom.[22] There are others who see the sharing in the sense of participating in the work of Christ in a more comprehensive manner in the sense that believers become members in such a way as to represent all Christ stands for. This would be in the sense that Paul declares the following in Ephesians, "Because we are members of his body" (Eph 5:30).[23] However, it is to be understood, the main matter at hand is whether or not this status remains applicable to each one.

The author of the letter indicates that it all depends upon whether or not one holds fast to their original assurance. The conjunction he uses "if indeed" (*eanper*) reinforces the condition required–*to hold fast to our original assurance until the end.*[24] The condition is similar to that in verse 6: "*if we hold fast to the confidence and boast in our hope.*" There are several issues that come out of any understanding of both these phrases. First, the clinging onto, has to be a lasting factor, which endures to the end. It is not sufficient to start well if this is not matched with perseverance. If there is failure to cling onto one's initial hope, then there will be no sharing in Christ. Paul warns the Corinthians of the possibility of receiving the grace of God in vain (2 Cor 6:1) and that is the same danger here. Second, what is meant by the beginning of "our assurance" or "the confidence"? Most scholars believe that it means the start of their life of faith and the way in which followers of Christ acted when they first believed.[25]

This understanding is backed up by what the author says in 6:11 where he writes about the necessity of showing the same eagerness to the full assurance of the hope they have, to the end. So, this eagerness has to be present from start to finish. Finally, what is the real sense of the Greek *hypostasis*–confidence or assurance? It occurs in 1:3, here and in 11:1. Hellenistic

21. Alford, "*Pros Ebraious*," iv.70 accepts the conclusion of Bleek. He says that the construction where the author includes himself in the consequence of any action, *metochos* with a genitive has to be translated as a partaker or sharer "of" someone or something and not "with."

22. Certainly, the kingdom is emphasized in 12:28. See. Bruce, *Hebrews*, 68; Guthrie, *Hebrews*, 111.

23. Owen on this verse 14, says we are joined with Christ: "that is, joined with him, united unto him. And this is that which the apostle puts to the trial, as the hinge on which their present privileges and future happiness did entirely depend." *Hebrews*, 3.

24. This conjunction is only used in Hebrews in the New Testament, here and in 6:3.

25. See Hughes, *Hebrews*, 152.

Greek, as cited by Alford, understood this word in the sense of "confidence," even if early scholars appear to have been unaware of the fact.[26] Guthrie likens it to a title deed, which the holder possesses proving legal rights.[27] In this way it would be similar to the premice or firstfruits, which is the Pauline way of demonstrating the proof of something which is yet to be fulfilled in the future. The Church Fathers saw it as the equivalent of "faith" or the substance of faith. It is certainly related here to holding firmly to the believer's share in Christ. So as Guthrie says: "So, long as we exercise faith we have the assurance that our share cannot be taken from us."[28]

v. 15 *"While it is said: 'Today, if you hear his voice do not harden your hearts as in the rebellion'."* This verse repeats verses 7 and 8 (Ps 95:7, 8) in terms of a summary or reiteration of what has been stated in order to underline its entire importance but also in preparation for what needs to be added to this warning in the following verses.

vv. 16–18 *"Because who was it who heard and were rebellious? Was it not all those coming out of Egypt along with Moses? But with whom was he angry for forty years? Was it not with those sinning, whose bodies fell in the wilderness? To whom did he sware that they should not enter into his rest if it was not the ones who disobeyed?"* The next three verses are made up of a series of questions all intended to underline the same answer showing that the disobedient were the object. All the questions point to issues directly raised in Psalm 95 but which were the very same as those to whom the letter was addressed here; so that the readers would immediately recognize exactly where they stood. The first phrase in verse 16 was translated by the translators of the KJV as a declaration rather than as a question. This was undoubtedly due to the influence, as Hughes says, of the Latin Vulgate.[29] However, it is clear from what follows, that what we have is a series of questions with the appropriate responses which reinforce the identity of those who were the target of God's anger. Therefore, there is little question but that this phrase should also be understood as a question rather than as a statement. The reader is meant to place himself in the place of the guilty party and read into the consequences their own end, if they continue to display the same disobedience toward God.

Those who came out of Egypt had been in bondage to Pharaoh and were set free as a consequence of God's power and intervention in the miracle at the Red Sea. This demonstrates that the fact of having experienced

26. Alford, *"Pros Ebraious,"* iv. 70.

27. Guthrie, *Hebrews*, 112.

28. Guthrie, *Hebrews*, 112.

29. See Hughes, *Hebrews*, 153 and n55.

miracles in the past and having participated in the glory of the events at the time together with Moses, was no guarantee that their future was assured. Similarly, any who had been set free from the bondage of sin through the redemption of Christ in the past, must not assume that their participation in his grace is automatic. Secondly, although God gave the Israelites manna in the desert for forty years and provided for their needs in an otherwise impossible time, that again, did not mean that they would all enter into his rest. All of them, as already stated, except for two, died in the desert and that is where their bodies were buried. This was because of their sin and disobedience. The author is saying that the past experiences that they may have enjoyed, will not prove that their end will be any better than those who died in the wilderness and missed out on God's promises; if they are disobedient to the Christ, in whom they trusted at first, they should not assume that they are safe, because disobedience today, has the same results as it did in that day.

Obedience is a theme that is central throughout the letter. However, it is not the mere following of rules but a conviction that comes from the heart of the individual, which gave birth to the hope and enduring confidence mentioned in verse 6. In the following chapter it is linked to faith (4:2). Thirdly, and really just a summary of all that had already been stated, is the clear declaration asking the readers to recognize who it was that would fail to enter into God's rest. With Moses it was all that rebellious generation; their outcome was just as God's word had said it would be. Obviously, the same would be the recompense for all who were disobedient among the recipients of this letter. Any teaching that once a person believes in Christ they will always be saved regardless of their behavior, is clearly untenable here.[30]

v. 19 "And we see that they were not able to enter [God's rest] *because of unbelief."* The reason for these people not entering God's rest was because of unbelief. Therefore, disobedience from the previous verses and unbelief,[31] go together in this presentation. One is equivalent to the other and both have the same result: that of exclusion from God's promised rest.

---

30. This is the position held by those who propagate the teaching of John Calvin. Of course, there is more to the question of salvation than any claim of faith, because the discussion as to the meaning of belief is not simple. However, the normal clear understanding of the message of this letter should clarify the sense in which this word has to be understood.

31. Note the similarity in the statement made in John 3:36, where believing in the son results in eternal life but the one who disobeys will not see or experience life but God's wrath. There, as here, belief and disobedience are juxtaposed and the consequences are also similar with the lack of rest being specified as wrath.

In terms of the *rest* which is promised to the follower of Christ today, any going back on a commitment to the "confidence" and "hope," which is a prerequisite (v.6), indicate an abandonment which is equivalent to disobedience and unbelief and has disastrous results. This is the lesson which the author wants his readers to grasp at all cost. More about this disobedience and the failure to enter the rest, follows in chapter four. The warnings given in this chapter underline the importance of an ongoing vibrant and obedient relationship between the follower of Christ and their Lord. There is no room for any lax approach to faith if the individual is to please God and expect to benefit from his promises.

4.

4:1-10 A rest, yet future, which not even Joshua could guarantee

v. 1 "*Therefore, let us fear, lest anyone of you who have been left a promise to enter into his rest, might be judged to have failed to reach it.*"[1] The thrust of this opening verse is that just because a promise is made regarding the possibility of entering God's rest stands, it does not automatically mean that all will benefit from it. The opening: "therefore," indicates that based upon what has preceded, action needs to be taken. The word "let us fear" (*phobēthōmen*) appears to be a commonly used construction at the time (see 2 Cor 11:3; 12:20) showing deep concern that something bad may occur. This exhortative model "let us," is the first of more than 13 such linguistic structures used in the epistle.

It is not the fear of an inevitable and dreadful outcome but an acute awareness that there are vital forces at work and the individual has to take important and ongoing decisions in order to avoid what will happen if there is neglect. Here it highlights the fact that there is more to fear than missing the "rest" which the generation under Moses and then Joshua (v.8) had failed to enter. There is now a dimension which is not "this worldly" and yet future, to which the author wishes to draw the readers' attention. It is this coming rest (eternal) which is at stake. The present readers and their ultimate destiny are the central factors here. The author wants them to understand that their future rest is in jeopardy. The present, not any historic event, is the matter at hand because it has future consequences. He is

---

1. The verb *hustereō* (here a perfect infinitive–*husterēkenai)*), has the sense of coming short of something, failing to reach something or being excluded from something.

making it very clear that there is a promise for them regarding their future and the rest which God has promised. Once more its accession is dependent upon conditions which may not be met and which then mean that there will be a failure to enter into what was promised by God.

The interpretation of the last phrase is not definite since the Greek *dokē* (the 3rd. person sing. pres. subj. of *dokeō*) can be understood in a number of different ways: Reckoned, judged, or considered. This would then mean that God, the Judge, would be the one who makes the decision as to whether or not the conditions have been met. It could also mean, "to seem" or "to appear," in which case the conditions are even more stringent than one may imagine. Finally, it could mean "lest anyone of you think" where it would mean that the appraisal is not necessarily correct. The subjunctive shows that the outcome is not yet fixed, so it is most likely that judgment is the thought in mind here; this would bring it into line with the words of 12:15 where the author writes about the danger of *"failing to obtain the grace of God"* and substantiate this latter understanding of missing the mark and being left outside the promises of Christ and *"the great salvation"* (see comments on 2:3 and extra notes). Once more the subject at hand indicates that a right mindset is vital for all who give themselves to serve God. The godly fear behind the motivation of all that is involved in loving God has to continue and grow and expectation increase throughout one's entire life. The reason for this is expanded upon in the following verses of the chapter.

v. 2 *"Because we have had the Good News preached*[2] *to us just as it was to them. But the word did not benefit those that heard because it was not mixed with faith in the hearers."* This verse opens with a verbal phrase that means "we have been evangelized just as they were." Most translations render this "we have had the Good News preached to us just as it was to them." Having been evangelized and having heard the Good News, the force is that, the consequences and the actions which have resulted, are now up to the individual. Obviously, the evangelization of Moses' generation was very different from that of the people who were reading this message. That generation had the opportunity of being delivered by the action of God from the slavery of Egypt through the miracles experienced; the *Good News*[3] for them was the possibility of entering subsequently into the promised land, which was theirs, had they obeyed and trusted. But they did not have faith in the message brought through Moses, so they missed out on the promise and the rest. There was no final benefit for them.

2. The verb *euangelismenoi*–having had the Good News preached–is a past participle.
3. The noun *Gospel* or *euangelion,* is not found in the book of Hebrews as such.

The phrase *"the word did not benefit those that heard because it was not mixed with faith in the hearers"* is rendered variously by scholars and translations because of the differences within the MSS of the Greek word that is preferred. The masculine singular *sunkekerasmenos* (having been mixed with) agrees with the masculine *logos* (the word) and *tē pistei* (the faith) is favored by many. However, a good number of MSS of considerable weight opt for the variant *sunkekerasmenous* ("the ones who were mixed with") qualifying the plural pronoun "those (*ekeinous*) who are the faithful." Either could be correct but since the significance of the preaching is made together with the matter of the hearing of the word and all in the context of faith, it is most likely that it is this application of faith to the message which is meant here too.[4] This is all similar to what is mentioned by Paul in Romans 10:14, where believing and faith are equivalent (from the same root in Greek *pisteuō*). This sense is also the simplest when it comes to the grammar used.

The evangelization of the present generation was a message of *Good News*, which dealt with the sin question through the redemption of Christ. It was about a future or "other world," into which all who trust in Christ should enter and have eternal rest. However, like the message to Moses' generation, it had to be mixed with faith in those who heard it. If the word (*logos*), which is the message here, is not acted upon, the evangelization became futile and ineffectual with respect to the hearers. It does not mean that the promise or the redemptive act of Christ failed but that the hearers do not appropriate what the promise offered and the conditions upon which it is made were not met. It needs to be remembered, as already underlined in chapter 3:7, that the hearing was the problem. They did not *hear*, in the sense that was required, meaning *to hear and to obey*. The lack of faith was the reason. In the same way that failure to hear, unbelief and disobedience go together, in this failure to attain the promised rest, so faith and hearing or obedience, result in its certain fulfilment.

v. 3 "*For we who have believed enter into that rest as he said: 'As I swore, in my wrath, "They will never enter into my rest,"' Although his works had come into being from the foundation of the world."* The hard-hearted

---

4. There are at least six different variant readings in the MSS relative to this word– *sunkekerasmenous*. The plural accusative, is the preferred in the most recent *Greek New Testament* (5th Ed. In this sentence, it gives the sense of "they were not united by faith with those who listened," whereas the first gives the thought that the word was not mixed with faith by those who heard it. For more on the argument see: Bruce, *Hebrews*, 70n4 and 255n119. See also Hughes, *Hebrews*, 157n62. The differences between the *nun* "n" and the *gamma* "g" can be accounted for due to the rule that the pronunciation of the "g" in front of the *kappa* "k" being verbalized as a "n" in Greek.

generation pictured in the Exodus, did not enter that rest but those who are alive today and have the faith to appropriate its promises, by following the conditions laid out, will enter into this rest. The "we" here is inclusive of all members of the believing community, which is known better as the Church. This is the new household or community of God. There is significance in the sequence of the participles here: those who have believed (*hoi pistuesantes*– aorist participle is a complete action) are entering (*eiserchometha*–present indicative) into that rest now, dependent upon the reality of the event seen as "having believed." The believers are just that, because at a point in the past they made a decision based upon faith, to trust Christ as Redeemer. It needs to be remembered that the word: "to believe" and "to have faith" in Greek, are from the same root (*pisteuō/pistis*), as indicated above in verse 2. These people believed and have already begun the journey which is neces- sary to fully enjoy what the rest is all about; provided that they continue and endure to the end, then the finality and perfection of what that rest means, will one day become a complete reality. At present it is partial and proleptic.

This rest is also God's rest, since Psalm 95:11 describes it as such. The link between God's resting and his creative work in Genesis is brought out by the addition to the verse of the words "*Although his works had come into being from the foundation of the world.*" Once God had completed the creation at the end of the sixth day, he entered into the Sabbath of rest and it is into this same rest that believers enter when they believe, even if not fully until they have completed their earthly journey, according to the conditions laid out earlier (3:6). Genesis 2:2 describes this resting of God from all his work, at the end of the creative process. Therefore, in Hebrews, God's rest is not only the rest of those who have completed their earthly sojourn but what God has had in place since the end of the sixth day as his own.[5] It must not be understood as a matter of inactivity but of completion.[6] This completion is accentuated when the Jewish authorities questioned Jesus regarding his healing people on the Sabbath and he replied: "*My Father works even now and I work*" (John 5:17). What he was saying was that even though the Father's Sabbath started long ago, he continues to be engaged in and with the creation he put in place. It is into this rest that the believers will enter fully in the future, provided that what they have entered into, upon belief in Christ, is demonstrated by their faithfulness; for it to be seen as such, their state of heart needs to give some clear indication and visible evidence proving that this faith is more than a verbal declaration. This is the

5. See Bruce, *Hebrews*, 73–74.
6. Guthrie, *Hebrews*, 116.

very thing that James talks about when he says that he will show his faith by his works (James 2:18).

vv. 4–5 "*Because he said this somewhere concerning the seventh day: 'And God rested on the seventh day from all his works' and again in this passage* [he said]: *'they shall never enter into my rest.'*" Following the way in which he introduces quotations in an imprecise manner earlier in the letter (2:6) and showing more concern for the content and meaning of the words than their original context indicates, the author reiterates first, what has already been said indirectly about the Sabbath day's rest in Genesis 2:2–3. The Jewish readers would have been well aware of the locality of the quotation. He is preparing his readers for the place where in verse 9, he will have even more to say about the Sabbath rest. Second, he goes back to Psalm 95, which he has already cited twice (3:11, 18). Its purpose being to show that even if some are not going to enter this rest, the possibility is still there and some will most certainly enter it.

v. 6 "*Therefore, since it remains for some to enter into it and those who formerly had had the Good News preached to them did not enter because of disobedience.*" The logic of the presentation in this and the next verse seems difficult to today's readers but the steps are actually clear enough, if they are followed through: God created a place which he calls his rest. This place is very much part of his plan. He still intends that there be those who will share in this rest with himself. Moses' generation did not enter it, so they were left out and never participated in the possibility of entering this rest, despite all the miracles they enjoyed during their lives and all they experienced along the way. However, this does not nullify God's plan and this place of rest is still open. This is evident as the same offer is made to the people who lived during David's generation, if only they would accept the same conditions which were made at first.[7]

The thinking proposes that God intended for people to enter this rest. The original target group to benefit from the promise was the generation of Moses' day, which left Egypt as a consequence of God's power and care. They were the ones to whom the Good News was proclaimed (they were the ones who were evangelized) regarding their deliverance and the promised land of Canaan (see the notes on verse 2 above). The reason for their failure to enter the promised land and their rest was disobedience.

But that is not the end of the story because some had to enter the promised rest or God's word would have been seen as void and as having failed. This leads to the next part presented in the following verse.

---

7. See Ellingworth, *Hebrews*, on this section, 35.

v. 7 "He again designates a certain day, 'Today' speaking through David after such a long time in words he had already written, 'Today, if you hear his voice do not harden your hearts.'" The apparent failure with Moses' generation is not the end of the story because God continues to address the issue in Psalm 95, some four hundred years after the Exodus fiasco; it raises the same matter once more. The author indicates that it was through David that the words were reinforced. Again, God appoints or sets in place a day. The word *horizō* has the sense of determining or putting something in place.[8] Here it is a certain day. The fact that David's name is mentioned here appears to justify the Davidic authorship of the psalm.[9] The significance is that after all that time, the offer of entering into this rest still stands. That meant that it was not exclusively for the Exodus generation, as by that time the nation was long settled in the promised land. They had relative rest during David's time but this was not the rest which was at the heart of the message in the psalm. Its repetition here is showing that in the same way that the "today" was extended to David's day, so likewise it was being extended to their own day, now in the epoch of the New Covenant of the Son; they needed to take heed to its offer, as well as its warning and not harden their hearts. The force of the constant and repetitive statements which may appear to be redundant to us today, is to get the attention of the readers in order that any necessary change could be enacted.

v. 8 "For if Joshua had given them rest, God[10] would not have spoken concerning another day after this." Joshua was the one who eventually led the nation out of the forty years of wandering in the desert into the Promised Land. It needs to be noted that the Greek: *Iēsous*, translated, Jesus in the KJV, should be translated Joshua (*Yehoshuach* in Hebrew) because otherwise it does away with the typology that the author intended. For the reader of the Greek text, Jesus and Joshua are one and the same name, and mean "Yahweh saves" or "Yahweh is salvation" but for those who do not read Greek there could easily be some confusion. Here the name is specifically intended to identify the man who eventually led the Jews into the promised land. The people at that time may well have thought that they had finally arrived in the land of their rest but what we have here is an affirmation that this was not the case at all. Certainly, their arrival in the land of promise, did give them some sense of permanence and security but the fact that Psalm

8. See Arndt & Gingrich, 584.

9. The Hebrew Massoretic text does not attribute an author to the psalm but the LXX adds David to its title.

10. God's name does not appear in the original but the pronoun is attached to the verb "he spoke" (*elalei*) so it is legitimate to add the implied word "God" for the pronoun here.

95 raises the issue again and that God uses these verses to give prominence to the real need, indicates that the land of Canaan was not the sphere of ultimate rest, which was indicated originally. That day was yet future as far as David's generation were concerned. Therefore, even Joshua did not manage to provide the promised rest.

v. 9 "So there remains a Sabbath rest for the people of God." For that very reason, the Sabbath rest, which is at the center of the hope of the people of God, remains a future reality. Here it is called a Sabbath rest or more literally a "Sabbath keeping"[11] (See *Appendix B*) because it is a participation of the individual together with God in the provision of the rest which he put in place and none other. The word used for Sabbath keeping (*sabbatismos*), does not appear anywhere else in the literature of that time and may well be coined by the author to highlight the particular nature of this rest as compared to anything which may have been understood earlier. It is found a little later than this letter, in the writings of Plutarch and the verbal form is present in the LXX, which was of course, translated well before this time.[12] Here this rest is qualified by the fact that it is only for *"the people of God."* This is then the eternal community or household of those who have finally qualified and demonstrated their ongoing loyalty to God. The result is similar to what is mentioned in Revelation 14:13, where the believers who die in the Lord are said to be blessed because *"they shall rest from their labors."*

v. 10 *"For the one who has entered into God's rest has also rested from his own works as God did from his."* This rest is God's and those who enter into it follow the same pattern as God himself followed. Once more this rest of God's, into which the true people of God have entered, refers to the termination of his creative work as depicted in Genesis 2. Some scholars have interpreted this rest in a manner similar to that of a thousand-year rest, resulting from a typological dependence upon what Peter says in his letter where he declares that a thousand years is as one day and one day as a thousand years (2 Pet 3:8). Following this reckoning, they would say that since God did his creative work in six days, the seventh or his Sabbath, is his thousand years of rest which is yet to come after the *Parousia* takes place.

11.. The Greek *sabbatismos* from the verb *sabbatizō*, to keep the Sabbath, gives the sense of Sabbath keeping. See. Arndt & Gingrich, 746 and Bruce, *Hebrews*, 72n13.

12. Plutarch, a Greek historian and philosopher who died c.120 A.D. in his *De Superstitione 3, Moralia,*166a and see Leviticus 23:32 in the LXX. It should be noted that those groups which emphasize the necessity of Sabbath keeping such as the Seventh Day Adventists, use this verse to back their mandatory keeping of the Sabbath today. The problem with their interpretation is the failure to grasp the entire context and thrust of what obedience and faith are all about and what the author is trying to impress upon his readers overall.

This will then be followed by the eternal age. This teaching was accepted by many during the period of the Early Church.[13] As ingenious as this may appear, this is not the thought of the present work.

The actual timing of the entering into the totality of this rest, is not stated here. Certainly, acceptance of God's plan of salvation through Christ is the doorway to this rest but that is only the beginning of what is involved. The following verse indicates that the fulness is yet future.[14] Verse 3 above, showed that "the believing ones" are entering into it but this does not mean that the fulness of all that this "rest" stands for, is already complete. After all, the next verse points this out when it emphasizes the measures that have to be taken. The narratives of following chapters like those in chapter 11, show that even the giants of faith recognized that they were "*strangers and pilgrims on earth*" (11:13b) who were looking for a heavenly country (11:16). The same chapter concludes that all these men and women of faith "did not obtain the promise" (11:39). Then the final verse of that much-loved chapter, declares that "*without us they should not be perfected*" (11:40). The author is saying that their rest was not achieved at their death and that it will only be fully realized together with those of us who are from the New Covenant. This indicates a divine plan which sees the completion of any entry in to the rest, as something which will only be fulfilled in at a later date. It will happen only when those of the Old and New Covenants, as members of the one household and one community, enter at what God sees, as the right time.

The theological suppositions regarding the timing have to be left out of the discussion here because they are not included by the author. The resurrection of the dead is not referred to in the letter, other than in terms of its fact (see 6:2; 11:35). However, the world to come or the age to come (2:5; 6:5) and the sphere of the heavenly (3:1; 6:4; 8:5; 9:23; 11:16; 12:22) most certainly are. So, the timing of the final and ultimate rest can only be associated with the reality of the latter and not with any earthly experience, even if initial entry into it is certainly possible and absolutely essential during one's earthly sojourn. This is underlined in the following verse.

13. It was expressed in the extra-canonical book of the *Epistle of Barnabas*, 15:4–8. See also Bruce, *Hebrews*, 74n20. The teaching of a millennial reign may be justifiable from Revelation 20 but it is not here. Biblical exegetes need to take great care not to transpose a teaching from one part of Scripture to another, unless there is clear evidence for such.

14. See Brown, *Hebrews*, 90.

4:11–13 An Exhortation to appropriate God's Rest

v. 11 "*Therefore let us be eager to enter into that rest lest anyone falls in the same sort of disobedience.*" In the light of this offer being made to enter into God's rest, a response is necessary. The exhortation here is to make every effort. The verb in Greek *spoudazō,* conveys the thought of eagerness, followed by the willingness to engage in whatever action is necessary to make the goal of this keen desire a reality. There is no thought here that there is room to sit back and wait for something to happen or to relax and let God do the work on one's behalf. Rather, there is the absolute conviction that whatever one has to do and whatever the cost, it has to be committed to and that without delay.[15] The fact that the author draws upon the same example as that presented in the earlier portion of the letter, regarding failure and hard heartedness, shows that danger was ever present. That attitude is what prevented the Exodus generation from entering their rest; it shows that the same problem of disobedience and failure, was ever lurking. The only way in which to counter the danger was to take immediate and determined action. This action may well include the possibility of pain and opposition; it must not be considered that it will always be easy. It calls for total commitment to the fulfilment of the hope mentioned in 3:6. This hope and this eagerness, calls for faith and trust in the Redeemer at every stage together with consistent and lasting perseverance.

v. 12 "*For the word of God is living and active and sharper that any two-edged sword, piercing as far as to divide soul and spirit, and the joints and marrow and able to judge thoughts and intentions of the heart.*" This verse is part of the warning carried over from the previous one. It is about God's word, his *Logos*. God's word is the revelation of his will and purpose. There are certainly parallels here with the Logos in John's Gospel but we must be careful not to read Johannine theology into the text.[16] The word of God in this context must be understood to refer immediately to the word which came to the people who were set free from Egypt and found themselves wandering in the desert of Sinai. They then disobeyed and suffered the consequences. It is the same word which was being shared with those of the Psalmist's day and here with those addressed in this letter. Here the author wishes to underline the significance of the Word of God as it relates to his subject.

If this passage were to be understood in the clear context of a theological statement related to Jesus, then it could be compared with the *Logos*

---

15. See Arndt & Gingrich, 771.

16. That is the task of those involved in systematics and not of exegesis.

theology of John and it is most likely that there are some parallels here. However, as already stated above, this is not the purpose of the author. His desire is to show how the Word of God is God speaking to mankind. This factor was made at the very start of the letter when the author makes it very clear that the God who spoke in the past through the prophets now speaks through the Son (1:2). It is the revelation of his will. Therefore, this verse clarifies the general manner in which all need to comprehend the significance of God's word. It needs to be understood that the word of God is not merely a written code but something living and engaging. It shows the true nature of the one who presents it to his creatures as it constantly searches their very soul and spirit. When that sort of language is used it is not in order to justify some doctrine regarding the nature of man but to demonstrate that the whole of man is reached and influenced by this Word.

The imagery of the sword is common in Scripture and it is often linked to the word that comes from the mouth of Christ (Isa 49:2; Rev 1:16; 2:16; 19:15, 21). This word penetrates the very heart of man so that it works away at his thoughts, even when he is not aware of what is happening. The soul and the spirit are the immaterial parts of humanity, while the joints and marrow speak of his material aspect. These descriptors show how the word penetrates every part of the individual; it is sharper than any two-edged sword. It divides between soul and spirit, joints and marrow as well as thoughts and intentions of the heart. These aspects are meant to show that there is no part of man and his being, beyond the influence of this revelation of God. The next verse highlights this.

The word brings subtle as well as radical change in every area of an individual's life because it is God's living word at work and thereby God himself at work. This word constantly calls for change, brings conviction, evokes hope and new purpose because it is alive and the means by which God speaks and provokes his people to do what is right. The similarity of the word and the two-edged sword is one which shows that it is able to penetrate to the innermost depts of the individual in order to bring about God's design. It is also most capable of revealing the deepest and most difficult emotions and motives as well as bringing about change within them.

In Scripture the sword is often an instrument of war and death (Isa 3:25; 13:15; 37:7; 51:19; Rev 6:4, 8; 13:10 et al.) but it is doubtful that there is any of that sense involved in the simile here. This does not mean that the significance of judgment and aspects relative to God's commands should not be seen here, as they certainly are part of the manifestation of himself to his creatures. In fact, the place given to judgment (*kritikos*) is most evidently part of the Word's role where it takes on a personified sense.

This verse is one of the favorites when it comes to looking at the anthropology of man and his composition but that aspect was never the intention of the author when he penned these words, even if there are some who depend upon it to reinforce their particular view of man's psychology but to attempt to justify such is to take a step too far.[17]

v. 13 "And there is no creature that is not totally open before him but all things are naked and stand open before the eyes of the one with whom we have to give account."[18] Here God and the word are linked in the sense that any action springing from the word, is the direct result of God seeing and knowing everything about each person. This verse reinforces the fact that the all-knowing and all-seeing God, cannot be deceived. In addition to this, the judgement mentioned in the previous verse, even if it does not occur during one's lifetime, will most certainly take place because it is definitely programmed to do so. In the light of this day of reckoning, behavior needs to be immediately adjusted accordingly.

4:14–10:18 Christ our Great High Priest

4:14–16 *Draw near to our Great High Priest*

After the strict warning of the preceding verses, this section encourages the reader to draw near to the only one who is in a position to fully understand the struggles of mankind.

v. 14 "Therefore, since we have a great high priest who has passed through the heavens, Jesus, the Son of God, let us hold fast to our confession." The high priestly role of Jesus has already been introduced in 2:17 and 3:1 without any clarification but here the entire theme is regarded in considerable depth. This High Priest is "great." This means that he is superior to all other high priests of whatever order. The immediate thought is that there is no other more excellent than he and he must be considered superior to all others. Part of the reason for this fact has already been intimated in 2:17 and is linked to the fact that no other priest was ever in the position to offer himself as the propitiation for the sins of mankind.

17. This is especially so when the subject of trichotomy and dichotomy are discussed. Soul and spirit are mentioned here but this verse is rather directed at the whole man which is how the Jews viewed the entirety of a person's character rather than as man divided into parts. That was more of a Greek perspective.

18. Note that *logos* here has to do with accountability and is used differently from the way it was first introduced in verse 12.

Again, earthly priests had to pass through the veil into the holy place to offer up the sacrifice but this priest has not passed through any terrestrial barriers but through the heavens to the throne room of God himself and the very seat of divine power. This has already been indicated in 1:3 where, after having provided the cleansing for sin, he is seated at the Right Hand of the Majesty on High. The use of the plural, "heavens" (*tous ouranous*) should not be understood in any way other than that in keeping with the Jewish concept of the nature of the heavens; it was always described in the plural. Now that he has passed through the heavens he is in the real sanctuary and not in any symbolic one as portrayed in the physical and terrestrial ones which were only types of the real. This heavenly aspect is expanded upon in 7:26.

Further, there is the fact of this High Priest's identity. He is Jesus, the Son of God. All other high priests were of human descent, imperfect and in need of cleansing for their own sin and imperfection. But this one is the Son of God. The significance of this Son has already been seen in the first chapter and he is the Son who is God himself (1:8). He is not only the Son of God but Jesus. The author wishes to underline the link between this Son of God and the man Jesus, as the person who fulfilled the earthly mission on behalf of mankind. As the Great High Priest, he is the heavenly Son of God and the earthly Jesus, all in one. Therefore, he is the perfect person to take on this great high priestly role. This title is used here and three other times in the letter (6:6; 7:3; 10:29) in a variety of contexts. Therefore, in every sense possible, this Great High Priest is far superior to all. Again, this aspect will be expanded upon when Aaron and Melchizedek are introduced (5:4, 6).

Because of the person of this Great High Priest, there is the exhortation: "*let us hold fast to our confession.*" (see 3:6). It has already been pointed out that the expression indicates the necessity of a firm and lasting grasp of something. In 3:6 the object of the grasp was the believer's confidence and hope. Similarly, here it is a synonym which is "the confession" which has already been mentioned in 3:1 (see the notes on the heavenly calling). Both statements reinforce the same subject and call for the reader to react accordingly, in a positive manner to all that the exhortation means. If any confidence or any expression of faith is to be meaningful and bring about a change regarding the danger which looms, the response which is called for, has to be immediate and tenacious.

v. 15 "*For we do not have a high priest who is not able to sympathize with our weaknesses but one who has been tempted in every respect like us, except that he did not sin.*" The fact of his superiority and that he has already passed through the heavens, does not in any way limit this High Priest's ability to sympathize fully with mankind's weakness. Some may have felt that his divinity left him in some ways aloof from the world in which the rest of mankind lived. The author of the letter wishes to make it absolutely clear that this is not the case. This is because, Jesus too, was just as we are, apart from one single factor and that is that he had no sin. The author has already indicated that Jesus was like his brethren; he had suffered in his life and had been tempted in the same way that all mankind is tempted (2:17, 18).

This verse confirms and underlines the reality of Jesus' humanity and all that being part of the human race automatically involves. This means that not only did he look like a man but he was as fully man as anyone and in every way, physically and mentally. The ways in which mankind is tempted and subjected to emotional trials as well as physical, were all known to him. However, this verse also highlights one major difference on his part; although he was human, just like us, there is one area of his life where he was different from all: he never failed in the tests and therefore was sinless. He was without sin and he did not sin, in spite of all the temptations that he encountered. Christ experienced the same temptations as us all but where we fail due to weakness, he never did. The victory he achieved, was in the final place, the victory over temptation. Because he did not suffer from a fallen human spirit the temptations would have been even keener than those felt by the rest of us. In addition, it is through the things that he suffered that he learned obedience, which was all part of the human experience which was required of him (see 5:8). The fact of his obedience is especially underlined in John's Gospel where it is linked to doing the Father's will (John 5:30; 8:26, 28 and notes on chapter 5:7–8.) and is part of what is intended by the fact of Jesus' learning obedience. The consequence of all this suffering is why he is able to fully sympathize, as he has passed the same tests. Had he failed he would not have been in a position to provide the propitiation which was necessary to satisfy the entire plan of redemption.

v. 16 "Therefore, let us draw near the throne of grace with boldness so that we may receive mercy and find grace for timely help." Therefore, as a consequence of knowing who our Great High Priest is, what he has experienced on our behalf, and the victory which he has provided, it is incumbent upon us to approach the throne of grace with boldness. Under the Levitical system it was only the High Priest, and that annually, that the place which stood for the presence of God in the Holy of Holies, could be approached. Now however, the one who is our Great High Priest, is seated in the heavenlies at the right hand of the Majesty on high (1:3). There is no longer the need to deal with the symbols of divinity in any earthly temple but with divinity itself in the true sanctuary, which the author calls the throne of grace. This is the source of all grace and mercy.

Again, when the High Priest entered the holy of holies annually, it was always with fear and trepidation because any indication of acting in an unworthy manner could result in instant death, as is indicated especially in Leviticus chapter 10:1–2 and 16 (especially Lev16:2, 13). Here the exhortation is to draw near to this throne of grace, which is in reality, to God himself, through Christ. He is this High Priest and the believer is to do so with boldness. The concept of drawing near to God is one which is repeated seven times in the letter. It denotes a close and bold relationship with God on the part of the follower of Christ, through his provision. The word translated from the Greek *parrēsia,* which indicates confidence and openness, indicates that there are now no barriers or limitations in this approach to God.[19] The thought is similar to that which was indicated by the veil of the temple being torn in two (Luke 23:45) indicating that the way to the holy of holies was now wide open. God's mercy seat is available, without any palaver and thereby the grace upon which all depend for timely help is freely available. This means that whatever and whenever the time, this grace is available upon the drawing near of the individual to God's throne. There is no longer any restriction in place and no annual ritual necessary, since at any moment the way is wide open.

19. Arndt & Gingrich, 635–36.

5.

5:1–4 Human qualifications for High Priesthood

This section deals with the human qualifications for the High Priesthood, specifically those which were associated with Aaron and his offspring.

v. 1 "For every high priest who is taken from among mankind, on behalf of mankind, is appointed with regard to things related to God; this is so that he may offer both gifts and sacrifices concerning sins." The first verses of this chapter immediately reflect the priesthood of the Old Testament where the first representative who qualified for the responsibility under review, was Aaron, as he was appointed by God himself. The High Priest, like all priests, has to be chosen from among the people to represent them. In the Old Testament period, that individual was a Jew who knew the conditions and circumstances of the people he was to represent before God. Since the one who is responsible for the selection and the appointing is God, it is he who is responsible for both these aspects and not mankind. This chosen person is selected from among mankind and not an angel but one who is totally identifiable with humans in every way. Note that the Greek word *anthrōpos* is not a male but a member of the human race, so inclusive of all people. This is important because this High Priest is all mankind's representative before God. Specifically, this person is expected to be a go-between man and God, so has to be perfectly acceptable to both parties. The initial High Priest, as with Aaron, was not elected by man but God and so there was no democratic selection or vote involved, even if by the time of Jesus, the system was changed and corrupted. The author of this letter is referring to Aaron and his line (5:4). His function was to offer both gifts and sacrifices. The construction of the sentence is such that the gifts and the sacrifices are closely related; they represent different forms of offerings made by man to

God for sins and also for thanksgiving. These gifts and offerings for sin are especially part of the work of the High Priest's annual responsibility on the day of atonement (9:7). Both words should be seen as covering the total duty of all the different offerings which were part of his mandate. Note that in 8:4 the word *gifts,* is inclusive of all the offerings.

vv. 2–3 *"He must be able to feel compassion for those who are ignorant and who are being led astray, since he is also beset by weakness. And because of this, he must be able to offer sacrifices for his own sins, just as he does for the people."* The High Priest was not to be an unfeeling and impassionate bystander. Rather he was to be full of compassion for the ignorant and errant, as an indicator of his own weaknesses. In 4:15 Jesus was able to sympathize with our weaknesses and here the earthly High Priest was the same. This weakness is the inheritance of all the ancestors of Adam. Any brief look at Aaron's history during the Exodus does not take long to highlight his weaknesses (Exod 32:2–6, 35; Num 12:1, 9). Nevertheless, he, like his brother Moses, did not hesitate to cry out to God for his mercy when the people acted in agreement with the rebellion of Korah, Dathan and Abiram (Num 16:22, 41, 47). It is the consequence of sin upon the whole race which requires sacrifices for all, including the High Priest himself. There are two kinds of sin mentioned here: those due to ignorance and those due to the fact that people have wandered from the path. For such there is the possibility of atonement and reconciliation. However, in the Old Covenant, for those who sinned purposefully or what is termed "high-handedly," there was no covering for sin (Num 15:30, 31). This meant that for the person who had a hard heart, which led to their apostasy, there was no means of reconciliation. Therefore, the sins of all who were guilty of ignorance and of wandering from God's pathway, would be satisfied by the High Priest's offering on the day of atonement, but those who had purposefully and blatantly rebelled should not expect that they would be included among those for whom the mercy of God would play a role. This teaching may seem extremely harsh, especially in the face of some recent teaching regarding the grace of God.[1] What it does demonstrate, is that in spite of God's offer of forgiveness, to take sin lightly is extremely dangerous.

v. 4 *"And no one takes this honor for himself, but the one who is called by God, indeed just as Aaron was."* One thing is very certain and that is that to be a high priest, the individual has to be appointed and called by God in the same way as was Aaron (Exod 28:1). During the later history of Israel, there were some individuals who were appointed to the high priesthood by the authorities of the day, including during the time of the Greek Seleucids

---

1. See notes on 12:14 and footnote.

and Roman authorities.[2] For example, the latter Hasmonean High Priests were ratified by the Roman Senate. However, the only ones who were really qualified and divinely recognized were those appointed by God.

5:5–10 *Christ's divine call and qualifications to be the perfect High Priest*

v. 5 *"So also Christ did not exalt himself to become a high priest but* [was appointed by] *the one who said to him: 'You are my Son. Today I have begotten you,'"* There are a number of qualifications necessary for someone to be a High Priest. The most important, as stated, is that the person has to be put in place by God. In the Gospel of John, the reader is reminded constantly that Jesus, the Son, has come as one sent by the Father to do his will and his works (John 5:36, 37; 6:44, 57; 8:16, 18 et al.). He is not self-appointed. The words of Psalm 2:7: *"You are my Son. Today I have begotten you"* have already been quoted in chapter 1:5. In that context they were seen as a declaration related to Christ's exaltation (see notes on 1:5). Here specifically, it is related to the day of his entrance into his office, on what can be considered the day of his coronation. That took place upon his exultation when he returned to his rightful place as the God/Man, after the resurrection. The matter that concerns us here, is his identification by the Father, that Jesus the divine Son was also placed in the office of High Priest on a continuing basis. This exultation was only possible after the humiliation of the cross and the emphasis is upon the fact that the office was not something which he chose but to which he was appointed by the Father. So, the series of events related to Christ's incarnation, his rejection and crucifixion, as well as his resurrection, and exultation, are all part of this glorification and appointment. However, these two verses, most importantly, bring together the divine Son and the human priestly person of Jesus.

v. 6 *"as he also says in another* (psalm) *'You are a priest for ever according to the order of Melchizedek.'"* As was indicated in the introduction, with regard to the way in which the author of the Epistle uses brief quotations from the Old Testament to introduce the entire context of the sections from which those quotes are drawn, so here.[3] The *"he also says"* is clearly referring to God who makes the declaration in Psalm 110:4, which is quoted

2. Vasile Babota, "The High Priesthood of Simon (142–140)," 225–267. For more on the improper appointment of the high priests during the years prior to Christ's birth and subsequent to his death see Bruce, *Hebrews*, 92n19.

3. See the Introduction and section 1. The preference for the text of the Septuagint (LXX) and the author's methodology in using the Old Testament.

here. There is a clear link between Christ's divine activities together with his power and his High Priestly work in redemption and mediation. In Psalm 110:1, which is not explained in depth here but is developed considerably in chapter 7, Christ is seated upon his throne, exalted at the right hand of God, awaiting the completion of the work he has undertaken during his earthly ministry. But in verse 4 of that same psalm, he is the eternal priest who identifies with Melchizedek. This identification of Jesus with Melchizedek is unique within the New Testament and this is the first occasion where it is found in this epistle. More will be said about Melchizedek in chapter 7.

All that needs to be said regarding him here, is that he appears in Genesis 14:18–20, as king of Salem, which is usually identified with Jerusalem.[4] Although there is little other literature upon which to base our understanding of him, he is clearly identified as being "priest of God Most High."[5] It may well be that the mystery surrounding this person is intentional, in the sense that the author wishes to add to the aura surrounding the person of Christ, as the one who sits upon the throne in heavenly places and is at the same time the everlasting priest. Psalm 110 becomes the foundation upon which the claims for the combination of the divine and the priestly ministry are identified in the one person of Christ, who is also the Son here in Hebrews.

Yet, once more, the nature of the ministry of Jesus and that of Aaron are compared as this ministry is eternal, while that of Aaron's was limited to his lifespan alone. Jesus' ministry has no terminus. When the author states that Christ is a priest forever and like that of Melchizedek, he is underlining the fact that his priesthood is not passing, like that of Aaron but of an eternal nature, like that of Melchizedek's. This means that both Melchizedek and Christ have continuing priesthoods.

v. 7 Still speaking of Jesus, we read *"who in the days of his flesh he offered up both prayers and supplications with strong cries and tears, to the one who was able to save him from death, and he was heard as the result of his reverence."* There are a number of significant factors in this section which from verse 7–10, is one long sentence in Greek. This means that these verses need to be seen together. The first is "In the days of his flesh" refer to the days of Jesus' earthly ministry as the incarnate One. This section highlights Christ's ability to sympathize with humanity as a whole. He too knew what it was like to suffer as a man and this verse highlights that fact. He was really

4. In Psalm 76:2 God's abode is named as Salem; in the parallel strophe of the same verse, it is called Zion, indicating the fact that it is synonymous. Josephus in his *Antiquities,* i. 180, identifies it as Jerusalem.

5. Here this is translated from the Hebrew: *El Eliyon* which is the same as *Yahweh* in Ps 18:13 and elsewhere.

a man like all others in this matter. This is important in the light of some of the false teaching at the time, that Jesus was not a real man but only a spirit being. As a man he too relied totally upon the Father for all direction and help. This is especially evident in the Gospel of John, as already noted (John 5:19, 30; 15:5 et al.); Christ's entire life and ministry was one of humiliation and submission to the Father, so that this verse could describe the entirety of that life lived under the direction of his Father. However, there is one occasion in particular, which is called to mind by the words of this verse and that would, as developed further below, be Jesus' prayer in Gethsemane on the night he was betrayed. The second, is the offering up of prayers and supplications but also has to bear in mind the fact of Christ's death. The expression "offering up" something in the letter, is nearly always associated with sacrifices (see 5:1, 3). Christ, as the perfect sacrifice, surpasses all Old Testament sacrifices, which were only shadows of things to come, of which he is the antitype or perfect fulfilment.

As already stated, the fact of Jesus offering up prayers and supplications to God, fits the occasion which Matthew describes, prior to the crucifixion when Jesus prayed in Gethsemane: "*Let this cup pass from me; nevertheless, not as I will but as you will.*" (Matt 26:39; see also Mark14:34–36). It was not so much the fear of death and pain that was the subject of his prayer but the fact of being the bearer of mankind's sin, which was so abhorrent to him and which caused these strong cries and tears. Some may ask how the "saving from death" was accomplished, since all know that Christ died upon the cross. It needs to be understood that the prayer was answered but not in the sense that he was spared the death of the cross. Rather it was that his death vanquished all evil and he rose again to be delivered from death and thereby became the deliverer of all who trust in him. In the light of the sacrificial aspect, Christ fulfils all requirements of everything that was portrayed by the sacrificial order in the Old Testament. He not only offers up prayers and supplications but himself. This has already been dealt with in 2:14, where it shows that the battle Christ had was with Satan himself.

Therefore, there was an affirmative response to his prayer in this sense that he was heard and the Father brought about the deliverance that was always anticipated by the Godhead. His victory over death was confirmed by his resurrection. As mankind's everlasting high priest, he is certainly in the position to know exactly the nature of the creature's feeble frame and he fully sympathizes and empathizes with his own at all times.

The term which is translated variously: because he feared, his godly fear, his reverence, is the Greek from the phrase "*apo tēs eulabeias.*" The correct rendition depends on the setting in which it is found. In this sentence it has to be viewed within the context of a prayer to God, so has the sense of the awe of and for God and his will. Fear on its own, is unsatisfactory. It is certainly not that Christ himself had fear of death. The phrase has to be rather the idea of divine reverence and trust in the entire plan of God, even though his death was to be the instrument of the victory and liberation that would follow.

v. 8 *"Though he was a son he learned obedience from the things which he suffered."* This was, as Bruce points out,[6] because Jesus was no ordinary son but the Son of God. Yet because of his High Priestly office he was not spared any suffering and in this case was specifically required to experience this dreaded form of death. As humans, it is required that obedience is something each one must learn. Human nature, under the yoke of sin, rebels at the thought of suffering. What would this obedience and suffering have meant to Jesus as the sinless Son of God? To answer this question, it needs to be understood that the obedience which was required and the suffering which was his lot, is part of entire mission of the Son, from his throne to the earth and back. All was subject to the fulfilment of the plans of the Father for the salvation of the universe. This required the incarnation and all that it entailed, including Christ's rejection by his own people the Jews; the success of the entire mission was only possible because of the Son's willingness to do what was required of him, including his going to the cross. If there are any specific texts from which justification for this obedience and suffering can be drawn, Isaiah 50:5–7 and 53:3–10, most certainly highlight both these aspects (see 4:15 above). The latter concludes with a verse which highlights the overall necessity for what had to take place in order to redeem mankind.

v. 9 *"And being perfected he became the source of eternal salvation to all those who obey him,"* The thought presented in the phrase regarding Christ's perfection, does not indicate that at any point he was imperfect in himself but rather, that he had fulfilled and completed what was required. He could only be seen to be perfect after having done all that was necessitated by this obedience and suffering; since without that, the salvation which awaited would never have been available. The requirements that made justification available to all, required Christ's sinless life and his sacrifice. Without them his mission would have been incomplete. Christ is the cause or the source and the reason (*aitios*) for all salvation, as the result of having completed the entire plan. Now that all is fulfilled by him there is a prerequisite for all who wish to participate in the salvation which he offers: total obedience.

This statement is not contrary to any Pauline doctrine of salvation by faith. Rather it is the confirmation of it, in different terms. Just as Christ was obedient so also obedience to Christ, the Great High Priest of mankind's

6. Bruce, *Hebrews*, 103.

salvation, requires that those who place their faith in him should never go back to their former way of life. There is no place for abandoning hope and trust in the only one who can provide salvation. There is a clear declaration that there is no hope for the salvation God offers, other than in Christ and by means of his provision. This obedience requires total surrender to him and his ways, nothing more and nothing less. The Jewish Christians to whom the author addresses this letter, are prevaricating. They have to set their faces like flint (see Isa 50:7), to follow Christ, even in the face of persecution and rejection. After all, this is just as Christ did in showing complete obedience to his Father and the mission that was ahead of him.

v. 10 So then, to complete this long and somewhat ungainly sentence and to summarize who this Son really was, the author concludes that he was the one: "*being designated by God a high priest after the order of Melchizedek.*" He is the one who is, as already stated in verse 6, the fulfilment of Psalm 110:4. The man about whom more will be said in chapter 7.

5:11–14 Failure to mature

v. 11 "*Concerning this[7] we have much to say and hard to explain since you have become dull of hearing.*" The author indicates that this matter, which relates to the priesthood, which is like that of Melchizedek, is of such a nature that much could be said about it but that what he has to say is hard to explain. This is not because the nature of its content is difficult but because the problem lies with his readers. Their difficulty is described in terms of a hearing problem. The author emphasizes the fact that have become *hard of hearing*. This expression is unique to Hebrews, although the thought is present elsewhere in Scripture (Matt 13:13; Luke 8:10.) This dullness is not highlighting a physical state or the consequence of something that is due to a basic lack of intelligence but because they have changed their attitude toward the person of Christ. The word *nōthros* (here the plural *nōthroi*) is only found here and in 6:12 in the New Testament.[8] The thought is not really that they are not able to hear but that they do not want to hear and put into practice what they hear. They have lost their zeal and desire. The fact that they have adopted this characteristic shows that this was not always so.

---

7. The Greek *peri ouch* can be taken either as a masculine in which case it would mean "of whom," referring to Christ or neuter "of which" referring to the entire priesthood of Melchizedek. Here it is more likely that it refers to the whole subject and not just to the person of Christ who is like Melchizedek.

8. In the LXX of Prov 22:29 it is found to describe slothful men.

v. 12 "For because of the time, you ought to be teachers, you need to have someone teach you again, the basics of the foundation of the word of God and you have become those who have need of milk not of solid food." Time has gone by. It would seem to have been a considerable time during which they ought to have been in a position to teach. The word translated "ought to" is a participle from the Greek verb *opheilō*, meaning that someone is under an obligation to do something.[9] The thought is that as an individual is a believer, he or she should then automatically be learning in such a way as to be able to pass on their faith to others. This should be automatic as they acquire information and understanding about their belief system and the person of Christ. However, rather than being in the position to pass on any understanding of what the author calls, the rudiments or the first principles of the word of God, they have stalled.

They need to be taught the basics of God's word again. The Greek word *stoicheia*[10] has the sense of the very basics or rudiments of any subject. It is the same word that is used in Galatians 4:3 for the equivalent of the ABCs of a subject. The author is really pressing home the fact that the readers have failed to learn their lessons well. Not only does he make it very clear that they need to learn these basics but he adds the adverb–*again*. In other words, they knew this at one time and have now forgotten what those basics were. It would appear that the author is being sarcastic here and wishes to drive home the point that they are dull of hearing or just plain lazy spiritually. They have failed to grasp the very beginning of what God's word is all about (compare the idea with what is stated in the first two verses of the following chapter). This state of infancy in their understanding is emphasized by the last phrase which says that they need milk and not solid food. Only the youngest of infants (*nēpios* is a baby not a young child) survive on milk. This same metaphor regarding people being milk drinkers, is used by Paul in 1 Corinthians 3:1–2.

This phrase has to be read in context, since elsewhere in the New Testament Peter writes about *"the pure milk of the word"* 1 Pet 2:2, as something being required of new born believers, meaning something that is essential and necessary but here it is used in the sense of showing the state of their belief being that of babies who have failed to grow up.

v. 13 "For everyone who lives on milk is unskilled with the word of righteousness for he is a baby." Those who are milk drinkers, the babies referred

9. See Arndt and Gingrich, 603.

10. For more on this word see Garrard, *Epistle to the Galatians*, 70, commentary on 4:3. It must have been a word in common use as both Paul and the author of this epistle use it in the same sense.

to in the previous verse, are literally *untested* when it comes the word of righteousness. This means that they do not have experience in it or are out of practice when it comes to the very basics. It needs to be remembered here that "righteousness" is not being used here in a Pauline manner. It is more in the sense of the Old Testament understanding where it refers to the direction given to what is correct and good and what needs to be put into practice. It is a matter of the principles that stand behind what righteousness represents or what is good and correct in God's eyes. The "word" here (*logos*) has the sense of the teaching about something and that is how it is used later in 6:1. So, these spiritual babies do not fully understand what God is saying to them about how they are to do things in his way and live according to his plan.

v. 14 "*But solid food is for the mature because their faculties have been exercised to distinguish both good and bad.*" The solid food, which is referring to the ability to be able to judge the reality of this righteous behavior as well as all that goes together with what all this priesthood stands for, is only possible for people who are mature or perfect (see the Greek words *teleiōn* here and *teleioteras* 9:11 which here have the sense of something that is complete or fulfilled). Maturity or completeness, and growth, is a common theme in the New Testament especially in Paul's epistles (1 Cor 2:6; 3:1; 14:20). In Ephesians 4:13–16 the theme is that of growth in order to resemble Christ and as here, the need to avoid continuing to live like children who are unable to discern the true nature of the winds of doctrine. People are only mature when they have had experience and are consequently, in a place to be able to discern correctly. Discernment requires the constant use of a person's rational abilities; that only happens with exercise and time. When these characteristics are in place, it is possible to immediately recognize if something is out of order or not.

6.

6:1–12 The need to move forward

The question of maturity is underlined in the following section. In practical terms this is mandatory in our day as there are many who call themselves Christians but who have an elementary understanding of Christian doctrine and depend mostly on a trust in their leaders for direction. This is based upon their personal charisma rather than their character and biblical absolutes. The time has come to get to grips with the implementation of scriptural truth and that with a passion founded upon truth and strong conviction that Jesus the Son must come first in all of life.

v. 1 "Therefore, leaving the elementary teaching of Christ, let us go on[1] to maturity, not laying again a foundation of repentance from dead works and of faith toward God," The "therefore" here, means that in spite of this lack of desire and the fact that they have been behaving like children rather than adults, it is time to move on. There is need to make some radical changes which require a different approach to that practiced currently. The elementary teaching of Christ is literally "the word of beginning of Christ" or the start of any teaching about Christ. The start or the rudiments are the same thing. In 5:12, the author used a different term to describe this foundational teaching (*stoicheia*), which, as was seen, had the sense of the ABCs. The thought is similar here. The significance is that it is time to move on and leave the fundamentals behind. The fundamentals are not bad and are necessary but there has to be progression. What then are these foundational or rudimentary matters?

---

1. The Greek *pherōmetha* here gives the idea of being borne along by something powerful and dominant.

It is significant that before the author lists these things, he brings a strong exhortation to his readers in which he includes himself; this is evident from the way in which the phrase is written in the first-person plural–*us*. The construction conveys the thought "Let us be borne along together to perfection" or maturity. It gives the sense that there is divine intervention which empowers the change that awaits them and makes it all possible. However, even if the Spirit of God is present to enable any required change, it is necessary for the individuals involved, to be open to submit to what God requires; they are not to be passive in what has to happen.

The items listed, here and in the next verse, as part of the foundational teaching include six areas which do not need to be established again. That fact alone shows that there was a time when this foundational teaching must have been undertaken. It is not therefore, a matter of a failure to put the foundation in place but a matter of moving on from the foundation to the superstructure. It needs to be remembered that in the Greek text, these two verses are part of the same sentence. These six areas are divided into three pairs. The first pair is repentance from dead works and faith toward God. Dead works most certainly need to be repented of. They speak of actions which lead a person away from God and result in death. Such terms are only used here and in 9:14. However, in Romans 6:21 and 23, after having written about behavior which was the fruit of sin, Paul made it very clear that those who were slaves to sin, were sure of death and that the wages of sin are death. This then confirms the same fact, using slightly different phraseology. Repentance from such works was absolutely necessary. Any relationship with God or with Christ requires repentance and a heart to turn from such behavior. Together with repentance and the forsaking of sin, there has to be new direction and faith placed totally in God. Although Pauline teaching on faith directed at God, is seen as an absolute necessity, it is presented very differently than it is in this epistle. The central place given to faith here, is nevertheless, without question. This is especially so in chapter eleven, where it is the evidence of trust in God in and for all of life's needs.

v. 2 "of teaching about baptisms and of laying on of hands, of resurrection of the dead and eternal judgment." The second couplet includes ritual washings and the laying on of hands. "Baptisms" is plural here (*baptismōn* not *baptisma*) so appears to indicate something more than initial baptism at the point of trust in Christ. Ritual washings were part of the Jewish religious behavior so it is most likely that this is what the author had in mind.[2] In 9:13 this ritual cleansing is elaborated upon further and the language there

2. For more on the significance of *baptismōn* see Hughes, *Hebrews*, 199; Bruce, *Hebrews*, 114–16.

clearly reflects the kind of language used in Ezekiel 36:25 "*I will sprinkle clear water upon you and you shall be clear from all your filthiness . . . and I will cleanse you.*" It needs to be remembered that ritual immersion was something carried out by Jews, especially during the period of the Second Temple.[3] Essenes and at least one group of Jewish worshippers at Qumran, practiced regular washings or baptism in a ritual manner and perhaps there were some in this Jewish-Christian following, who were taken up with similar practices.[4] These baptisms are certainly not necessary nor legitimate today, other than the initial baptism which is an indicator of obedience to Christ's command in Matthew 28:19.

The Laying on of hands was something carried out regularly during the religious rites of the Old Testament, as in Numbers 27:18–23, where the transference of divine authority and blessing is indicated. It is also common in New Testament writings in a number of different contexts, not only requesting blessing but matters such as praying for the reception of the Holy Spirit (Acts 8:17), the conveyance of the gifts of the Holy Spirit (Acts 8:17) and while praying for the sick to be healed (Acts 28:8). However, it needs to be noted that there are also occasions where the reception of the Spirit, gifts and healing took place without this practice being observed (Acts 2:3, 4; 5:16). It is also a sign of the committal of an individual to service or a specific task (Acts 6:6).

The last pair of requirements in the list of things that require progression is the matter of resurrection of the dead and eternal judgment. The resurrection of the dead is especially elaborated upon in the New Testament, as the consequence of Jesus' being raised from the dead. It is the central theme of this New Covenant and apart from the historical records related in the Gospels, it is constantly alluded to in the Epistles especially by Paul in 1 Corinthians 15 and by Peter in 1 Pet 1:3 and 3:21, and the author of Revelation 20:5, 6. It is the believer's hope and without it, the central reason for the Christian faith would be missing, leaving Christian teaching empty and meaningless.

Nevertheless, it is not exclusive to the New Testament because it was very much the teaching of the Pharisees (Acts 23:8), and is taught specifically in texts such as Isaiah 26:19 where it is written: "*Your dead shall live, their corpses shall rise . . . and the earth will give birth to those long dead.*" Daniel 12:2 has a similar teaching. It also links in with eternal judgment because it states: "*Many of those who sleep in the dust of the earth shall awake,*

3. See Pfann, "The Essene yearly Renewal," 1.

4. For more on baptism and the practice of many within Judaism at that time see Daube, *Rabbinic Judaism*, 106–140.

some to everlasting life and some to shame and everlasting contempt." The last part of this verse makes it very plain that the resurrection has two very different outcomes, depending upon the way in which individuals have lived their lives. This is because the previous verse shows that everything is fully known by God and all who belong to him are *"found written in the book."*

Therefore, to summarize all that has been said regarding what the author has depicted in these triplets, it can be affirmed that none of these teachings are exclusively Christian or unique to the NT. A good Jew could say a hearty Amen to all of these matters and would have a good grasp of what they all meant, just as could a non-Jew, who had placed their trust exclusively in Christ. All these teachings are foundational and would have been known to both groups. The problem is, nevertheless, that to be a Jew who was supposedly a Christian, there are certain aspects within each of them which make no sense without total allegiance to Christ. For example, when the Christian reads Daniel 7:13–14 and sees the one like the Son of Man coming to the Ancient of Days from whom he receives all dominion, glory and kingship, he knows automatically that the text is referring to Christ. He can grasp from the text that Christ is the Judge at the end of time, who will decide everything and everyone's outcome. So, the eternal judgement of which the author writes here, is in his hands. Any possibility of rejecting this Son of Man, would automatically exclude the individual from the possibility of participating in his eternal kingdom. One's own damnation would automatically be sealed for eternity and that due to their own decision. The final meaning of all that follows and what is stated outright in verse 6, is decided here. Anything that resembles what is included under apostasy, is out of the question for anyone who thinks logically.

v. 3 "And we will do this, if indeed God permits." What exactly is the author saying when he states that he will do this if God permits? Since he has already made it quite clear that he does not want to lay the foundation all over again and that he wants them, together with himself, to be borne along to maturity by the Holy Spirit (see v. 1), this must mean that: If God Makes it possible and there is no reason why he will not, they would do all that is necessary to not remain as milk drinkers. There is, in other words, engagement required by believers in the carrying out of what God wills. In spite of the debate among scholars as to its meaning, this phrase would make most sense if it is understood in this way. If people are going to move on with God, as their enabler, they need to put the superstructure in place, which Christ wants them to build. To do this, zeal, right understanding, and action are required. Those who are designated as "we" here, must not remain in this dangerous and listless state of the basics but make progress and go on to maturity in Christ. There is no place to go back to the past and the shadows. Since this progress is what God desires of all his children; it is expected that there will be advancement and maturity but the next verse shows that there is nevertheless, danger for those who are not willing to follow the advice. It should be noted that the author is not saying that it is not necessary to have the correct foundation but that once the foundation is in place there has to be change and progression.

vv. 4–6 "*For it is impossible for those who were once enlightened and tasted the heavenly gift and have shared in the Holy Spirit and tasted the good word of God and powerful works of the coming age and fall away, to be renewed again to repentance, as they are actively crucifying the Son of God again and putting him to open shame*" (see *Appendix C* on the matter of the impossibility of apostates repenting, also the notes on 10:26).

The "for" (*gar*), which is present at the commencement of this verse, links what has just been stated and what is to follow. The theme of apostasy, which was first introduced in 3:12 and which is raised again twice in the letter (10:26–31 and 12:25–29), is the reason for the dogmatic statement here. The declarations made here are difficult for many to grasp, in the light of the teaching regarding God's forgiveness, grace and mercy. First, it needs to be seen that the author uses the word *impossible* (*adunaton*) four times in the letter: here with regard to apostasy and repentance; in 6:18 with reference to God being unable to lie; in 10:4 where it is impossible for the blood of animal sacrifices to remove sin, then finally, it is impossible to please God in any way without faith (11:6). This makes it very clear that there are conditions applicable, which have to be met in the circumstances of life, for all followers of Christ. If they are not, then the impossibility prevails and rules.

Here, the author is adamant that there is an impossibility attached to the state of the individuals who are guilty of apostasy or as is stated here, those who fall away (*parapesontas*) after they believe. The aorist of the verb shows that the action is to be seen as complete. It leads to an irreversible situation which makes it beyond question to consider the possibility of any future repentance on the part of an apostate. One may state that nothing is impossible with God but in this instance, it is clear that there are limits to the application of God's offer of grace. If the grace of God which brought redemption to an individual, was then blatantly spurned, subsequent to the application of all its benefits, then the condition for its re-enactment can never be met. They cannot be renewed again to a place of repentance (*palin anakainizein eis metanoian*). The language is very clear, even if it is unpalatable to many; it cannot be explained away.

The detail given here in Hebrews is that there are several criteria which would indicate that this impossibility is set in place and at the point of being enacted but has not yet occurred. *These individuals were once enlightened.*

Enlightenment has already taken place for them. Enlightenment takes place when the meaning of the word of God, which is declared to an individual is fully grasped. The nature of this is further repeated in 10:32. Light is synonymous with truth and truth is God's message of salvation; therefore, enlightenment is the comprehension of God's truth made known through Christ (John 1:7; 3:21). Christ himself is the light, lighting all who come into the world (John 1:9), so to embrace him is to be enlightened (John 8:12). Those who are enlightened are "sons of light" (John 12:36).[5] To be enlightened therefore, automatically assumes some meaningful comprehension of the person of Christ, his message and his will. It is not a mere ritualistic pronouncement of being a follower without conviction and comprehension acknowledged in a mechanical manner. The thought then is that the individual who was previously in the dark, was enlightened and then rejected the light to return to the darkness. This process of enlightenment is not something which can be repeated. Elsewhere in scripture, there are specific warnings given about certain kinds of sin which are unpardonable. Jesus himself talks about blasphemy against the Holy Spirit being one of them (Matt 12:31), so this sort of warning is not unique here.

To underline the nature of this enlightenment, a list of participles is added, all of which develop what this enlightenment means.[6] These people who are in danger of falling away, *"have tasted the heavenly gift."* What then is the tasting of the heavenly gift? Bruce, in the same way that he suggests that enlightenment is as seen above, thinks that it may refer to baptism and that this tasting of the heavenly gift may refer to the Eucharist.[7] However, if we see how the phrase has its origin in Ps 34:8, where the psalmist states *"O taste and see that the Lord is good,"* we note the tasting aspect is used elsewhere in the New Testament; it is more likely that it refers to having participated in something divine in a deeper and more meaningful manner. An example would be as in 1 Peter 2:3, where Peter uses the word to describe the experience of the individual with Christ and the rich blessings which flow from that relationship. Here, the heavenly gift (*dōrea*), must be understood in the sense of a spiritual gift;[8] it encompasses all that is part of

---

5. Justin Martyr, *First Apology*, 61:12–13.; 65:1 writing in the middle of the second century says that "enlightenment" equates to baptism for believers in the church at Rome. As interesting as that may be, it is hard to demonstrate that this is the sense here. See Bruce, *Hebrews*, 120n39.

6. See Spicq, *Hébreux*, II. 150.

7. Bruce, *Hebrews*, 120–21. It is also added to the description given for the participation at the breaking of the bread in Acts 20:11 where the participle of "to taste" (*geusamenos*) is used.

8. It needs to be recognised that *dorea* here, points to all that is related to salvation.

salvation, which has its origin in heaven and is dependent upon the person and work of Christ. Again, these same people *had become those who shared in the Holy Spirit*. The term *sharers of* or *participants in* (*metochos, metochoi* or one of its forms), has already been used in this epistle (1:9; 3:1, 14 also 12:8). So, the sharers or participants are also the tasters of these things.

The construction makes it clear that this enlightenment included the grace of the work of the Holy Spirit. To have experienced the person and or the gifts of the Holy Spirit, indicate that the individual was no mere nominal follower of Christ. It is not evident as to exactly what is meant by being sharers in the Holy Spirit here, as the Holy Spirit is first of all the one who brings about regeneration in all its aspects but he is also the one who distributes the various gifts which are elaborated upon by Paul in his first epistle to the Corinthians chapters 12 and 14. Anyway, to have shared in him and his gift of life, most certainly demonstrates a vital communion with God which is no unilateral or superficial relationship. It has to be far more than participation in baptism or the eucharist which are outward acts.

The last of the participles incorporates two strands. There is the fact that the person has tasted of the *"good word of God and the powers[9] of the age to come."* With regard to the tasting, something similar to what was stated above must be understood here. That means there has been a full and meaningful experience which would have left a very deep impression on one's mind and which could not simply be discounted or explained away later. Consequently, the first thing they experienced here was the *"good word of God."* It was indeed the good word, which opened their understanding and left room for the Holy Spirit to bring the conviction necessary for someone to believe in Christ. It was good because its entire content is from God who is good and who seeks only what is good for all his creation (Mark 10:18; Luke 18:19; 1 Tim 4:4). It is again good because it is the content of the message of the Gospel and correct teaching (Acts 8:12, 35; 10:36). Finally, it is also good because it opens spiritually blind eyes and the door to salvation with all that that term includes.

They benefited positively from that word, at least initially, even if now they doubt it. The second part of that tasting was the experiencing *"of the powers of the age to come."* When the word of God is declared, God acts in such a way as to perform miracles. These include salvation itself which is inclusion in God's eternal plans. However, in addition to this, the gifts of

---

Pneumata on the other hand, especially as they are described by Paul in 1 Cor 12, speak only of one aspect and that is the Holy Spirit's gifts.

9. The word *dunameis* is translated *powers* here but elsewhere it is translated miracles, as in 2:4. See also Acts 8:13.

the Spirit include: healings, prophecies, signs and wonders all of which have taken place. It is not necessary here to elaborate upon the eschatological aspect of what this means but the author is saying that the consequences of the powerful works of God in the present, are only partial evidence now, of what will be in the future. That aspect will be clearer when the Kingdom of God comes in all its fulness. These powers are, in Pauline thinking, the firstfruits of things to come (Rom 8:23).

The author adds to the reasons related to the impossibility of any renewed repentance for apostates. If this were to happen it would be the same thing as asking Christ to repeat his work upon the cross, all over again for them personally, because it had not worked the first-time round. That is what is meant by the phrase: *"they are actively crucifying the Son of God again and putting him to open shame."* It reinforces the fact that to reject Christ, after having believed, is to trample under foot all that the crucifixion represents; at that point there is no possibility of any personal vindication once the decision to reject his work and his person has occurred.

vv. 7–8 "For the land which has drunk the rain which often falls upon it and produces crops suitable for those whose sake it is farmed, receives blessing from God. But if it bears thorns and thistles, it is disapproved and near to being a curse; its end is for burning." The author uses what is the equivalent of an agricultural parable to drive home his message. This kind of procedure is common especially in the Old Testament. There are some similarities here with Isaiah's fruitless vineyard (Isa 5:10) but its consequences go even further than those in that narrative. They are more representative of the curse which was proclaimed against the earth and its consequences in Genesis 3:17b–18. The people who fall away are like the land which has received the blessings of the rain and provision from the hand of God. But instead of producing good fruit, as would be normal of land that is cared for by any farmer, it bears thorns and thistles and ends up being cursed and burned. That burning is damnation and eternal judgment.

v. 9 "But although we speak in this way beloved, we are persuaded of better things regarding you, things related to salvation." From this verse the author changes his approach. He is clearly offering his readers a way of escape from the terrible outcomes described in the first part of the chapter. Rather than seeking their loss and destruction, here are words of concern which demonstrate a heart of longing to see a reversal in their behavior. The author calls them *beloved,* which is unique here in this epistle. It is a tender term which calls for a rapid change in their approach so that relationships with God and with one another may be restored, in spite of the harsh warning that has gone before. Although this word is not found elsewhere in the epistle, it is used commonly in the Pauline literature (Rom 9:25; 11:28; 12:19;

16:5, 8, 9, 12; 1 Cor 4:14 et al.), by James in 1:16, 19; 2:5, Peter in 1 Pet 2:11; 4:12 and by John in 1 John 2:7; 3:2, et al., as well as Jude in verses 1, 3, 17 and 20. This shows that it was common to use it in believing circles, to address those of the Christian family. The force of the words is aimed at bringing the readers back to their senses and awakening them from their spiritual lethargy. The author wants to encourage them to swift and appropriate action. He intimates that there is still something within them related to salvation as a whole, which would indicate that there is hope and that they have not yet crossed over the line of demarcation described. Further, the way in which the words are penned, appears to show that the author has a good knowledge of his readers. This means that he is more than a distant acquaintance. He knows about their past, as is evident from the following verse.

v. 10 "For God is not unjust to be forgetful of your work and your love which you have shown for his name, having served the saints and are still serving." The ground of this persuasion in the verse is based upon two factors: God is not unjust and the readers' works are important. God is not some harsh and uncaring God. He knows all about the lives each one lives out and is aware of the trials and works of the past. He knows of the love and passions of the heart surrendered previously in acts which were carried out in favor of the saints and, as the author states here, in which they continued to be involved. In fact, they engaged in these works in an ongoing manner. These works were being carried out for his name (*eis to onoma autou*), which indicates that all these works of love were done in favor of God's service and person. They demonstrate some form of faith and trust was the motivation behind them; again, the works were primarily directed toward those who belonged to the Christian community: the saints (*tois hagiois*). This behavior is all taken into consideration in God's estimation and appraisal of what has taken place in a person's life; he will certainly do what is right. It does not make any difference that the actual nature of those works is not listed, as it is the heart behind the works which is the matter at hand. These works were not perfunctory.

v. 11 "But we desire each one of you to show the same eagerness to (possess) *the full assurance of the hope unto the end."* Having declared positive words of encouragement, the author continues in the same vein, calling for the manifestation of animated and eager lives, that demonstrate not merely some acts of service, even if there was love behind those. More is necessary and when he voices this in terms of "we desire" (*epithumoumen*) he is giving vent to strong feelings of his own. The strength of this word comes out in some of the translations: New English Translation: ". . . we passionately want . . ."; New English Bible " . . . we long . . ."; Wycliffe Bible ". . . we covet . . ." The readers need to have some of the same passion and earnestness that goes together with meaningful convictions attached to faith in Christ and his service. The word translated eagerness or diligence, in Greek, is *spoudē*. It would indicate a state of mind which would be the very opposite of the lack of zeal and diligence mentioned in the next verse (*nōthros*). It is doubtful from what the author writes, that there is any clear evidence that this diligence is present or that there is any full assurance actually being manifested. This is the matter he touches upon once more in 10:22, where again, it is linked importantly to faith. If this lack were not the problem, it would not have been necessary for him to write about it so passionately here. Obviously, hope and faith, both of the same nature and from the same root in Greek (*pis*), are not therefore in evidence here. That is why the readers need to manifest the full assurance of all that it means and continue on in that fashion until the very end.

v. 12 *"That you should not be sluggish,*[10] *but imitators of those, who through faith and steadfastness, inherit the promises."* That "you," the readers, should not be lethargic. The thrust here is that there is most certainly an active role to be played by the believers in Christ. Engagement with Christ in a manner which demonstrates one's faith and obedience to the teachings of Scripture, is required. It must be remembered that this zeal has nothing to do with the earning of one's salvation but it is the opening of the individual's own person to the moving of the Holy Spirit so that the individual becomes God's instrument in his salvation plan. Imitation of other believers who have run or who are running the Christian race, is something which is recommended in several New Testament texts (1 Cor 4:16; 11:1; I Thess 1:6; 2 Thess 3:7, 9) and is alluded to further in chapter 13:7 of this letter. Paul tells the Ephesians to be imitators[11] of God. One of the easiest ways to learn anything is to imitate people who are known examples. However, to imitate someone or something, requires a close relationship and rapport with that person or thing. Here, there must have been those who were in a position to pass on to their disciples or peers, the required models to follow. This imitation of the right kind would only happen if they were to abandon any sluggish attitudes and mimic true faith and steadfast behavior. In the very next verse, we see that Abraham is one of those who these Hebrew Christians should imitate when it comes to faith and steadfastness.

The word which is so often translated patience, is the Greek *makrothumia*. It conveys more of the sense of longsuffering and perseverance, than

---

10. The Greek *nōthros* has the sense of having "no push" or no energy or enthusiasm as already mentioned.

11. The translation is from the Greek plural of *mimētēs* the word from which we get our English word mimic.

it does of patience and waiting for something to happen. It calls for active engagement in all the goals and purposes that are related to the teaching and message of the Gospel of Christ. This engagement must occur during the waiting period before the end is reached. Of course, there is patience but it must never be understood in the sense of mere passive waiting for something to occur. In one way, the inheritance about which the author has more to say (9:15; 11:8), has already been entered into, from the moment of the acceptance of Christ's lordship but its final and complete fulfilment, is future and therefore, only those who meet the criteria which is encouraged throughout this letter, will be the final beneficiaries of all that this inheritance promises. The promises are all that is involved in the salvation mentioned in verse 9.

6:13–20 God's sure promises

The first cursory look at this section may give the impression that it is out of place in this treatment but when we continue on to the next chapter and what the author has to say about the priesthood of Jesus, which is similar to that of the order of Melchizedek, then the reason becomes clear. The central theme is that of God's faithfulness and the fact that all who trust in him can be completely certain that what he has said will happen. His word is sure and cannot be changed. It is like the anchor which is imbedded in the bottom of the ocean that will hold the ship, even when the storm is raging and the waves are roaring (v.19).

vv. 13–14 "For when God made a promise to Abraham, since he had no one greater by whom to swear, he swore by himself, saying, 'Surely I will bless you and multiply you.'"[12] Abraham was always considered to be the supreme example of a man of faith, both among the Jews and early Christians. So here too, as already mentioned above (v.12), he becomes the model to follow. On more than a few occasions God made promises to Abraham concerning his future posterity and other blessings that would be transmitted through him to the generations to come (Gen 12:1–7; 13:14–17; 15:4–6, 18–21; 17:1–8, 16 et al.). Abraham was faithful in spite of the many setbacks in his life and he did not give up but persevered. In Genesis 22:16–17, after Abraham had not withheld the offering of his only son Isaac, the Lord called to Abraham and said "By myself I have sworn says the Lord," and "I will

---

12. The Hebrew structure of the Greek comes through here as the phrase reads literally, even if it is not grammatical: "if surely blessing, I will bless you and multiplying I will multiply you." (ei mēn eulogōn eulogēsō se kai plēthunōn plēthunō se). It is a construction which emphasizes the facts related to what God will certainly do; there is no doubt at all about his word being fulfilled, as it will be abundant or without measure.

indeed bless you and I will make your offspring as numerous as the stars of the heaven and as the sand that is on the seashore." This is the reference to which the author alludes here. What he is saying is that there is no one greater or more dependable than God himself. The numerous offspring of which he speaks, is not merely the physical offspring as we see from what Paul writes in his Epistle to the Romans 9:6 and Galatians 3:16 but all those people of faith, like Abraham, who make up the spiritual offspring. They, like their predecessor Abraham, will all have a heart to persevere. The author is saying indirectly that the blessings promised to Abraham are also theirs but they need to make sure that the perseverance which was characteristic of Abraham, must be part of any enthusiastic steadfast service on their part (see v.12), if they wish to benefit from God's sworn oath to Abraham.

The question of the swearing of an oath (Greek *omnuō* or *omnumi*), as it is understood here, conveys the thought in human terms, that the words invoke a higher power or a divine person, to back up what is stated. This is not common in English, other than perhaps in some legal contexts, especially related to bearing witness to truth. However, there are still cultures and languages where this kind of invocation, calling for the backing of a higher power is made.[13] Usually, swearing, in modern English, is associated with foul language, which most certainly is not what is meant here. God is saying that he stands behind whatever he declares and that his word is totally dependable, just as he is. After all, who is more reliable than he?

The nature of the oath which was sworn, although written here in Greek, represents a Hebrew style which is absolute even if it commences with the words "*ei mēn*" or "If indeed" because it has the sense of something that is most certain and is consequently going to happen even if all indications may appear to be contrary.

v. 15 "And in this way, having been steadfast, he received the promise." The steadfast perseverance of Abraham that the readers are called to imitate (v.12) was certainly something Abraham was required to manifest during the long years prior to the birth of Isaac but subsequent to the promise being made.

His steadfastness and trust in God are evident even when he was called upon to offer up Isaac as a sacrifice; he was obedient and was willing to do what God commanded, even when he recognized that the future and the numerous descendants who had been promised depended upon this miracle child (Gen 22:10–12). The significance of this aspect is mentioned

---

13. A number of Central African languages have specific words linked to this kind of oath which have nothing at all to do with coarse language. The Luba of Katanga in the DRCongo use the term: *kutyipa muptyipo* for "to swear an oath." In English swearing an oath appears to come from the Anglo-Saxon custom of calling upon a deity to bear witness to a statement and affirm its veracity.

again in chapter 11:17–19. Here the verse emphases the importance of faith and trust on an ongoing basis. Of course, although the immediate application of God's promises to Abraham were fulfilled partially in the days of Genesis, the ultimate fulfilment awaits the future, with Christ, his offspring and God's eschatological kingdom. Only then will the fulfilment of the promise, as the author points out in 11:39, become a reality because it awaits the addition of all the offspring in order to be completed.

v. 16 *"For people swear by what is greater* (than themselves) *and the oath is the conformation* (of) *an end of all disputes."* The author looks at human convention here as the basis of what oaths are all about. Because people cannot be trusted to do what they say, the oath is supposed to be the guarantee that validates any agreement made. The oath is supposed to incorporate something or someone greater than oneself to stand behind the words and make sure that they will be enacted. The one who is greater, would be the divine or human superior, who would then become the guarantor that the oath is fulfilled. If this greater person or power were absent, then the oath would be pointless, as there would be no way of assuring that it would be accomplished. When Jesus taught his disciples, he said that their "yes should be yes" and their "no be no" and that there should be no need to have to have an oath (Matt 5:37). In other words, followers of Christ should be seen to be absolutely reliable and trustworthy. But as far as the convention of the day was concerned, oaths were supposed to be binding; once pronounced, they seal the matter in the eyes of all who participate in the matter and no modifications to what was stated would be permitted.

v. 17 *"So when God resolved to show more assuredly to the heirs of the promise the unchangeable nature of his purpose, he guaranteed it with an oath."* Here, the one making the oath is God himself, as already seen in verse 13. Although it was not necessary for God to sware an oath because when God speaks, his word is always final and trustworthy. However, in this instance, he submits himself to human convention, in order that all should understand perfectly, the reliable nature of what was declared. The words translated, "resolved more assuredly" (*perissoteron boulomenos*), indicate strong resolve on the part of God and show that although they were initially addressed to Abraham, they were intended for the heirs who would follow. That means it was addressed to all who would be partakers of the promises made to Abraham; these heirs or seed,[14] needed to understand the significance of what was sworn in terms of their own participation in the outcome of the promise. So, all who were of Abraham's progeny of faith

14. It has already been noted that these heirs are not the physical but the spiritual seed of Abraham, and include all followers of Christ.

and perseverance, including these Hebrew readers and the generations of believers in Christ who were to follow in Abraham's steps, were and are the heirs of this oath (Gal 3:29).

v. 18 *"so that through two unchangeable things in which it is impossible for God to lie, we who have fled for refuge, might find strong encouragement to take hold of the hope which is set before us,"* What then are the two unchangeable things? Firstly, God's promise made and founded on who he is and secondly, the oath that God made to substantiate it. This means that it is not the individual's own ability that is the important thing, even if it is required that each individual keep focused and steadfast, God is not going to fail. The fact of "the impossibilities" in this letter has already been mentioned in verse 4. This is one of them. God cannot ever lie because of his attribute of truth, which is an intricate part of his character and person. So, all he has to do is make a declaration and it is automatically the truth. This one has to do with conditions laid down relative to the inheritance of the promise given to Abraham. The author includes himself in the action in which he depicts those as having fled to God for refuge. The Greek word *kataphugō*, used here and also in Acts 14:6, is used of someone fleeing for refuge. It indicates that only God is seen to be a place of safety, both from the present and for the future. In the light of what was said about the need for earnest steadfastness (v.12), this verse may imply that there are some who have not fled for safety but who need to do so because they are exhorted to take hold of the hope set before "us"; this also infers that some had not fled nor taken hold of the hope set before them. Others, however, have done just that. To take hold of this hope, requires a determined will and the appropriate action, already designated. The hope that is set before them is the fulfilment of the promise given to Abraham and his heirs. Hope is another important factor that is raised at least seven times in the letter (3:6; 6:11, 18, 19 (x2); 10:23; 11:1 (as a verb)). It is expanded upon in the next verse.

v. 19 *"which we have as an anchor of the soul both safe and firm and which leads into the inner side of the curtain* [in the sanctuary]." Hope is likened to an anchor, only here in the New Testament. So, this hope keeps one absolutely firmly attached and immovable with respect to their trust in God. The Greek word *asphalē* is used in the sense of something being completely firm, safe and sure.[15] Hope is this anchor which means that even when the storms of life bear down upon a person, the hope of all the promises made here, will mean that they will not be moved. We are taught not to mix metaphors in English but this does not appear to be a problem for writers of Scripture. So, from the anchor of hope the reader is transferred inside the

---

15. Arndt & Gingrich, 118.

heavenly tabernacle. Hope leads to the inner side of the heavenly sanctuary, where the final and complete fulfilment of all that Christ's work means, will be realized. The author is using language which would have been familiar to the Jews, who knew about the earthly temple and its structure. It had a curtain separating the holy pace in the sanctuary from the holy of holies. Here, it is no longer the earthly sanctuary, which is the subject but the heavenly, where, as was stated in 1:3, Jesus has entered and sat down *"at the right hand of the majesty on High."* This fact is further mentioned in the next verse where hope in the promise, the theme that was first raised in chapter 5:5–10 about Christ and his being high priest, is reiterated.

v. 20 *"Where Jesus, a forerunner on our behalf, has gone, having become a high priest forever according to the order of Melchizedek."* The author has just stated that Jesus is in the holy of holies on a permanent basis. This seals the significant matter that Jesus has become the eternal High Priest, interceding on behalf of his own in such a manner as to have no limitation in his representation of them before the Father. Christ's High Priesthood is forever, unlike that of any High Priest who has ever gone before; that automatically elevates him to a level never previously anticipated. This means that this role is in place, not only now while his followers are linked to the earth but also in the future, when they will be together with him and the Father in the eternal state.

Therefore, any thought that following Christ and his teaching, is of secondary importance and that abandoning him would ever be a possibility, needs immediately to be reappraised and the appropriate remedy applied. The other factor is that, if Jesus is the forerunner or precursor, then he is the first of a number. The others who are designated to follow are included by the author as "us" as he has gone there on "our behalf." This makes it evident that Christ's person has made a way for all who belong to him, to also enter behind the curtain, into the very same presence of the Almighty. From Matthew 27:51, it is known that the curtain of the temple was split from top to bottom, showing that in Christ's death, the way was now opened into the holy of holies, in order that this entry would be possible; therefore, the thought is not a new one. This verse brings the reader a full circle from the introduction of Melchizedek in 5:6. There the author had much to say about Jesus in 5:11. It was difficult to make known because of the readers' dull state of mind; consequently, they were not able to fully grasp the significance of what Christ's priesthood, modelled on Melchizedek's order, was all about. The parenthesis has challenged the readers regarding their need and it is now supposed that they have had the opportunity to rethink what was involved and apply any correction needed.

7.

Melchizedek's order of Priesthood 7:1–28

As already seen, Melchizedek was introduced in 5:6 and 10 (see the notes on those texts). It was stated there that the context from which the subject was first drawn, is that found in Psalm 110 but it is necessary to go back to Genesis 14:18–20 for the only other biblical mention of the name apart from here in Hebrews. As Ellingworth notes, Melchizedek is the very first priest mentioned in the entire Bible and it seems that for this reason the author has chosen to use him to highlight the role of his service and liken it to that of Jesus.[1] There are other non-biblical texts, such as those at Qumran, where one of the scrolls found in Cave 11, portrays Melchizedek as a heavenly king with armies.[2]

It seems that in a manner somewhat similar to the approach Paul uses in Romans and Galatians, where he goes back to a time prior to the granting of the Law and where individuals like Abraham displayed faith and purity of religion in service to God, so here the author of the Hebrews uses this mostly unknown patriarchal figure to highlight the same fact. As a type of Christ and the perfect priestly example, he is presented in order to highlight the excellence of the high priestly office.[3] The whole purpose appears to be that this mysterious individual represents a priesthood, which Christ portrays perfectly. This is a priesthood which was previously unclear, even if it is mentioned in Scripture. So, what was previously an enigma and not fully understood, now is the center of the discussion. It is important to remember

1. Ellingworth, *Hebrews*, 52.
2. van der Woude, "Melchisedek," 354–373.
3. See Spicq, *Hébreux*, II, 180–81.

that although Melchizedek may consume our immediate interest, he is not the focal point of all that is intended: Christ is, with his priestly order.[4]

It needs to be understood that the methodology used to prove the author's theme regarding the superiority of Jesus' priesthood, could be easily identified by modern scholarship as being allegorical or at least bordering on what is allegorical and therefore be disallowed. However, again, in the light of the conservative view of the inspiration of all Scripture, including both Old and New Testaments, and although the procedures followed here by the author of the letter would mostly be disallowed today, what has been written and what is made of the passages in hand, have to be viewed as God's word. It is not mere allegory but the work of the Holy Spirit. Therefore, even if the author seems to be reading between the lines in the Old Testament passages upon which he depends, he is clarifying the nature of the person and work of Christ, by means of this otherwise obscure individual: Melchizedek and his role in history.

v. 1 "For this Melchizedek, king of Salem, priest of the Most High God, was the one meeting Abraham returning from the slaughter of the kings and blessed him." Who is this Melchizedek? We have seen him, as noted earlier but some repetition is necessary. The author does what we have to and that is go back to the first biblical occurrence of the person under review. In the Genesis narrative, Abraham is caught up in a dispute involving the kings of Sodom and Gomorrah with their overlord (for the entire narrative see Gen 14:1–24). They rebelled against Chedorlaomer from Elam and consequently he came to the Jordan valley with other kings allied with him, to put an end to their defiance. He carried off many prisoners including Lot, Abraham's nephew. Abraham was by that time, a man of considerable means, so he gathered together his own men, pursued the enemy, defeated them and retrieved all the captured people, as well as a considerable amount of booty. This booty not only included what had previously belonged to Lot but items which had originated from the kings of Sodom and Gomorrah, as well as from the alliance of Chedorlaomer, which had been overthrown by Abraham's troops. This routing of the enemies is summarized in the phrase *"returning from the slaughter of the kings"* (Gen 14:17).

It is at this point that we are introduced to Melchizedek. Upon the return of Abraham and his army they meet up with the king of Sodom but also with this king called Melchizedek, who is the center of attention in this section of Hebrews. He is introduced as *"King Melchizedek of Salem . . . priest of*

---

4. A simple but excellent, even if not intended to be scholarly (it certainly does not lack scholarly insight), treatment of this section, is found in Tom Wright, *Hebrews for Everyone*, 69–73.

God Most High" Gen 14:18). After bringing out bread and wine for Abram (note he is still called Abram[5] at this point in time) he declares: *"Blessed be Abram by God Most High, maker of heaven and earth and blessed be God Most High"* (Gen 14:19, 20). This man has the Hebrew name, Melchizedek, which when broken down into its component parts, means: "king of justice" or "righteousness." Therefore, he is *king of righteousness.*[6] The next significant fact is that he is also king of Salem, the town which we know better as Jerusalem.[7] The location of his dwelling place is not of great consequence to the author of the letter. Salem is, through its cognate form, the same as *shalom* or peace, which means that Melchizedek is also *king of peace.* This makes him the king of righteousness and peace. Therefore, linked to this individual is both kingship and priesthood; in addition, is the fact that this individual is evidently the priest of the Most High God (*el 'elyon*). This is the same name which is later represented by the name Yahweh; here *Most High God,* is in place prior to the revelation of God's name *I Am,* to Moses.

The fact of Melchizedek's blessing of Abraham is important, as he is the greater who blesses the inferior, as is noted in verse 6 of this chapter. The matter of his bringing out bread and wine in the Genesis account is not a factor here, although there may be some theologians who would like to make a big thing of this in an effort to highlight the Christian teaching related to the Lord's table. The author avoids any such matters here and likely with intent, as one could then go on to maintain that this may maintain Melchizedek's service of Abraham which would in turn, infer that Abraham was greater than he. Any examination of the text has to adhere to the way in which the author of Hebrews develops the theme, in order to avoid any possible allegorical interpretations which would not highlight his purpose. The importance of not introducing anything which is not part of the original text or being in the mind of the author, will be understood in the next verse.

vv. 2–3 "And to him Abraham divided a tenth part of everything. On the one hand, he is first, by the interpretation of his name, king of righteousness and then king of Salem, which is king of peace. He is without father, without mother without genealogy, having neither beginning of days nor end of life, but resembling the Son of God he remains a priest continually." After rescuing Lot, Abraham gives tithes to Melchizedek of all the booty he had gained during the overthrow of the kings. This shows that the latter's priestly line

---

5. It should be noted that no New Testament author uses the form Abram for Abraham.

6. This is how the text in Hebrew is interpreted by both Josephus and Philo the Jew. *Leg. Alleg.* III, 79.

7. For more on the link between Salem and Jerusalem see Bruce, *Hebrews,* 136n16.

was recognized by Abraham and was in place long before any Levitical priesthood, ever existed. After all, the Levitical priesthood was only put in place years later, when the Law was given to Moses. This priestly order then predates everything related to the Law and must be seen as what its Levitical precursor was. Melchizedek received this tithe, which shows that he had the right to do so. Again, he is both king of righteousness and king of peace. In emphasizing the interpretation of the names of this person, the author is highlighting the parallelism between him and Christ, who bears both of these titles and attributes [see *Appendix F* on the question of tithes].

The next statement is the one which is most commonly misunderstood and which has led many to believe Melchizedek to be some angelic being or to depict Christ in some way. That would be in a manner similar to the Christophanies of the Angel of the Lord, who appeared to Abraham prior to the destruction of Sodom and Gomorrah. What needs to be remembered is that any careful reading of the Old Testament, endorses the importance of family lines recorded in scripture. It is possible to follow all the important lines, including those of the Levitical priesthood, as well as the kings, back to their founders. Their genealogies had to be verifiable for them to qualify for their specific functions, whether priesthood or kingship. But when it comes to Melchizedek there is no way at all of following his line as none is given. The author is not saying that he does not have a father or mother or that he did not die but that, unlike Aaron's line, where anyone could check up on his ancestry, here that was out of the question.[8] In other words, even if he did belong to a priestly line during his day, that is not associated with anything recognized or recorded and there is nothing about his background, his parents, his birth or his death in Scripture. Yet, if Abraham, the father of the Jewish nation, as well as of all the faithful, gave him tithes, that would prove that Melchizedek's priesthood must have a line superior to his own, or from which the Aaronic priesthood descended. In modern rational thinking, it is not possible to prove anything from silence but silence here is exactly what is used to prove to the readers what the author has in mind here. For him the fact that nothing is written about this man's genealogy, proves that his priestly legitimacy resembles that of the Son of God in perpetuity.

The important phrase the author uses here reads: *made like* or *resembling the son of God*. In the Greek it is: *aphōmoiōmenos*[9] *de tō huiō tou theou.*

---

8. The ability for any claimant to priesthood to be able to validate their ancestral links was essential as is seen in Ezra 2:59–62 where some who could not prove their families or their descent were excluded.

9. This is the nominative singular past participle passive of *aphomoioō*. To make something like something else. See Arndt & Gingrich, 126.

It is the only time in the scripture that the word *aphōmoiōmenos*, appears. It has the sense of being made like, resembling or being similar to something or someone. It needs to be understood that Melchizedek's priesthood is likened to that of Jesus the Son of God and not the other way round because the priesthood which is under review is not Melchizedek's but that of Christ, even if at the moment it would seem that the important figure is that of the former. In the thought of the author, his presentation shows that there is no succession for the priesthood of Melchizedek because nothing is mentioned regarding it. When it comes to Christ's priesthood, it is perpetual because of who he is and what is stated about him as the Son of God (6:6) and also from the very start of the letter (1:2); after all, his character is exactly that of the Father and he has once more, taken up his place at the right hand of the Majesty on High (1:3). The whole thrust of the section is dependent upon this fact of Melchizedek's priesthood being like that of Christ's. Spicq, citing Javet, says that in reality, the whole of the Melchizedek episode is really demonstrating that this man is like a mirror reflecting the true person and work of Jesus.[10]

v. 4 "But see how great this man was to whom the patriarch Abraham gave a tenth of the spoils." Abraham was the friend of God (2 Chron 20:7; James 2:23) and the father of the faithful, according to Paul (Rom 4:11, 16), yet here the author paints things in a different light. Instead of starting with the priority of the man who is the patriarch—Abraham—he underlines the priority of Melchizedek. This verse is stating that the greater of the two is this man to whom Abraham gave tithes. Of course, the Jews all knew of the greatness of their patriarch Abraham and gave him great honor. But here we have someone who seems to outrank him by the very fact that Abraham gave Melchizedek tithes from the spoils of war, rather than receiving honor from him. As stated, the tithes he gave came from the spoils of the war against the kings who had taken Lot captive, together with those from Sodom and Gomorrah.

vv. 5–6 "And although, on the one hand, the sons of Levi who received the priesthood have a commandment to take tithes from the people, that is from their brothers according to the Law, although they descend from Abraham, on the other hand, the one not reckoning his genealogy from them, is the one to whom Abraham tithed and he blessed him as he had the promises." The purpose of this verse is to show the difference and superiority of two priesthoods. The one which descends from Aaron is Levitical and the other belongs to Melchizedek. The Levitical priesthood descended from Abraham via Aaron and depends upon natural descent. It has the right to impose the

10. Spicq, *Hébreux*, II, 184.

giving of tithes upon its own brothers who are, like themselves, descendants from Abraham. So even within the family of Abraham there are categories of honor or privilege and responsibility. However, even if all the sons of Levi are priests, not all qualify for service, as there were physical qualifications that had to be met. This means that even within Levi there are divisions. So, what is the author saying? That although all the Jews were descendants of Abraham, not all were part of the priesthood with the same rights. There were factors which differentiated between the members of that priesthood and their functions; although all were Levites and had the right, according to the Law, to receive tithes from the family of Abraham (The Jewish nation).

Then, on the other hand, there is the priesthood of Melchizedek, which has no mention made in it of genealogy or descendants, so it differs from the earlier one. Yet, if it is understood that this priesthood received tithes from Abraham, even though there was no law which enforced it, it is not the same as the Levitical order that came afterwards. The giving of the tithes by Abraham was a matter of his own will and an action resulting from his recognition of Melchizedek's superiority as the priest of the Most-High God. The Greek word showing that Melchizedek *received* tithes from Abraham is in the perfect tense (*dedekatōken*), which indicates that the consequences of that action continue to have an impact even until the readers' time and beyond, showing the lasting nature of this priesthood. Again, this decision by Abraham, the patriarch and founder of the nation and its established priesthood, to give the tithes, resulted in him being blessed by Melchizedek. This was on the grounds that as Priest of the Most-High God he had the authority to pronounce God's blessings. Both the giving of the tithes and the bestowing of the blessing, demonstrate that one who gives the tithe is inferior to the one who receives them and the one who bestows the blessing is greater than the one who receives it. This is underlined in the following verse.

v. 7 *"So beyond any dispute the inferior is blessed by the superior."* Abraham paid the tithe to the superior who then blessed him, so Melchizedek and his priestly order has to be considered superior. As far as the author is concerned, the facts here demonstrate that there is no argument which would uphold the superiority of the Levitical priesthood. Therefore, Melchizedek's priesthood, which is the type of Jesus', which is about to be explained further from verse 11, must be seen to be superior.

v. 8 *"Here, on the one hand, mortal men receive tithes but on the other hand, is the one of whom it is witnessed that he lives."* The way in which the author pens the words when he opens this sentence with the word *"here on the one hand"* and then *"there on the other,"* is intended to compare two very different kinds of priesthood. The first is the Levitical priesthood, which is one which depends upon men who, from one generation to another, die. When one of them dies he has to pass on his tasks to his offspring. This continues *ad infinitum*. The procedure of tithing therefore, continues in this system. However, when it comes to Melchizedek, there is no mention of his death or the end of his priesthood. The author uses the phrase that he is "*the one of whom it is witnessed that he lives.*" The Greek for this: *marturoumen hoti zē*, is, according to the author, saying that the Scriptures, to which he is referring, give him the authority to make this claim; even if the reader believes that, once again, there is much that is being read into the descriptions in the original texts.[11] Nowhere is there any mention of Melchizedek's death and so for the purposes of this argument, there is no thought of the end of the priesthood which was his. This is exactly what the author wants to establish, even if today's reader may question the logic of the whole argument.

vv. 9–10 "*And in a manner of speaking, even Levi who receives tithes, paid tithes through Abraham because he was still in the loins of his ancestor when Melchizedek met him.*" For those who may object to the way in which the author introduces the next thought and who think that what he is saying is questionable, he starts out with the phrase: "in a manner of speaking" or "one may say."[12] For the purposes of his argument, the author is saying that Levi, who through his progeny, now receives tithes under the system of the Law, in fact, paid tithes to Melchizedek. This is the case if the solidarity of all the descendants of Abraham, which the Jews accepted, is taken into consideration and most certainly all Jews would have understood this. Paul used this kind of logic when he presented his Adam theology (Rom 5:12–14) and the solidarity of all mankind in sin is due to him; therefore, the methodology is not out of place in Jewish thinking. In spite of the emphasis upon Melchizedek and his priesthood, nothing more is given in terms of his identity. This is because the only thing that really counts here is the fact that his priesthood represents one which is unlike that of the Aaronic line and is more like that of the priesthood of Christ, which is at the heart of all the author wants to highlight. No more needs to be said, once that is understood by the reader.

v. 11 "*Therefore, if perfection was available through the Levitical priestly office (because under it the people were supplied with the Law), what further need was there for another priest to arise after the order of Melchizedek, rather than one called after the order of Aaron?*" This verse, although it is presented

11. The same verb is used in 7:17 and 10:15 to uphold scriptural authority for a statement. See Guthrie, *Hebrews*, 162 who makes this same point.

12. This expression is not found elsewhere in the New Testament.

in what Ellington calls a rather "tortuous" manner,[13] is important for a number of reasons. First, it makes it very clear that the letter was originally intended for Jewish readers. If there ever were any doubts as to this fact, they are put to bed here. Non-Jewish readers would not have considered the Levitical code to be perfect, and mostly it would not have even been a factor to them, either as unbelievers in the Jewish God prior to their conversion or as converts to Christ by faith.[14] Unlike the context of Paul's letter to the Galatians, where the Judaizers had been at work among the new converts in Galatia in an attempt to force Law-keeping upon all followers of Jesus, there is no thought that the same was the issue here.

Second, is the matter of perfection or completeness (Greek: *teleiōsis*) [see *Appendix D*] and all that this word means; it is certainly central to what the author seeks to promote in the whole letter and what he assumes as achievable only under the new priesthood of Christ. This perfection cannot be attained through the Levitical priesthood because, as the author has been pointing out, its very foundations in Aaron and Levi, were preparatory and transient, as compared to the possibilities of the sort of priesthood envisaged under Melchizedek. When the author writes "*if perfection was available through the Levitical priestly office*" he is clearly stating that it was not. It is not because the Law was faulty or that God had made a mistake somewhere but because of the very nature of man and his sinful nature it has resulted in death. This argument is somewhat like that of Paul in Romans where he says that the Law is, because it comes from God "*holy and just and good . . . but I am fleshly, having been sold under sin*" (Rom 7:12, 14) and that is where the weakness lies.[15] Here the author has shown already that the Law came with that regime linked to the stage of infancy under which many of the readers found themselves (5:12). It was not able to usher in the perfection that God demands. So, the Law was not going to bring about this state of perfection, even if at that time it allowed those who were imperfect to have a way of approaching a perfect God. The Levitical priesthood and the Law were all wrapped up together and were inseparable but perfection was never going to be the outcome. Here the readers are told that because this perfection is not possible under Aaron's regime, there is the need for another person (Jesus) who was like Melchizedek, in order to carry on the kind of priesthood he had initiated, which is of course, a different order altogether from that of the Law.

---

13. See Ellington, *Hebrews*, 56.

14. See Bruce, *Hebrews*, 114–15.

15. See Guthrie, *Hebrews*, 164.

v. 12 "*For when there is a change in the priesthood, there is by necessity also a change in the law (that) takes place.*" It has already been pointed out that the Law and priesthood go together (v.11) but rather than say that the Law has been changed so the priesthood naturally has to change too, the order in which the presentation of the argument is made is reversed. The Aaronic priesthood, which the author has presented as being only introductory and preparatory, together with the Law, was meant to serve as a teacher, and was never going to be able to deal with or take away sin totally (10:11). The whole system was inadequate. So, it is not just the Law that has to be changed but the entire system of the priesthood which goes together with it. If one remembers Jesus' words about the fact that he did not come to change a jot or tittle of the Law (Matt 5:17.18), then it is necessary to realize that it is the procedural matters of the Law or the ceremonial practices, which are associated with the Law here that are in mind; this is why Christ came to enable this perfection through his own priesthood. It is his priesthood which was promised in Psalm 110:4; all this makes Christ the "*priest forever after the order of Melchizedek*" who has changed the Aaronic order for this one. It alone, makes perfection possible in every sense of the word.

vv. 13–14 "*For the one of whom these things are spoken is one who has partaken of* [shared in] *another tribe from which no one served at the altar. For it is perfectly clear that our Lord sprung*[16] *from Judah and concerning that tribe, Moses said nothing regarding priests.*" The one of whom these things were spoken is the person in verse 11, who would be, according to Psalm 110:4 "*another priest to arise after the order of Melchizedek.*" This one would be the eternal priest. He is the Lord in the next verse. Here he is identified as coming from a line which has nothing to do with priestly and sacrificial service at the altar. He is not of the Levitical line, which was formerly the only family permitted priestly service, according to the Law of Moses.[17] The phrase "*the one who has partaken of*" from the Greek verb *meteschēken* from *metechō*, is from the same verb seen earlier in 2:14 (see

16. Most translations have something like "descended" here in order to show Christ's human descent. However, the word *anatetalken* is a perfect from *anatellō*, meaning to spring up, and is best rendered arisen or ascended. It fits in better with the synonyms *anistasthai* (v.11), to raise up or rise up and is the word from which we get *anastasis* or resurrection. From the same root and having the same meaning, this immediate context is *anistatai* (v. 15), showing Jesus' arising to take his place in the new priesthood after Melchizedek's line.

17. It should be noted that although the Law specified only the descendants of Levi and Aaron should act as priests, there may be the apparent exception of Samuel who acted as priest during his entire lifetime (see 1 Sam 3—25) Although his father was an Ephraimite by residence his actual tribal descent is not simple and from 1 Chron 6:33-38 it is possible to suggest that he was a Levite.

notes) when the author was talking about how Jesus partook of or shared in (*metescheken*), human nature. This would indicate that he was not really of that tribe because he was the heavenly man, who shared in human flesh and here, he shared in Judah, in spite of his heavenly origin. The purpose of this sharing was so that he would fulfil the promises made to David and be his greater son, who would in turn become this perfect priest after the order of Melchizedek.

The belief that Jesus was from the tribe of Judah is substantiated here, in the phrase saying that it is perfectly clear that our Lord descended from Judah. But as Guthrie points out, it needs to be remembered that in the New Testament, although this link is inferred in Matthew 2:6, it is only mentioned as such, here and in Revelation 5:5.[18] Jesus is of course, also identified as the greater Son of David (Matt 9:27; 12:23; 20:31; 21:15; Luke 1:32; 3:31 et al.) and of the house of David (Luke 1:27), the most famous representative of that tribe. There is nothing in the Old Testament writings which would legitimize anyone from Judah participating in Israel's sacrificial order. Bruce suggests that the main factor here is the drawing of the distinction between the earthly and heavenly orders[19]or what was temporal and what is eternal. Consequently, the imperfect is temporal with all its limitations, while the heavenly is eternal, final and perfect.

vv. 15–17 "And this is even more abundantly clear when another priest arises according to the likeness of Melchizedek who has become a priest, not on the grounds of the legal commandment concerning human descent but the power of an indestructible life. For it is witnessed of him, 'You are a priest forever, after the order of Melchizedek.'" During the Old Testament period there was no priest of the Aaronic order who fulfilled the requirements of the endless priesthood promised by the Psalmist's words in 110:4, *"You are a priest forever."*

So, when the author says that this is abundantly clear, to what is he referring? Obviously, to what he has already stated in part in verse 3, that Christ's priesthood is without end. The author is saying that in the Aaronic priesthood, people die and their work comes to an end. That kind of priesthood is not satisfactory in that it can never be continual or complete, even if it has the legal code and the right human descent from Aaron to back it up. However, Christ's ministry meets all the criteria of Melchizedek's because it has no end. This demonstrates the power of God and an indestructible life since his life goes on forever and therefore, so does his priesthood.

18. Guthrie, *Hebrews*, 164–65.

19. Bruce, *Hebrews*, 147.

To underline what he wishes to get across to the readers, the author makes his declaration in two ways: when it comes to fitting into the necessities of the legal code under the Law of Moses, Christ is disqualified, because he is not from the Levitical line. However, when it comes to the nature of the priesthood he possesses, he is the only one who is qualified; this priesthood is like himself: indestructible and all powerful. The declaration that his life is indestructible is evident from the fact that even if he died because of man's sin, he rose again, demonstrating that he was without sin and perfect as mankind's unique representative. This automatically elevates his priesthood above that of the Levitical order. Christ is the antitype or the fulfilment of the type depicted by Melchizedek because, not only is he the everlasting and perfect High Priest but, as was stated at the very start of the letter in chapter 1:2–3, he was before Melchizedek, as the Son who made the worlds and who then came to deal with the sin question. Now Jesus, the Son, having completed his earthly ministry, has returned to his rightful place at the right hand of the Majesty on High and combines within his person both this eternal priesthood, as well as the eternal kingly role, together with its power; consequently, he fulfils the promises made regarding the one who would be the greater Son of David (1 Kings 9:5).

vv. 18–19 "*For on the one hand, an annulment of a preceding commandment occurs because of its weakness and uselessness. For the Law perfected nothing; but on the other hand, a better hope is brought in by which we draw close to God.*" The author likes to compare different sides of an argument. Here the comparison is with two different kinds of priesthood. So "*on the one hand,*" is firstly referring to the priesthood attached to the Aaronic and Mosaic Law. The author states that it has been annulled or scrapped for two reasons: it is weak and it is useless. The Law could point out the right direction and its requirements but it could not grant the necessary life after which the person follows. It needs to be remembered that the author is referring specifically to the whole sacrificial system with all its rules and regulations. These may appear to be very strong words but they are to be understood in the sense that the Law and the system it stood for, could not achieve what was required in terms of the individual who wanted to draw near to God. The procedures which have to be followed, did not and could not, perfect anyone. The whole presentation resembles what Paul says when he talked about the Law and its inability. It could not change the heart of man and man himself is the weak link because of sin (Rom 7:10–13). The author is not saying that the Law itself is done away with but when it comes to looking for a way to enter into a meaningful relationship with God, it is not going to bring about the required result and it is, for this reason, that it is annulled.

"On the other hand," refers to the alternative, which is the relationship by faith and the hope that follows because of God's grace. When the individual casts him or herself upon the mercy of God, this new rapport will follow. This hope has already been mentioned in 6:11 and 18. It grants the desire and impetus necessary to continue in the face of difficulties and what is unknown. It is also something that is portrayed in 10:23 as part of the believer's entire confession, as what is at the heart of active faith in 11:1; this is because by faith, the reality of God is such that it brings about the proximity of all that this relationship represents. This could never happen through obedience to the legal code.

vv. 20–22 *"And this was not without an oath; for on the one hand others who became priests became such without an oath. But he on the other hand had an oath made by the Lord who swore to him and will not change his mind saying: 'You are a priest forever.' Accordingly, Jesus has become the guarantor of a better covenant."* The author is bent on extracting from the texts all that is possible, in order to show the superior nature of this new priesthood. He does this because it is foundational to his argument from the Old Testament. He is saying that God swore an oath when this new system was instigated. His word alone would have stood because he always backs up what he says but here there is the additional guarantee of the oath God made, which was already mentioned in 6:17 and which was drawn from Psalm 110:4. There never was any oath made when the Aaronic order was put in place but there was an order given, which is the equivalent of a commandment because, after instructions regarding the nature of the tabernacle and its contents, God told Moses *"bring near to you your brother Aaron and his sons with him from among the Israelites, to serve me as priests"* (Exod 28:1 NRSV). That was all which demonstrated that this Levitical priesthood was enacted. So, the priesthood put in place with the oath, needs to be seen as superior for that reason.

This order of Melchizedek, which is now the priesthood of Jesus, has subsequently been demonstrated to be the one which has overtaken this regime, which although it appears to be something new to its Jewish readers, is in fact, the earlier and superior one. Christ is, as the one who has been the perfect and superior High Priest, its guarantor. There are several important matters in this brief verse: Initially, there is the fact that the author uses the word covenant (*diathēkē*), the first of thirteen times (although it is understood indirectly more times than that) in the epistle. Much more will be said about this covenant in the coming chapters but it is superior as is the priesthood with which we are concerned. God is certainly involved in the main covenants, with which the readers of the Old Covenant will be familiar, as he is the one who is central to them being put in place. At their instigation God made promises, mostly with conditions and usually there was some sort of procedure including the cutting in parts of animals and the shedding of blood, which was part of their enactment bearing testimony to their certainty.[20] Second, there is the name of Jesus, which in the Greek is placed in the emphatic position at the end of the sentence. The last time his name was mentioned in the biblical text is in 6:20 but here the purpose is to highlight his identity as the head of this Melchizedekian priesthood, about which the author has had much to say. It is all in anticipation of the superior covenant that he has put in place in the following chapters and which is part and parcel of the same. Third, is the word translated as guarantor (*enguos*). It is found only here in the New Testament, although it is found in other documents of the day.[21] Jesus himself is the surety for this new covenant, which is, unlike the old covenant, superior and not passing away. If all of these factors are taken together, and they must be, then they reinforce the superior nature of this priesthood, as well as this new covenant, headed up by Jesus.

v. 23 *"On the one hand, the former priests were many in number because they were prevented by death from continuing* [in office]." The significance of a continuing priesthood runs throughout this chapter but here it is linked to the question of the difference between the Aaronic priesthood and that of Jesus. Therefore, once more the author uses his comparative constructions to present the material he has in mind. It was necessary to have a lot of priests under the Aaronic order because as already stated, death meant that they were not able to continue in office; that they had constantly to be replaced as they passed away. Therefore, beginning with Aaron, who was the first to be the head of the regime put in place under Moses, each one had his own successor when their lives came to an end. Perpetuity was not a possibility. Josephus the Jewish historian says that from Aaron to Phanas, at the fall of the second Temple, which took place in AD 70 when the Roman legions destroyed Jerusalem, there were eighty-three high priests.[22] So the author is correct in pointing out that mortality was the difficulty associated with this priesthood.

v. 24 *"But on the other, because he remains forever his priestly office is permanent."*[23] On the other hand, death was not a factor when it came to

20. In Hebrew you do not make a covenant; you "cut a covenant."

21. See the apocryphal book of *Ecclesiasticus* (*the Wisdom of Jesus the son of Sirach*) 29:14–16 where it is used both as a verb (to stand as guarantor) and a noun (the guarantee).

22. This may have been on 4 August AD.70 (or the 9th day of Av). See Flavius Josephus, *The Antiquities of the Jews*, L.20, chapter 10.1.

23. The Greek *aparabatos* has the sense that something is permanent and

Jesus because he had already conquered death by the resurrection, although this aspect is not mentioned until 9:28 and then only indirectly. The only matter that is mentioned here is his permanence and that his priestly office is also permanent. The fact that Jesus is alive forever, means that his priesthood never has to be handed over to another. Since this High Priest is also the Son, who is seated at the right hand of the Majesty on High in perpetuity, there is no question about his priesthood being anything other than permanent.

v. 25 *"Consequently, he is able to save completely, those who approach God through him for he is always living to intercede on their behalf."* Jesus, the antecedent of "he" and highlighted in verse 22, by reason of his permanent priesthood, is able to save completely, those who approach God through him. There are a number of significant factors here. This is the first time in the epistle that his ability "to save" has been mentioned and that with the qualifier "completely." Since Jesus' priesthood is eternal, some translations have added something like "forever' (ERV; GNT; NASB; NLT) and this is true but the emphasis here is upon the complete nature of the salvation, rather than the ongoing nature of it. The saving and the salvation include an array of benefits, which are outlined throughout the scriptures and which culminate in the promises which unfold in the New Heaven and the New Earth (Rev 21:1–22:5).

The next important factor is Jesus' mediatorial role. In verse 19 the drawing near to God through this new priesthood has already been mentioned. Here, this approach is what is important. Any communion with God the Father is through Jesus, who, as the High Priest who never dies and who is already seated at the Right hand of the Majesty on High, is in the best position possible to be able to carry out his work of interceding on behalf of all who approach God in this way. There is no possibility of any rupture in the mediatorial role with this eternal High Priest in place, in the way that there would be with human intermediaries. They come and go and are suddenly cut off, due to their own mortality. This intermediary and intercessory office of Jesus, is not new to the New Testament here, as it is evident in Paul's writing in Romans 8:34,[24] where interestingly the context is, as here, one of Christ's death and resurrection. It is also clearly portrayed in Acts 4:12 as the only means of salvation through him. The nature of this intercessory activity of Jesus is not elaborated upon in this text but it must be seen as the continuation of the sort of intercession of Jesus for individuals

---

unchangeable; see Arndt & Gingrich, 80.

24. Interestingly, the matter of intercession in Romans 8:26 is followed by intercession on the part of the Holy Spirit for the saints (Rom 8:27).

like Peter and of all his followers as a whole (Luke 22:32; John 17:9–26), while Jesus was still engaged in his earthly ministry. Part of the intercession must include the provision of the absolute salvation which he grants to all who approach God through himself. The significance of approaching God together with acceptance by him, include the faith and obedience which was stated earlier in the letter (see notes on 4:16).

v. 26 "*For it was indeed fitting that we should have such a high priest, holy, innocent,*[25] *pure, separated from sinners and having become higher than the heavens.*" Not only is this new priesthood superior because of the factors outlined above but it is superior because of who Jesus is and was. The Greek word (*gar*) which introduces this verse links what went before with what follows. Christ was in every way able to represent man as the perfect man but here there is the aspect of the differences between this man and all the rest of mankind. Up until now we have had the similarities but now, we need to grasp the dissimilarities.

To introduce this aspect the author says that *it was fitting,* meaning that it was necessary. He has already used this phrase earlier in the letter in 2:10, when the necessity of Christ's death was raised. There, it is stated that *it was fitting* for him to be completed through his suffering. Here *it was fitting* that he should, as our High Priest, be different from us in the things that are listed. After all these attributes are the opposite of those in fallen humanity, which are the result of mankind's sinful rebellion against God in Adam. This list differentiates us from this High Priest and shows his superiority when compared with sinners; this demonstration also underlines the less than perfect status of the previous priests who were part of the Aaronic priesthood. Note that the author includes himself in this affiliation to the new High Priest and his priesthood. To be part of it, it is necessary to be a convinced follower of Jesus so as to be able to include oneself in the "we" of this verse.

The first three items on the list immediately differentiate Jesus from all other members of the human race. He was and is *holy*. Holiness is here what he was as an individual. He was this before all else. He did not have to become holy as others may strive to be. He reflected all that is holy because he was a perfect reflection of God as God (1:8), even though he became a man. Even as a man this holiness remained part of who he was. John describes this holiness in the form of the *Logos* who was God and who became

---

25. *Kakos* is the opposite of the word that is used here and refers to someone who is bad, evil and dangerous because they are of such a nature. So *akakos* shows that the person is innocent in the sense that they have no evil, are harmless and are totally good and pure. The person who is qualified by this word has no fault with them at all and cannot ever be accused of a failure in any area of their person or life.

human and lived among mankind. At the same time, John says that they, that is his disciples, saw his glory (John 1:14). Glory is more than holiness but it is certainly not less and speaks fully of God alone. Holiness has no negative aspects attached to it whatsoever. Second, Jesus was *innocent*. The word translated innocence here (*akakos* see note 25) gives the impression of being totally guileless, harmless and without any possibility of evil or wrong. It does not have any thought of ignorance as it may in a human setting. Christ could never be accused of anything that was not absolutely correct in all his ways. Third, he was *pure*. This Greek word (*amiantos*) can be rendered pure, unstained or something that has not been contaminated. So even if he was called a friend of tax collectors and sinners, although he lived among mankind and shared his humanity within the context of those who were sinners, he was never contaminated by them. Purity marked everything he thought, said and did.

To emphasize what all these three things mean when it came to his priesthood the author states he was *separated from sinners* or unlike sinners. This, is in spite of all his similarities to man in order to be their representative as the perfect High Priest. This comparison is similar to what the author stated earlier in the letter where he said that Jesus was *in every respect like us except that he did not sin* (4:15). Paul says the same, when he draws a picture of similarity and dissimilarity in his letter to the Romans when he says that in order to deal with the sin question: "*God sent his own Son in the likeness of sinful flesh . . . condemned sin in the flesh*" (Rom 8:3). That meant that Jesus was like man in every way and his humanity was the same but, in the resemblance, he was not a sinner even if he was "like sinful flesh." Jesus' personal qualities were such that he was unlike mankind in his nature and this separated him from the ordinary nature of man. The phrase "*separated from sinners*" does not mean, as some have suggested, that Jesus has been elevated to heaven and now is *separated from sinners* on the earth or that he was somehow immune to sin while he was on earth.[26]

The last part of the verse: *having become higher than the heavens*, immediately speaks of Jesus' exaltation, which was introduced in chapter 1:3. Here it underlines the victory following his earthly ministry and anticipates what is to follow in chapter 8. As the Son who descended, to use the words of Paul, to describe what our author is saying here, he is now the one who "*has ascended far above all heavens*" (Eph 4:10; for further parallels to this event see Phil 2:9; 1 Pet 3:22 et al.). The descriptor used by Paul in Ephesians is almost the same as that used by the author of Hebrews. It shows that Jesus'

---

26. For the various views concerning this phrase, and those who opt for them see Hughes, *Hebrews*, 273–75.

might and authority, surpasses anything associated with the fallen state of earth and its inhabitants, including that of the Aaronic priesthood which was most assuredly ensconced upon the earth. It also, immediately, brings to mind the background upon which this exaltation is superimposed: the resurrection and victory over sin. Christ now assumes his rightful place, not only as Son but as eternal High Priest. The expression "higher than the heavens" has its background in Hebrew thinking, where there were different levels of heavens in their cosmology and the heavens refer to the sky and above.[27] The expression "the Kingdom of heavens" (*hē basileia tōn ouranōn*) which is found in Matthew's Gospel at least 13 times (see Matt 13:33 et al.) illustrates this plurality of what was understood as more proximate to earth to what was further away and that God's rule extended over all of these levels. This therefore means above all, what is either physically related or distant to man and his world. But the main thought here is that this elevation of Christ takes him to the highest level possible of any sphere known to mankind. The emphasis is not limited to direction, distance or height but to jurisdiction, power and authority over all God's creation. Consequently, nothing is over him or greater in any way. This places him as Lord over all (see Eph 1:22) so that all is subject to him.

v. 27 "*Who had no daily need, as did the high priests, first to offer up sacrifices on his own behalf then for the sins of the people, for he did this once for all, when he offered up himself.*" Here Jesus is compared with the earlier high priests or those of the Aaronic order. However, there is a difficulty in the interpretation of what is written here in terms of being carried out *daily*, since the High Priest only offered up sacrifices annually on the Day of Atonement (Lev 23:27–*Yom Kipur*) for the sins of the people and not daily. Some have suggested that the author was not very familiar with what took place[28] but in the light of his clear familiarity with the LXX and the whole ceremonial procedure (see 9:7) it is highly unlikely that this view can be accepted. Others suggest that although the High Priest only offered up that particular type of offering once a year, that he was also involved in offering

---

27. This view of cosmology may appear to be unique among nations but there are similar views among groups in the wider world and even in Africa today. The Luba people of the high plateau land in the Democratic Republic of Congo would speak of the sky (*mulu*) but really where does the sky start and where does it finish? So, for them there is a closer sky and the more distant skys giving the idea of different levels or skies (*madiulu*). Similarly, the Bemba people of Zambia talk about *miulu* in the plural to distinguish different spheres within the heavens, Even in French the difference between heaven "*les cieux*" (plural) and the sky "*le ciel*" (sing.) is vague. The context informs one as to which is in mind.

28. See Rohr as cited by Spicq, *Hébreux*, II. 201.

up other sacrifices such as flour offerings and that also the daily offerings made by all the priests under his authority were indirectly made by him or implicated him in some sense.[29]

All this tortuous reckoning can be avoided if, as Guthrie says, we take the statement *"who had no daily need"* to refer directly to the entire ministry of Jesus.[30] His continuous ministry and intercession on behalf of his people, has already been underlined in verse 25. He is now in the heavenly places at the right hand of God and has already obtained all the access that could possibly be required to intercede for his people before the throne of God. He has no need to constantly offer sacrifices, either for himself or for the people. That sacrifice and all the offerings required under the old priesthood have already been satisfied, once and for all, when Christ went to the cross and offered himself by paying the debt for the entirety of mankind's sin and failure. Therefore, his service as a whole, which includes his sacrifice, is complete, although, it continues eternally when it comes to the matter of intercession. The fact that his service is complete, makes it absolutely clear that there is no further necessity of any sacrifice. This is contrary to other sacrifices, which under the Aaronic system, have to follow the Levitical instruction and order. As already noted, they will never be complete or perfect but for all who understand Christ's role, they should be regarded as having long since been cast aside. Christ's sacrifice never can and never will be repeated. Its efficacy is beyond all question and to attempt to repeat it would be to totally snub the grace of God in the provision already made.

v. 28 "For the law appoints men who are weak as high priests, but the word of the oath which came after the law (appoints), a Son who has been made perfect eternally."[31] In this statement the author brings together everything he has said in verses 26 and 27. The one who is the perfect holy and undefiled High Priest, does not need to follow the Levitical order of priesthood to fulfil the requirements of the Law of Moses to head up Melchizedek's order. He is now carrying out what was always his rightful role as the Son. The High Priests, under the Law, had the same limitations as everyone else, because of sin. This is what the first part of the verse is saying when it states that *the Law appointed those who were weak*. Those human priests were beset by sin and its consequences. This order of priesthood has been

---

29. See Spicq, *Hébreux*, II. 202. Spicq sees the terms used in *Hebrews* here as presenting a radical difference between the daily sacrifices of the Aaronic High Priest and Jesus' unique offering of himself.

30. Guthrie, *Hebrews*, 171.

31. Note that the KJV concludes the verse with the words: *"the Son, who is consecrated for ever,"* which is not correct because the Greek *teteleiōmenon* means completed or perfected, never consecrated.

superseded by the perfected one, which has been put in place for eternity, as the result of God's oath. It seems that the last part of this statement is chronologically out of order because here the oath comes later than the Law (Ps 110:4) when it is apparent it was made originally to Abraham (6:13) prior to the Law. It seems that what is meant is that when Christ is ensconced as High Priest, it is subsequent to the role that had been exercised by the Law under the Aaronic order. This is of course, because Christ's role as High Priest could only take place after his incarnation, crucifixion, and glorification.[32]

When God did this, he sent the only one who was fit for the task and that was his Son who had to take over the role of the head of this new order. This means that the priesthood, which was earlier described as that of Melchizedek, is in fact that of the Son. The enigma is, that although this priesthood appears to supersede the Law, in reality it predates it because it was prefigured prior to it in Melchizedek. Nevertheless, now, because of Christ, all has been made complete.[33] This is because he carried out all that was required of him; therefore, his priesthood can never be replaced by another. Consequently, the priesthood which was dominated by man's weakness has now been replaced by a new and perfect one, which reflects the Son in every way. Because of who he is, his priesthood is also eternal and complete. Christ is the one and only priest of this priesthood who is seated in the throne room at the Right Hand of the Almighty. It is he alone to whom all followers come and this gives them all the assurance they need in every matter of life.

32. See Guthrie, *Hebrews*, 172.

33. This making of Christ complete is, as already noted, relative to all that he as the incarnate God/Man had to accomplish and nothing to do with any imperfections in his character or person.

8.

The new covenant 8:1–13

The author continues to compare two very different systems or covenants in this next chapter. They are described under what was introduced in chapter 7:22 as, a *better covenant*. The methodology is to look at the earlier covenant and what it involved and then, to progress to the new, so as to demonstrate its superior status. The readers of the letter would have been familiar with the first covenant, which was based on Moses' Law and the Aaronic priesthood; so, from there the author shows them how they need to abandon their hope in what was always only an interim regime. It awaited what was the perfect and everlasting ministry of the kind initiated by Melchizedek, as seen in the previous chapter; the new is now clarified under this updated new covenant and put in place by Christ. So, the presentation moves back and forth from what is old, earthly and imperfect, to what is new, heavenly and complete. However, at the same time, it moves from what was known and existing, to what was previously unknown and beyond anything previously comprehensible or possible. The content of this chapter and the theme which continues through to 10:18, is concerned with the way in which Jesus, this High Priest, carries out his ministry and the way that this new covenant relates to Christ's own people.

 vv. 1–2 "*Now the point of what we are saying is that, we have such a High Priest who is seated at the right hand of the throne of Majesty in heaven, a minister of the holy things and of the true tabernacle[1] which the Lord*

---

1. The Greek word *skenē* is usually translated in Scripture as sanctuary or tabernacle because of its association with the tabernacle and the Holy Place. However, in simplest terms it means nothing more than a *tent*. It is its associations which gives it its full sense as the sanctuary and obviously as the temple was later constructed to

erected and not man." There is some discussion among scholars as to how the Greek word *kephalaion* (what is rendered here as: *now the point*) should be translated. In the writings of the classical Greek authors, it is often used to underline *the main point* or *thing* but, it is also used in the sense of *being the summary* of something.[2] Here it may be either of the first two but it may also be, as Bruce suggests, a gathering of thoughts concerning what this is all amounts to or is leading up to, as it will be clarified in this chapter regarding the superior ministry of Jesus and his covenant.[3]

The superiority of the Melchizedekian priesthood and hence, that of Christ's, of which that was the type, has now been demonstrated but its nature is now going to be described. It has already been shown that the Aaronic priesthood has been overtaken by a superior one. This is all centered upon the High Priest–Christ–who is now in place permanently. It has already been mentioned from chapter 1:3 that the Son *made cleansing for sin* and then *sat down on the right hand of the Majesty on High.* But here there is some recapitulation because now the Son is highlighted as the High Priest. Both are drawn together into one. Whatever was stated with regard to him earlier, obviously also applies to this High Priest here. Unlike the high priests of the Levitical line, who live and work in what the author describes in verse 5 as the *"shadow of the heavenly things,"* this Jesus is seated in the real holy place, where he shares the very throne with the Almighty. *Majesty* as already stated in 1:3, speaks of God's divine person.

There is no distance between Jesus and the Father. As already noted, Lord is the name the LXX uses for Yahweh. He is one with the Almighty and not restricted to any annual entrance into the Holy of Holies, as earthly priests would be. This is because he is on the throne with the Almighty in the very heavens themselves. The earthly tabernacle or tent, was a man-made construction but this is the place which God himself put in place. The author draws a picture of God building something which, no matter how elaborate it may be in terms of human endeavor and beauty, is compared to

---

integrate this temporary tent its full force is now understood as referring to that edifice which is better known as the tabernacle. See John 1:14 –the word. . . tabernacled among us, tented among us, or lived among us.

2. See Arndt & Gingrich, κεφάλαιον–*kephalaion,* 431 where he includes for the for the first: Plato, Thucydedes, Philo and others; for the second: Cyranides, and *the Oxyrhynchus Papyri,* et al.; the English translations differ: along the lines of " *the main point"* see NASB, ESV, NIV, NRSV, RSV and others; Coverdale [old English is used] "Of the thinges which we haue spoken, this is the phyth"; Darby, "a summary of the things of which we are speaking"; J.B. Phillips, *New Testament,* "Now to sum up"; Wycliffe Bible, "a recapitulation."

3. Bruce, *Hebrews,* 161n1 and 163n16.

the inferior construction of mankind. This is the real, and final sanctuary, rather than any imitation of it. And this is where the perfect High Priest is to be found.

It may appear that there is a contradiction in the verse because, on the one hand, the High Priest is described as seated in the heavenlies and on the other, as ministering in the tabernacle relative to the holy things. First, the fact of being seated is as already seen, a contrast with the ministry of all servants of God who stand and who never complete their service. That is linked to their imperfection and the fact that the human aspects of what are required are never complete or perfected. Christ, on the other hand, has completed his earthly service in his once for all atonement provided for sin but as was seen in chapter 7:25, he is constantly making intercession on behalf of his own. So, the sacrificial aspects are complete but his service continues.

The Greek word used here for *ministry* or *service* is *leitourgos*; it is the same word from which we get the English word *liturgy*. It conveys the idea of any kind of work which is relative to the service of or for a god. Here, obviously, it indicates God working, on behalf of his people. In this regard and especially in his intercession, provision and involvement, Christ's work is never complete. It will not be complete, at least, until the New Heavens and the New Earth are in place. Even subsequent to that, he will be available to all the redeemed. His proximity in the *actual* or what the author calls, *the true tent* (sanctuary) in the New Creation, will be even greater than ever before because, by then, all his followers will be present with him in the same location. Even if that aspect is not highlighted here in this chapter, the concept of the Heavenly Jerusalem (12:22) and the continuing city, is part of the hope of the letter (13:14). This true tabernacle is presented with the goal of distinguishing it from the temporary tabernacle which Moses erected. It is *true* because it is the real, actual and eternal construction, put in place by God and unlike anything which Moses and the artisans put in place (Exod 25:8–43; 26:1–27:19; 31:1–11).

The matter of the *true tabernacle* (tent) is interpreted variously by scholars. Some see it as the body of Christ, others as the Church or the spiritual temple, where the Holy Spirit dwells, others of the Catholic persuasion as the Virgin Mary, and others a perfect holy of holies beyond the heavens.[4] I personally tend to agree with Hughes, that we are to look at the question in the light of the exegesis of this letter to the Hebrews, rather than

---

4. For a cross section of these views and their explanations see Hughes, Excursus II: "The Meaning of 'the true tent' in Hebrews 8:2 and 'the greater and more perfect tent' in Hebrews 9:11." *Hebrews*, 283–90.

from the perspective of Pauline or other theological perspectives, related to the tabernacle. If the normal exegetical procedure is followed,[5] then what the author states here about the true tent, as well as what he says in 9:24 about Christ entering into the tent that is not made with hands, must indicate that the tent and the sanctuary are the same thing. It means that Christ is now in heaven where the true sanctuary is located and not here on earth. After all, the earth is associated only with man-made edifices and artifacts.[6] Again, all comparison in these chapters is relative to the two priesthoods and their representatives. The one is earthly and passing, while the other is heavenly and eternal.

v. 3 "For every high priest is appointed to offer both gifts and sacrifices; therefore, it is necessary for this priest[7] *to have something to offer."* The service of those who were appointed or put in place, as High Priests, was to watch over the whole priesthood and its functions but specifically to officiate in the presentation of gifts and sacrifices. The High Priest had to have something to offer up. The construction in Greek of "*it is necessary for this* (priest) *to have something to offer*" includes the aorist subjunctive of the verb *prospherō, prosenenkē,* (may have something to offer or to sacrifice); it shows that it was an imperative that something be offered. If nothing was sacrificed, then any forgiveness would be impossible and in addition, if it was not offered up by the appointed person, it would not be acceptable. This point has already been made in 5:1 and is repeated here.

Even if the nature of these gifts and sacrifices are not detailed here, it would have been understood by the readers of the letter that the most important of these would have been the annual offering on the Day of Atonement. However, when it concerns Jesus, there is no mention made with regards to any actual offering, although it was certainly touched upon in the previous chapter verse 27, where the offering up of himself was clear; more will be said about this in 9:14. The reader of the New Testament and the Gospels knows that Christ's role was part and parcel of the reason for his

5. This means that normal exegesis requires procedures which seek the sense of the words *in situ* rather than the pursuit of a theological outcome. The theological outcome must depend upon what is found from the examination of the words and their interpretation and not vice versa.

6. Hughes, *Hebrews,* 289–90. Of course, this does not mean that Christ does not have any influence over the earthly domain as, like the Father, he is omnipresent; what the author wants to emphasize is that in this context Christ is already in the heavenly domain, unlike the many priests who only ever entered the symbol of that sphere when they entered the holy of holies in the physical tent annually.

7. The word *priest* is assumed from the pronoun "this one" (*touton*) depending upon the High Priest mentioned at the start of the verse, although it is not recorded as such.

incarnation and in the final, his entire ministry on earth led up to this offering of himself. This means that the *something* (Greek–*ti*), when referring to
the other High Priests has to be applied to their offerings; when it is seen as
applied to Christ, is indeed, the offering up of himself.

v. 4 *"Therefore, if he were on earth, he would not be a priest, since there
are those who offer gifts according to the Law."* Jesus' ministry was not an
earthly one. It is important for the readers to understand this. The focus
in this argument is about a ministry that surpasses anything that has to do
with his earthly ministry. It has already been pointed out that Jesus comes
from the wrong tribe and he could not be seen to qualify for the priesthood
according to the demands of the Law. His priesthood is therefore, not an
earthly one and he would not have fitted into that one anyway. However, as
has been already mentioned and, as his priesthood is in the heavenlies, this
is not a difficulty. This priesthood automatically shows that it is superior
to the earthly; consequently, it does not have the limitations of the earthly
imposed upon it by the Law.

v. 5 *"They serve a copy and shadow of the heavenly things, as Moses
was ordered[8] when he was about to complete the tabernacle: For [God] said
'see that you make everything according to the pattern shown to you on the
mountain.'"* The priestly order of Aaron served as a copy and a shadow of
the heavenly or the real, that has been already mentioned. Everyone knows
that a copy is not as good as the original from which it was made. Similarly,
a shadow cannot exist unless there is an object, which like a mirror, is there
to reflect what it resembles. However, the shadow is never the same as the
actual object itself, which is the reality causing its shadow to fall on something; in addition, it is often distorted and unclear. Both the copy and the
shadow help people to visualize the reality of which they are only visual aids
but they never can be mistaken for the actual objects themselves. Therefore,
both words impress upon the reader the fact that whatever the Aaronic
priesthood managed to achieve, it never managed to fulfil the substance
behind the copy or the shadow. The essential fact is the existence of the real
or the substance which exists.

Moses had been shown the reality of the heavenly tabernacle while he
was on the mountain, as God revealed that to him (Exod 25:9, 40; 26:30;
27:8). From the original texts, the matters were numerous and very detailed.
Consequently, he was ordered by God (*kechrēmatistai* see note below and
11:7) to replicate that pattern or model in the earthly, which had to be put

8. The Greek word *kekrēmatistai* (3rd p. sing. perf. ind.) from *chrēmatizō* is used
to show some sort of divine disclosure in the sense of an instruction which has to be
obeyed. It is therefore, sometimes translated as an instruction, order, or warning; it is
understood as always coming from God.

in place. It is not clear exactly what Moses saw but what was put in place was intended to be based on the original pattern and there is no indication in Scripture that after he had carried out his instructions God was in any way displeased or that the replica was unsatisfactory.

The earthly tabernacle was intended to indicate God's residence among his people on earth but the truth is, that as God is spirit and omnipresent, he is not restricted to any one locality and even Solomon was aware of that (1 Kgs 8:27). The earthly tabernacle could therefore only mean that it was supposed to help the people have some sort of idea of the glories of the heavenly reality. The details which were underlined in the instructions given, must however, indicate the reality of which the shadow or the copy is an image and which is certain and absolute. Ultimately, the author is saying that the priest of the Aaronic order operates in the shadows or the copy of the real but that Christ, ministers in the real or actual heavenly tabernacle as he will point out in the following verse. The real was what Moses saw while on the mountain. That was what he was instructed to copy.

It is evident that many people in our day love pomp and ceremony. They love getting dressed up and being part of big occasions. The author here tells us that all this pomp and ceremony of the Old Testament was nothing more than that. He calls it all a matter of "shadows." Where the format and the procedures become the priority in Christian living then the point being made has been missed. God is looking to drive home the significance of who Christ–the Son–really is and what serving and following him involves. He is the Great High Priest of a new covenant that is not taken up with figures and ceremony. Outward acts and forms are not what count but are meant to help us understand what it is that God really desires and that is hearts that are totally surrendered and subject to the Almighty. This is what is at the center of the thrust being presented by the author of the letter here (see verse 10).

v. 6 "But now he [Christ] *has obtained a more excellent ministry in as much as he is mediator of a better covenant which has been enacted on better promises."* Now Christ has moved from his service and the offering up of himself in the earthly sphere, to the perfect domain. He has obtained a more excellent ministry. The Greek word *diaphorōteras,* translated here by "more excellent," has been seen earlier in 1:4, where it was with regard to the Son's name being more excellent than that of the angels. Here it is in connection with the far more excellent ministry than that of the Aaronic priesthood. Of course, it is intended to highlight the superior nature of the ministry in which Christ is involved, which in turn accompanies the superior covenant which the author is about to elaborate upon. In fact, the reality is that the entire letter is aimed at demonstrating how Christ is more excellent in every area. The ministry Christ has is more excellent now because, although it was certainly necessary for him to commence this work upon the earth as the High Priest of those who live there, it has moved in totality, to the heavens, amidst the reality of all that was previously depicted. This excellency is linked to what the author describes as *a better covenant*. The reason why it is described as being better here is that it is based upon better promises (see vv. 8–12).

If the question is asked what it is that makes the quality of this covenant better, there are a number of factors involved. The very first is already inherent in the fact that the mediator is not just any ordinary man but the Son, who is God himself (1:3); it is he who, as has already been stated, is present in the heavens in the true sanctuary, rather than in any copy of the real (8:1). Then there is the nature of this covenant which is about to be described in the words from Jeremiah 31:31–34.[9] Within this covenant are a number of factors which will be examined in the appropriate verses. Before that is done, it is necessary to say that in this mediator, as has been seen earlier in this letter (2:17; 3:1), we have someone who is not aloof in any way when it comes to the rapport he has with those who are his followers. In the synoptic Gospels, Jesus was denigrated in the eyes of his opponents when he was described as being, among other things: a friend of sinners (Matt 11:18; Luke 7:34). Without realizing what they were doing, they were actually affirming the nature of his intimate relationship with those who otherwise would have been cast on one side and rejected. This covenant is superior because it brings God and man into a place of friendship and union surpassing anything possible under the old covenant. Much more is brought out with regard to this superiority in the following verses from 8–12 cited from Jeremiah 31:31–34.

v. 7 "For if that first covenant had been faultless, there would not have been any place [need] for a second." This second covenant is also better than the first, simply due to the fact that it is new. If the former had been sufficient and met all the criteria God had in mind, there would have been no need for it to be replaced. The first covenant depended upon the Law to make it work. This Law was not deficient but as already noted, man was and therefore the Law was not and could not perfect mankind. This aspect has already been seen in Paul's explanation of the fault or weakness of the Law in Romans 7:8–14, being man's sinful nature and inability to keep the Law's requirements. The Law was always external and its accomplishment always just out of man's reach. This is why the new covenant was required because it would bring about the changes necessary to change mankind's nature and abilities.

9. Note that in the LXX the reference is found in Jer 38:31–34.

vv. 8–12 At this point the author quotes from his source: Jeremiah 31:31–34

The Background to Jeremiah's prophecy about the days that are to come

When Jeremiah gave this prophecy, the people of Israel had lived in a state of disobedience for years, since the time of David's reign. Most of this was manifested in one form or another of idolatry but it also included matters such as the sacrifice of one's children. The wickedness of Jeroboam, whose biblical designation was the one *"who made Israel to sin"* (1 Kgs 14:16 et al.) was soon followed by the sin of the kings of Judah like Manasseh, who was instrumental in making his people carry out sins worse than those practiced by the people that God had driven out from the land prior to their overthrow by the children of Israel (2 Kgs 21:2, 9). In spite of a few godly leaders like Hezekiah and Josiah, godlessness spread throughout the land. The kingdom of Israel was the first to go into exile in Assyria at the time of Pekah and Hoshea (2 Kgs 15:29; 17:6). It was not that much longer afterward that Nebuchadnezzar besieged Jerusalem and took away all the population of Judah, apart from the poorest in the land, to Babylon (2 Kgs 24:1, 10, 14; 25:11).

Jeremiah prophesies prior to much of this later disaster occurring. These prophecies were about the future and especially about the return of the people of Judah and her restoration from captivity. They came after a dream he had received from *"the Lord Almighty, the God of Israel"* (Jer 31:23–26). In 31:27 he prophesies again using the phrase: "The days are coming," which clearly speaks of the future (see Jer 30:3), telling the people that both those of the house of Israel and Judah will be reestablished in their land and each one would be responsible for their own sins without having to pay for the sins of their parents (Jer 31:27–30). It is at this point that the new covenant is introduced. Its mention clearly relates to a change like no other in Israel's history.

v. 8 "For finding fault with them he says: 'Behold the days are coming, says the Lord, when I will put in place a new covenant over the house of Israel and over the house of Judah.'

Despite the discussion regarding the correct reading to the introduction of this verse and whether or not the fault mentioned here is related to

the people or the covenant itself, the fact is that when the words were originally uttered, Israel lived in a state of disobedience counter to the covenant of
God. Since the whole context is one which deals with the inadequacy of the
first covenant in Jeremiah, it is most likely that the fault is with the covenant
rather than with the people alone. The reckoning related to the argument is
expanded upon in the footnotes.[10] As already seen the fault is not just because
the covenant itself was the only matter at hand but the fact that mankind's
nature was never going to be changed by that covenant (see notes in the previous verse). The difficulty with the reading: "He finds fault with them" (*autous*)
then appears to go against the thought of the inadequacy of the first covenant
even though it is preferred by the majority of commentators today.[11]

Yet included in the presentation one cannot avoid the fact that disobedience was very much part of Israel's historical record and the people
cannot be exonerated from the blame that accompanied their conduct. It
was not that many years later that the whole nation was swept away into
captivity as a consequence of God's displeasure. The quotation from verses
8–12, is cited as the very word of God, as the author states *"For finding fault
with them he says:"* then the words of the prophecy commence. The *"He
says,"* refers to Yahweh himself, even if the prophecy is found in Jeremiah's
declaration because his words are considered to be those of God (See Jer
1:7b–10). Three times in these verses, the emphasis upon what the Lord is
saying is underlined to show the significance of the one who stood behind
what is promised and its absolute nature. This emphasis upon the word and
God himself in the Old Testament, is the way in which the author introduces many of his quotations from the Scripture in this letter (see 10:15).
Finding fault with the nation, indicates that Yahweh was not at all satisfied
with the way in which the nation as a whole behaved, when it came to their
failure to keep the first covenant God had made with them.

Although the original statement made by Jeremiah was prophetic and
therefore looked to the future, here it is no longer; it is already in place

10. There is fairly strong support for both *autous* and *autois,* the first being an
accusative plural and the second a dative plural. Both can be translated "with them"
but the first gives the impression that the fault is with the Children of Israel while the
second with the covenant itself. Since the previous verse has just spoken of the need
to change the first covenant for something different it would be logical that the second
would make more sense here. But since the following verses demonstrate Israel's failure to keep the covenant and their disobedience therefore *autous*–with them–should
be maintained. In reality then there are faults on both sides. For more detail on the argument see Hughes' examination of the text in his commentary; *Hebrews,* 298–99n19.
The reading in *The Greek New Testament,* opts for *autous.* But there is considerable
favor given to *autois* by a good number of early MSS.

11. See Spicq, *Hébreux,* II. 240; Montefiore, *Hebrews,* 140; Bruce, *Hebrews,* 170.

because it has been fulfilled through Christ. It is necessary to go back to
Jeremiah's day, which was anything but desirable for the nation. It was a
day of turmoil following the people's disobedience and hardness of heart.
God promises something very different in the days to come. The first readers of the prophecy were aware that the promise was for the future but in
this letter the author wants his readers to understand that what had been
promised by God through his messenger Jeremiah, was already activated.
To reject it would be equivalent to rejecting what God had declared under
the regime in which these readers claimed to trust. It is doubtful that they
had understood what that prophetic word meant and that it was for them.
It is necessary therefore, for the author to go over the verses step by step, so
that they would grasp their implication. The whole declaration also makes
it very clear to all concerned, that any attempt to adhere to the old covenant
was never going to be satisfactory, either from God or man's perspective.
The original prophecy told of a time that would come when the people of
Israel, in its entirety would have a new covenant as the authority over them.
That meant that the one which was in place previously would be obsolete.
Clearly, the Mosaic covenant would no longer play a role.

There are a few other issues present in this verse.[12] First, this covenant
is put in place by God himself, as he indicates when he says "*I will put in
place*" or "*make*," this new covenant. This indicates that God himself sees
the necessity of something very different from the first as the result of man's
weakness and inability. In his establishing this covenant he knows that the
failures of the first would be met by the grace and enablement that would accompany the last. Second, Israel incorporates all the people of God, so even
if the first proclamation was understood of the people of God in the Old
Testament, it would need, in the day of the Messiah, to have broader connotations and include all the followers of the Messiah or as Paul sometimes
calls this new creation–the Church–the Israel of God (Gal 6:16). There is no
explicit indication of the formation of any new entity such as the Church in
the original prophecy given by Jeremiah; anything along those lines would
however, have to be understood in the present from what transpires in the
overall teaching of the New Testament regarding God's people, including the
words of Jesus to Peter in Matthew 16:18. There Jesus spoke about building
his Church and those words began to be fulfilled subsequently, on the day of
Pentecost. On that day, we have a clear link both with the inauguration of the
work of the Holy Spirit, who fulfils the words of Jeremiah's promise, as well as
the words of Jesus and the commencement of this new construction which

12. For more on the original prophecy as it appears in Jeremiah see the points
highlighted by Feinberg, *Jeremiah*, 218.

is called the Church. Jeremiah's words may indicate a healing or reconciliation between those of Judah and those of Israel[13] and the forging together of God's people that would be certain in the future. Third, there is no indicator in the prophecy of Jeremiah relative to the amount of time that would pass before this new covenant would be enacted but the chronology indicates that it would have been approximately 600 years.[14] This period is not of concern to the author. For him, this word regarding a new covenant, goes in tandem with messianic promises and the age to come.

v. 9 'Not like the covenant which I made with their fathers in the day when I took them by the hand to bring them out of the land of Egypt; because they did not continue in my covenant and I disregarded them, says the Lord.'

This new covenant is directly distinguished from the covenant made at Sinai, when God led the people out of Egypt. It is not to be like the Sinai covenant. The possibility of the intimacy between God and his people is displayed in God's words that "I took them by the hand to bring them out of Egypt" (Jer 31:32). He acted as a caring Father taking his children by the hand to give them assurance, having just delivered them from the bondage of Egypt. However, this taking of the people by the hand, shows primarily, that without God's direct intervention, that deliverance and all that it involved, including the parting of the seas and the destruction of Pharos's army, would never have been possible. That covenant was put in place in Exodus 24:1–8 when the blood was sprinkled upon the people by Moses and accepted by the voice of all the people. The details from the same chapter in Exodus 24 are part of story in the coming chapter (9:18–20). Yet, within a matter of days of having made that promise, the people broke the covenant and were making a golden calf to worship in the place of God (Exod 32:1–10). So, when the fact of their infidelity is added in the same sentence, their fickle nature is immediately highlighted, as well as the failure of that covenant.

When the Lord says that he *disregarded them*, he means that he no longer heard their cries for help when they got into trouble because they had failed through obstinacy and unwillingness to put into practice the things God insisted upon. There is more than a hint here that the *longsuffering* and *eagerness* which was called for in 6:11, 12, together with the *continuation* in the terms of the covenant mentioned here, are essential in any meaningful

---

13. It is necessary to remember the constant friction between Israel and Judah and the very clear divisions between them through large portions of their history.

14. Jeremiah's call to service was in the 13th year of the reign of King Josiah (c.627 BC.) and he was still prophesying at the time of Jerusalem's capture by the Babylonians during king Zedekiah's reign in 586 BC.

relationship between man and his God. It was obviously absent in any attempts of the people to keep the earlier covenant.

v. 10 'For this is the covenant which I will make[15] *with the house of Israel after those days says the Lord: I will put my laws into their minds and I will write them on their hearts, and I will be their God, and they will be my people,'*

The nature of this new covenant is now given. There is certainly both continuity and discontinuity in what is described in these verses. The covenant is similar but also dissimilar to the Sinai covenant. What took place there should remind the readers of what should have been and what could have been but which failed because of their inability to obey. The most significant matter is that the Sinai covenant was based upon external rules and regulations which had to be followed. There are three major differences with the previous covenant outlined here in these verses:

i) *The internalization of God's laws.* God promises here that the law will, in the new covenant, become internalized. Instead of laws being written on tablets of stone which then had to be consulted and the matters remembered, they would now be written on minds and hearts of his people. Minds would be changed so that they fully grasped the significance of the way in which God sees things so that their intellects would be different than they had been previously. But this is more than intellectual redirection, it would also bring about a different heart and desire.[16] This covenant was new because it could change the heart, something that the old could not do. When something is heartfelt it is constantly on one's mind. Its significance does not fade away because its compelling force drives one forward. This new covenant would open the door to that kind of realization of what God meant to each of his followers. God's people would not only comprehend his ways but they would know what was necessary as well as well pleasing in the purposes of God and want to do those things, not by constraint but because of the relationship in which they found themselves. Keeping God's laws would be the spontaneous fruit of joy, love and appreciation in recognition of the greatness of the grace of God and his person.

This leads to the second main difference which is part and parcel of the first:

ii) *A deep and personal knowledge of God in a vital rapport with him and he with his own.* The first covenant constantly underlined the distance

15. The Greek states literally: *"this is the covenant which I will covenant with the house of Israel"* the first being a noun and the second a verb.

16. The change of heart and mind is similar to what John reports in Jesus' words to Nicodemus when he tells him that he needs to be born again. (John 3:7). That *new birth* involves the work of the Holy Spirit bringing about a total reorientation of the person's thinking regarding Jesus and the nature of his person and work.

between God and man. This one demonstrates his proximity. It has already been noted that the whole understanding of law would be motivated in a different way so that rather than have an external force as the reason for actions carried out, it would be a deep inward desire springing from a relationship with God himself, which would be the driving force. The desire to do what pleases God springs from knowing him. That means being like Abraham, who was a friend of God and being close to him because he resides within. This aspect of his residence or being his temple and the coming of the Spirit after the resurrection of Christ, is not so clear here but in the light of what John says in his supper discourses (John 14–16), this means having a vibrant relationship with God through his Spirit. He now will live within the individual, enabling each one in every aspect of life. This knowledge of the Almighty is not based upon ritual but a heart that recognizes the individual's indebtedness to their God, in and for everything. When the individual grasps the reality of God's love, forgiveness and care, then service is not based upon form and ceremony but upon an exciting realization of God's person and the desire to surrender one's life to him completely. This results in an intimate relationship of trust and obedience, where the love of God for man is mirrored by man's love for God, even if the level of reflection could never be the equivalent of the Almighty's for his creatures. A correct relationship with God also results in a correct relationship with one's fellows. When this happens, as Jesus stated to the scribes who were attempting to trip him up, the requirements of the greatest commandment are to love one's God and one's neighbor as oneself, are fulfilled (Mark 12:30–31).

This new relationship with God is underlined by the words of Ezekiel, in a context very similar to that of Jeremiah's, when God says of his people: "*I will give them one heart, and put a new spirit within them; I will remove the heart of stone from their flesh and give them a heart of flesh so that they may follow my statutes and keep my ordinances and obey them. Then they shall be my people, and I will be their God*" (Ezek 11:19 NRSV). The main difference in this text, is the granting of the Spirit which is highlighted in John's passage related to the Spirit/*paraklētos*. When this dependency upon God is real and evident, then the people who fall under this level of grace begin to realize what it means to be God's people. There is no doubt but strong conviction and faith is placed in their unique patron.

It needs to be underlined that being called God's people (*laos*) indicates a very particular and special relationship which is of great importance in any understanding of the nature of the Church in the New Testament.[17]

---

17. The artificial distinctions which ecclesiology have introduced between the so-called *clergy* and *laity* have to be reappraised and seen as human additions if the true

Being called God's people is not new. This aspect is promised as early as Exodus 6:7, when God promised Moses the deliverance of the nation from Egypt saying: *"I will take you to be my people and I will be your God."* This same refrain is voiced in the New Heavens and the New Earth in Revelation 21:3 in an eschatological context, when once more the final outcome of all God's work is made known at the start of the new age: *"And I heard a loud voice from the throne saying, 'Behold, the dwelling place of God is with man. He will live with them and they will be his people and God himself will be with them as their God.'"* By this time the people of God are his completed and perfected saints for all eternity; they are the ones with whom he shall reign.

v. 11 *'And each one will not teach his neighbor and each one his brother saying: "Know the Lord;" because all will know me from the least to the greatest of them.'* During the period of the old covenant, it was only those of the priesthood, the prophets or selected individuals who could know God and his thoughts in any meaningful way. The majority of the people had to follow their leaders if they were to do what was warranted. This verse highlights the fact that under this new covenant, dependency upon human intermediaries would no longer be necessary. The categories which had been in place previously would be abandoned. The individual now has intimate knowledge of and, communication with God. Each could communicate directly with God without priests or other mediators. That is the thought behind what is stated here. It does not matter who you are, great or small, rich or poor, slave or free person, there is nothing to hinder this relationship in terms of what God has put in place between himself and the individual who wants to seek after him.

iii) The third factor here is *the matter of God's mercy and his forgetting of the individual's sin.*

v. 12 *'Because I will be merciful toward their iniquities and I will remember their sins no more.'"*

From the earliest times God revealed his mercy to his people as it is part of his nature and person (see Exod 33:19; Ps 51:1); so, this is again nothing new, but in this new system his mercy dominates the reason for the giving of the new covenant. It is the overruling reason behind all his actions (this emphasis on mercy is clearly elaborated upon by Paul in Rom 9 through 12:2). The intricacies of Christ's coming to earth and giving himself for mankind's sins clearly lies behind the granting of God's mercy and pardon for sin, even though this aspect is not highlighted here (see Rom 9:16). But it is certainly included in the author's statement made in 1:3 regarding the Son who provided *"cleansing for sins"* where the cleansing

---

nature of God's people is to be fully understood.

is the propitiation for mankind's sin. Without question, the mercy of God, which is manifest in his forgiveness of mankind's sin, depends upon this. This is at the heart of this new covenant. After all, as the author states in chapter 9:22, without the shedding of blood there is no pardon for sin. It is this remission of sin which allows the benefits of this covenant to become a reality so that all mercy and pardon of sin is possible, only because of the sacrifice of Christ.

v. 13 *"In that he speaks of a new* [covenant] *he has made the first obsolete.*[18] *And what is becoming obsolete and growing old is ready to disappear."* The quotation from Jeremiah is at an end and the author adds his own conclusion to what the Lord said through Jeremiah. The word "covenant" is not actually mentioned in this verse but it is most certainly understood in this comparison between the old and the new. The first is, according to the author, *already obsolete*, as he uses a perfect tense to describe its state (*pepalaiōken*) but then he goes on to say that it is in reality, *presently becoming old*. That means that although in reality, it is no longer in place, in practice it is slowly growing old to the point that very soon it will no longer have any role at all, like a person growing old and about to die. This indicates that although, in God's economy, it was already finished, in the way which people were concerned, some still adhered to the old and its precepts. Realistically, it is fading away because the last phrase of the verse says that it is growing old and about to vanish.

Some scholars believe that the author had in mind the presence of the Temple worship which continued for a considerable time after the resurrection of Christ until its destruction by Titus.[19] There is no proof that the temple was still in existence when this letter was written but whatever the historical situation was at the time (see the date of the letter in the introduction to this study), the system attached to the old covenant was getting old and about to vanish away. The sooner the readers could grasp the reality of the situation the better. The message is clearly: Let the old vanish and do not keep clinging onto something that no longer has a role to play in pleasing God. If it is true that the Temple at Jerusalem was still in existence when the letter was written, then this would add to the weight of thought which maintains that it was written prior to its destruction which took place in AD 70.[20]

18. The verb *peplaiōken* is a perfect of *paliaioō* which in this context means to be obsolete, abrogated or superseded. So, the first covenant is more than just something that is old.

19. Hughes, *Hebrews*, 302.

20. For more on the dating of the letter and the argument related to this verse and the continuing place of temple worship see Carson, Moo & Morris, "Hebrews."

9.

Earthly based worship surpassed by the heavenly 9:1–22

The earthly tabernacle is a symbol of the heavenly tabernacle and together with its regulations and worship was never meant to be permanent. Now that the new covenant of the Messiah has come and the old has become obsolete, so too, the entire system which accompanied it. This includes the earthly tabernacle with all its outward forms, which no longer have any role to play.

v. 1 "Therefore, even the first covenant had regulations for worship[1] and an earthly holy place." It needs to be noted that although the word *covenant* is missing in the Greek text, it is not out of place to add it in the translation here. It has been at the heart of the discussion since 8:6, so when the author writes about *"the first"* there is no doubt that he is referring to this same covenant, which has been and is once more compared with that same Sinai covenant. The first part of the section is dealing with the nature of the sanctuary and the procedures followed in the worship that was part of the first covenant. The Greek word translated regulations (*dikaiōma*),

---

399–400. If the logic of the argument presented in this letter is followed through, it would be unlikely that the author would not have mentioned the destruction of the temple had it already taken place. It is true that one is not supposed to argue from silence but the points which are made related to the worship would most certainly have called for such mention to be made, if indeed that event had already taken place.

1. The Greek verb *latreuō* and its cognate *latreia* is usually translated as service from the verb "I serve." However, because it is so closely linked to religious adoration, it is also translated "worship" and when attached to an individual who is involved in religious service it has the sense of a "worshipper." These are the ways in which it is used in this present section of the letter.

has a number of meanings in the New Testament. Paul uses it with regard to the righteous demands of the Law or the regulations related to the Law and its being kept properly (Rom 8:4). It is significant that its basic sense is associated with righteousness or rightness and here with divine service, which is in this context, the correct way of worship. In this instance, the worship is associated with the correct procedures that have to be carried out in the earthly holy place. The author wishes to specifically point out the fact that this covenant relates to what is earthly and temporal. Therefore, he wants his readers to see that even the nature of the holy place here is earthly and not heavenly. If this is understood, then the fact that the whole system which he has just pointed out in the previous chapter as being a copy and a shadow of the real, is once more, being designated as having a quality which is earthly; it is therefore, far from being ideal.

The priests who have just been included in what is happening in this temple (see 7:27–28), are obviously involved in this earthly or less than perfect, holy place. It is once again going to be compared with the holy place in heaven. From what is stated in the next verses it is evident that the author wants the reader to understand, that when he talks about the tent in verse 2, he does not have the later, semi-permanent structure of Solomon's temple, in mind or even that of Zerubbabel or of Herod. He is writing about the original mobile structure made according to the order of Moses (see Exod 25:1—27:19). He wanted to show that its entire structure was never intended to be permanent and that is why it had to be replaced with the new and permanent covenant.

v. 2 "For a tent²(tabernacle) was furnished, the first in which were the lamp-stand³ and the table and the bread of Presence.⁴ This is called the Holy Place." A tent was prepared. The word which is sometimes translated *tent*, sometimes *tabernacle* (see notes on 8:1–2 and footnotes on *skēnē*), here means tent because it indicates the very first tent which was erected by Moses. Likely the author did not wish the readers to think that he was talking about the later sanctuaries, which may have been considered to have had a more durable nature, even if they were earthly too. The Greek word *katekeuasthē* (aorist passive) from the verb *kataskeuatzō*, can mean to erect, to build, to

---

2. The Greek word *skēnē* is translated literally: tent. However, here it is used in the sense of the "tabernacle" which is part of the greater edifice. It is used in this way throughout this portion of this letter. Therefore, the words tent and tabernacle are used synonymously here.

3. This is not a normal lampstand but translates the Hebrew seven branch candlestick or *menorah*.

4. The Greek reads: the presentation of the loaves.

make ready but also to furnish.[5] Since in this context, furnishings are part of the central point being made in the verse, this is how it is rendered here. But this does not exclude the assembling of all that is part of this entire construction. The courtyard is not mentioned here, only the first and second parts, which are pictured in terms of the two separate tents or sections. In Exodus 25:10—27:21 the description of all that is found in these holy places commences with the ark in the Holy of Holies or the Most Holy Place and then works outward to the tents; here the order is reversed. Therefore, the author starts with the first or the outer court, which was known as "The Holy Place," which he does not describe in any detail. It was entered from the courtyard. There is no description here of the tent itself.

Here in the first compartment, there were three items or different kinds of furniture. Other than their presence, again no description or reason for their being there is given. The first is the lampstand. This is no ordinary lampstand but the golden lampstand bearing seven distinct arms and cast from one single piece into what is better known as the *menorah* (see Ex.25:31–40; 37:17–24). Secondly, there is the table overlaid with gold and upon which the bread of the Presence was placed (see Exod 25:23–28; 37:10–15.). As Bruce points out, the table and the bread of the Presence are to be viewed as one and not as two separate items because they are so closely linked and because the bread had to be constantly replaced.[6] None of the extras that went with these items are mentioned, such as the poles that were used to carry the table or the plates, bowls or flagons etc. The altar of incense is not mentioned. There is no mention either in this verse or the next as to the role played by any of the items which are given, as there was when Moses was told to make them initially. It must be assumed that the Jewish readers were aware of that factor and did not have to be reminded. This entire area, in what is called the first tent or the first section is called merely: holy (*hagia* a neuter plural) but usually translated "the Holy Place."

vv. 3–4 "*Behind the second curtain was a tent called the Most Holy Place, having a golden incense altar and the ark of the covenant covered on all sides, in which were a gold jar containing manna, the rod of Aaron which budded and the tablets of the covenant.*" The curtain here is called, the second. It separates the two tents or compartments from each other (see Exod 40:21). It was intended to make it impossible for anyone in the first section to be able to see the ark of the covenant in the second. It was made of blue, purple

---

5. See Arndt & Gingrich, 419.

6. Bruce, *Hebrews*, 183. The table was approximately one meter long by 50cms (19.68ins.) wide and 75cms. (29.52ins.) high. It had rings and handles so that it could be carried and also plates, dishes, flagons and bowls.

and crimson yarn, specially woven together with linen (Exod 26:31–33). It is called the second because the first was a screen of similar colors and finely embroidered at the entrance from the courtyard into the first tent from the outside (Exod 26:36); it is not mentioned here or in the previous verse. This second section or tent, is called the "Holy of Holies" or the "Most Holy Place"; in Greek this is: *hagia hagiōn*, without any definite article. The author describes this section of the whole edifice as a separate tent, just as he did the first section. However, it needs to be understood that the two tents have to be regarded as being inseparable and this is the reason why they are sometimes described as the outer and inner chambers.

The furnishings here in this second tent are listed as: the golden incense altar and the ark of the covenant. There is some difficulty concerning the nature of the first object, which in Greek is called *thumiatērion;* this is normally a place or an object used for burning incense. It is never used in the LXX of the altar but of the censer itself.[7] However, it is used of the altar of incense by both Josephus and Philo[8] and since the altar is a major part of the furnishings it would be strange if it was not mentioned in this context. For that reason, most scholars believe that this term is applied here to this altar of incense, as a unit and not just as a censer.

The second difficulty is the matter of the location of this altar of incense. In Exodus 30:1–6 the nature of this altar is described but it is definitely described as being "in front of the curtain that is above the ark" (Exod 30:6); Exodus 40:5 merely mentions that this altar should be set in front of the ark of the covenant but apart from that there is no more precision. So how is it that it is described here by our author as being part of the second tent or chamber when it was clearly in the first tent and where daily sacrifices were offered not just on the day of Atonement?

There are some scholars like Moffatt who believe that the author was not accurate when it came to the actual layout of the tabernacle.[9] This is most unlikely since if his description was in any way defective, his reckoning as a whole in the entire letter could and would logically be discredited. Jews at the time would have known the layout of the tabernacle, so if the author had misrepresented its setting, the readers would have been the first to react against anything that was incorrect. Even in Luke's narrative regarding the ministry of John the Baptist's father Zechariah, when he is in the

---

7. It is found in the following LXX references. 2 Chron 26:19 (note that it is also connected with *thusiastēriou* at the end of the verse, were it means altar of incense); Ezek 8:11 & iv Macc 7:11.

8. See Josephus, *The Wars of the Jews,* v.5; Philo, *Heir of Divine Things?* xlvi, xlvii (226, 227).

9. See Moffatt, *Hebrews,* 114–5.

Holy Place burning incense, mention is made of him being by the altar of incense with the Angel who appeared to him (Luke 1:11, 12) but this would have been in the Holy Place or the first chamber.

There is another unlikely suggestion that has been accepted by scholars and that is that rather than referring to the altar of incense, the author is focusing on the censer similar to what Aaron used to minister the incense in Numbers 16:46.[10] There are several difficulties with this explanation: the first is that as the High Priest had to bring it into the Holy of Holies burning with incense already on it when he entered the chamber; it is unlikely that it was kept in the Holy of Holies, which would necessitate an entry to collect it prior to entry with the burning incense. Second, the small items kept in either chamber were not of note in this narrative and it would be, as already noted above, a major omission to leave out the altar of incense completely, since it was one of the major permanent items.[11] As Hughes points out, there is no mention made in the Old Testament of a golden censer.[12]

Interestingly, in the extra-canonical writing known as *The Apocalypse of Baruch* (vi.7) a number of important items are listed: "And I saw him [an angel] descend into the Holy of Holies, and take from there the veil, and holy ark, and the mercy-seat, and the two tables, and the holy raiment of the priests, and the altar of incense."[13] The significant thing here is that this document from about the same date as Hebrews, shows that according to the thinking of the time, the altar of incense is certainly associated with the Holy of Holies.

It is more likely that the association between the altar of incense and the ark of the covenant has to be understood as being so close, that the two are inseparable, in the same way as the two chambers are inseparable.[14] Its placement is always with regard to the propitiation of sin and it is placed in such a way that the incense burnt on it is directed to pass through the

10. This is the view of some scholars including Alford, in consideration of the way in which the golden altar (*chrusoun thumiatērion*) is used in the *Mishna*, are convinced that this refers to the censer itself rather than any altar of incense. Alford, "*Pros Ebraious*," iv. 161.

11. See Spicq, *Hébreux*, II. 249 who also includes the matter of the permanent items in the tabernacle.

12. Hughes, *Hebrews*, 311.

13. *The Apocalypse of Baruch*, vi. 7.

14. Guthrie suggests that the participle "Having" (*echousa*) should be understood in the sense of "'belonging to' rather than 'standing within,'" because it is placed across the entrance to the Holy of Holies and could therefore be considered to be part of it. 183; Alford also says that "having" (*echousa*) is "somewhat ambiguous in its meaning here and cannot be understood as meaning 'containing.'" In "*Pros Ebraious*," iv. 161.

curtain toward the ark of the covenant. Numbers of evangelical scholars understand the matter in this manner.[15] Finally, and more importantly, the actual placement of the items is not the central matter but the fact of the activities carried out by the High Priest as they are compared with those of Christ our present High Priest.

The rest of the verse is concerned with the other major item in the Holy of Holies which was the ark of the covenant. It contained the manna, Aaron's rod which budded and the tablets of the covenant. It needs to be remembered that the items contained in the ark would have been those which were present during the earlier stage of its existence including the time of Solomon's temple but not what was there during the later times when the author was making this declaration. This is because after the destruction of Solomon's temple, at the time of Nebuchadnezzar king of the Chaldeans in 587 BC, no more is said regarding the ark.[16] The author refers all the items which would have been present originally. The fact that the altar, the ark and the jar were either gold or covered with gold, is emphasized to highlight not only their worth but appearance. Aaron was ordered by Moses to put an omer (approximately 2.3 liters (just over half a gallon) or a tenth of an ephah) of manna to be placed before the Lord in front of the covenant, according to Exodus 16:33–34; this was in order to remind the Israelites that God had provided for them during their wilderness wanderings but there is no further instruction in this regard.

When the children of Israel rebelled against Moses and Aaron, the Lord ordered that all the leaders were to identify their rods and place them in the tent before the testimony, together with Aaron's rod. His was the only one which budded, indicating that the Lord had chosen him. That proved that he alone possessed God's authority. All the other rods were removed from before the testimony, except Aaron's. The purpose was that all should see that it had budded after which it was replaced "before the testimony" (Numb 17:1–11). The "testimony" is synonymous with the ark of the covenant and that is why some translations say: "before the covenant."[17] There is no indication that it was actually placed within the ark. The important thing is, again, not the exact location but the proximity and it is quite reasonable to think that for safekeeping, both the urn with the manna and the rod were placed in the ark for safekeeping during the wilderness wanderings.

---

15. See, Spicq, *Hébreux*, II. 250–51; Bruce, *Hebrews*, 186–87; Guthrie, *Hebrews*, 183; Hughes, *Hebrews*, 312–13.

16. Legends abound but they are unreliable and cannot be trusted. By the time of Solomon's temple, the ark contained only the tablets of the covenant.

17. See NRSV.

The tables of stone upon which the covenant of God was written, were also within the ark. They were the tablets containing the Law which Moses had received upon Sinai. There is no contradiction with what is written in 1 Kgs 8:9, stating that only the two tablets of stone placed by Moses in the ark were present by the time Solomon's temple was dedicated because a lot of time had passed since the items listed above were noted. In the meantime, the Philistines had also been in charge of the ark for a time when some items may have gone missing (1 Sam 4:11; 5:1, 2 et al.).

v. 5 *"And over it were the cherubim*[18] *of glory overshadowing the mercy-seat. We cannot now speak of these things in detail."* Over the ark were figures of angelic beings called cherubim;[19] they represented the guardians of the glory of the person of God. The glory (*doxa*), as already mentioned, is representative of and synonymous with God himself and his person and it is often associated with the Holy of Holies. This is where God promised that above the mercy-seat he would meet his people and communicate with them (Exod 25:22). The lid of the ark was called the mercy seat or the place of propitiation (*hilastērion*).[20] The Greek word is the same used by Paul in his letter to the Romans 3:25 to describe the propitiatory offering of Jesus on behalf of those who believe in Christ as Savior. In that sense Christ becomes the mercy-seat where, through his own offering and sacrifice, he brings mercy and forgiveness to his people. In this context the author does not apply this as did Paul, although the thought could not have been far from his mind in the penning of the word, especially of verses 12, 14 and 21 et al. The mercy-seat was made of pure gold and was a solid lid. On the day of Atonement, it was upon this mercy-seat that the blood of the victims was sprinkled as a sin offering, for both the people and for the High Priest himself.

Although the author appears to want to underline the significance of the glory associated with this regime and its practices, he concludes any discussion on the nature of the Holy of Holies and its contents by simply saying that no more detail was going to be given in this regard. He intimates that much more could be said but that would not help in terms of what needed to be said. In the same way that the author makes it clear that he would refrain from development of the subject, the danger of becoming

---

18. Note that the qualifying verb "are," here in the past tense, is required here rather than "is" because cherubim are plural beings.

19. For the original descriptions of these beings and the mercy seat see Exod 25:18–22; 37:7–9. Note that the plural of cherub in Hebrew is cherubim.

20. The Greek means *"a propitiating thing."* It is the same word used by Paul in his Epistle to the Romans, 3:25 (see the notes in 1:17 and extra comments).

over allegorical needs to be avoided. This allegorization is what happens in any attempt to develop further than is necessary, what has been written.[21]

v. 6 "Now when these things had been put in place on the one hand, the priests were going continually into the first tent accomplishing their worship." There was, without doubt, great splendor attached to all the ceremony that accompanied everything related to the tabernacle, the temple and the rituals which were associated with them. This first covenant required exact fulfilment of all the procedures that had been put in place on the part of the priests. But one of the remarkable failures in all that took place, was that everything had to be done through the people's representatives. Here they are the priests. The fact was that on a continual and daily basis (note the phrase: go continually or at all times), the priests were fulfilling their duties in the first tent.

In reality, the continuity meant, twice a day, every day (Exod 29:38, 39). Individual worshippers could not themselves approach. Here in this context, it is not until chapter 10:19–22, that the follower of God is informed how they are able to have free access to the very presence of God himself by the blood of Christ. This means that the formality and procedure of the past, does not make up for the desire or ability of the individual to experience fully the reality of any communion with the actual presence and person of God following Christ's priestly work. Again, although the priests were allowed to enter the first tent, that was the limit and as far as they could go. They could not go as far as the Holy of Holies; therefore, that covenant was severely restrictive and limiting. It meant that even priests were kept at a distance from the presence of this Holy God.

v. 7 "But on the other hand into the second (part of the sanctuary) the High Priest alone goes once a year, and not without blood which he offers on his behalf and for the unintentional sins of the people." Unauthorized entry to the second tent could result in death (Num 4:20) and even the High Priest was permitted to enter the Holy of Holies but once a year, on the Day of Atonement. In addition, that entry took place only after he had carried out all the required measures that had been put in place (Lev 16:2–28). The rules relative to entry into the Holy of Holies highlighted the fact that the first covenant added to the limitations imposed upon any worshipper to draw near to a Holy God. They made it very clear that even the High Priest,

---

21. Some groups, especially among earlier Pentecostals, were known for their allegorical interpretation of such details. The danger with that methodology is that when something always means something else other than what is written, then it can always be turned to mean whatever the interpreter desires. The rule is that when there is allegory involved there is usually a clear indicator that allegory is intended as with Paul in Galatians 4:24.

as a mortal, was in danger of transgressing the conditions required for anyone to come close to God; even he had to spill blood on behalf of his own
failures. If that were the case, and it was, how much more difficult would it
be for those who were not part of the chosen priesthood? When the High
Priest did have entry to the second tent and the Holy of Holies on this tenth
day of the seventh month,[22] it was necessary among other things, to enter
with the blood of a goat for the unintentional errors or acts of ignorance of
the people and the blood of a bull for himself (Lev 16:1–16). All the other
matters, including the clothing to be worn by the High Priest and the burning incense, are not mentioned here.

It should be noted that the word *agnomatōn*, translated here as "unintentional sins," indicates sins which are committed in ignorance and not
blatant rebellious acts. This shows that sins of this rebellious category would
not be atoned for. The blood of the bull was to atone for any of the High
Priest's own sins and had to be sprinkled upon the mercy seat, as well as
in front of it, together with the blood of the ram for the people's transgressions.[23] This latter action only underlined the fact that there was no one
who fully met the conditions God requires for any intimate relationship
with himself; this was all because of mankind's sin. In this regard, the first
covenant only reinforced the distance between man and God. The procedure also shows that the sins and errors which are carried out are never
fully atoned for and that is why there needs to be at least an annual purging
of all sin.

*vv. 8–9 "By this the Holy Spirit shows that the way into the holiest of
places had not yet been manifested while the first tent was still standing (this
is figurative of the present age[24]) according to which both gifts and sacrifices
are being offered that are not able to perfect the conscience of the worshipper."*
The author of this letter is very clear that what was written in the Old Testament was revealed by the Holy Spirit. This is another of the texts within the
writings of the New Testament which highlights the role of the Holy Spirit
in the transmission of Scripture (2 Tim 3:16). Any difficulties in understanding the words and terms that are written here in these verses have to be
understood in the light of the fact that the author is moving back and forth
from the literal facts to the symbolic meaning which he wishes to draw from
them; this is clear when in verse 9, he states openly in parenthetical form,

22. It is known as *Tisherie* by the Jews and usually falls between September and
October.

23. There is no mention made by the author with regard to the role of the scape-
goat which was sent off as part of the ritual into the wilderness bearing the sins of the
people.

24. The Greek *kairos* indicates a specific or appointed time here.

that this is a parable for the present age.[25] It is here, therefore, that there is understandably room for disagreement among scholars in the way in which these verses need to be understood.

Therefore, when the author says that *"the way into the holiest of places had not yet been revealed while the first tent was standing,"* he is not just talking about the actual physical tabernacle but about the ability of the individual to enter freely into the presence of God in the heavenly tent, as long as the first covenant was in place. This becomes even clearer from verse 11. Before one can make such a statement it is necessary to back up and look at the literal sense of the words before the interpretation can be applied.

In literal terms, what does the phrase "the holiest of all" (*tēn tōn hagiōn hodon*) mean? The Greek could be read to mean "the way of the saints" or "holy ones," but since the immediate context is linked to the holy place (*ta hagia*), as in vv.12, 24, 25 and has already been used as such in verse 3,[26] it refers to the most holy place or the inner chamber, where the presence of God dwells above the mercy-seat. In this regard a number of scholars believe that it refers here to the first or outer tent, which is equivalent to the Holy Place. However, in this instance, it means the way into the Holy of Holies[27] because it represents, not just the outer tent but the system as a whole, which was related to the first covenant.

Those who insist that what the holy place stands for here, has to be relative to the first tent and not the entire complex, maintain that the author is saying that as long as this first tent was in place, there was no way to obtain an entrance to the second tent or the Holy of Holies. Therefore, it is the first tent itself which is the barrier, with its priestly functions and sacrifices. The difficulty with this understanding is the failure to see the symbolic nature of the words as they relate to the heavenly reality which was awaiting fulfilment when Christ the High Priest, after the order of Melchizedek, would eventually be revealed. He was, after all, the one who tore the veil in two from the top to the bottom, on the day of his death (Matt 27:51). That speaks symbolically of doing away with the separation between the two tents. Accordingly, it also made a way for all believers to have direct access to the heavenly tent or the real Holy of Holies, on a permanent basis. No longer is the access restricted to selected representatives, special days, ceremonies and prescribed rules.

25. See Ellington, *Hebrews*, 73.

26. It must be seen as a plural neuter relating to the place which here is the holiest of holies and not a masculine plural genitive relative to people who are saints.

27. See Bruce, *Hebrews*, 194.

If the above is grasped, the first tent is meant to represent, not just the first literal earthly Holy Place or the first tent situated in front of the entry into the Holy of Holies but the entire system which stood for the first covenant. This is because, as the author says in verse 9, this is a parable (*parabolē*–for the author's use of *parabolē* in this letter see also 11:19). For the author, the Levitical system with its rules and regulations, not just the tabernacle, stands for all he is describing and what was in place at the time. He is adamant that the first covenant prevented free access to the most holy place on the part of the people of God. The verse nevertheless, spoke of a day when all would be open and when that access would be available when he says "*that the way into the holiest of holies had not yet been manifested*." As long as the first tent or system was in place and adhered to, this entrance to the holiest of places would be impossible.

At this point, the author indicates that the entire procedure in this ceremony and its repetitive nature within the first and second tents at that time, were only symbols of the reality that needed to be fulfilled. They involved the gifts and sacrifices but were incapable in real terms of making anyone perfect. They could never bring about any actual changes in an individual's conscience regarding their relationship with God. The sacrifices and gifts indicated outward actions but did not change the heart of the people making the offerings. They had to be repeated continually because of the fact that they did not usher in perfection; therefore, people needed to be reminded constantly of their sinful state by repeating them. The main difficulty with the worshiper was his or her own conscience; only when that was in right order would any approach to God be meaningful. Continual ritual was only of an outward nature, no matter how spectacular it may have appeared. In reality, all the spilling of blood of animals did nothing to change the reality of the distance between man and God.

v. 10 "But deal only with food and drinks and various washing, regulations for the body which are imposed until a time of the new order."[28] The author is linking what took place in the procedures related to the first covenant as having little, if any bearing, upon the actual state of reality in the bearing between a person and their God. When food and drinks, washings and other matters are included here, it is clear that there is more than the immediate matter of what went on in the sanctuary that was in mind. There is nothing directly related to food in this section other than in this verse.

---

28. The Greek *diorthōsis* is translated variously: improvement and reformation but when it is used to depict contrast it is "new order" and this is certainly the sense here. See Arndt & Gingrich, 198.

This meant that the author must have been thinking of something other than this immediate context yet related to the first covenant.

Leviticus chapter 11 has a lot to say about food and the categories of animals which could be eaten. It also mentions the water which had been polluted by dead animals should not be drunk and a variety of other matters related to washings; so, it is likely that this is the sort of thing of which the author was thinking. What he is saying is that while keeping all these rules may well help when it comes to hygiene, it had no bearing on spiritual realities.

These rules were external, never internal. They were imposed until the time of "the new order" or "the reformation." This word from the Greek *diopthōseōs,* is only found here in the New Testament and gives the impression of a "new order."[29] In other words, the whole system of the first covenant, with its rules and procedures, was to be considered from the start, as only ever being temporary. It awaited the reality that was to come in the future, linked to the new order. This new order is the order under the second or final and perfect covenant, put in place by Christ. This covenant would completely reshape the concept of worship and the individual's relationship to God. The outward and physical symbolism which was portrayed in shadows and copies of an earthly nature, would be replaced by the inward and spiritual character of the heavenly reality. Forms and procedures if they are not followed from a heartfelt desire to please God have no real meaning in true worship.

vv. 11–12 "*But Christ has appeared as a High Priest of the good things that have come*[30] *through the greater and more perfect tent not made with hands, that is, not of this creation but he entered once for all into the holy of holies, not through the blood of goats and calves but through his own blood, having obtained eternal redemption.*" But now that Christ, who is the High Priest already mentioned in previous chapters (2:17; 3:1; 4:14, 15; 5:5, 10; 6:20; 7:24–27; 8:1), has come, he is the one who has ushered in the good things, that in this verse, are described as having already come. This means that believers now are already part of the inheritance of all that it means

29. See Arndt & Gingrich, 198.

30. See the textual variants "the things that are about to come." The reading *tōn mellontōn* indicates a yet future coming, is most likely present due to the fact that there is a tension in the fulfilment of the realization of the promises made with the fact that Christ has already come and made their accomplishment a possibility. This together with the declaration of 10:1 which speaks about good things to come would result in a redactor making changes to the original *tōn gnomenōn*–have come–being changed by a copyist. The majority reading including the Syriac as well as some early Fathers and MSS opt for the "the good things that are come."

to be a follower of Christ. However, in everyday life it is not apparent that these good things have come. How is this to be explained?

Perhaps the simplest way of understanding what this means is to consider a passage in Paul's Epistle to the Ephesians which touches on the same matter. In the first chapter of that epistle (Eph 1:3), Paul tells his readers that they have been blessed by God the Father with "*all spiritual blessings in the heavenlies*" through Jesus. He continues by explaining that this involves what he calls "an economy of the fulness of time" (Eph 1:10), which has to do with gathering everything together in and under Christ. That system includes the followers of Christ who have become part of God's inheritance (Eph 1:11). The whole passage goes on to explain what they have already during, what Paul explains as present, in "the now." However, this is also in spite of the fact that what they have is also, "not yet" fully achieved. The reason for this is because what they have is only the firstfruits or "earnest" (*arrabōn*) of what is to come (Eph 1:14). This tension explains why although they potentially possess everything belonging to that future regime and are positionally "seated with Christ in heavenly places" (Eph 2:6) they do not see it all yet.[31] This situation is the same here in Hebrews. The total fulfilment awaits the *Parousia* of Christ.

It is most likely that this tension and the lack of its understanding, is what has led to a textual variant in this verse in some MSS related to the tense and timing of the *good things*. Some MSS have followed the reading *tōn mellontōn* meaning: "the good things that are about to come" as though they were yet future but the most commonly accepted reading follows the reading of the *Greek New Testament*[32] which states, *tōn genomenōn*–"have come" (see the discussion also present in the footnote 28). The good things may not yet be in place fully for the followers of the High Priest but he has come and the good things are now already dispensed in part, awaiting their completion in the future.

The tent or tabernacle, that Christ entered, is not that earthly one, which was only a copy or symbol of the real belonging to this present creation (Heb 8:5). The writer calls this heavenly tent "*the greater and more perfect tent not made with hands.*" Christ, this High Priest, entered the perfect tabernacle, which was put in place by God himself; so, it is far superior to any earthly copy. Further, this holy of holies, which is the actual residence of God Almighty, unlike the earthly, which was entered after the sacrifice of the blood of animals, was entered by Christ subsequent to the offering of his own blood. The point being made here is the value of the propitiatory price

31. See Garrard, *Ephesians*, 28–29.
32. See *The Greek New Testament*, 734.

paid in terms of the blood of animals as compared to the blood of this High Priest. This was the blood of the Son, the perfect one, who had become man but was the image of God's glory; therefore, the sacrifice was perfect (1:3–4) because it was offered by the sinless Son of God. That is why this perfect sacrifice, happened only once for all, and never needs to be repeated.

The earthly High Priests had to carry out this procedure on an annual basis because their imperfect animal sacrifices, could never atone for humanity's sin. But now there is no further need for any other blood sacrifice of this nature to ever be offered again. The redemption price has been paid in full. It is secure for all who accept Christ as their redeemer. This verse also makes it very clear that the former system with its temporary and oft repeated sacrifices was only applicable to this earthly creation while that of Christ's transcends all earthly and physical barriers, opening up the way for an eternal and spiritual reality in the heavens.

vv. 13–14 "*For if the blood of goats and bulls and the sprinkling ashes of a heifer, sanctifies those who are polluted, brings about sanctification for the purification of the flesh, how much more the blood of Christ, who through the eternal Spirit offered himself without spot to God, will purify our*[33] *conscience from dead works in order to serve the living God?*" The examples of the sacrificial place of animals and the sprinkling of their blood, either generally or on the day of Atonement, would be a direct reference to what was required to bring about the covering of sin. The blood of bulls, heifers, goats and any other animal, only represented the giving of life of a person for that of another, as has already been referred to indirectly in verse 7 (Lev 16:2–22). In Numbers 19:2–10 mention is made regarding the red heifer, the sprinkling of its blood and the role of its ashes in providing the water for cleansing and purification of people and articles (Num 19:9). All of these procedures were ceremonial and required of God's people under the first covenant. The author wishes to make it very clear that under the first covenant there is no doubt that the blood of these animals and the rituals which followed, were effective in bringing about the outward sanctification of the people (the purification of the flesh) who carried them out. But what was pictured in this animal blood and ceremony was just that: it was outward and based upon obedience to outward regulations (It becomes clear as the presentation continues that the *flesh* is equivalent to what is outward in the same way that the *conscience* signifies the heart or inward and spiritual side of the individual). Westerners who live in the 21st century may not grasp the

---

33. The textual evidence for *hēmōn*–our–and *humōn* –your–is almost evenly divided. Theologically, there is no difference in the meaning, other than if it is the first, the author includes himself in the argument.

concept of this ritual cleansing but the passage has to be understood in the light of the concept of the people to whom it was addressed and who most certainly would have known what all this meant during their day.[34]

There is now a comparison made with those procedures and those following the sacrifice of Christ. The author asks the question: How much more would the blood of Christ be effective? First, although there is mention found in other New Testament writings of *the blood of Christ* (1 Cor 10:16; Eph 2:13; 1 Pet 1:2, 19; 1 John 1:7; Rev 1:5) this expression is found only here in Hebrews. Obviously, this blood is superior to that of animals, as already indicated in v. 12 above because it is the blood sacrifice of the sinless Son, who is the only one who qualifies to atone for mankind's sin.

Again, considering the comparison of the two sacrifices, the animals had no say in their role as they were taken and sacrificed according to the will of those who offered them, whereas with Christ this was a *self-offering* or an offering of himself; he gave himself up to be the offering, knowing fully what it all meant and what was required for this offering to be made. This aspect of Christ offering himself, is evident in passages such as John 10:17–18, where Jesus declared that he laid down his life and that no one took it from him. This whole sacrifice, even if it is not recorded here, required, as Paul makes it clear in Philippians 2:5–8: the incarnation, the life of suffering and rejection, culminating in the crucifixion and the subsequent resurrection, for it to be possible and efficacious.

The meaning of the phrase "*through* [the] *eternal Spirit*" is debated by scholars. In Greek there is no article. Does this refer to Jesus' own spirit? This is the view of several like Spicq who writes that this is:

> . . . by virtue of his very personality or of his own power, of a transcendent value, which assured him of a life and an eternal priesthood even by means of death, and which we are entitled to identify with according to ch. 7:16, 14, to the divine nature . . . . this eternal divinity is designated by πνεῦμα [*pneuma*], because his nature is "spiritual" (Jo. iv, 24), but also in contrast to σαρξ [sarx] from [verses] 13–14[my translation][35]

---

34. There are still those of other faiths who rely heavily on cleansing rituals prior to worship but in the light of Christ's comments about the inner man being the source of sin and the fact that these rituals are outward observations, they do not change the mind, the heart or the relationship with God himself and are therefore not a factor when it comes to biblical faith.

35. Spicq, *Hébreux*, II, 258–59. This is the view of others like Hughes, *Hebrews*, 358–59.

If "eternal spirit" does refer to Jesus' own spirit, then it speaks of his sacrifice being far beyond anything mankind could offer, as he is not only man but God, as is evident from 1:2–3. This would mean that his offering is infinite. It would make perfect sense in the light of the eternal redemption he provides, in verse 12.

The second possibility is that the "eternal spirit" should be understood to mean the Holy Spirit. The Holy Spirit has already been mentioned on several occasions in Hebrews in calling out to God's people to repent (3:7) and in bringing enlightenment granting grace (6:4). It is therefore, likely that the thought of his role is not far from the mind of the author, who sees Jesus in the light of the Servant of Yahweh, upon whom the Spirit of the Lord rests to enable him to fulfil all his earthly ministry (Isa 42:1).[36] That same servant fulfilled all that was required of him and the passage in Isaiah 53:3–12, certainly covers this same aspect of his self-sacrifice, as presented in this chapter. Whichever is correct, it is not out of the question that both aspects fit what our author wishes to emphasize.[37] It is obvious that Christ is eternal in himself, as are the consequences of his sacrifice. This means that his priesthood is also eternal. Its eternal nature is guaranteed in spite of Christ's death. The eternal ministry is guaranteed by the victory of the resurrection, which now, after the offering of the sacrifice establishes the continuity of Christ's priesthood.

The next major point in this verse is the nature of Christ's sacrifice being without blemish. The Greek word *amōmos* is translated either "without blemish" or "without blame" in the New Testament (see Eph 1:4; Col 1:22; 2 Pet 3:14). The ideas run together. All Old Testament sacrifices had to be from animals that had no blemish or natural fault of any kind (Exod 12:5; 29:1; Lev 1:3; 3:1, 6; Num 6:14 et al.). This underlined the fact that for any sacrifice to be acceptable to God, it had to be whole and perfect. The prophet Malachi reports the displeasure of the Lord when the people brought the torn, lame and sick animals as offerings (Mal 1:13) because they could never be acceptable to God. Christ's character and actions were without blame before man and God (Isa 53:9 applied in 1 Pet 2:22; Heb 4:15) so that once more he qualifies in every way to provide this offering of himself.

Lastly, this sacrifice, unlike that of the animals, which only brought about external or "fleshly" cleansing, is able to get to the very heart of man's sin question, which resides in his inner being and conscience (within his heart and soul). It changes his way of thinking and rather than worrying about what things appear to be, it is concerned with their very essence and

36. Bruce, *Hebrews*, 205.
37. Guthrie, *Hebrews*, 190–191 tends to opt for both these aspects being combined.

the motivation from which all thoughts and actions spring. When Jesus was criticized by the Scribes and Pharisees with regard to his disciples not washing their hands before eating, he responded by pointing out that it is not what goes into the mouth that defiles a person but what comes out of the mouth because that shows what is in a person's heart (Matt 15:10–11, 18). This heart or conscience, can only be purified when the relationship brought about by Christ's redemptive sacrifice is appropriated by the individual. True worship, which follows, is only possible when outward acts are no longer seen to be the driving force as they were for the majority under the first covenant.[38]

This cleansing is also a work of the Spirit of God who provides the means for the individual to please God. The *dead works* from which mankind are cleansed are the actions which spring from a state of heart that is polluted as a consequence of sin. *Dead works*, as seen in 6:1, need to be repented of; this is only possible when the individual appropriates the sacrifice of Christ in recognition of who he is and what he has done on their behalf. Otherwise, people remain dead in their sin (Eph 2:1, 5; Col 2:13). In the same passage in Ephesians, Paul states that these believers have been made alive, who previously were dead. In the passage in Colossians 2:13, the reason for them having been made alive, is that they have been forgiven all their trespasses. The context of death, forgiveness and Christ's sacrifice, all fit together in all these passages, underlining the fact that any work which is performed outside this new relationship, is a dead work, irrespective of how correct it may be in terms of fulfilling ceremonial niceties. This underlines the fact here that *dead works* are any works carried out in a state of disobedience, outside a meaningful relationship with the living God. Rather, all mankind's works have to be motivated by the recognition of the sacrifice of Christ, this supreme High Priest, after the order of Melchizedek who is the author of this new and perfect covenant.

When the relationship is correct, then the main reason for the reconciliation between God and the individual becomes obvious: It is their service or worship (*latreuein*) of the Living God, which is no longer outward but from the heart; otherwise, it is all outward and meaningless, no matter how it may appear.

---

38. There were many who, under the first covenant, were undoubtedly driven by love for God and who understood that procedures were not going to gain them any favors before the Living God. David was one such and his many psalms give evidence of that.

Christ the mediator of a New Covenant 9:15–22

This section from 9:15–22 develops what has already been stated about the Old Covenant as well as the New. It highlights the role of Jesus as the mediator of a better and eternal covenant.

v. 15 *"Therefore, he is the mediator of a new covenant so that those who have been called may receive the promise of eternal inheritance, since death has occurred that redeems them from the transgressions under the first covenant."* Christ's role, as the High Priest, has already been pictured from the earliest in this letter (2:17) but here the significant matter is the subject of his being the mediator of this better new covenant. The subject is still centered upon this second covenant but here it is better because of the mediator who has already been described as the sacrifice for sin in the preceding verses.

The covenant under review is the one which has been put in place by this mediator. It enables those who had the promises from the first covenant to receive all that was theirs from that time until now to become a reality but on a permanent basis. All was due to Christ's death because it was only possible after the shedding of the blood of the victim and its death for the new covenant to be regarded as effective. The *therefore*, at the start of this verse, links together what the author has already been describing previously, to show why Christ, whose actual name is not mentioned but understood, became the mediator of this new covenant. The whole purpose of Christ was to bring about the redemption (*apolutrōsis*)[39] of transgressions. This was formerly not totally possible for those who lived under the first covenant in the way that it is now with the new one. However, subsequent to Christ's redemption, the eternal inheritance can be passed on to all those who have been called.[40] This shows not only its present efficacy but its retroactive power to deliver those who fulfilled the requirements under the first covenant. The phrase related to the "redemption of transgressions" here, has the very same force as that mentioned in 1:3, where the author describes the work of the Son in terms of having made "cleansing of sins" (*katharismon tōn harmartiōn poiēsamenos*).[41] When there is the redemption of sins there is at the same time complete forgiveness, as Paul declares (Eph 1:7). So,

---

39. *Apolutrōsis* is the payment required to acquit someone or to set them free from some form of debt. That is why it is seen as the payment to set free a slave or to redeem them.

40. Forgiveness took place under the first covenant but the procedure had to be constantly repeated, as has been stated in the previous verses, because the nature of the sacrifice was not absolute but is it now with Christ's sacrifice.

41. See the same in Moffatt, *Hebrews*, 126.

without this mediator, who became the sin offering, full forgiveness would never have been a possibility.

There are at least two questions which arise from the construction in this verse: First, who then are those who have been called? In 3:1 this a heavenly calling (see note 3:1) which indicates that the source of any calling is divine, showing that the initiative comes from God in the call. It is not limited to those of any single nation but made to all who are open to the work of God's Spirit. Here, those who are called include all who are believers (*hoi keklēmenoi*); the perfect participle shows that they have been called at some time in the past and must be aware of that call. This call is not limited, as mentioned above, to those who were called during the epoch of the new covenant, as the work of Christ and his redemptive offering is, as this verse states, effective for all those who were called under the first covenant. Clearly all godly Jews from previous generations are included as well as those who are followers of Christ, the Great High priest during this present dispensation.

Second, what then is the nature of the eternal inheritance? Promises made to those who lived upon the earth were usually made in terms of earthly reward such as security in their dwelling and continued posterity, as was the case of the promises of God to Abram (Gen 13:15–17) but mortality limited any promises to time. This promise however, transcends time and translates to what the author has previously called a heavenly calling, as the first of 6 occurrences speaking of the heavens in the letter (see notes on 3:1). He uses the word in terms similar to those used by Paul (Eph 1:3, 20; 2:6). In this way the promises are not merely earthly but indeed eternal. They would include the promises which are described in Revelation 21:1, 2 under the New Heaven, the New Earth and the New Jerusalem and which relate to God's future plans, not only for individuals but for his entire creation.[42]

v.16 *"For when there is a will[43] it is necessary to establish the death of the one who made the will."* There is considerable debate between scholars as to the correct translation of the Greek word *diathēkē* in this verse (see *Appendix E*). The first question that requires an answer is how is this word to be understood on its own? Most scholars accept that it is an agreement or arrangement[44] made by one party who has the overall power. Moulton and Milligan state that it is imposed by the superior party and either accepted

42. This does not mean that there are not promises which Christians can accept as relative to their time on earth as well as those which are yet future.

43. The same Greek word *diathēkē* means will or covenant.

44. Bruce, *Hebrews*, 210.a "settlement."

or rejected by the party to whom it is offered.[45] From a biblical perspective, when God makes a covenant (*diathēkē*), it is his unilateral decision, dependent upon his divine person and grace, since there is nothing outside his own will that forces him into any agreement. The agreement here is called a covenant and its purpose was to enable a special relationship between himself and the people of Israel.

Therefore, even his first covenant, which was a based upon the keeping of rules, was, in fact, a demonstration of his mercy.[46] The difficulty here is that of the way in which this word should be translated into English because Greek speakers during the first century would not have had a difficulty understanding its nuances. Up until this point in the entire letter of Hebrews, *diathēkē* has been translated as *covenant* and this is the way it is translated in the LXX where it is the rendition of the Hebrew *berith* (covenant). Since the argument, up until present, has been related to the comparison between two covenants, the old and the new and since *diathēkē* (covenant) is the accepted translation of the Hebrew *berith* (covenant) as stated, is it not right that the meaning of the original use of this word needs to be what is considered the normal meaning here?

The question is not as simple as it may at first appear. Anyone who has had anything to do with translation work learns very quickly that one word does not always mean the same thing when it is transferred to another language and indeed, even in the same language; it can have a variety of meanings depending upon the context. When this epistle was written *diathēkē* had several meanings, including both *covenant* and *testament* or *will*. In fact, most Greek speakers at the time would have understood it as a will. Some scholars, like Westcott[47] are adamant that since the entire argument here relates to two different covenants that this is the way in which *diathēkē* needs to be translated throughout.

But there is an immediate difficulty if it is understood as a covenant because the author states that "*where there is a diathēkē there is of necessity the death of the one who made it.*" However, this is not correct, since it is not necessary for the one who puts the covenant in place to die before it becomes effective. When God made a covenant with Abraham (Gen 15:1–18) and

45. *Moulton and Milligan, Vocabulary,* 148 see *diathēkē* as universally understood "with absolute unanimity" by Greek speakers as referring to a last will and testament and he believes that Greek speaking Jews at the time would have understood it in the same way; see also G. Quell & J. Behm, "διαθήκη"[*diathēkē*] in *TDNT,* II, 106–134.

46. John 1:17 is very clear that the Law was given by Moses and grace and truth by Jesus Christ but God in his mercy transmitted the Law via Moses so it must be understood to show the mercy of God to man in spite of his faults and failings.

47. Westcott, *Hebrews,* 300–302.

later with the people of Israel as a whole (Exod 24:3–8), there is no question of any of the participants dying, even if it was ratified by the spilling of blood of animals. This action did not represent the death of either party, as Westcott suggests.[48] Likewise, the covenant between God and Noah (Gen. 9:8–17) required no death. However, what we have here is another kind of agreement. One which is better known as a testament or will because a will only comes into effect when the one who made it dies. This certainly fits the present discussion. The Greek word *diathēkē* is the same but the concept is better known to us in English, as a will in this particular instance. This is the reason why it has been translated in this way here in verses 16 and 17.

v. 17 *"For a will only takes effect upon death since it is not in force while the one who made it is still alive."* While an individual is alive, he or she is able to give gifts to people freely, as they please. This is evident from Jesus' parable in Luke 15:11–32, where the wayward son requested his share of his father's inheritance while he was still alive. But when the matter is one which concerns a will, everyone knows that as long as the person who made the will is alive, the will is not yet in force. The author had just spoken of Jesus putting a new covenant in place by paying the redemptive price for mankind's transgressions but also of Jesus becoming the mediator of an eternal inheritance in verse 15. The first requires his death and the second his presence and ongoing intervention, so how do all the factors go together?

In the first, the matter was the question of the redemptive price where blood is spilled to cover the sin of mankind. Christ was the equivalent of that sacrificial lamb when he died upon the cross. Now the author wishes to convey a different aspect which deals with the same work he has undertaken but from the perspective of a will. As the one who has been the initiator and implementor of this plan, he has the final word as to what it is that the ones who are to receive the benefits of the inheritance will accrue. Before the benefits are distributed, he has to die. This Christ has done. But unlike any ordinary testator, he was the God/Man and although he died to fulfil the requirements of the one who is able to grant this eternal inheritance, he has also vanquished death and returned to be the mediator and guardian of the better covenant on a continual basis. So, he is both the one who lays down the conditions for the inheritance and then becomes the mediator who ever lives to oversee and be the guarantor of all that needs to take place.

This is where there are some scholars who feel that the analogies of life related to testators, executors and mediators fail.[49] Bruce clarifies the matter when he writes: "all analogies for ordinary life must be defective when

48. Westcott, *Hebrews*, 267.
49. Nairne, *The Epistle of Priesthood*, 365.

they are applied to Him who rose from the dead and is thus able personally to secure for his people the benefits which He died to procure for them."[50] He died so the benefits fixed by him cannot be changed subsequent to that death; they rest in perpetuity as that is the way in which wills work.

If this is understood, then Christ's work is both a covenant in the sense of the Old Testament as well as a will in the sense that what he determined can never be changed and in spite of any apparent failures from the human perspective; his resurrection and victory over death quash any apparent enigmas.

v. 18 "*For which reason not even the first covenant was inaugurated without blood.*" In what appears a rather difficult form of logic, the author suddenly returns to the first covenant and for the moment leaves the matter of the second to one side. Nevertheless, there is a link because it has just been established above, that the covenant Christ put in place, was inaugurated by his death and the shedding of his blood. The word covenant is not mentioned in this verse but is again, most certainly supposed, when the author states "*for which reason not even the first was inaugurated . . .*" where the "first" is the covenant made in Exodus 24:5–8 and where blood was sprinkled to inaugurate the covenant. The particular form of *diathēkē* is once more clarified, since there is again the matter of blood and sacrifice, which is not associated with the making of a will. The Greek word translated *inaugurated* here, is *enkekainistai* which means literally: to renew something, and as Guthrie suggests, it really has the sense of renewing what was required in the application of this covenant.[51]

vv. 19–20 "*For when every commandment had been declared by Moses to all the people in accordance with the Law, he took the blood of calves and goats with water and scarlet wool and hyssop and sprinkled both the book itself and all the people* saying '*This is the blood of the covenant that God commanded you.*'" The reference here is clearly drawn from what transpired in Exodus 24:3–8. Moses was required to write the words of the Law as well as announce them to the people after which there was the sprinkling of blood upon the altar, and the people. The part relative to the sprinkling of the blood has already been alluded to in verse 13 above. Some of the details differ from the Exodus account. What is recounted here with regard to blood being sprinkled upon the book, as well as the blood of calves and goats and the matter of the scarlet wool and hyssop, is not part of the Exodus narrative. However, there has already been the mention of goats and calves in vv. 12, 13 and crimson and hyssop are mentioned in Lev 14:4, all reinforcing

---

50. Bruce. *Hebrews*, 213.

51. Guthrie, *Hebrews*, 195.

the sacrificial character of what took place.[52] The extra details need not become the focus of attention because the most important factor is that of the sprinkling of the blood.

v. 21 "And similarly he sprinkled with blood both the tent and all the vessels used in worship." The procedures added here are not part of the Exodus narrative but it can be supposed that it is not outside the bounds of what took place, since in Leviticus 8:10–11, the anointing oil was used to anoint the tabernacle and its contents and there was the blood of a bull smeared on the horns of the altar as well as on its base (Lev. 8:14–15). Josephus wrote that blood was sprinkled on the tabernacle together with oil and it is apparent that this tradition is what is related here.[53] As in the previous verse, the emphasis is upon the importance of blood in the covering of sin and in purification.

v. 22 "And according to the Law, almost everything is cleansed by blood and without the shedding of blood there is no forgiveness of sin." When the author states that under the Law or according to the Law, he is speaking of the entire system in place under the Law of Moses. The blood is central to forgiveness. There are some exceptions as the word *schedon*–"almost"– indicates. In cases of the severe poverty of the worshipper, an omer or the tenth of an ephah of flour could be offered (Lev 5:11)[54] and some things were purified by water (Num 19:7–8; 31:23b) or fire (Num 31:23a) but in general, this was the established rule which all understood and exceptions did not set aside the rule.[55]

In Leviticus 17:11 Yahweh tells Moses: *"For the life of the flesh is in the blood; and I have given it to you for making atonement for your lives on the altar; for, as life, it is the blood that makes atonement."* This is the point that the author is making in his entire discussion here. For anyone who is a follower of Christ this principle is at the heart of their belief. Without Christ's sacrifice there would be no forgiveness of sin, so the symbolism established under the Law is fulfilled in Christ. Note that although the word "sin" is not found in the Greek at the end of the verse, when remission or forgiveness is the subject of the phrase, it is automatically understood that

52. For further views on the additions see: Bruce, *Hebrews*, 214–216.

53. Josephus, *Antiquities*, 3.8.6. "And when Moses had sprinkled Aaron's vestments, himself, and his sons, with the blood of the beasts that were slain, and had purified them with spring waters and ointment, they became God's priests. After this manner did he consecrate them and their garments for seven days together. The same he did to the tabernacle, and the vessels thereto belonging, both with oil first incensed, as I said, and with the blood of bulls and of rams, slain day by day one, according to its kind." https://www.fulltextarchive.com/page/The-Antiquities-of-the-Jews3/

54. This would be approximately the equivalent of 2.3 liters or 0.5059 gallons.

55. See Hughes, *Hebrews*, 378.

"sin" is what is forgiven. For this reason, it is perfectly legitimate to include it in the translation.

Christ the perfect and final sacrifice 9:23–28

This section resumes a theme that was initiated earlier in 8:2 where Christ is portrayed as a minister in the tent which the Lord set up and not man. In other words, in the heavens, where the true tabernacle of God is present.

v. 23 *"Therefore, it was necessary on the one hand for the copies of the heavenly things to be cleansed with these (rituals) but on the other hand the heavenly things themselves by better sacrifices than these."* The "therefore," links the thought that there is a parallel between what has just been described under the ceremonial rituals and symbolic images related to what is required in the purification of the earthly and the heavenly. Nevertheless, the entire process relative to the heavenly has to be seen as superior. It needs to be understood that the author is not saying that the objects in the heavenlies have to be cleansed, as were the objects in the earthly tabernacle, nor indeed that the heavens themselves have to be cleansed. But the earthly creatures who are called to enter this heavenly sanctuary have to be cleansed by something that is far superior to any earthly ritual or they would never qualify to gain entry to the real tabernacle, which is God's dwelling place.

The copies of the things in the heavens were cleansed by the rituals just described, especially by blood. However, they did not, as already described in verses 8–9 and 14, deal adequately with the conscience of sinful mankind. Something better was required to accomplish that kind of purification which would change the heart of man. The plural "sacrifices" does not in any way convey the thought that there needs to be a multiplicity of sacrifices to bring about the required result. It merely underlines the fact that all those symbolic and ritualistic sacrifices carried out repeatedly in the earthly tabernacle, could never satisfy God's demands.

v. 24 *"For Christ has not entered into holy places made with hands which are copies of the true things but into heaven itself, now to appear in the presence of God on our behalf."* For Christ did not enter any earthly holy places which were only copies of heavenly but into the real one as already mentioned in verse 12 and that is where God himself resides. The "for" at the start of the verse, highlights the difference in the procedures followed by the earthly and this heavenly High Priest. Earthly holy places were concerned with the copies and necessary for practical reasons on the day of Atonement; however, Christ is now in the actual eternal dwelling of the Almighty

(1:3). This is the holy place or heavenly tabernacle; it is the definitive goal to which all other images pointed.

Again, not only did he enter the heavens in some temporary fashion, as did the earthly High Priests, only to vacate the Holy of Holies after they had fulfilled their momentary annual duty; that would require the same sort of entry at another point in time, a year later but he entered (*eisēlthen* aor. ind.) to take up his rightful and permanent place there as the High Priest in permanence. In this manner he represents his own people before God continually. If the word "entered" is understood properly here, it represents the end of the first covenant with all its symbolism. It closes the door immediately to any future need for the entire system supported by the Levitical rituals. The earlier holy places were part of the Law with all its shadows of the real that has been achieved. The words *now* (*nun*) and *to appear* (*emphanisthēnai* aor. infin.), enforce the present and ongoing mediatorial work of Christ before the Father on behalf of those who have committed themselves to him. This is evident from the use of the pronoun "our," which means that he does not mediate for all but for those who belong to him, having accepted his redemptive sacrifice on their behalf. Spicq suggests that this pictures a pastoral role for Christ and that this is all based on his sacrifice upon the cross.[56]

v. 25 "*Nor in order to offer himself frequently in the manner in which the High Priest enters into the Holy of Holies year by year with blood of others.*" The earthly model of the sanctuary and the day of Atonement required the procedure to be repeated annually by the High Priest. The expression "year by year" which is used on several occasions, shows that the author is thinking constantly about the repetitive nature of the sacrifice on the Day of Atonement. The repetitive nature of this activity on the part of the High Priests has already been mentioned (v.7). If an action has to be repeated, then it is evident that it is not final or complete. The contrast with what happened under the first covenant is what the author wishes to underline here. Christ entered into the permanent holy of holies and this was only possible as the consequence of his own blood sacrifice, not that of animals' blood as with the High Priests of the first covenant.

When the High Priest entered the earthly holy of holies, there was one activity that was required and that was to make the required offering on behalf of the sins of the people. Therefore, the entry and the offering are also part of one single activity and must be seen as such. With Christ, the entry and the sacrifice also go together, even if the sacrifice is not specifically mentioned in the verse itself. The fact that he did not enter with the blood of

56. Spicq, *Hébreux*, II. 268.

others automatically demonstrates that he entered with his own blood and therefore speaks of his sacrifice as being part of the entry. This action of Jesus is not something that necessitates repetition because this is the final and complete sacrifice as the next verse underlines. In fact, the next verses clarify this whole emphasis of the perfection of Christ's sacrifice and priesthood.

v. 26 *"Since that would have required him to suffer repeatedly since the foundation of the world. But now he has appeared once, at the end of the ages to do away with sin by the sacrifice of himself."* If Christ was required to carry out this procedure repeatedly, he would have had to have kept doing this over and over again since the world was created but he did not. People do not live and die repeatedly as the following verse indicates. So, the concept of someone living and dying repeatedly is nonsensical, just as such a concept of Christ having to die over and over again would be nonsensical.

In three consecutive verses and for the purpose of demonstrating the finality of what Jesus did, the author uses the word "once" to qualify actions which have been carried out. Christ appeared once. His mission was unique at what is called the end of the age. This Son who in the very first verses of the letter is identified as the one who has spoken on behalf of God, fulfilled what was required to reconcile sinful man with God by coming to earth to make the whole plan possible. It was not something to be repeated and it was completed perfectly, just as the will of God should be. It was also something put in place for the end of the ages as without this happening, disorder and chaos would continue to reign. It is only because of this perfect sacrifice of the Son, who is also this High Priest after the order of Melchizedek, that the transition from the present age to the perfect age to come can be contemplated.

The phrase *"at the end of the ages"* (*epi sunteleia tōn aiōnōn*) is unique to this letter but it is an extension of what again was introduced at the beginning of the letter when God spoke directly to us *"in these last days"* by the Son (see notes on 1:2). It is slightly different because it emphasizes the end of this period and coincides with Christ's sacrifice and victory over sin. Spicq says that this also ushers in the new world which is the messianic era in which the readers of the letter live.[57] Paul uses the expression *"the ends of the ages have arrived"* (*ta telē tōn aiōnōn katēnteken*) in a context which indicates a similar experience for those who are participants among the Corinthian church, to show that they too are living at a time when this transition has already begun. Obviously, it is Christ and his work alone which has brought about this transition, which is at the same time a fulfilment of all that was prophesied in the past.

---

57. Spicq, *Hébreux*, II. 269.

vv. 27–28 "*And just as it is appointed for man to die once, and after that comes judgement, so also Christ having been offered to bear the sins of many, will appear a second time, not to deal with sin but for the salvation of those expecting him.*" There is one appointment which God has ordained which needs to be understood absolutely. Every person upon the earth must die and subsequently be judged for their behavior. The author expands upon this later aspect in chapter 10:27–31 (see notes). Both John and Paul make it very clear that the judgment for believers does not include condemnation (John 5:24; Rom 8:1) but the fact of a judgment for all, including believers, is also certain (Rom 14:10; 1 Cor 3:12–15; 2 Cor 5:10).

Likewise, Christ was appointed to die once. Again the "once" is significant. His work is singular and absolute. However, this appointment is different from that of mortal man because it is linked to his incarnation, his ministry and his sacrifice. He too, although God, became man for this specific purpose of bringing salvation. His death is not just the consequence of the mortality of mankind which follows the disobedience of sin but the obedience of a perfect life laid down on behalf of all those who here are designated as "the many" and who are "expecting him." In other words, he died once voluntarily, as the once for all sacrifice, necessary to atone for the sin of all who believe in him. In the light of the previous verses the author wishes to underline the *once for all* nature of the sacrifice and death of Christ and its complete satisfaction in terms of atoning for sin. There is no other sacrifice or atonement needed ever again.

This last verse ends with a declaration of an eschatological hope and a promise for all who have placed their faith in Christ (see 10:37). He is going to come again but not to offer any further sacrifices. This time when he comes, he comes to bring in the fulness of the salvation which God has planned. This will be more than anything which can be experienced in the present age but the fulness of all that is possible once the totality of rebellion and sin have been entirely removed from God's creation; this is when the New Heavens and the New Earth will be fully established (Rev 21:1–2).

However, even if the death of Christ has the possibility of atoning for the death of all, it is also clear that there is a condition for its application and that is that people have to be expecting him. There is the necessity of identifying with Christ and his work. The teaching of universalism is not justifiable from this verse. The thought is to encourage eager participation in the hearts of his followers during their earthly lives so that the eagerness which accompanies the willingness to longsuffering of which the author wrote in earlier chapters, may be evident in the faith of all believers (3:14; 4:11; 6:11 et al.).

10.

The former system was only shadows and types: With Christ the reality is now here permanently 10:1–18

One may consider that the preceding treatment regarding Christ's superior sacrifice, would suffice but the author wishes to drive home his point that the Old Covenant and all its rituals, including its priesthood, is totally inadequate.

v. 1 *"For the law has a shadow of the good things to come, it is not itself the exact image of these matters; it can never, by the same sacrifices which they offer continually every year, perfect those who draw near."* Verses 1 and 2 are one long sentence in Greek and this accounts for a variety of translations in different versions of the English. The Law here includes, not just the decalogue but the entire system handed over to the people under Moses and specifically the procedures to be followed for worship. The author contrasts the covenants in terms of a shadow (*skian*) while the actual thing is described as the icon (*eikona*). The Law was a mere shadow of what were the good things to come. An icon is something which is the exact replica of the original. For example, Paul calls Christ the icon (*eikon*) of the Father (Col 1:15). Consequently, whoever has seen the Son has seen the Father, as Jesus informed Philip (John 14:9). Similarly, the new covenant is the very image of the heavenly reality. The good things that have come, have already been mentioned in 9:11. They include all that has been described from 8:5, relative to the superior heavenly tabernacle. That means everything that is superior in the letter when compared to the first covenant with its imperfect priesthood and worship. The former things were all shadows of what the author calls *"the things to come."* Shadows cannot exist without the reality of the objects that cast them, so it cannot be said that the Law was completely without purpose or effect. However, it was, as already seen, only preparatory and incomplete.

The question may be asked how it is that in 9:11 these things are spoken of as having already come, while here they are yet future? (In part, this question has already been dealt with in the notes on 9:11, 12). The most commonly accepted response is that although these things have come since the completion of Christ's sacrificial work and his resurrection, they have not come in their fulness; the fulness awaits the completion of the age and the return of Christ. Some scholars suggest it means nevertheless, that a good number of better things have already come upon the earth because of Christ and that is certainly correct. They would include such as the actual priesthood of Christ which is already in place. This has after all, already replaced the old priesthood under the first covenant. But Christians still await the coming of heavenly things related to the perfection that will only come when Christ comes again, so that there is a built-in tension. This is the equivalent of what we have now and what we do not have yet as in Paul's description regarding the sons of God in Romans 8:16–24. In this, all the Law is a shadow, meaning that it only foretells what the real would be like. It could never be the real thing itself.

Again, as has already been stated from 9:25, the continual necessity of something having to be repeated, indicates its inadequate nature. Now that the real is here in the new covenant and set in place by the Son, there is no longer the need for the repetition. The shadow has been dispensed with and *the real* is here. The same sacrifices offered yearly have been replaced by the one–all sufficient sacrifice of Christ. To fail to recognize this is the equivalent of snubbing his entire sacrifice and priesthood. It means that the purification, which was sought through the many animal sacrifices but which never was sufficient, has finally been fully achieved by the blood of the perfect substitutionary victim: Christ the perfect man. Since his sacrifice is perfect, those who identify with it can be counted perfect. It has already been noted (see notes in 2:10) that the verb *teleioō* (I am perfect) is a favorite of the author's. The Law was never going to achieve this perfection in anyone because it was ceremonial and outward but the covenant of Christ was all sufficient and well able to bring perfection because it resulted in the inward change of the heart required by God. The people who are called *"those who draw near"* (*tous erchomenous*–sometimes translated *"those who approach"*; 4:16; 7:19, 25; 10:22 et al.) are the individuals who have placed their hope in Christ and thereby benefit from the perfect sacrifice and all its consequences. They are included among those whose faith is described in the following chapter.

v. 2 "*Otherwise would they not have ceased being offered, since the worshippers, once they have been purified, would no longer have any conscience of sin?*" The construction of the sentence (remember it is the continuation from the beginning of the first verse) is that if it had been possible for all the repetitive offerings to make someone perfect, then there would be no need to continue with them. They should have stopped under the old system but they did not and there is no such thing as complete and non-repetitive cleansing under the first covenant. If perfection is achieved, one does not have to keep making new offerings. If you do then it means that what you have been doing is unsatisfactory and incomplete. The worshippers who were part of the Levitical system, should have arrived at the point where sin was removed from their consciences but this is not what happened. The worshippers continued to have consciences dominated by the problem of sin, as it was part of mankind's very nature; they had no means of overcoming it. If the earlier annual and ongoing sacrifices had really cleansed man's sin, then it would no longer be a problem and there would not be any need to continue the process annually but it is only Christ's sacrifice that can, once for all, blot out mankind's sin. In any case, the old system continued and it did not deal with the sin question or the conscience.

Bruce suggests that the wording of the presentation infers here that the system of continual offerings was still in place when this was written, indicating that the Temple at Jerusalem was still in place and that this would reinforce a date for the letter prior to AD 70.[1] This may be true or it may just be that too much is read into the construction.

v. 3 "*But in them* [the sacrifices] *is the remembrance of sins every year.*" When sacrifices are made for sin, it is only logical that there is the remembrance of the sins for which they are offered. Consequently, all that the annual sacrifices do is remind the worshippers of their weakness and sinfulness. It is supposed however, that the offerings would be accompanied by the appropriate attitude of heart, resulting in sorrow for their faults and an attempt at corrective action on their part. The most important action would be one of prompting the need for repentance and the desire to overcome whatever the sin may have been. In the case that what was carried out was merely ceremonial and there was no change of heart, then the offering would be considered baseless, as far as God was concerned. There would be no grace granted by God for the offering itself. In other words, there would be no forgiveness if their hearts were not right.

---

1. Bruce, *Hebrews*, 227.

v. 4 "*For it is impossible for the blood of bulls and goats to take away sins.*" Most readers today[2] would have no difficulty accepting this statement because the whole question of sacrifices of animals for humans and the shedding of blood is not part of the thinking of our generation. However, for people who lived at that time and in that culture, such a declaration could well immediately set them against everything the author wished to say. In chapter 9:13–14 the author had already made a comparative statement regarding the efficacy of Christ's sacrifice over that of animals; that of the first covenant was only capable of an outward cleansing. However, the argument was building and here it is declared unequivocally that these sacrifices have no role in the removal of sin. This underlines the absolute impotence of the first covenant to deal with man's sinful nature, even if it was able to satisfy the outward and ceremonial requirements of Law keeping.

As early as the days of Samuel the prophet makes it very clear that obedience and a right heart were more important than animal sacrifices (1 Sam 15:22) and the psalmist declares that it is sincerity and declarations from the heart as well as true praise, which are more important than burnt offerings (Ps 50:8–14). Again, that is why David calls out for God to create in him a clean heart and to enable him with a new and right spirit (Ps 51:10). This indicates that what the author is saying here was long understood by true worshipers of God among the Jews.

vv. 5–7 "*Therefore, when he* [Christ] *came into the world he said: 'You did not desire sacrifice and offering but you prepared a body for me; in burnt offerings and sacrifices you have not taken pleasure.' Then I said, 'Behold, I have come to do your will, O God as it has been written concerning me in the scroll of the book.'*" The author applies the words of Psalm 40 which are normally called a Psalm of David and following the method he has used from the commencement of the letter, takes what seems to have been applicable in a different setting in order to apply it in a very specific way to another. Here the speaker of the words is Jesus himself.

The *therefore* (*dio* or as a result), at the start of the verse, links what has just been stated in the preceding verse, to the life and ministry of Jesus. It is relative to the inadequacy of the first covenant to be able to deal with the sin question. The assumption that this verse refers to Jesus, is without doubt, although his name is not given; it is supported by the form of the verb (*legei*) which means "he says." After all, this whole discourse is the continuation of what was stated in 9:28 where Christ was "*once offered*" to deal with the sin question. When did he say this? When he comes into the world. That

---

2. There are still some places in the majority world where sacrifices are offered by followers of indigenous religions but they are far fewer as time goes by.

is when he voluntarily took on human flesh at his incarnation, all was a prerequisite to the offering of himself. When these words are attributed to Jesus, he had already begun his mission, as in his word here he declares to the Father: *"but you prepared a body for me"* (*sōma de katērtisō moi*), the aorist tense showing that the action had already been accomplished. This part of the verse is cited in the form which is represented by the Greek in the LXX, rather than by the Hebrew in the Masoretic text; the latter reads *"ears you have dug for me,"*[3] which is an idiom referring to God fashioning man's ears as part of his whole person. His body becomes the instrument necessary to carry out the divine mission of salvation. Without Christ's act of obedience to the will of the Father in taking on this body, and all that it stood for, everything pictured in the previous copies and shadows of ministry and sacrifice under the first covenant, would have been meaningless.

Although the word incarnation is nowhere mentioned as such, it is certainly clear that this is what the expression "coming into the world" means; it is certainly to what "the preparation of a body" for him, refers. The aspect of obedience and Christ's earthly work is highlighted throughout his entire ministry, especially in the John's Gospel, where, as already stated, Jesus does nothing other than what is the will of the Father (John 5:19, 30 et al.). This incarnation and this mission were the whole reason for his coming to earth as a man; it was to do God's will in order to surrender himself as the only satisfactory sacrifice to atone for mankind's sin and that is exactly what he did (see John 8:42).

Another matter of great significance here, is that Jesus' words to his Father, register the fact that the Father was never satisfied with the animal sacrifices offered over the entire period of the first covenant. There are four specific terms which the Psalm employs to encompass the sacrificial requirements of the entire Levitical system: they are sacrifices (*thusia*), offerings (*prosphora*), burnt offerings (*holokautōmata*), and sin offerings (*peri harmartias*); yet these were all inadequate. Here the author includes them all to reinforce his point regarding the heart of mankind. This was because the keeping of the letter of the Law in the carrying out of the requirements of the Levitical system, including all its sacrifices, was regarded by many Jews as all that was required. Rather, God was looking for

---

3. An expression which means "you have given me receptive ears" (REB) or "you have given me an open ear"(NRSV); Bruce, *Hebrews*, 232–33, notes that even if the Hebrew version had been used it would have served equally well, since it is used to describe the Servant of Yahweh in Isa 50:4–5 who listens and obeys the Lord, which is the same as to do the will of God that is the main thought here; Moffatt, *Hebrews*, 138, sees the LXX as a mistranslation of the Hebrew original but says that in fact it does not make a lot of difference because the overall meaning is not changed.

repentant and contrite hearts which represented a correct inner attitude on the part of all worshippers.

The phrase *"in the scroll of the book"* (*en kephalidi bibliou*), in Greek is literally the knob at the top of the rod around which the manuscript was rolled. However, it is a phrase which stood originally for the *Torah* or the books of Moses but then for the entire Old Testament scriptures.[4] For the way in which it is applied to Jesus' words, it reflects all that pertains to what God has included under Scripture relating to his life and ministry. This is the way the phrase: *"it is written,"* which is found often in the New Testament (as in Matt 2:5; 4:4; 11:10; 26:24; Rom 1:17; 3:10; 8:36; 9:13 et al.), is interpreted to mean that whatever needed to be revealed in Scripture can be regarded as having God's stamp of approval upon it. It must be considered to be authoritative.[5] In this particular verse the author is saying that Jesus declares that his submission to the Father and his coming to earth were all aimed at fulfilling what was necessary to put this new covenant in place, as is underlined in the next verse.

vv. 8–9 "When he said above, 'You have not desired nor taken pleasure in sacrifices, offerings and burnt offerings and sin offerings' (all of which are offered according to the Law) then he said 'Behold I have come to do your will.' He does away with the first [covenant] *in order to establish the second* [covenant]." Once more the author repeats what has been stated in the first verses of the chapter. Although those sacrifices were all important in the first covenant and the people needed to offer them under that regime, they were only symbolic. They did not satisfy God's demands and the author is adamant that they gave God no pleasure and were not what he wanted ultimately.

So, Jesus states here that he came to do what was necessary to satisfy the requirements of the first covenant and to put an end to it. This is because it was unsatisfactory and incomplete. He needed to establish the final or second covenant sealed by his own sacrifice and blood. The word translated "to do away with" (*anairō*), when related to a person, usually means to kill or destroy someone (see Acts 16:27) but here it is clearly removing completely the regime which was in place previously because the two covenants could not co-exist. One is reminded in Acts 2:46 et al. that after the death and resurrection of Jesus, the Jewish believers continued to frequent the temple. This apparently continued until its destruction in AD 70. There is

---

4. See Ps 39 (40):7 and Ezek 2:9. There is some debate on the part of scholars as to its meaning but in most contexts, it stands for the entire Old Testament scriptures. Spicq, *Hébreux*, II. 306, suggests that this is the same as the Hebrew ספר~במגלת (*bimgillat sefer*). Literally: "In scroll of book."

5. See Guthrie, *Hebrews*, 207.

no clear indication however, that they participated in any of the sacrifices, as this would have been immediately contrary to the entire purpose of the Covenant of Christ.[6] Some among the readers of this epistle were tempted to reintegrate among the Jews who were still offering sacrifices.

v. 10 "By that will [of God] we have been sanctified through the offering of the body of Jesus Christ, once for all." In the previous verse, the words of Christ as applied to Psalm 40 regarding his having come to do God's will, are now what have been accomplished. He came, he fulfilled God's plan and he gave himself as the perfect sacrifice, which alone is able to set apart (sanctify), once for all, sinners who have trusted in him. It is significant that here, the author describes the action relative to this sanctification as complete (hagiasmenoi esmen–literally: we stand as having been sanctified) where the perfect passive indicates a complete and continuing state. Probably, he uses this structure in the same sense that Paul would describe the believer as righteous in Christ (Rom 5:17; Phil 3:9), even if we are not yet ourselves righteous but are being made righteous through the continuing process of sanctification. He does not say any more about this aspect and it is necessary to remember the earlier warnings given regarding the need not to have hard hearts (3:8) or hearts full of unbelief (3:12) and that the readers needed to be ready, looking out for Christ's return (9:28). Of course, this belief is an act of submission to the will of God and an indication that there is an integration into the plans of God. The ceremonial aspect of outward display has gone together with the covenant of the Law. Now the conscience, and the desire of the worshipper sets a new course to follow God wholeheartedly through Christ. This sanctification is therefore of a spiritual nature, although it also requires some sort of outward evidence, which in terms of James' thinking, could be elaborated upon in terms of the works that follow faith (James 2:14, 17–18).

The offering of the body of Christ is central to this sanctification. It is his offering of himself that alone makes it possible. Without the cross, it never would have satisfied the demands of God regarding the shedding of the blood of a perfect man for the sin of mankind. Once more, the absolute efficacy of this offering is declared with the addition of the Greek word which means once for all (ephapax). There is no longer any need to ever again look for any other sacrifice to atone for sin. Remember Jesus' words on the cross: It is finished (John 19:30). There is nothing more that needs to be done on God's part.

6. von Harnack, What is Christianity? 79, says that at the beginning of the Church Age the sacrifices did not disappear immediately but they did within a very short period and indeed, prior to the destruction of the temple. The reason was that people understood what the death of Christ meant.

vv. 11–13 *"And on the one hand, every priest stands ministering daily and often offers up the same sacrifices which can never take away sins but this (priest) on the other hand, when he had offered one sacrifice for all time, sat at the right hand of God waiting from then until his enemies be made a footstool for his feet."* The author reminds his readers of the efficacy of Jesus' offering as compared to that of all other offerings made under the first covenant, in order to drive home the significance of Jesus' unique offering in verse 10. There are a number of issues which are highlighted here, most of which, apart from the first, have already been mentioned directly or indirectly, elsewhere in the epistle: first, under the Sinai covenant the priests who made the offerings stood because their work was never finished. Second, they continually offered up sacrifices of a similar nature. Third, the sacrifices could never satisfy the sin question and were unable to deal with the problem at hand.

However, when it comes to Christ, who here is called *"this (one)"*–*houtos*–(v.12) there is no need to stand. He sat down because he had completed his work in one fell swoop. There is clearly another reference here to Ps 110:1 (see notes on 1:3 & 13) where *"The Lord says to my lord, 'Sit at my right hand until I make your enemies your footstool.'"* When Christ had offered up himself and completed his self-offering, he returns to his rightful place in the heavens in the presence of the Father and takes up his position at the right hand of God (see 1:3). His work was complete and totally successful. Unlike the continual requirements of the Aaronic priests, who never completed their work and who were therefore required to continually offer more animal sacrifices, Jesus offered up one single sacrifice and the work was done. This single sacrifice was all that was ever required and there is no need for any other. Not ever! There is no ongoing sacrifice of Christ in the heavens as some have taught.[7] The only ongoing ministry of Christ is his priestly intercession for his own as already stated in 7:24–25.

As already stated in earlier passages referring to this same Psalm 110:1 (see 1:3 &13), the making of *"your enemies your footstool"* relates to the ongoing work of Christ in the world to complete all that is necessary to usher in the Age to Come. It includes the fortification and direction of the Church in all its tasks under the direction of the Holy Spirit but has nothing more to do with any sacrificial aspects. The declaration also indicates that the

---

7. The translation in the Latin *Vulgate* of the Greek verb *prosenegkas,* is an aorist participle, showing something that is done and complete; it has been rendered by a present participle in Latin (*offerens*), giving the impression that Jesus is continually offering himself as a sacrifice in the heavens. For more on this see Bruce, *Hebrews,* 239n67. This is likely why some have wrongly held to the idea that Jesus continually offers up sacrifices in heaven on mankind's behalf.

enemies of God, whoever they may be, have to deal with this High Priest, in all their attempts to frustrate God's plans. Paul writes about these enemies and speaks of death being the last of them. Therefore, what we have in the phrase is the complete assurance of victory which is going to be finalized at the end of this age (1 Cor 15:25–28). Ultimately, no opposition to Christ is going to be able to stand. Finally, unlike the multitude of animals and other sacrifices since the instigation of the first covenant, all of which could never take away sins, this one was completely successful. The resurrection proved that to be the case and is proof of its acceptance by the Father. Christ's place, seated at the right hand of God, demonstrates once more, his total supremacy over anything that could have been implicit in the first covenant. This High Priest is the Son himself. Every single point raised as ineffective under the first covenant is supplanted by Christ in the second.

v. 14 "*For by one offering he has perfected for all time those who are being sanctified.*" The fact is that all the endless sacrifices since their initiation from the days of Moses, had never been satisfactory and those who attempted to become sanctified or set apart to God's service never achieved their desire. This verse informs us unequivocally, that Jesus' once for all sacrifice, instantaneously fulfilled all the requirements. It brought about an immediate action (*teteleiōken*–he perfected or completed) which as a perfect tense, shows that the result is already in place in an ongoing state or in perpetuity. In other words, the consequences of this sacrifice are immediate and can never be expunged. It may appear inconsistent that the verb referring to those who are being sanctified–*hagiazomenous*–which is a present continuous tense but it needs to be remembered that people from every generation until the return of Christ, need to have this perfection applied to them continually; Christ's work is complete even if its application is continuous.

vv. 15–17 "*And the Holy Spirit also witnesses to us, for after he had said, 'This is the covenant I will make with them after those days says the Lord: I will put my laws on their hearts and I will write them on their minds and their sins and their lawless acts I will no longer remember.'*" The words, which are originally the words of the prophet Jeremiah in chapter 31, have already been seen in part in 8:8–12. Here they are ascribed to the Holy Spirit. This same procedure has already been used in 3:7 where the words of the Psalmist in 95:7–11 are attributed to the Holy Spirit. Again, the words in verse 16 are slightly different than in 8:10. Some of the differences have deep significance while others do not. Firstly, the quotation commences with "*This is the covenant.*" It is now in place. All that was foretold in the earlier has been accomplished. In the earlier quotation the emphasis was upon God making the promise of a new covenant in the future, which would bring about a new relationship with his people. Now the emphasis is upon the fact that the promise has been fulfilled and this new relationship is operative, meaning that everything that is related to worship and the heart of the worshipper is already different. There is no need any longer, to live in the land of shadows, symbols and types. The believer's sins have been forgiven and forgotten under this new covenant made by Jesus.

The second difference is that the author has changed what will transpire in terms of the hearts and minds but the overall meaning is not changed in any sense because the two are used interchangeably in Scripture and this is a well-known methodology, especially in the parallelism of Psalms. The significance of the work of the Spirit here is that the internalization of God's will has become a reality in the lives of all who are under this new covenant. Ceremonies and rituals are no longer of importance, unless they are ordered by the Word of God such as baptism and the Holy Communion. Finally, the sin question has been totally dealt with by the unique sacrifice of Christ, which leads us to the words of the next verse.

v. 18 *"Now where there is forgiveness of these, there is no longer offering for sin* [required]*."*

The new covenant has already provided the forgiveness which was sought through all the multiple offerings of the past, under the first covenant but which were never fully acquired. Now that it is in place, there is no more place for any further attempts to satisfy God in this way. Sin offerings are a thing of the past. This new High Priest has provided all that could ever be required. Up to now the author has underlined the fact that those who worship God, as followers of this High Priest, are fully sanctified (v.10) and consequently perfected (v.14) and fully forgiven (v.18).[8] All of these factors would have been impossible under the first covenant.

This verse brings the reader to the end of the theological arguments related to the Old and New covenants and the superior person and state of the new High Priest, who is Christ.

Encouragement to Worship, Faith and Perseverance
10:19—12:29

Based upon all that he has said previously, the author sets out in this section to encourage his readers in the application of meaningful worship, which all that has gone before now facilitates; this is so that the benefits will become real (10:19–25). This encouragement is followed by a stern warning (10:26–31) and a call to remember the past and act accordingly (10:32–39). The

8. See Ellingworth, *Hebrews*, 90.

entire section from verse 19–25 in Greek, is one long sentence, although modern translations vary greatly, some breaking it into as many as seven. The way in which the author presents this section, demonstrates a significantly entreating attitude, in which he identifies himself with his readers using terms like "let us . . ." and "brothers". Spicq suggests that it may well be that rather than having the intention throughout this epistle of teaching his readers, the author is far more concerned with encouraging them.[9] Obviously, that encouragement has the purpose of immediate and ongoing changes in attitude and behavior because of what the outcomes may and should be.

A New and Living Way to worship 10:19–25

vv. 19–20 "Now therefore brothers, since we have confidence to enter in to the holy of holies by the blood of Jesus, which he opened up for us, a recent and living way through the curtain, that is through his flesh" The "therefore" is dependent upon all that has been written up to this point including the theological argument relative to Christ's High Priestly activity. The author, as already mentioned in the introduction to this section, uses more inclusive and gentler language in his approach to his readers here, calling them brothers. This is by no means the first time he has written in this manner (3:1, 12 & 6:9). *Since we have confidence,* shows that he included himself within the group of those who have this confidence; the confidence which was never an option for the worshippers under the first covenant, is now certain for all participants under this new covenant because of the blood of Jesus. The nature of this confidence (*parrēsia*) has already been seen as early as 3:6 (see notes) and is mentioned again later in verse 35 relative to the believer's reward. Its presence indicates courage and boldness because all doubt and inability have been replaced by absolute certainty under this new covenant.[10] It is the same boldness, which according to Paul, gives the believer access to God (Eph. 3:12) and so certainly means the very same thing as here, where the holy of holies in the heavens is the goal of one's entry to participate in the worship of God. This is the place of the presence of God and not the copy in the earthly tent where only the Aaronic High Priests were qualified to enter.

The Greek word *enkainizō* (here in the aorist), translated as part of the phrase *"which he opened up for us"* means, to inaugurate something or to make something possible. Again, the author includes himself in the

9. Spicq, *Hébreux*, II. 315.

10. For more on the breadth of meanings of *parrēsia* see Arndt & Gingrich, 635.

benefits available to his readers when he uses "*us*." Christ has made this way, providing the entry through the curtain which here is pictured as his own flesh. There is considerable debate among scholars as to the meaning here of "*through the curtain, that is through his flesh*." The first part of the difficulty is, in what way is the curtain to be understood here? Usually, it is understood as a barrier to the Holy of Holies. If that is what it means here, then when it is linked to the body of Jesus it would infer that his earthly body was a barrier to the heavenly sanctuary. However, there is nothing to indicate that while he was on earth, Jesus was in any way limited in the communion he enjoyed with the Father in heaven, so this is unlikely. One other possibility here is that the curtain does not represent a barrier to the author but rather the route to "the way." After all, when the High Priest entered into the Holy of Holies annually, the curtain was no barrier to him. In other words, once it is opened there is a clear path to the presence of God. If this is the correct sense, by his sacrifice, Christ becomes the direct way to opening the curtain in a manner which is similar to him being the door/ gate in John's Gospel (John 10:7, 9).

We know that at the death of Christ, the veil between the inner and outer sanctuaries was rent in two, indicating the removal of any barrier to the presence of God (Matt 27:51). Since the *curtain* and the *body* of Christ are identified here in connection with the new and living way, then it makes good sense to understand this phrase in terms of the sacrifice of the body of Christ being the means by which the barrier between God and man is removed. Christ's humanity made all this possible. Without it there would have been no acceptable sacrifice for mankind. Chapter 2 has already established the need for his incarnation. The body of Christ and its offering to God, create a new and living way. If the curtain was the barrier, then when the sacrifice was made, it was removed. After all, the author has just said that the blood of Jesus opened up this recent living way.

Most translations have rendered the Greek *prosphaton,* in the phrase: "a new and living way" by the English word as: "a new." It is a word which appears only here in the New Testament and has the sense of something that is recent or which was not previously available.[11] It is clearly meant to differentiate this covenant with the previous one because Jesus alone is the one who made it possible. In addition, not only is it recent but it is a living way. This is because Jesus is alive and is constantly available as intercessor on behalf of all his own. Again, it is living because it is ongoing in its

11. Arndt & Gingrich. 726. Originally the word had the sense of something that had just been killed but it took on the sense of something that was recent or new. It occurs in LXX, Ps 80:9 (English 81:9 where it is translated "strange") Eccl 1:9 "nothing new under the Sun."

efficacy. Spicq proposes that this new and living way is dependent upon faith or grace.[12] Certainly, both of those factors are primary in making Christ's work available to his followers and the benefits depend totally upon this sacrifice. We know that followers of Jesus were known as those of "The Way," in the earliest days of the Early Church (Acts 9:2; 19:9, 23; 24:14, 22), which is not surprising as Jesus declared in John's Gospel (14:6) that he was *"the way, the truth and the life."* This metaphor would certainly go together with the symbolism present here where the subject is access to the heavenly tabernacle and that Jesus is the only one who makes this way available. But here the way is primarily the provision or the means of access, which Christ has made available for entry into the presence of God but it could also be pictured as Jesus himself.

v. 21 *"and having a great high priest over the household of God"* Jesus is here called a Great High Priest as he was previously in 4:14. His greatness is evident in the fact that he is the only man to ever enter the Holy Place permanently and that through the offering of his own blood. Of course, all the other factors related to his priesthood have already been described in the course of the letter and the fact that not only is he the perfect man but also the Son of God who is presently seated at the right hand of the Majesty on high, adds to his greatness. The language here recalls what was stated in 3:2–6, first of Moses being over God's community and then of the Son, who was both faithful and being over the house. The house here, as there, represents God's people. Here this Great High Priest is most definitely in charge of God's house and all its people.

v. 22 *"let us draw near with a true heart in full assurance of faith, having had our hearts sprinkled (clean) from an evil conscience and our bodies washed with pure water."* As was seen as early as 4:1, the exhortative style of the author is nothing new but here it becomes the focus of this long sentence from verse 19, where three times the readers are encouraged to immediate and forthright action: *"let us draw near,"* which he has already stated earlier (see 4:16), *"let us hold fast"* (v.23) and *"let us consider how to stir up one another to love and good works"* (v.25). This drawing near to God is part of the new way just described above. It was not possible previously but now that Christ has made this access possible it should not be neglected. The whole context of approaching God during the Levitical system was pictured in terms of worship. To grant God his proper place, something that had been lost from the time of Adam, the restorative work of Christ was required. This means that the relationship which was lost, now is found. Worship is no longer a ritual which follows outward ceremony but is the means of

12. Spicq, *Hébreux,* II. 315.

giving back one's life to God in totality and enjoying what was intended by God from the start in a very intimate and genuine manner. This verse is encouraging the reader to participate fully in this renewed relationship with God in his heavenly sanctuary.

To do what is required in this approach there are a number of conditions: First, the heart of the follower of Christ has to be one which exhibits truth or sincerity. Show or pretense is not going to suffice. Sincerity demonstrates the reality of the individual's actual state. Second, there has to be an attitude of full assurance of faith. The phrase which translates "*in full assurance of faith*" (*en plērophoria pisteōs*) goes with the boldness or confidence mentioned in verse 19 but the full assurance of faith, is what opens the door to the reality of the communion between God and man. Faith here, is similar to the hope described in 6:11; so; there is little difference in the outcomes since both originate from the same verbal stem in Greek (*pis*) and have a similar thrust because in the New Testament, hope is based on faith. The nature of the faith is going to be developed considerably in the next chapter but here it is a necessary part of this new relationship. Third, "*having had our hearts sprinkled (clean) from an evil conscience.*" This is the work of the Holy Spirit.

Under the Levitical order, the sprinkling of blood upon the altar and the mercy seat was required to bring about the redemption and forgiveness necessary for forgiveness (see 9:7). However, here the ceremony is replaced by hearts submissive to God and consciences which have been purified. The significance of the inner man and the conscience have already been indicated (see notes on 9:8–9, 14). This cleansing has to result in an inward and moral renewal which aligns the individual with the purposes of God. The expression "sprinkled" indicates more than merely getting wet. It speaks of enacting a cleansing process and it is for that reason that in the translation here "clean" is added; it is not redundant but indicates the result brought about by the sprinkling. Fourth, "*and our bodies washed with pure water.*" Most scholars accept that this is a reference to water baptism. After all, the ritual washings of the priests prior to their engagement in the sacrificial offerings are well known (Exod 29:4; 40:3–32). Nevertheless, the way in which this is to be understood is not without difficulty.

All the previous conditions are inward and spiritual. Would it not now be contradictory to say that this outward rite of water baptism has to be fulfilled prior to the believer's entry to the heavenly sanctuary? Water baptism is certainly enjoined upon believers in scripture (Matt 28:19) and assumed to have been the norm (see Acts 2:38). This is something, the importance of which is often disregarded by many Protestants in the Western Church today. Any careful examination of texts such as that in Romans 6:3–4 result in the conclusion that all believers in the Early Church were baptized as soon as they understood the meaning of the decision they had taken to follow Christ. It would appear that rather than look at the question here as that of an outward action, it has to be considered as the consequence of an inward one, where inward change results in outward action. This means that it is viewed as the heart leading to an act of obedience and identification with Christ. In Ephesians 5:26, a verse also in the context of Christ's sacrifice on behalf of the church, Paul writes about the church being washed with water but then adds that this cleansing is identified with the word. This would mean that the word is the instrument the Holy Spirit uses to bring about a change in heart and that, in turn, leads to a new way of thinking and behaving. Similarly, in Ezekiel 36:25–27 Yahweh tells Israel: "*I will sprinkle clean water upon you and you shall be clean from all your uncleannesses . . . and I will cleanse you. A new heart I will give you, and a new spirit I will put within you; and I will remove from your body the heart of stone and give you a heart of flesh. I will put my spirit within you.*" (NRSV) There is no doubt in these verses, that what is promised is the work of the Holy Spirit who resides within and who actively changes the optic as well as the spiritual understanding of the individual far beyond anything that could be enacted by mere rites. This latter text most certainly aligns completely with the promise made in Jeremiah 31:31–34, which is behind the promise made here to the Hebrews from 8:9 and reaffirmed in 10:16–17. Whatever, the meaning here relative to the washing of bodies with pure water, the thinking and the resultant actions are intertwined so that the cleansing is an internal factor brough about by the Holy Spirit, just as the verses noted have promised.

v. 23 "*Let us hold fast the confession of our hope without wavering for the one who promised is faithful.*" This verse returns to the exhortation initiated in the previous passage. It is not the first time that the author has emphasized the importance of this steadfastness or grasping hold of something with all one's strength (3:6, 14). It is apparent from all that was stated earlier, as well as what is repeated here, that there is great uncertainty on the part of the readers.

The Greek *aklinē* (unwavering) demonstrates that there is a lot of *wavering* present in the minds of the readers. This word is another of those used only here in the New Testament. Christians cannot have a shaky faith. There has to be certainty and not doubt. Those who go back and forth are those who do not manifest true hope in the one who is their Great High Priest; they live in this shaky state. They cannot therefore, have certainty in what it is that they believe and what faith means in their day to day lives. They are told that they have to hold fast to this confession of their hope and this is only possible if the confidence (*parrēsia*) which was mentioned in verse 19 is real and present. Confession here, is much more than verbal assent, although it is certain that open verbal confession is clearly part of belief and needs to be made boldly and unashamedly. It needs to be manifest in an open lifestyle which confirms what it is that is hoped for. It is the certitude which stands behind any verbalization of what one believes. The same must be said regarding the full assurance of faith, discussed in the previous verse, which here must be worked out, not just in a verbal confession of hope but in a demonstration of one's entire lifestyle. Faith is usually directed in specific areas but here the confession of hope, which is under review, is inclusive of all that God has promised. So, it is all that the teaching of the Christian faith means and stands for (as in Jude *v.3*). It is in this instance, far broader than faith because it incorporates all that God has planned for the future, including all of which believers are yet ignorant; this holds true even where parts of this divine plan have already been revealed in Scripture in sufficient detail to grant light and encouragement which enable believers to continue practicing their beliefs, even if that is in an imperfect manner.[13] The assurance of hope does not depend upon the individual alone. Now that the Holy Spirit resides within and has become the one who enables all to take place, it should be natural that followers of Christ should be able to place their full trust and hope in God who made the promises which have been fulfilled. In fact, the next chapter is an extension on the matter of faith and God's faithfulness.

vv. 24–25 "*And let us consider how to stir up one another to love and good works not neglecting to meet together, as is the habit of some, but encouraging each other and even more so as you see the Day drawing near.*" This verse commences with the second exhortation which is concerned with "*let us consider . . . one another.*" The confession involves a passionate conviction which leads to involvement in such a manner that it is not possible to avoid being taken up, not only with God but with those who are of the household of faith. One's faith cannot be confessed or declared in isolation and because, as was stated in the previous verse, it has to be more than words, it is demonstrated in actions. This consideration is one which encourages provocation but of the right kind. Usually, provocation is considered in a negative way (3:8) but here it is to provoke what is good and positive.

13. The full comprehension of what all the revelation of God in scripture means with regards the future is only going to be possible after the *Parousia* of Christ and the completion of the new creation. But there is sufficient information in the present for followers of this revelation to be able to live in such a manner that they conform to the will of God in the present age. There is no excuse for believers to ignore what is already clearly known and is now part of their present hope.

This is stirring up fellow believers to three specific actions: Love, good works, and in gathering together. This appears to demonstrate that the right kind of behavior is not necessarily going to happen automatically in every case among Christians. There has to be direction and encouragement given through teaching and example. The gathering of believers together is also a necessary part of Christian worship because it is only when this gathering takes place that correction and admonition can take place.[14] It must be remembered that when this letter was written, the circumstances of the present day, would not have been in place. People lived in close proximity to each other. They would gather in each other's homes and not travel long distances to attend a place of worship as many do today. Life was very much lived in close communities, so that not only did people worship in community, they lived their social lives in the same communities. In this way it was considerably easier to know what was happening in other people's lives. When people needed counsel and admonition it happened in the gatherings where openness prevailed in every area. Love was practical in terms of help and concern, the sharing of food and involvement in other people's difficulties such as comfort at times of bereavement and contributions where people lived in poverty. This was what was regarded as real fellowship.[15] Good works were the fruit of love. The last element here is related to the gathering together of believers. It would appear that this gathering is for more than social reasons but for worship. The word *episunagōgē* means merely the gathering together of the believers, in spite of what some scholars have tried to extract from its presence in this verse.[16] The readers are specifically told that they should not stop gathering together. There may be reasons why this was the case. There were times when the political authorities were anxious to identify all who were followers of this illegal

14. Any thought that worship in front of a TV or by means of recent forms of media would be satisfactory to the demands of this verse, could never be considered as meeting the criteria which are inherent here for needing to gather physically, even if in some circumstances today they are the only means of understanding what fellowship is for individuals in isolation.

15. This kind of fellowship is still practiced in many majority world nations and especially in rural contexts where many of the social aspects of life are orchestrated by and from the local churches. Obviously, proximity is a major factor in facilitating such behavior. In Western nations where many travel long distances or miles/kilometers to their normal places of worship, this aspect becomes more difficult. Also, in mega churches where people seldom know their fellow believers in any depth, apart from those in any cell group to which they belong, this sort of behavior is immediately rendered difficult.

16. For some of the different views on the meaning of this word in this verse see Hughes, *Hebrews*, "Note on the Meaning of *episunagōgē* (10:25)," 417–18.

sect (*religio ilicita*)[17] and therefore to be identified as a member could prove dangerous. Others may have grown tired of attending and may have been put off by the presence of non-Jews who met with them. It is unclear exactly what the reasons were.

One thing is clear and that is active community is essential to vibrant faith; isolation is not part of Christian life and when the gatherings took place there was to be exhortation. Exhortation is any sort of encouragement to the right kind of behavior and belief. As already stated, exhortation to the right kind of conduct has just been recommended when it comes to helping those in need. Here that could include contributing toward physical or social needs but it could also be because there was hesitancy in faith and belief. The qualifying addition *"even more so as you see the Day drawing near"* has to be understood as referring to the Day of the Lord as that was a common theme in early literature and "the day" or something very similar, is found referring to the same day elsewhere in the New Testament (Acts 2:20; Rom 13:12; 1 Cor 3:13; 1 Thess 5:2; 2 Thess 2:2 et al.). There is the thought among some scholars that there may have already been indications in Judea at that time, of the disruptions that led to the destruction of the temple in AD 70 and that was what was in the author's mind here.[18] But it is more likely that the coming of the Lord or the *Parousia*[19] is what was the matter foremost in the author's thinking because that was the day of hope for all followers of Christ. However, the day of the Lord is not only a day of hope for the faithful it is also a day of judgement; therefore, all needed to be prepared for that day.

A dire warning regarding willful sin 10:26–31

This is an ideal juncture to introduce an urgent warning where *the Day of the Lord* has just been mentioned. It may well be that the threat of deserting the gatherings normally held by believers, has become the launch pad for this next section.

17. Under Roman law certain religions were legal *(religio licita)* and others illegal *(religio illicita)*. Judaism was legal but once the authorities identified Christians as not being part of what they understood as the Jewish faith, they were regarded as illegal.

18. For more on this aspect see Bruce, *Hebrews*, 256.

19. The *Parousia* is the technical Greek word which indicates the second coming of Christ.

v. 26 *"For when we go on sinning[20] willfully,[21] after receiving the full knowledge of the truth, there no longer remains a sacrifice for sins."* Warnings relative to indifference and apostasy have already been given from the earliest in this epistle (2:1–3.; 3:12; 4:1–7; and most recently in 6:4–6; see *Appendix C*). As hinted at in the introduction to the section above, it is appropriate that having spoken of the dangers associated with the failure to gather and exhort one another on a regular basis, is the fact of the return of Christ and the Day of the Lord. This event, even if its fulfilment is doubted by many in church circles today, is certain in spite of the fact that millennia have passed since it was promised. This Day is one when God's action will be seen by all. This action will be evident on the one hand in the granting of grace and mercy to his own but on the other hand, it will be a day of retribution for all who have turned their backs on his call to change. This is especially so for those have had total disregard toward Christ's person after having benefited from his pardon. Eschatology is not developed greatly in this epistle but the aspect of retribution is most certainly not excluded.

The warning here is one of deliberate sin. In the original language the word relative to the deliberate nature of the sin (*ekousiōs*–deliberately) is the first in the Greek sentence, which adds weight to its importance; it is followed by a present participle meaning: *"continually go on sinning"* (*hamartanontōn*). The construction shows that the individual is indifferent of or completely uncaring about the sin for which he or she is guilty; its practice is an act of rebellion yet the person deliberately continues to engage in it, in spite of the knowledge that it is wrong. Under the Old Testament sins which were committed in ignorance could be atoned for (Num 15:27–29) but as already stated, if anyone acted in a "high-handed" or deliberate manner, then there was no atoning for their sin (Num 15:30–31). In this verse the author emphasizes the fact that someone who has received full knowledge of the truth, meaning that they have comprehended what their faith is all about and who then goes back on that earlier decision, is the one who is in mind here. Such individuals had been taught and understood the significance of the message they had embraced concerning Christ. There must have been a well-established body of truth available in Christian circles by that time, so that it would have been impossible for followers of Christ to have claimed ignorance in this regard.[22] Consequently, anyone

20. *Hamartanontōn* is a present participle which therefore shows that the action or presence of sin is ongoing.

21. *Ekousiōs* the adverb from *ekōn* showing spontaneity and customary behavior here.

22. The matter of the nature of this body of material is irrelevant. It does not matter whether it was an oral or literary body. On this "definable body of doctrine" see

who had made a decision to follow Christ and then subsequently rejected his message, could not expect that there would be any possibility of the remission of their sins. Such rejection is an indication of blatant apostasy. This is the same message that has already been openly declared in similar terms in 6:4–6. Anyway, in spite of the great debate related to "the unpardonable sin," any rejection of the truth related to Christ on the part of those who previously embraced it, must most certainly fit, whatever that phrase conjures up in one's mind.

v. 27 *"But a fearful expectation of judgement and a fury of fire that is about to consume the adversaries."* The result of this kind of behavior is described in this verse so that all should understand the alarming but not exaggerated terms. If the first covenant had severe and drastic punishment for the blatant sinner, the thought must be, how much more for the person who has embraced the truth of the second and subsequently rejected it? This text does not describe the nature of the judgment, other than that it is executed with a passion on God's part. The phrase "the fury of fire" is a rendition of the original "the zeal of fire" (*puros zēlos*) or "fiery zeal" (see the notes on 12:29). It is intended to demonstrate God's anger and most likely the indication of great pain and anguish which is to come upon the guilty parties. Judgement, in the sense of absolute condemnation and punishment, is certain for all apostates and those who continue to sin knowingly. The concept of the judgment is evident in the progressive manner in which it is emphasized over the following verses. To reject Christ's sacrifice, is to knowingly invite upon oneself the judgement that is required by God for sin; that is what happens here. The rejection of Christ and his offer is totally illogical. What makes this judgement even more drastic, is the fact that the person has gone from being a believer, who had their sins covered by the sacrifice of Christ, to being an unbeliever with no possibility of any mercy; this about turn, is all as a consequence of their own deliberate decision and rebellion. Judgement has already been determined as stated in 9:27 but the outcome of that judgement here, is due to the individual's own choice. It is because they have rejected the light they previously had.

The language our author uses here regarding the fury of fire, recalls passages such as Deut 4:24 *"For the Lord your God is a devouring fire,"* (see also Deut 9:3; Isa 26:11; 33:14) being evident in the use of the expression the "zeal of fire" in this passage. This underlines the fire of God's passion on the day of his wrath (Zeph 1:18).[23] It is inescapable and inevitable for all who

---

Guthrie, *Hebrews*, 219.

23. The cleansing role of fire is also present in the work of the Holy Spirit as promised by John the Baptist (Matt 3:11 & Luke 3:16).

have behaved in this way. The force of the simile where fire is used, cannot be escaped.

vv. 28–29 "Anyone who disregarded the Law of Moses dies without compassion on the word of two or three witnesses. How much worse do you think the punishment will be deserved, by the one who has trampled underfoot the Son of God and has considered the blood of the covenant by which he was sanctified, profane and has outraged the Spirit of grace?" The entire thrust of the presentation here in this warning is to show that, if under the Mosaic regime the rejection of God's conditions were ignored, there were severe consequences, how much greater will be the punishment of those who blatantly disobey this final and perfect offer in Christ's sacrificial work?

The author points out an example taken from the Law of Moses and specifically from Deuteronomy 17:6, where the context is concerned with someone who worships other gods. The sin is therefore a matter of idolatry in the midst of the congregation. Provided that there is sufficient evidence to prove the matter of guilt, meaning that there needed to be at least two people, if not three, who could verify the charge, then the perpetrator is put to death by stoning. Another case worthy of the death penalty is given in that same chapter (Deut 17:12).

If therefore, under the first covenant, this strict retribution for rebellion was judged in such a severe manner, how much greater will be any retribution for this greater failure? The question is put in terms of, *"How much worse do you think the punishment will be . . .?"* For a start, the first punishment is the loss of earthly life. What could be worse than that? It is implicit that it is eternal life that will be lost. The nature of the death is also implicit from what has just been said in the previous verses, where God's anger is exhibited in fiery condemnation, picturing not just death but pain and agony. The descriptor used for punishment is the Greek word *timōria;* it is another of the words used by this author which is not found anywhere else in the New Testament but which specifies punishment related to general judgement and condemnation. It is the consequence of the latter. The duration of this punishment is not something that is dealt with here.

The reason for the punishment is given as having been guilty of three major offences: First, having *"trampled underfoot the Son of God."* To trample someone underfoot is to treat them with total contempt. It is to declare that they have absolutely no value and it is also the same as declaring that you are far superior to them in every way. Since Jesus is the one who is the subject of this action it can be assumed that those who are guilty of this kind of action were at one time submissive to him but have become antagonistic to the degree that they now are not just indifferent but have become his open enemies. This understanding of the meaning of apostasy, certainly would be justified by the wording here. Declaring war on God can only be considered as the greatest of follies possible for anyone. Second, the guilty have *"considered the blood of the covenant by which he was sanctified, profane."* Those who have blatantly turned away from Christ, ignore the fact that they were previously sanctified or set apart because of Christ's blood poured out on their behalf. After all, it was this blood offering, which was the means of bringing in the new covenant that has already been demonstrated to be far superior to anything that existed under the first. But worse than that, they now consider this blood sacrifice *profane.* The way in which the word can be understood, profane means something that is common and of no particular significance or worse yet, as something that is not holy and therefore without any divine function or authority. It is therefore, treated with equal disdain as treading Christ underfoot. To do this would be equivalent to rejecting the entire new covenant.

Finally, these same people have *"outraged the Spirit of grace."* Again, we have another word that is found nowhere else in the New Testament. *Enubrizō* is found elsewhere in the literature of the day and translated as either *to insult* or *outrage* someone. Here the one who is outraged is the Spirit of grace[24] or the Holy Spirit, who is the one who brings about the incorporation of an individual into the people of God when they repent and believe in Christ. Obviously, to outrage him is to cut oneself off from the grace that he grants and when that happens, forgiveness, as well as spiritual life itself, is impossible. The result is the same as that Jesus warned of in Matthew 12:31, when the Pharisees accused him of doing miracles by the power of the devil. He told them, in as many words, that to associate the work of Christ with the devil is to blaspheme against the Holy Spirit and for that there is no forgiveness. Once the Spirit's grace is withdrawn there is no hope for anyone, only the certainty of condemnation. To outrage the Spirit of God is to immediately distance oneself from any possibility of forgiveness or salvation and to pit him against you with drastic outcomes.

There is nothing to actually say that there are among the readers, those who have gone as far as to be guilty of the above behavior. However, it is evident from the nature of the presentation that the danger of doing so is real. If not, the warning need not have been included in this epistle. In addition, the fact that similar warnings are repeated, appears to justify the fact that there may well be those who are treading a fine line and who need to

---

24. This is the only place in the New Testament where the Holy Spirit is directly called the Spirit of Grace.

be reminded of the impending danger if there is not some radical change in thinking and behavior and that without delay.

v. 30 "*For we know Him who said 'Vengeance is mine. I will repay.' And again 'The Lord will judge his people.'*" At this point the author quotes from two verses in Deut 32:35, 36 where Yahweh speaks to Israel through Moses in a context which is primarily directed at Israel's disobedience and their being deserving of God's punishment. He includes himself in the address as he has done earlier, when he says, "*For we know Him who said.*" He still sees the readers of his letter as valid members of the community and not outsiders, which may appear strange in the light of the harsh things he is saying. The first adaptation of the quotation is from Deut 32:35, which states, "*Vengeance is mine, I will repay*" and the second from verse 36, "*The Lord will judge his people.*"[25] Here the main thought is that God himself, as the one who is offended, will most certainly do what is right in the end. Again, no one is going to escape their just reward because God is the Just Judge. Judgment has two aspects: reward for the upright who have embraced God's mercy and received his pardon and then retribution for the wicked who have turned away and shunned his offer. In the final, the judgement of God has to do with redressing everything that is out of order and replacing it with the perfection which alone is ultimately good enough for the proper functioning of his eternal kingdom. For those who have benefited from the light and gift of God only to turn away and shun all at the end, there is certainty of a greater degree of punishment because with greater knowledge, comes greater responsibility. This brings the matter to a conclusion in the next verse.

v. 31 "*It is a fearful thing to fall into the hands of the living God.*" Fear is a matter which is frequently referred to in the epistle (2:15; 4:1; 11:23, 27; 12:21: 13:6). This is often because of the consequences of going against the will and person of God. On the other hand, boldness and fearlessness is also an attribute of those who trust in God and do not fear man (13:6). In the context of this verse fear is the outcome of dissent and flagrant disobedience.

---

25. The form of words used here in the first part of the quotation, is the same as that used by Paul in Romans 12:19 but with different contexts in mind. Scholars point out that the form used here is similar to what is found in the Jewish Targums of Onkelos and the Samaritan Pentateuch, rather than in the LXX, which reads "I will repay in the day of vengeance" and more like the Hebrew in the Masoretic text, which reads "Vengeance is mine, and recompense." Shrenk, in *TDNT* II, 446n4, thinks that there may have been a Greek translation which is not the same as the LXX, in existence at that time and that may have been the source of some of the differences in what we perceive as today's LXX. It is possible that there was a well-known version in circulation at the time which both authors are using.

The expression "*to fall into the hands of the living God*" refers to becoming subject to Yahweh, who unlike all the gods of the nations, is the one True God and who is Living not dead. He has already been given this title in 3:12 (see notes) and 9:14. Because of who he is, he is able to enact whatever judgment he pleases. Those who reject him while they are living, will come face to face with him in the future; according to the Revelation of John, every person will receive their just reward (Rev 22:12). This means however, that the unbelievers and all who have not been covered by the pardon of Christ's sacrifice, receive their just recompense in the lake of fire, which is the second death (Rev 21:8). When David sinned against God in the numbering of the people, he was given three choices regarding the way in which he should be judged (2 Sam 24:12). In a state of distress and repentance he responded: "*let us fall into the hand of the Lord for his mercy is great*" (2 Sam 24:14). David recognized the justice and mercy of God in the midst of judgment. The lesson there, is that God certainly does what is right and if someone deserves it, punishment will certainly be meted out to them but at the same time, God is a merciful God as well as being just. Therefore, whatever happens will be appropriate. However, the wicked will not escape the hand of the living God, even if they think they will and, in their case, that will result in terrible punishment.

Remember the past; never go back but press on 10:32–39

As in the earlier section where warning required clear language on the part of the author to underline the dangers associated with lax behavior (6:4–8) there was a gentler approach which followed, calling for diligence (6:9–11); so too here, the harsh words are followed by encouragement to continual steadfastness.

v. 32 "*But remember the former days when, after you were enlightened, you endured a great struggle with sufferings.*" The first thing is the importance of remembering. The word which the author uses (*anamimnēskō*), is found only here in the letter; it has the sense of reminding someone about something; so, it is focused on recalling things from the past. Here the readers are called upon to specifically remember the former days, when they were enlightened. The subject of enlightenment has already been dealt with in 6:4–6 (see notes). It speaks here of having the light of God awaken within the individual, the truth of the message of Christ; this is so as to embrace its Savior as Lord and Redeemer. When it comes to what has happened in the past, people tend to have selective memories; the pleasant ones are first to surface but here it is apparent that when these Hebrew believers first turned to Christ, they must have suffered considerable opposition and persecution. The language (former days or first days) implies that the readers of this epistle had been followers of Christ for some time and were not new converts. The word describing the nature of the struggle is only found here in the New Testament and is the word from which we get the English *athletic;* in Greek it is *athlēsis.* So, there was an "athletic struggle" going on; this caused the suffering that resulted. They had endured opposition but if we look at what is written later in 12:4 they had not spilled blood and there had been no martyrs among them. Bruce says that this would rule out their having been from Jerusalem because from the death of Stephen to the death of James the Just (Acts 12:2) at the time of the high priest Annas in AD 62 there had been martyrs in that city. Also, as early as the reign of Nero in AD 64, Christians had been martyred in the stadia at Rome; that would then eliminate the readers being from there.[26] That is, unless the letter was written earlier than AD 64, which is unlikely. It is not clear which specific events may have been the cause of our author's comments here. All that is clear, is that these Jewish converts to Christ had suffered considerably and endured under persecution of one kind or another at that time.

v. 33 *"You were exposed[27]to both reproaches and persecutions and became partners of those who conducted themselves like that."* In this verse the specific nature of the suffering is described. The word translated "exposed" (*theatrizomai* only found here in the New Testament) has the sense of being portrayed as part of some theatrical or public display. In this context the abuse in the form of verbal reproaches (plural of *oneidismos.* See 11:26; 13:13) and physical persecution results from this open display. The use of the word "reproach" is often associated with the reproaches of Christ as in Romans 15:3 where partnership with Christ is similar to what is apparent here and what is encouraged from believers. Here, this reproach is in the context of becoming partners with those who are of like faith and not being ashamed of what it is for which they stand. Again, these reproaches are accompanied by some sort of physical tribulation (*thlipsis*). The word used for this trial is common throughout the New Testament. The concept of being sharers (*koinōnoi*) or partners, in the sufferings of Christ is also well known (Phil 3:10) just as is fellowship among Christians in all circumstances (Acts 2:42; 2 Cor 8:4; Phil 1:5; 1 John 1:7). The concept of being sharers together with Christ has already been seen earlier in the epistle (see notes on 1:9; 3:14) and the thought of both sharers (*metochoi) and partners (koinōnoi*) is one. The identification with others of the same faith can easily lead to the

26. Bruce, *Hebrews,* 267.

27. See Josephus, *Antiquities,* 1, 47 & 20, 117.

same sort of reproach and suffering as those who are targeted by opponents and this is clearly what they had learned in the past. They had not been ashamed to identify with believers previously, even if it jeopardized their standing in society.

v. 34 "For you shared the sufferings of those in prison[28] *and you accepted with joy the seizing of your belongings knowing that you have a better and remaining possession."* The specifics of what has been mentioned previously are now enumerated upon (for more on the practicalities of sharing with those in prison see notes on 13:3). This partnership had led to suffering with those who had been imprisoned (See note below on the textual variants here). That means that in their fellowship with others, they had been identified with those who were in prison for their faith in Christ. There is no actual example of what this really meant but there was sympathy shown for those in prison. The Greek construction (*sunepathēsate,* the aorist of *sumpatheō*–the word from which we get the English: sympathy), indicates the most profound participation in the suffering of the imprisoned, although the word itself is usually translated as having compassion for or sympathizing with someone. Their pain and misfortune are born personally by their fellows. Likely this would refer to Christians visiting others in prison to encourage them and even to take them food.[29] This was no light matter. Imprisonment of Christians was not uncommon; much depended upon the particular views of local authorities in any area. It was not until much later that there may have been more of a blanket approach to what to do with Christians on the part of the Roman State.[30]

Part of this persecution included the seizure of their belongings. The circumstances of the way in which this was done is not mentioned. The

28. Some MSS have "in my bonds" (*tois desmois mou*) or imprisonment (including Aleph ℵ). It is considered that this came about because it was thought that since Paul was the author, he must have been referring to his own imprisonment. Consequently, it is believed that this reading must have originated from Alexandria which held strongly to the Pauline authorship of the epistle. The Greek NT (5th rev. ed.) has included *tois desmiois* (to those imprisoned) in its text as the most strongly supported reading with what is called the second degree of certainty {B}.

29. I have lived for long periods of my life working in nations such as these, where unless visitors, family or church members provide food to prisoners, they can starve to death.

30. There was local persecution of Christians in Rome at the time of Nero between 54–68 AD, followed by more general persecution under Marcus Aurelius between 161–180. Then there was a slight break with more persecution during the time of Decius 249–251 and Gallus 251–253; however, the worst period of persecution was instigated by Diocletian from about 303–11 because it became widespread throughout the Roman Empire.

fact is that they accepted it with joy. This would be the kind of reaction enjoined upon them by James in 1:2. Other Scriptures come to mind such as the words of Jesus in Matthew 5:10 which speak of the blessing of those who are persecuted for righteousness' sake because the kingdom of heaven is comprised of such. Again, in Luke 6:22 Jesus told his disciples that they were blessed when they were hated and reproached for the sake of the Son of Man because they could rejoice in the fact that they would have great reward in the future. This hope was certainly very real and evident during that time in the Early Church when Christians were treated with great antagonism by many in authority; often they had little to look forward to under their circumstances. Their better possession was the heavenly reward and it was very real to them.

v. 35 *"Therefore, do not throw away your confidence which has a great reward."* They have been called to look back to the days when they endured all treatment just described and remember how they were in fact joyous over the fact that they were counted worthy to suffer on behalf of Christ and his testimony. They went through it willingly but now have doubts. Are they going to throw it all away? No! The boldness they had was based upon the reality of their experience of Christ and faith in him. They must continue to manifest endurance and never give up. There is a great reward not only in the future but now; the verb "has" (*echei*) a great reward, is in the present tense showing that the reward has already started but they need to be tenacious if they want to participate in its completion. The race which they run is not yet complete and they will have run in vain if they give up at this point.

v. 36 *"For you need endurance so that when you have done the will of God you may obtain the promise."* Again, endurance, perseverance and clear purpose, are all part of what is necessary to carry out the will of God. Life is not simple and there are many times when it appears that everything is going in the wrong direction. But this does not indicate that one is abandoned by God and forgotten. This fact is underlined later in 13:5. The author emphasizes what is needed: endurance. Some translations have used *patience* to render this word (*hupomonē*)[31] but it is not the best, since endurance is in no manner passive and nowadays patience is mostly understood as just waiting for something to happen. However, patience is certainly also a part of the central thought. Perhaps the best rendition would include both words so: *patient endurance.* This is part of the life of faith and the demonstration of what it means to trust God, even when things do not appear to add up. The doing of God's will, is the purpose of all who follow Christ. That was what Christ

---

31. *Makrothumia* and *hupomonē* are in many ways similar and both give the idea of perseverance, endurance and patience. See 6:12; 12:1.

did in coming to earth to pay for the sin of man. This *will of God* which needs to be enacted by all, differs for each individual but it is in carrying it out that the true worship of God is fulfilled. It has already been seen that Christ came to do this will of God (10:7–10); his total obedience to the Father was manifested throughout his lifetime. The proof of his fulfilment of this will, was his death upon the cross. The verses earlier in the chapter, demonstrate the endurance (*hupomonē*) of Christ who then becomes the example to follow for all who believe in him. If the totality of the promise is to be obtained, endurance is an absolute necessity because it enables the believer to maintain faith in God alone, in the face of all opposition. At the end of one's life, the reward is granted which is guaranteed by God through Christ.

vv. 37–38 "For yet a very little while and the one who is coming, will come and will not delay, but my righteous one will live by faith, and if he draws back my soul has no pleasure in him." These two verses are a combination of quotations from the Septuagint, mostly from a passage in Habakkuk 2:3–4 but including the briefest phrase from Isaiah 26:20 *"for a little time"* (a rather different phrase in the Greek, where there is a doubling up of the comparative *osos* is included: *"hide yourself for a very short time"–apokrubēthi mikron oson oson*). The author's inclusions are added and the text is applied differently here, targeting the readers of this letter. The thought from the original context (Isa 26:11, 20) is one of certain judgment coming and that God was going to act. But here the emphasis is of the coming reward. In the former text in Habakkuk, it was the vision that was to come at its appointed time but here it is *"the one who is coming,"* who is Christ. He too has an appointed time and when that moment in God's plans is right, nothing will be able to stop it. It is absolutely certain. This is a clear declaration of Christ's return and all within the context of the need for endurance on the part of his followers. The focus is the accomplishment of God's long-term promises. Therefore, both here and in the next verse, which speaks of destruction, this coming is associated with the settling of scores and making things right.

The next part of the quotation from verse 38, is one which is found twice elsewhere in Paul's writings in Rom 1:17 and Gal 3:11, to set out the theme of his entire argument that the only way to please God is by faith. This subject would also make it an apt introduction to the chapter which is to follow, as it emphasizes the significance of faith in the life of all believers. However, here the righteous one does not have reference to the Messiah, as in the original quotation. It needs to be remembered that the "one who is coming" in Old Testament thinking, was always the Messiah (see Matt 11:3). Here the righteous one, is the believer in Christ who lives by faith. Faith is the sign of the reality of any decision the follower of Jesus has to make and maintain. The next part of the declaration is that this follower has no room to draw back or give up the position he or she has previously held; there is no room to act in a way contrary to what was originally their descriptor. If there is a drawing back, God will show no pleasure in that individual. Once again, the warning is clear of the displeasure of God for the recalcitrant and backslider.

v. 39 "*But we are not of those who draw back and are destroyed but those who have faith to preserve their lives.*"[32] Once again, using inclusive terms in order to identify himself with the readers, the author says that "we are not of those who draw back." From 4:16 the emphasis was upon the ability of the individual to draw near to God through Christ. This is the opposite, where people draw back and leave the place of security in Christ; consequently, the outcome is their destruction because they lack faith. The result of drawing back is destruction (*apōleia*), not just the fact of being lost but total ruin and devastation. Destruction[33] is the recompense for all who are the enemies of Christ (Phil 3:19; 2 Pet 3:7). In Philippians 1:28 it is the opposite of the gift of salvation and eternal life for the believer. Destruction is what happens when God no longer has pleasure in someone (v.38) so they become subjects of his wrath. Note that destruction in the context does not mean annihilation but total ruin at a conscious level for eternity. In other scriptures it is included under eternal punishment (Matt 25:46; 2 Thess 1:9; Jude 1:7).

In the entire letter, warnings abound but there is no clear declaration, in spite of all of them, that anyone had actually gone too far in their behavior or that they had crossed the line when it came to their laxity of behavior and faith. Some appear to be very close to that position but there is still time for correction. It is important to note that the author is not denying the possibility that someone who has at some time followed Christ, could end up as one who has lost their faith and become retrograde. However, these Hebrews have not yet reached that point. Faith is necessary on a continual basis because it indicates that the believer is living in a state of perseverance, in a demonstrably active manner.

---

32. Note that *psuchē* in the Greek text which is normally translated "the soul" needs to be understood here as the life of the person and not just their soul or inner spiritual being.

33. Destruction (*apōleia* the accusative from the verb *apollumi*–to destroy or ruin) is the equivalent of rendering something totally useless, making it unfit for purpose, and bringing about its total ruination. In Scripture it often describes the nature of eternal punishment. It does not have the sense of annihilation or the cessation of existence in Scripture.

11.

Faith 11:1–40

The previous chapter ended with a strong emphasis upon the necessity of endurance in the Christian life. It has just been stated in the last verse and it needs to be remembered that chapters and verses are not part of the original biblical text and that these people are not those who draw back from Christ. In other words, it clarifies all that apostasy would mean for the unfaithful and the very different outcomes for those who have faith in God and his word. This is then the reason for the development of this entire subject in this chapter and in fact, is a development of how endurance is only possible when faith is at work.

Whenever, Jewish leaders of the past wanted to convey a point of importance to their audience, they tended to go back to the history within their own scriptures, in order to draw from them the foundational aspects which they wanted to establish. This methodology is especially clear from the narrative of Stephen before the council in Acts 7:2–53 but also in other passages such as the discourse of Peter on the day of Pentecost (Acts 2:14–21 and of Paul at the synagogue in Pisidian Antioch (Acts 13:16–41). This same methodology is followed by our author here, where he presents a catena of people and events related to Israel's history who illustrate lives of faith in the face of opposition and circumstances which appeared to be insurmountable. Spicq points out that it is remarkable in itself, that none of the original passages used in the citations given in this chapter, actually mention faith as the source of the individuals' success, so the way in which the author uses these citations is completely original to this writing.[1]

---

1. Spicq. *Hébreux*, II. 335. Obviously, this is due also, to the direction of the Holy

The purpose of the author in this chapter and its examples, is to demonstrate that people of faith from the days of the Hebrew scriptures and those of faith in the same God today, are the same and have the same requirements in terms of everyday life. There is one continuous link between the believers in the Old Testament and those who live under the New Covenant. They were faithful and enduring, just as believers today need to be. As the last verse of the chapter indicates, they had not yet received the promise, as those under the New Covenant have. But even those of the New Covenant have received the promise in part. Nevertheless, it is only collectively that those of the new and old can be made perfect or complete.

It should be noted that in spite of their faith, those of the former covenant did not acquire all that had been promised because the promise depended totally upon Christ and his fulfilling what was necessary to set everything in place through his incarnation and death. Therefore, despite the wonderful things which did take place because of their faith in the One who makes all possible, the future still beckoned. Faith together with belief, must continue to be part of the endurance of every believer until Christ's second coming.

Another important factor that needs to be underlined from this chapter, is the way in which the author presents his argument, using the names and identities of individuals from different periods of the biblical record. Their integration validates the historicity of the original narratives from which they are drawn, including the subjects which concern them.

The nature of faith: 11:1–3

v. 1 "*Now faith is the assurance of things hoped for, the proof of things not seen.*" Faith here, without an article, is the reality or assurance of things that are hoped for. It is not just something that is part of the Christian experience but also key to the lives of those who followed God in the Old Testament. This verse is not so much a definition of what faith is but rather what happens when faith is present. It brings about the reality of the thing which is hoped for. The faith here is directly associated with *hope* which, as already seen in 10:22, comes from the same verbal stem. The one works in tandem with the other. The NEB has translated this phrase "Faith gives substance to our hopes," meaning that when faith is present, something that has no existence in the present time, nevertheless becomes a reality. That means it becomes a reality in the mind and experience of the one who believes, whatever it is, that is hoped for. This is not some qualitative or mystical

---

Spirit in the formulation of the argument overall.

explanation as to the character of faith but the believer's indication of trust in a message given by God, which is therefore totally dependable and which can be accepted without any doubt.[2]

In Paul and John's writings people are called upon to believe in Christ or to place their faith in him; although the emphasis here is slightly different, the meaning is similar because the message of God through Christ is the same. In other words, God stands behind his message and validates it. It is not hope in hope or faith in faith that is called for but faith in the one who stands behind the message and who brings about what has been promised.[3] The word translated *reality* or *assurance* in Greek is *hypostasis*. It has a number of different connotations but basically it gives the understanding of something that is foundational.[4] *Hypostasis* has already been seen in this letter in 1:3 and 3:14. In the first reference it refers to the Son bearing the exact reality of the person of the Father, while in the second it is used in the context of the necessity to hold fast to the reality of all that is related to the foundation laid in Christ's person.

There is a parallelism between the two phrases which qualify the nature of faith here. Therefore, faith is both the:

"*assurance of things hoped for,* and
proof of things unseen."

This means that faith is assurance and proof of the thing that is unseen and hoped for. That thing in turn, either belongs to the future or the heavenly realm. The same link to the unseen is mentioned in verse 7, relative to the coming destruction of the flood. In the second strophe faith is the equivalent of proof, evidence or conviction (*elenchos*[5]) of what is not seen,

2. This may appear to have parallels with the teaching of the so called "Name it and claim it" teaching of the "Word of Faith" teachers but it is not the same. This is because it is not the proclaimed word of the believer which creates the thing sought after but the fact that the trust in God who has spoken is totally reliable and brings the matter to pass. Therefore, it is trust in God that is the important factor.

3. The so called, "word of faith message," of some groups is very different because it sees faith as having its own abstract existence. Biblical faith is only real because it is placed in God's divine person and word, since he is the One who brings into being what he has declared.

4. For four variants on its meaning see Hughes, *Hebrews*, 439–40; Moulton & Milligan give an array of meanings which they point out as "somewhat perplexing" but nevertheless present the idea of "something that *underlies* visible conditions and guarantees a future possession." *Hebrews*, 660.

5. Arndt & Gingrich, 248; Moulton & Milligan, *Vocabulary*, 202. Interestingly, the verb *elenchō* has the sense of bringing conviction as when someone shines a light on something, to show its true character (see Eph.5:11). To do this, the object under observation changes from being subjective to something absolute and therefore, evident

meaning that although the things which are not visible as yet, they will in the future become visible or tangible. This happens in the same way that the things that are hoped for will become real and take on existence. The unseen includes the entire domain which is presently beyond man's ability to grasp in terms of the present visible and physical world. It can, however, be hoped for in the light of knowing, only because trust in the God introduces a new dynamic and dimension (a heavenly one) in the heart of the believer. In theological terms, this is a true knowing of God or Gnosticism[6] because it is an experiential knowledge based on a relationship with God and not just an intellectual understanding.

To use the sort of language that the author of this epistle has already employed, it could be stated that faith is required in the period between the transmission of the promise in the word or message and its realization. The thing with which the faith is associated is brought about in the future (it may be almost instantaneously or some considerable time afterwards), according to God's timing. Faith keeps the hope alive in the heart of the believer until God brings it to pass. Furthermore, faith maintains the reality of the thing hoped for by the follower of God, in such a vivid way, that it is never doubted; its force enables the believer to continue in the face of all physical and natural phenomena which tend to deny the possibility of its promise being accomplished. The lists of people which follow give evidence to what this verse declares here.

v. 2 "For by it, men of old obtained commendation." The Greek phrase itself states that *"the elders obtained witness;"* this is because this faith was central to their lives and gave them the fortitude to persevere. The context of the chapter refers to those of old (*hoi presbuteroi* literally: the elders) who are mentioned in this section; they are not just any elders but the people of faith noted in this passage. They had witness born to them recommending their conduct and state of faith before God and man. There is no actual mention made in this text of God commending them, as some translations have recorded here, but in the context of the word of scripture as a whole and the inclusion of their names by the Holy Spirit, there is proof of the fact that God has commended them. In addition, what is written regarding Abel (v.4) indicates that God bore witness to his gifts so we can extrapolate from that comment, as well as from the context, that this divine witness applies

---

in the true sense, which demonstrates proof of whatever claims may be made. In this way, the unseen with which the faith agrees, is in this context, transformed into the object itself.

6. In Theology, Gnosticism is usually understood as a false teaching regarding knowledge leading to salvation but this kind of knowledge in Hebrews is experiential and based only on knowing the giver of life.

to all those in the list.[7] Interestingly enough, their names are included in what follows in chronological order, showing how, throughout history God has been active in the lives of his chosen ones, to bring about his purposes. All these people are his instruments and each one underlines the significance of faith.

v. 3 "By faith we understand the universe was created by the word of God so that the things that are seen are not made out of what is visible." This verse confirms the divine creation of the universe and validates the Hebrew/Christian understanding of the origins of the earth. Faith and understanding go together. Faith illuminates the understanding in the unseen sphere. Faith facilitates and activates understanding but the opposite can also be stated and that is, where there is no faith, the understanding remains inactive or steeped in ignorance. For those who do not believe in God, the world and the universe, are the consequence of chance.[8] They have to be because, from their perspective, God is non-existent and cannot therefore be the agent of creation. However, for those who believe in Him, that he should make the physical out of the intangible is not a difficulty. God spoke the universe into being, because, as has already been stated in 1:2, he made the ages (*aiōnes*) through the Son. The word *ages*, includes all that comes under what would be understood as the universe of time and space. *Word* here, is not exactly equivalent to the Johannine *Logos* (John. 1:1–14) which emphasizes the incarnate Christ, even if there are certainly a number of strong parallels. Here it is the aspect of God's creative and spoken word, as in in the beginning, bringing things into being, as in Genesis 1:3, it is recorded: *"Then God said, 'Let there be light'; and there was light."* This is clearest in Ps 33:6, 9 (LXX 32:6, 9), where it is the spoken word of God which is the agent of creation and which brings the heavens into existence.

In fact, it is this word of God which, as already stated in verse 1, is the basis underlying the possibility of all faith and its fulfilment. So that, just as faith in the yet unseen future is required, it is also necessary to grasp the significance of how the visible creation, of which mankind is a part, points to the Creator God. He is the one who in the past brought it all into existence by his word. So, there is a lesson here, that in the same way that this present creation came into being by God's word and was formed from

---

7. It has already been pointed out several times in the letter by the author that the role of the Holy Spirit in validating Old Testament verses, is vital and the same is therefore assumed here (see 3:7; 9:8).

8. The entire teaching of the evolutionary hypothesis is based upon this legacy of chance, even if it is presented under the guise of science "falsely so called."

nothing,[9] so too the final form of the future Kingdom,[10] which is not yet visible, will become exactly what God has already promised, when he speaks the word at the right time in the future. The author is underlining the understanding that what will happen in the future, goes together with faith in what happened in the past. The significance of faith in God as Creator is certainly of primary importance in the Revelation (Rev 4:11; 10:6; 14:7). This factor affirms his mastery over all things. In this verse, creation and the new creation go together and the Son, as the agent through whom the worlds were made (1:3), is also integral to making substance out of all that is presently unseen.

In the following verses the individuals mentioned cover three specific periods:

a) From the creation to the flood (11:4–7);

b) From Abraham to the Exodus (11:8–29);

c) From the entry to the promised land to the intertestamental period (11:30–38).

Examples of people of faith from the Hebrew scriptures 11:4–40

This section deals with people of faith starting with Abel.

v. 4 "*By faith Abel offered to God a more acceptable sacrifice than Cain, by which he obtained witness that he was righteous. God commending*[11] *him because of his gifts and through it* [faith], *although he died, he still speaks.*" Abel is the first person on the list given as part of this number of the faithful examples from the Hebrew scriptures. There is much discussion among scholars as the to the reason given in Genesis 4:4–5 for God accepting Abel's offering and not Cain's. Some see this as a matter of the giving of a life being more acceptable than that of the giving of what was representative of the earth[12] but this cannot be correct because elsewhere in scripture the firstfruits of the harvest are not only acceptable but required by God (Exod

---

9. This nothingness, is how mankind understands the essence from which man comprehends God's creation. In Genesis 1:2 where what is written regarding the earth being "formless and void," this is represented by the Hebrew phrase *tohu webohu* (תהו ובהו).

10. This future Kingdom is presently here in its embryonic form since the victory of Christ over death but it is not yet fully manifested.

11. Literally: God testifying, or witnessing with regard to his gifts.

12. Philo, *De Agricultura*, 22; *De sacrificiis Abelis et Caini*, 88; Josephus, *The Antiquities of the Jews*, i. 2. 1.

23:19). The reason must be rather the attitude of Abel's heart as compared to Cain's. In Genesis when Cain displays anger after the rejection of his offering, God tells him: "*If you do well, will you not be accepted?*" (Gen 4:7). This indicates that it is not just the matter of the offering but that there is something more that is not enlarged upon behind the rejection. It must point to the attitude behind the giver of the offering that was either acceptable or not.[13]

Here the reason given for the acceptance of Abel's offering is that of his faith. That would indicate a heart of trust and thanksgiving. The nature of Cain's heart is soon manifested in the killing of his brother. In John's epistle the author says that Cain killed his brother "*because his works were evil but his brother's righteous*" (1 John 3:12). Since works are the fruit of the heart this would ratify what has been stated above regarding his having a heart and mind out of order with God.

In a manner somewhat similar to that employed by Paul when he talks about Abraham being reckoned righteous or made just because he believed (Rom 4:3), so here witness and commendation is given to Abel, as being just. In this he is compared with his brother who most definitely was not. That fact is substantiated, as already mentioned in Genesis 4:8, when he killed his brother. This verse is the only one, as already mentioned in the notes on verse 2, where the bearing of the testimony or the commendation to Abel is attributed directly to God. The reason given here is as to the nature of the gifts offered, together with the attitude of heart behind the offerings.

One wonders how the acceptance of Abel's offering was recognized. After all, Cain was certainly aware of its acceptance and of the fact that his own had been rejected because as a consequence he went away and fumed. It was commonly accepted by Christians from the second century, that when Abel presented his offering, fire came from heaven and consumed it but not Cain's. This aspect which appears nowhere in scripture, was included in Theodotion's Greek version of the Old Testament in Genesis 4:4, where the phrase "God sent down fire" (*kai enepurisen ho theos*), replaces the Masoretic text for '"the Lord favored" (וישע יהוה).[14] It was also held by

13. See Bruce's comments on this that it is not the material content that is important in any offering but the expression of the heart behind the giver. *Hebrews*, 283.

14. This can be found in Fridericus Field, *Origenis Hexapla*, 17; this view was held by Jerome, *Liber quaestionum hebraicarum*, P.L. xxiii, 944; Chrysostom, *Ad Hebraeos*; Homily xxii. 774, wrote: "It is said, that fire came down and consumed the sacrifices. For instead of ['And the Lord] had respect to Abel and to his sacrifices' (Gen. iv. 4), the Syriac said, 'And He set them on fire.' "; Jerome, *Quoestiones in Genesim opera*, iii. 379 Col. 1616 "How could Cain know that God *accepted* his brother›s *offering*, and

a number of the Church Fathers, as well as those during the mediaeval age that God sent down fire and a number of scholars today favor this concept.[15] It would appear that the reason for this is an interpolation on the grounds of what happened elsewhere when offerings were made in the Old Testament (Lev 9:24; Judges 6:21; 1 Kgs 18: 38; 1 Chron 21:26) but there is no clear indication either in the text itself or here in Hebrews that this is what happened and if this were the case it seems that it would have been mentioned somewhere in scripture. Therefore, the matter of God sending fire must remain as nothing more than conjecture.

God's acceptance of the gift that Abel offered, relates therefore, to his righteous ways and the fact of his faith. He was right in his actions and heart and consequently God accepted what he presented. Cain was neither righteous nor a man of faith and his offering was not accepted. The last part of the sentence does not directly mention "by faith" but "by it." To what then does the "it" (*autēs*) refer? It could go back to the earlier part of the sentence and speak of the sacrifice but it is more likely that it is to the faith and for that reason a number of translations (RSV, NRSV, NASB, ESV et al.) have translated the pronoun as "faith." By this faith which resulted in his righteous behavior and his right attitude of heart in the offering which he gave, even though he is dead he still speaks. The phrase "he still speaks" (*eti lalei*) is a present tense, showing that death did not have the final word and his actions continue to bear witness without limit, over time.

There are a number of interpretations of these words, such as that of Bruce who sees the author of the epistle as presenting Abel "appealing to God for vindication, until he obtains it in full in the judgement to come. The idea in that case is paralleled in Rev. 6:9–11, where the souls of the martyrs cry aloud for vindication" which will take place at the end of time at the judgment.[16] There may well be something which needs to be considered here in the light of Gen 4:11 and the words of God to Cain that Abel's blood cries out to him from the ground. More needs to be said in this regard in 12:4. However, in the light of verses such as 16 of this chapter, it is more likely that the emphasis here is upon the testimony of his faith and its importance, even as it is recorded here. This means death cannot put an end to the promise claimed by faith. It is, therefore, a challenge to all who follow in the same footsteps as Abel, to live as he did. One thing is certain, that in

rejected his own, unless the translation which Theodotion has given be the true one? –and God sent down fire upon Abel's and upon his sacrifice; but upon Cain and upon his sacrifice he did not send down fire."

15. Note that this interpretation is also held by a number of recent authors including Spicq, *Hébreux*, II. 342–43; Alford, *Hebrews*, iv, 211; Kendrick, "Hebrews," 148.

16. Bruce, *Hebrews*, 286.

spite of the seeming defeat related to his death, Abel's faithfulness shows that it does not have the final word.

vv. 5–6 "By faith Enoch was taken up [was removed] *so as not to see death and he was not found because God took him. For before his being taken up he was commended*[17] *for having been well pleasing to God and without faith it is impossible to please God. For it is necessary for the one who approaches God to believe that he exists and that he becomes the one who rewards those who continually seek him."* With Abel we have a faith which nevertheless ends in apparent failure and his death at the hands of his own brother. Nevertheless, as already noted, this is not the way God sees the matter. Here with Enoch, we see that faith, for him, has a very different outcome in terms of the end of his earthly existence. There is not a lot in scripture written in the Genesis record about Enoch, only 4 verses (Gen 5:21–24). His faith is given as the reason for his being removed from the earth without seeing death. The next verse has more to say in this regard. The only clear statement here is that he was translated because God took him.

Once more the author of the letter follows the Septuagint when he writes "*Enoch was well pleasing to God,*" rather than the words of the Masoretic text "*Enoch walked with God.*"[18] The two are not contrary since to walk with God, is to please him and vice versa. In Micah 6:7, 8 the question is asked: What it is that God requires? Is it the abundance of sacrificial rams and rivers of oil? The response is No! What he seeks for is the performance of justice the love of kindness and "*to walk humbly with your God.*" Justice and humility show confidence in God alone rather than in one's own ability but the walking with God again demonstrates close relationship, which is obviously what was central to Enoch's relationship here. The outcome is a realization of total dependency upon God. This is Enoch's model. Elsewhere in the New Testament he is mentioned as part of Luke's genealogy (Luke 3:37) and again in Jude vv. 14–16. Enoch was removed by God and unlike Abel, did not see death. In this way, it could be said that he is a symbol of the first fruits of those believers who will be alive at the time of the return of Christ, who will not see death but be changed instantaneously, as he was (1 Cor 15:51–57; 1 Thess 4:17).

Many interpreters of prophetic literature, especially those who focus on Revelation 11:3–11, see the two witnesses mentioned there, as Enoch

---

17.. See the remarks in the previous verse relative to testimony being given to Abel. The same is true here.

18. "And Enoch walked with God." Genesis 5:22 LXX text: *euēpestēse de henoch tō Theos;* & Masoretic text: ויתהלך חנוך את~האלחים–*weythalek Hanoch eth haelohim,* The extra canonical writings of 1 Enoch 1:9; 71:14; Jubilees 4:17; 10:17 and Ben Sira (Ecclesiasticus) 44:16 have more to say on Enoch from a Jewish perspective.

and Elijah because both were caught up by God but nothing of that nature is ascribed to Enoch by the author here. The mere fact of his faith and his trust in God are given as the reason for this removal from the earth. The significance of drawing near to God, has already been presented on several occasions throughout the epistle (4:16; 7:19, 25; 10:1, 22), where intimacy with God and engagement in his purposes are the priority. This most certainly was the experience of Enoch in what the Genesis record depicts as already stated, as walking with God. The mention of the necessity of having to believe in God's existence, in a letter to Jews, may seem unnecessary but the emphasis is upon something more than mental assent that God has some role in the universe. What is required is a vital participation in his purposes, which depends totally upon a close and ongoing relationship with the Almighty and not mere following of procedures and outward forms. In this relationship there has to be a continual and meaningful pursuit of God and his purposes, which means a bending to his will and complete obedience.

The historical era needs to be remembered, as it is not all that long after this time that the corruption and antagonistic attitude of mankind results in the flood with Noah. Enoch stood out from his generation in every way by choosing to follow after God the way he did. This is only possible where faith is integral to any relationship. The outcomes of such faithful and active seeking are God's rewards. The nature of the reward here for Enoch, is in part at least, his being translated without seeing death but that is not the end of the matter, as we see from the other examples which follow.

v. 7 "By faith Noah, being warned by God concerning things not yet seen, in reverent fear, built an ark for the salvation of his household by which he condemned the world and became heir of the righteousness that is the result of faith." The narrative concerning Noah is very well known. It is compelling in terms of demonstrating his faith in the word of God and like both Abel and Enoch, he walked with God and was the first person in the Bible who is directly designated as righteous (Gen 6:9). Noah received detailed orders from God (Gen 6:13–7:5) and the record states, "Noah did all that the Lord had commanded him" (Gen 6:22; 7:5). In this verse the construction, "in reverent fear, built an ark" (eulabētheis[19] kateskeuasen kibōton) shows that the fear here is godly fear and reverence, brought about by faith in the word that he had received from God. It is this faith which then results in his obedience and engagement in the construction of the ark. The work required to build the ark would have taken many years and without doubt, he would have faced much mockery and opposition from his neighbors, especially as

---

19. From the Greek verb eulabeomai which is not common in scripture. For the noun eulabeia see 5:7; 12:28.

this construction would have been carried out far from any large body of water; in spite of that, he faithfully carried out what he had been told to do and pressed on with the building. In this he demonstrated his unwavering faith in God and his word regarding what was, as far as he was aware, something that God had indicated would take place in the future (as yet unseen). The fact of a worldwide flood would not have been easy to grasp.

Peter depicts his actions as making him a preacher of righteousness (2 Pet 2:5). His actions were a constant witness to all who lived during his day and yet they failed to repent of their ungodly behavior. Just before he was ordered to enter the ark with his family, God tells Noah that of all his generation, he alone was righteous (Gen 7:1). This attribute was demonstrated though his faithfulness and obedience, regardless of any verbal declaration he made; his was a life of faith. There are two important and very different outcomes which are the result of this faithful testimony over many years in the building of the ark. On the one hand there is the salvation of his family and the human race and on the other, the condemnation and judgement of the wicked, who failed to listen to the message Noah proclaimed. In this there are parallels which Jesus himself drew between what happened to the generation that lived in Noah's day and those who will be alive when the Son of Man comes again at his *parousia* (Matt 24:37–39). That is when the people of God will receive their final reward but the wicked will receive the judgement which they are due. For Noah the reward was that he became the means of the salvation, for humanity. Then to return to the significance of faith and his lifestyle, Noah becomes the heir of righteousness; this verse clearly links righteousness and faith in a way which is similar to what Paul does in his epistles (see Rom 4:11; 10: 6; Phil 3:9). Both are intricately bound together and again, his perseverance proved their veracity throughout the entirety of his life.

v. 8 "By faith, when Abraham was called to go out to a place which he was about to receive for an inheritance, obeyed and went out not knowing where he was going." There is no actual mention made in the Genesis record of faith being part of the experience of the three former individuals included by the author of this epistle but when it comes to Abraham there is no question that his faith and belief were very much part of the narrative. Genesis 15 relates the discourse between Abram and Yahweh and the former being told to count the stars as he was promised by God that his offspring would be as numerous. Then verse 6 states of Abram: *"And he believed the Lord; and the Lord reckoned it to him as righteousness."* Abraham has already been introduced in the letter from 6:13, so it is not at all out of place that he should be granted as much room as he is in this present narrative; certainly, it is far beyond anything given to the other heroes of faith.

Jews as well as Christians, saw Abraham as their supreme example of piety and faithfulness and the former saw him exclusively as their father (Matt 3:9) while Paul declares that he is the father of the faithful (Rom 4:16) so, more than any national hero.

The first part of what is written concerning Abraham in this verse, relates to his faith and obedience. Faith, obedience and action go together. Faith is not a mere intellectual acknowledgement of something but belief which results in action. This is what James means when he writes that *"faith without works is dead"* (James 2:14, 17). Abraham's faith was far from being passive. He was called to leave his residence in Ur of the Chaldees and to go to Canaan (see the context of Gen. 11:31 and 12:1–4). He did not know where it was that he was going or what it was going to be like when he got to this new inheritance but he obeyed God and went. If the Genesis record is kept in the back of the reader's mind, the entire time of his "going" was marked by steps of faith and the demonstration of his obedience and sincerity in continual acts of worship, with the building of altars along the way (Gen 12:8; 13:4, 18). In Genesis this going, is depicted as something that took place in stages (Gen. 12:9) and over an extremely extended period, which was that of his entire life from the time of his call until his death.

Not only was he obedient in the going out from where he had been called but he was also anticipating an inheritance or a land which God had promised him. It is one thing to receive a promise when the designated inheritance is understood and known but it very different when the promise is totally unclear. It shows that Abraham's faith and trust in God as not only the promise maker but the giver of what is good, was stamped upon his heart. This part of his faith was therefore based upon the *assurance of things hoped for* and *not seen* in verse one.

vv. 9–10 "*By faith he lived in a land of promise as a foreigner, living in tents with Isaac and Jacob the joint heirs of the same promise. For he was looking forward to the city which had foundations of which God was the architect and builder.*" Even when he was living in the land which had been promised to him after his return from Egypt, it was never totally his. The Greek word *parōkēsen* shows that he lived as a stranger in the land. *Sojourner* is probably the best word to use here because it shows the lack of security and the transient nature of one's residence, but nowadays it is viewed as archaic and hardly used. He lived in Canaan as a nomad, in tents and as a foreigner among people who never accepted him as one of their own. In fact, while he was alive, the only piece of land that can be really regarded as his own, was the cave he purchased from Ephron the Hittite, at Machpelah near Hebron; he purchased that in order to have somewhere to bury his wife Sarah (Gen 23:16–20). This was the situation, even when Isaac and Jacob were eventually added to his line and lived in the same territory. There is never any indication that he had any permanent dwelling place. The declaration shows the nature of his continuing faith and willingness to obey God because there is no indication that things ever got any simpler for him once he arrived in this land of promise. Again, there is no mention that he ever thought of returning to Ur, not even for a visit.

The statement that Abraham lived in tents with Isaac and Jacob, is at first sight difficult, in the light of the chronology of the time (see Gen 26:1). However, if it is understood that the emphasis, which is clear in verse 10, is that of their status as foreigners, then the chronological aspect is not the point being made. They all understood that they were looking for another final and yet future destination, which was central to the promise made. This is again underlined when the author details in verse 13 that they all died in faith awaiting the fulfilment of the promises.

The author states very clearly that Abraham was looking for a city which was unlike anything of human origin but designed and built by God. This would have been despite the fact that after Lot had separated from Abraham and taken the best of the land. Yahweh had told him to look all around him: north, south, east and west, and that all the land would be his and his offspring's forever (Gen 13:14–15). He sensed therefore, automatically, that there was much more to God's promise than any earthly kingdom. In the end, not only was he a stranger in Canaan but upon the Earth. There was faith in far more than the visible and material about him. It is unlikely that Abraham understood all that was involved in the unseen future but the author, in the light of his understanding of Christian teaching, can see the picture of this promised land in a far clearer manner. What is being described fits perfectly with the teaching of Revelation 21 and 22 where the spiritual interpretation of the facts that are seen are far more important than any literal understanding of what is depicted. Whatever is to be grasped of those passages, the thought it is the same here and that is that God is the architect and builder of that city. As architect or designer (*technitēs*), he is the one who plans all that has to do with this future city and its nature and as builder or creator (*dēmiourgos* only found here in the NT), he is the one who makes it happen, exactly as he desires.

v. 11 "*By faith Sarah herself received power to establish a posterity, even though she was past the age* [of conception] *since she considered the one who had promised* [to be] *faithful.*" This verse is a parenthesis in a discussion relative to Abraham and this needs to be remembered as the words which tell of Sarah's faith seem to go against the normal understanding of the Genesis record. When she laughed at the words of the Lord to Abraham, that she would have a son, she laughed to herself (Gen 18:10, 12), clearly doubting the words she had just heard. When the Lord asked her why she laughed she denied that she had because she was afraid (Gen 18:13–15). Later, at Isaac's birth, her laughter became an expression of great joy and wonder (Gen 21:6). It is apparent that after reflection and in accord with the last phrase in this verse, which says that she considered the faithfulness of the God who had promised her that this would happen, she did believe and changed her view on what she had considered previously to be impossible.[20]

Therefore, in spite of any initial doubts, she did give birth to Isaac, which shows that she like Abraham, did have faith. Scholars disagree as to the meaning of the Greek phrase *dunamin eis katabolēn spermatos elaben*, so that it is translated variously: "she [Sarah] received power to conceive seed" and "she received power to establish a posterity." Those who hold to the first interpretation state that it means the *establishment* of seed or *conception* of seed. On the grounds that it is the man who produces the seed and not the woman, the first is contested. But the woman does produce ova, which is then fertilized by the man's seed and the niceties of biology are not the question at hand in the presentation. However, the second is the more likely, if seed is understood in the sense of posterity, which is, as several scholars point out, how the word (*spermatos*–seed/offspring) has already been used in Gen 12:7, as well as later in this same chapter (v.18), including multiple times in Galatians 3:16, 19, 29 and elsewhere.[21] Certainly, it was necessary for Sarah to receive supernatural power (*dunamis*) to change her dead womb, so that she could bear a child but that aspect followed the promise of God, which made the entire maternal function possible.

The Greek *katabolē*, means *foundation* or something put in place and that is how it is used in the other ten places where it is found in the New Testament; so, it is unlikely that it should be understood differently here.[22] Because of the inclusion of Sarah in the midst of a long passage that speaks of Abraham, numerous scholars debate the text, some suggesting that the phrase is an addition.[23] However, if it is taken together with what is stated in the next and inclusive statement relative to both Abraham and Sarah, there should be no difficulty in accepting what is stated. After all, Sarah has to be seen as being an intricate part of what the fulfilment of any promises made to her husband would be, since she was to be the bearer of the

20. See the comments made by Spicq, *Hébreux*, II. 348 with regard to Sarah's initial unbelief.

21. Alford, "*Pros Ebraious*," iv. 216; Hughes, *Hebrews*, 473.

22. Matt 13:35; 25:34; Luke 11:50; John 17:24; Eph 1:4; Heb 4:3; 9:26; 11:10; 1 Pet 1:20; Rev 13:8; 17:8.

23. For comments on this view and some of those individuals involved, see Hughes, *Hebrews*, 472 and n39.

promised offspring and without her it would not have happened. If this verse is properly understood, Sarah is the mother of a people as much as Abraham the father of the same.

v. 12 "Therefore indeed, from one man, and him as good as dead, came descendants as numerous as the stars of heaven and as innumerable as the sand which is by the seashore." Although there can be no doubt that the words "from one" refer to Abraham, being in the masculine, the role of Sarah and the fact that she has just been described as being past the age of childbearing, both have to be viewed collectively as one body. He was as good as dead in the matter of the possibility of childbearing, as was his wife. Together they were not under any normal circumstances, ever going to bear a child. Yet, now the author looks at the reality of the consequence of what happened following Isaac's birth. The number of the posterity that came into being, due to the fulfilment of this promise of God and the faith of the individuals involved, resulted in exactly what was stated in Genesis 15:5 and 22:17–children as numerous as the stars of heaven and the grains of sand on the seashore. The Jews of the day would have regarded this multitude as being that of Abraham's physical descendants but Paul includes within the "seed" or posterity, Christ and all those who are his followers (Gal 3:7–9, 16, 29), adding a new dimension to the numbers incorporated within the miracle that took place.

v. 13 "All these died in faith, not having obtained the promises but seeing and greeting them from afar off, and confessing that they were strangers and exiles on the earth." *"All these,"* refers to all who have been listed, specifically those from verse 8. They had a promise given to them and they lived in faith of its accomplishment but never did see its fulfilment. From the mention of death, it would seem that having lived their earthly existence without achieving what they hoped for, something had gone very wrong; apparently, there had been a complete failure. For the majority of the human race, death is counted as the terminus, so that if achievements are to be valid, they have to be realized during one's earthly existence. Nevertheless, this is not the hope of those who trust God, as the author of the letter keeps saying. The heavenly or unseen dimension, is the reality for which these people sought and they were very much aware of it, as is declared in the opening verse of the chapter where the substance for which they hoped is not associated with their time on earth. Although this hope was as yet unseen, it was most certainly real. Therefore, the promises remained integral to their faith and hope; these factors only reinforced the fact that their destinies were not earthly.

The fact that he considered himself a stranger was the confession of Abraham's lips when as already stated, he purchased a burial plot for his wife from the Hittites (Gen 23:4). The language that these people of faith saw and greeted the promises from afar and that they realized the nature of their transitory sojourn in Canaan, meant that they were not limited by the physical boundaries of life and death. They then understood that they were on a journey as strangers and exiles and the next verse underlines that fact.

v. 14 "For those who speak like this make it clear that they are looking for a homeland." The author interprets the actions and words of the patriarchs (as mentioned relative to Abraham in the previous verse) in terms of the recognition of the limitations of earthly existence and a recognition of something much better and longer lasting in a domain where proximity to God would be the answer. The patriarchs were in what was apparently the promised land but they did not live as though they had arrived. The continual wanderings of the patriarchs show in the most vivid manner that they never felt that they had found what they were looking for in terms of the permanent status of a homeland. The author here presents this search not in terms of the physical but the spiritual homeland.

v. 15 "And if on the one hand, they remembered where they came from, they would have had opportunity to return." If they had seen their homeland in terms of Ur or Haran in the Chaldees, they could have returned there but they understood that that was not their homeland either. Abraham was adamant when he spoke with his servant tasked with finding a wife for Isaac, that he should most certainly not take Isaac back to Ur (Gen 24:6) as there was never a thought of returning to Chaldea. Even if Jacob did return to Haran to find a wife, the dream at Bethel (Gen 28:12–15) promising him that God would bring him back, did not let him settle there and later upon the command of the Lord (Gen 31:3) he returned to Canaan. Even Jacob's dream was an experience that must be considered central in his growing awareness of the inferior nature of any earthly existence because after this encounter with the Lord, he is filled with a mixture of fear and awe (Gen 28:16–17). The heavenly dimension and the person of God awaken within him a desire for more of the God and the heaven toward which the ladder gave access. All these people of faith knew that earthly residency was never going to be permanent (This is the same as David's experience Ps 39:12b).

v. 16 "But now on the other, they desire a better one, that is a heavenly one. For that reason, God is not ashamed to be called their God for he has prepared a city for them." Any earthly desires aimed at an earthly fatherland, are overridden by a greater desire for something far better. In this instance, the present or what is "seen," is recognized for what it is: inferior and passing. Faith has opened their hearts and spiritual eyes to see what was otherwise invisible. Because of their right state of heart and mind, these people automatically identify with God who likewise identifies fully with them.

Adam and Eve were rejected and expelled from God's presence in the garden because of disobedience and their desire to be in charge. Here there is an abandonment of the creature to God himself, as well as to his purposes. Therefore, God reciprocates fully by returning to the original plan he had for communion between himself and his creatures. This makes citizenship a possibility for God's followers, in a new and heavenly city which he has prepared for them. The fact that God has prepared this city for them, shows that they have not yet taken up their residence but this is assured in the future, as it is for all of God's people. In this context God identifies with these patriarchs as elsewhere when he calls himself the God of Abraham, Isaac and Jacob (Exod 3:6 see also Jesus' words in Matt 22:32), showing that death does not sever this relationship. The distinction between heavenly and earthly has already been seen on several occasions in the letter (see notes on 3:1) but its most significant meaning here is the distinction with anything that is seen and earthly. It is identified with the fulness of God's presence and perfection. It is also the place of future permanence for all of God's people.[24] This heavenly city is not described in any manner in the epistle but is identifiable in Revelation chapters 21—22.

vv. 17–18 "By faith Abraham, when he was tested, offered up Isaac and the one having received the promises was offering up his only son, of whom it was said that: 'In Isaac your offspring shall be named.'" Once more Abraham takes center stage. After having seen part of God's promise accomplished in the birth of Isaac, God called upon Abraham to sacrifice him. This was indeed the ultimate test[25] of his faith because all the promises for the future depended upon Isaac (see the notes in v.19). In spite of this, Abraham went ahead and was carrying out the command he received.

The verb "offered him" (*prosenēnochen*–3rd p. sing. perf. of *prospherō*) shows a complete action, so as far as God was concerned, the completion of the offering was executed. This same thought is present in the recounting of the narrative in James 2:21 where the Greek *anenengkas* (aor. participle of *anapherō*) again shows a complete action of the offering up of Isaac. It needs to be remembered that Isaac was bound and Abraham was at the point

---

24. In spite of the differences in the way the expressions: "heavenly places" or "heavenlies" are used by NT authors there is a commonality which exists between them all. Some of the clearest appear in Paul's Epistle to the Ephesians. See from 1:3 and elsewhere. The unpublished dissertation by Bannon, "The Heavenlies" in Ephesians," is highly recommended reading on this subject.

25. The word *peirazomenos*, is a present passive participle of *peirazō*, meaning to test or to tempt, depending upon the context. In James 1:13 it means to tempt. But there, where it says that God temps no one, it is in the sense of tempting someone to do what is wrong.

of carrying out the action necessary to bring about his death when he was stopped by the angel of the Lord (Gen 22:9–12). This meant that as far as God was concerned, he had done what was required of him and offered him up.

Prior to this, Abraham obviously believed that since the promise was that Isaac was the child through whom the promise would be accomplished, that God would bring about a miracle, as the next verse indicates. This test was beyond anything God would ask his own to carry out because the killing of one's offspring was something practiced by the worshippers of Baal and Molech (Jer 19:5; 32:35) and regarded as an abomination to the Lord (2 Kgs 16:3). Nevertheless, Abraham was quick to do what God requested of him, even if he was aware of all that must have seemed against logic and what was going through his mind at the time. All that he was thinking of was obeying God; the matter of trusting him was his sole preoccupation. He still had faith that whatever was going to happen would take place through this same son. Of course, Isaac was not his only son, as he had already given birth to Ishmael but the promise made and the covenant was through Isaac alone (Gen 17:19, 21).

v. 19 "*He reckoned that God was able to even raise him from the dead from which, figuratively he did.*" The fact of Abraham's "reckoning" here shows that he had thought at length about what his actions meant and realized that in the natural course of events, after having offered up Isaac, the only way for him to be able to continue to be the one through whom the promise was going to be fulfilled, would be some act of God, such as raising him from the dead. When Abraham had left his two servants behind on the way to the mountain, he had ordered them to wait while he and Isaac would go and worship and then return (Gen 22:5). He had no doubt that he would return with his son.

The phrase qualifying the possibility of God raising Isaac from the dead: "*which figuratively he did,*" has been the subject of considerable debate among scholars. This is not the first time that the author uses this sort of construction with the Greek word *parabolē* (figure or parable) involved, as already seen in 9:9, where the earthly tabernacle was indicative of access to the heavenly. From the earliest times the parable/figure here has been seen by Christians as a type of Christ coming back from the dead. Most certainly, this is what the meaning has to be here, since in real terms, although Isaac did not die, in God's eyes Abraham had been willing to sacrifice him and had carried out the action in his heart. Therefore, his was the equivalent of a resurrection for Isaac and that is how the expression should be understood.

The extremes of interpretation by such as Augustine[26] and Origen[27] were never intended here, even if there are most certainly some valid parallels in the teaching of scripture as a whole.

v. 20 "By faith Isaac blessed Jacob and Esau relative to things to come." The next mention of faith is that of Isaac and his blessing of his two sons Jacob and Esau. The narrative behind what happened (Gen. 27:27–40) is not viewed as important but the fact of his faith and his blessing of the brothers is. This, together with 12:16, is the only place in the New Testament, apart from what Paul says in Romans 9:13, regarding the choice between Jacob and Esau, where Esau is mentioned. It seems that the author, both in this verse and the next, is concentrating on the fact that the blessing conveyed to children at the end of one's life, indicates their faith in the one responsible for all provision and guidance. The significance of transferring blessing, either from God or to one's offspring is considered as of great importance and value in biblical writings (Gen 31:55; 35:9; 48:15, 20; 49:28 et al.). It appears to have become a custom at that time that when the head of a house was about to die, he would muster the family and bless their offspring, relating what would happen to them in the future.

v. 21 "By faith when dying, Jacob blessed each of Joseph's sons and worshipped over the head of his staff." Once more, at the point of death, Jacob blesses his grandchildren. One matter which is not mentioned in either v.20 or v.21 is the way in which the one who receives the blessing of the firstborn[28] here, is not the physical firstborn but the one God has designated as preferred. This shows that the faith of the father appears to operate in combination with the sovereignty of God.

The author cites from the Septuagint rather than the Masoretic text, from something which had happened earlier when Jacob made Joseph

26. Augustine, *De Civitate Dei,* on this passage in Book xvi, 32 comments on the "similitude" and state as that as Isaac carried the wood on which he was to be offered, so Christ carried his cross. For him the ram caught by the horns in the thicket represents the crown of thorns on Jesus before he was sacrificed. This kind of allegory only exemplifies the extremes common in the allegorical school and the dangers of reading into what was written in ways that were never intended.

27. Origen, *Genesis Homily VIII*, 140–41;145 allegorizes in a manner similar to Augustine; see the previous footnote. He sees Isaac as a type of Christ but also the ram as representative of Christ.

28. The name "firstborn" was usually an indicator of the first male child born to a family; the one who would have the rights of leadership and benefits in the family. However, sometimes the firstborn male had his rights passed to another because it was God's will that the other child become the head of the family in the future. This was the case with Jacob who was physically the second after Esau but who usurped his place in God's plan.

swear that he would not bury him in Egypt (Gen 47:31). In the Masoretic text it reads: "Then Israel bowed himself on the head of his bed" while the Septuagint reads: "And Israel worshipped leaning on the head of his staff." The reason for the difference in the renderings is easy to find. The Hebrew *mittah*–bed–in the Massoretic text, has been read as *matteh*–staff–and translated as the latter in the Greek of the Septuagint by *chrabdou* in that text. It needs to be remembered that the pointing in the earlier texts was not present in the Hebrew indicating that the consonants *mth* in Hebrew, would have been the same. The outcome is not different because the activity of worship while bowing is what is significant.

v. 22 *"By faith Joseph, coming to the end of his life, made mention of the exodus of the Children of Israel and gave orders regarding his bones."* At the end of Genesis and just prior to Joseph's death, he foretells the eventual exodus of the people when he tells his brothers that at the time of God's intervention, they are to carry his bones away from Egypt (Gen 50:25). The word "exodus," in spite of its significance in the history of Israel, is not common in the NT and it is only used here of the departure from Egypt.[29] There is nothing to indicate that Joseph knew this would be a century and a half later but it is nevertheless a promise of ultimate release from the bondage of Egypt. Although most of his adult life, from the age of seventeen (Gen 37:2), had been spent in Egypt, he did not recognize it as his motherland. This removal of his bones, did indeed take place at the hand of Moses, as had been promised (Exod 13:19); he was buried finally in Shechem, after the people settled in the land of promise in Jacob's own property. As indicated earlier, that was the same plot of land purchased by Abraham to bury Sarah (Josh 24:32). This promise, like those before them, was based on his faith in the word of God.

v. 23 *"By faith Moses, when he was born was hidden for three months by his parents because they saw that the child was impressive and they did not fear the decree of the king."* The next series of verses relates to Moses, who next to Abraham, was probably the most highly regarded individual of all among all the whole Jewish nation. However, this verse actually speaks of the faith of his parents. The Genesis record actually focusses mostly on the actions of the mother and the sister (Exod 2:2–9) but the author includes the actions as being those of the parents collectively, following the plural verbs in the Septuagint which say that "and having seen that he was striking/impressive they hid him three months" (*idontes de auto asteion espepasan auto mēnas treis*). The hiding of Moses for three months was followed by his being placed in the papyrus basket. The fact of Moses appearance:

29. It is used twice elsewhere in Luke 9:31 and in 2 Pet 1:15 of death.

"the child was beautiful" or "the child was striking/remarkable" may seem coincidental but it is mentioned again in Stephen's sermon in Acts 7:20. The word Greek word *asteios* can be understood in a number of different ways as referring to something that is pleasing to the eye, striking, well put together or beautiful.[30] There was obviously something about this child that was especially remarkable to the parents. The faith of the parents is evident in their refusal to submit to the order of the king to kill all males because they decided rather to trust God.

vv. 24–25 *"By faith when Moses grew up, he refused to be called the son of Pharaoh's daughter, choosing to be badly treated with the people of God, rather than having the enjoyment of sin for a time."* Josephus tells a story of how Moses was presented to Pharaoh by his daughter and that the king hugged him and placed a crown upon his head but that Moses threw it upon the ground and trod upon it.[31] Whether or not the story is accepted as reliable does not really make any difference to what our author has to say here. It is certainly evident that he preferred to be identified with the people of God and as a consequence had to flee from the courts of the king. His background as a young man growing up in the context of receiving preferential treatment, is not enlarged upon in the biblical record but it is certainly assumed in terms of his being the adopted child of a princess in Egypt; the context of what the power and luxury of royalty meant for all closely associated with any pharaoh at the time, would automatically have assumed such advantages.

This is then rejected by Moses when he saw the unjust treatment of his own people who were also the people of God. Although he was brought up in royal surroundings, it is most likely that through the contacts with his own family from his youth, that he was aware of his real identity. There came a moment when he knew that he had to make a choice as to his future. In the Exodus narrative, that choice had to be made when he understood the nature of the forced labor and mistreatment of what Scripture calls "his people." The moment came when he saw an Egyptian beating one of "his kinsfolk" or a fellow Hebrew and it was at that point that he decided enough was enough (Exod 2:11–12). The author calls this Moses' moment of choosing to be badly treated with (*sunkakoucheisthai*–choosing *"to be badly treated with"*– only found here in the NT), the people of God. The choice was made, even if the wisdom of the manner of its initial manifestation is questionable.[32] Stephen says that Moses thought that his kinsmen

---

30. See Arndt & Gingrich, 117.
31. Josephus, *Antiquities*, ii. 9.7.
32. This is obviously the killing of the Egyptian.

understood how God was going to use him to bring them deliverance but that they did not (Acts 7:25); therefore, even at that point, prior to his en-counter with God at the burning bush, he did not yet have a strong sense of calling.

According to this verse, the choice also involved, not only his kinsmen but the privileges of holding onto what is depicted in terms of, the passing or fleeting pleasures of sin. During his youth Moses must have come to a place of knowing and trusting God and it is this knowledge which led to the faith resulting in his strong and focused actions.

v. 26 "*Considering the reproach of Christ greater riches than the trea-sures of Egypt for he was looking to the reward.*" The reason for Moses' deci-sion is given here in terms which are not the simplest in the light of normal hermeneutics and the person of Christ. There is nothing clear in the context of the time of Moses that would suggest what we see here. But if we remem-ber that the name Christ (*Christos*), is the equivalent of "the anointed one" or the Messiah, as already seen in 1:9, much of the difficulty disappears. The thought is that, the abuse he suffered here, was in the name of God's anoint-ed One, who we know in the New Testament, as Christ the Messiah. There are other verses, including Ps 89:50–51, which speak of the Lord's anointed being taunted and of the insults of those who insult the Lord falling on God's servant. That psalm is certainly viewed as a Messianic psalm, as is Psalm 69:9, which also includes the matter of insults falling upon God's ser-vant. The author seems to be indicating the reception of abuse for the sake of serving God's anointed, is part of being faithful to him. Certainly, this thought is applied to Moses here, both in his standing up for the purposes of God in confronting Pharaoh in the name of God but also in the opposition he received from his own people. That happened prior to the Exodus, when his own people doubted his declarations that God had sent him and again later in the wilderness when they constantly complained against him (Exod 15:24; 17:2–3; Num 12:1, 8). In Moses' case, this reproach is attributed to his embracing the faithful service of Christ, rather than living the life of luxury. The latter would have automatically followed any conformity to a life Egypt would have offered him. He was looking for a reward that had nothing to do with earthly recompense, in the same way as those people of faith who had gone before him.

v. 27 "*By faith he left Egypt not fearing the anger of the king for he en-dured as seeing he who is unseen.*" The faith of the previous verse is associ-ated here with Moses' leaving Egypt when he was at all times under threat from Pharaoh. There are two main schools of thought as to the occasion of this leaving of Egypt.[33] The first links it to Moses actions when he killed the Egyptian and fled to Midian (Exod 2:15), while the second to the final Exodus at the head of all the people when they finally left captivity, subsequent to the plagues. There are difficulties with both views. With the first, the narrative in Exodus 2:14 says that Moses was afraid when he realized that what he had done was widely known, while here it is stated that he did not fear. If the second view is accepted, that it refers to the final Exodus, the endurance mentioned here which would go better with the forty years in the wilderness. But it does not appear to fit. Again, chronologically, why is this mentioned prior to the Passover when the exodus was subsequent to the Passover?

Some use the strength of the verb "he left" (*kateleipen,* the aorist of *kataleipō*), which means more than merely "to leave" but *to abandon,* as a complete and final action, to prove that this must have been the second occasion when the Exodus took place. This is because on the first occasion he later returned to Egypt to rescue his kinsmen, indicating that the first departure was not final. However, it appears that it is necessary to grasp that, as he has throughout the letter, the author interprets the narrative and thereby raises issues which may not be identifiable in the original episode. He does this to underline the facts he wishes to reinforce. If this is understood, then the only way to deal with the question of chronology raised in the following verse in a satisfactory manner, is to see this "leaving" as primary applicable to the first departure, even if there are aspects which also fit the final Exodus. Although, there was initial fear, when Moses realized the consequences of what he had done and it meant that he had to flee, at least for the present, there was a stronger sense of faith and trust in the person of God. This faith and trust in God, by far surpassed any fear of man and was responsible for his entire ministry as well as his leadership of the whole nation. It is this that the author wishes to highlight.

It was that sense of faith that enabled him to endure the many long and weary years looking after herds in the deserts of Midian. The word "he endured" (*ekarterēsen,* 3rd person sing. aor. of *kartereō*) is found only here in the New Testament.[34] It identifies Moses' perseverance in the face of conflict. It certainly describes the Midian period better than what took place when he was in dialogue with Pharaoh later, considering its duration; although it cannot be denied that the period of dialogue with Pharaoh

33. The first is represented by those who favor the leaving of Egypt as referring to Moses' departure to Midian including: Bruce, *Hebrews,* 321; Hughes, *Hebrews,* 498–99; Alford, "*Pros Ebraious,*" iv. 225. et al. The second as the departure at the Exodus itself: including Calvin, *Hebrews,*11:27; Owen, *Hebrews,* 11:27.

34. See Arndt & Gingrich, 406; Moulton & Milligan, *Vocabulary,* 322.

was certainly fraught with danger. Moses' willingness to endure was based entirely upon his understanding of what was yet unseen. Even after his encounter with the God, who is unseen and who had nevertheless appeared to him in the wilderness at the burning bush (Exod 3:2–4:17), his steps were driven by faith in God's promises and commands.

v. 28 "By faith he kept the Passover and the sprinkling of the blood so that the Destroyer of the firstborn should not touch them." The Passover has always been of the greatest importance for Jews and not least for Christians, as Christ is pictured as the sacrificial lamb (John 1:29, 36) and it was immediately prior to the Passover that Jesus was crucified. Moses had received directions from Yahweh in the clearest of terms regarding the Passover and the sprinkling of the blood on the doorframes of all Israelite homes (Exod 12:7, 13). He had already seen how God had fulfilled all his promises in the former plagues in Egypt but his transmission of the orders of God, prior to this final miracle, was without doubt an act of faith. This was because the coming action, unlike the previous plagues, would touch all the firstborn in the land, whether Egyptian or Jew. Here the Destroyer of the firstborn, is the one who will be responsible for this action, while in Exodus 12:23, it is the Lord himself who commands the destroyer. It was the action of the Destroyer and the death of all the firstborn of Egypt which was the deciding factor for Pharaoh in finally bringing him to the place where he agreed to set the Children of Israel free.

v. 29 "By faith they went through the Red Sea as on dry land, which when the Egyptians tried to do, they were drowned." At this point the faith mentioned is not just the faith of Moses but the faith of the people as a whole. However, Moses was certainly very much part of that national belief because, when the people saw the army of Egypt behind them and the sea in front of them, they were greatly afraid. Moses was the one who told them: "Do not be afraid, stand firm, and see the deliverance that the Lord will accomplish for you today; for the Egyptians whom you see today you shall never see again" (Exod 14:13 NRSV). He then urged them forward to cross as on the dry land when the Lord parted the waters of the Red Sea.[35] The Hebrew states that the Children of Israel went on dry ground,[36] which considering the fact that this was normally the bottom of the sea, was indeed another miracle, since even the withdrawal of the sea would normally have left the ground full of mud. The collective faith of the people, which was their

---

35. The Hebrew text reads: yam-suph–Reed Sea (Exod 13:18) but the Septuagint calls it: hē eruthra thalassa–The Red Sea.

36.. The Hebrew reads: ubene Yisrael halku bayyavvahsha–but the children of Israel went on the dry ground.

response to Moses' encouragement, was also obedience to the word of God himself and that was what resulted in their great deliverance. The miracle of the dividing of the waters was nevertheless a miracle, dependent totally upon the power of the God who was behind the action and the words.

When the Egyptians tried the same crossing shortly afterwards, they were drowned. It is worth noting that in spite of this mention of collective faith on the part of the nation at their departure from Egypt, there is no further example of any national event when anything similar was evident during their next forty years of wilderness wandering.[37] In fact, the contrary was true. It was a time of disobedience and failure to believe God and his spokesman Moses. That entire period is omitted by the author, who here wished only to portray the aspects related to the exercise of faith.

This verse brings the narrative to the end of the people of faith associated with the patriarchs and Moses. The years of the Children of Israel in Egypt are now at an end and find themselves in the promised land without any mention of what happened at the Jordan even though that could have been an occasion used to emphasize faith in action; it is left out by the author.

v. 30 "*By faith the walls of Jericho fell, having been encircled for seven days.*" The next step takes the reader immediately to Jericho, which could have been one of the largest towns the people of Israel would have had to overthrow if their conquest of the land was to be successful. It was also the closest to their entry since crossing the Jordan. This fall of the walls of Jericho came about as the result of obedience to the command of God. The people were beginning their settlement of the land but that required conquering the inhabitants and the first major town they encountered after crossing the Jordan was Jericho. Its walls were formidable and it seemed that it would not be possible for this, ill-equipped group that had spent the last forty years in the wilderness, to be able to breach this fortress city. The tactics followed made no sense at all to the human mind. How could circling a city for six days and then another seven times on the seventh day, accompanied by a blast on the trumpet, bring about its conquest? (Joshua 6:3–5). The walls did fall down, just as God had said, once the conditions imposed were fulfilled. There was nothing in the carrying out of the order, other than obedience and faith in the word of God, that was responsible for this action. The faith was that of the people collectively, even if it was mostly as the consequence of one man's direction: Joshua, they obeyed.

The archaeological evidence for the fall of Jericho is hotly debated by specialists. There are those who state that the evidence does not align with

---

37. There were miracles but never like this one and they always took place at the instigation of God and Moses.

the chronology of the time, while others believe that the evidence confirms the biblical record.[38] Bruce's comment however, is most apt in spite of the inconclusive evidence when he says: ". . . the forces that operate in the unseen realm, such as the power of faith, cannot be dug up by the excavator's spade . . . but our author ascribes their fall to the power of faith."[39]

v. 31 "By faith, Rahab the prostitute did not perish with those who were disobedient, having received the spies with peace." It may seem strange that a prostitute should be included in the list of those who are mentioned as people of faith. She was neither a Jew nor a person of high moral standing, yet here she is given as an example of a person of faith. In fact, this incident demonstrates God's mercy without limit. What took place when the spies visited Jericho shows that the people of the area were well aware of all that Yahweh had done to bring the Children of Israel from Egypt to Canaan and that there was a great fear that had come upon them all (Josh. 2:9–14). But Rahab had understood, not only responding in fear but had given refuge to the spies as well as abetting their escape, rather than surrendering them to the city authorities; all this was as an act of faith. This action is used by James to show that faith is far more than words (Jas 2:25). Rahab[40] is of considerable importance because there is little doubt but that she is the person mentioned in Matthew 1:5 who is in the direct line of Christ, as the wife of Salmon and the mother of Boaz.

The next verses conclude the subject which has majored on the significance of faith and obedience since the beginning of the chapter. There is now a change in the approach to the presentation, as the climax is reached.

v. 32 "And what more shall I say? For time would fail me to tell of Gideon, Barak, Sampson, Jephthah, of David and Samuel and the prophets." The names on this list all belong to the period after Israel's entry into the promised land. There is nothing specific recorded in terms of each one's accomplishments, as they would be assumed from the biblical text.

The six people mentioned are introduced by the rhetorical question: *"And what more shall I say?"* This gives the impression, either that the list already given should be more than enough to get the message across to the reader regarding the entire matter of faith or that the lack of space does not allow further development. Although the people who are included here

38. See Windle, "Discoveries at Jericho,"; Wood, "The Walls of Jericho" 36–40; Aust and Ashely, "Jericho."

39. Bruce, *Hebrews*, 327–28.

40. There is a different spelling for her name in Matthew's list but as Bruce points out, the *chi* [χ] in Greek better represents the Hebrew Ḥêt [ח] in her Hebrew name *Raḥab*, in Joshua 2:3 than the ā in Raáb in Greek, as it is rendered here and in James. Bruce, *Hebrews*, 329n229.

represent major periods of Israel's life they do not do so in equal measure and they are not given in chronological order. The first four come from the earlier period of Israel inhabiting the land: that of the Judges (Gideon, Jud 6:11–27; Barak, Jud 4:6–16; Sampson, Jud 13:24—16:30; Jephthah, Jud 11:1—12:7), while the last two on the list–David and Samuel–are from the commencement of the monarchy and the first prophets. The later period is altogether left out other than in the generalities which follow in the next verses and most likely come from the extra canonical writings.

The order of presentation appears strange, since in the biblical narrative Barak comes before Gideon, Jephthah before Sampson and Samuel before David.[41] In terms of any significant roles played, Gideon overcame the Midianites with a force of 300 men with nothing but torches in their jars (Jud 7:7, 19–22); Barak seems like an unlikely candidate because he did not want to go to battle with Sisera, the commander of king Jabin of Canaan's army, unless Deborah the prophetess accompanied him (Jud 4:2, 8) but he did go and was victorious in the battle. In spite of his questionable moral character, Samson served the purposes of Yahweh during a bleak period in Israel's history (Jud 14:4; 16:30). Jephthah may appear to be another unlikely candidate as the son of a prostitute, once driven from his own family (Jud 11:1); he then became the head of the people and commander of the army of Gilead (among the tribes who lived in trans-Jordan) bringing about a great defeat upon the Ammonites (Jud 11:11, 33). David with all his foibles, was nevertheless a man of great faith and love for Yahweh. He certainly gave great evidence of his trust in God and his promises; this was clear in his willingness to stand up to Goliath (1 Sam 17:32, 37, 45–51) and later, especially during the time when he was being pursued continuously by Saul, he refused to lay his hand upon him but left his case in the hand of God (1 Sam. 24:4–6; 26:6–12).

Samuel had the hand of God upon his life from his earliest years and was an outstanding leader, as well as a strong prophetic voice, who kept the nation on the right path during his entire ministry. He is not the first prophet as there were others before him like Moses, who talked face to face with God and received his commands but of those who are known as prophets in the land, he became the first of an outstanding number who followed. The prophets are not named here but would most certainly include all those in the canon of scripture who have books named after them, as well as others like Elijah and Elisha.

vv. 33–34 "*who by faith overcame kingdoms, brought about justice, obtained promises, stopped the mouth of lions, quenched the power of fire,*

---

41. See Bruce, *Hebrews*, 331.

escaped the edge of the sword, were made strong out of weakness, became mighty in war, made foreign armies yield." All these people of faith included in this text, are noted for different aspects of the factors recorded. This does not mean that they all accomplished each of the items but at least one of them and most, more.

The first group mentioned here is comprised of those *"who by faith overcame kingdoms."* It may appear strange that faith is associated with military conquest but it needs to be remembered that the period during which this took place was when the Children of Israel were settling in the land and their victories were attributed to Yahweh, who enabled them to overcome the pagan peoples who they were intended to replace. Of those mentioned in the list: Gideon (Jud 7), Barak (Jud 4), Sampson (Jud 13:24–16), Jephthah (Jud 11), and David were involved in military battles by which they overcame their enemies and enabled the settlement of the land.

The next group are recognized for establishing justice. This would have included those mentioned in the book of Judges but also men like David who is reported to have *"administered justice and equity to all his people"* (2 Sam 8:15) as well as Samuel, who although he is primarily remembered as a prophet/seer, was also one who judged the people and administered justice both on his circuits throughout the land at Bethel, Gilgal, Mizpah, as well as in his permanent residence at Ramah (1 Sam 7:6,16–17).

All of them were involved in obtaining promises which God had made to them and to the people as a whole. Those promises were given in regard to what was necessary during the life of the people at that time, so that although it is mentioned later in verse 39 that they did not receive the promise, there is no contradiction because, that verse refers to the ultimate heavenly or unseen promise which was yet to come. Here, what God had said happened. When it comes to shutting the mouths of lions, the first person that comes to mind is Daniel (Dan 6:22). In that verse it was actually God who sent his angel to shut the lions' mouths but Daniel was the one who by faith lived through the experience and trusted in God so that he would not give up on his times of prayer, regardless of the threats made against him. But there were others too, who like Samson (Jud 14:5–6) and David (1 Sam 17:34–37) who carried out powerful deeds overcoming lions with their bare hands.

Those who *quenched the power of fire* clearly refers to Shadrach, Meshach and Abednego (Dan 3:23–26). It is not clear as to which incident the author had in mind when it comes to the expression: *"escaped the edge of the sword,"* since that is a common Old Testament expression, showing that someone escaped death. It is used in Moses' testimony to his father-in-law Jethro, when he says: *"The God of my father was my help, and delivered me from the sword of Pharaoh."* There are other passages where escape from death is noted, particularly that of David (1 Sam 19:10; 2 Sam 15:14). Others would include Elijah who escaped from Jezebel (1 Kgs 19:2–3) and Elisha who was delivered from the army of the king of Aram (2 Kgs 6:12–19). But this could refer to any occasion when God's servants were delivered.

The phrase: *were made strong out of weakness,* could apply to many individuals and occasions during the period referred to in this text. Of those whose names appear, Sampson is the clearest example. In spite of what appears to be total failure and impossible circumstances, he committed himself to God and brought down the house upon the heads of the Philistines. In his death he killed more of his enemies than the total of all those numbered during his entire life (Jud 16:28–30). There are others like Gideon, who could be considered as applicable here; this is because he considered himself as the least in his clan and his clan as the weakest in Manasseh (Jud 6:15). Yet through him, the might of God was manifest and deliverance from the Midianites was achieved. Nevertheless, he has already been mentioned in the list, so it is not certain that he was envisaged here. Hezekiah's life was lengthened when he was at the point of death so he would certainly qualify for the list (2 Kgs 20:5–6). Some scholars mention Judith from the apocryphal writings but there is no direct reference to her, even if she fits the criteria.[42]

The following phrases speak of power and success in overcoming those who were Israel's enemies, so that the context is that of war. These people *"became mighty in war, made foreign armies yield."* Individuals here would include men like David in his battle against Goliath as well as in his many battles (Ps 18:17–18, 29, 34–35, 37–42, 47–48) and Joshua as well as the other judges who put the enemies of Israel to flight. It is also very likely that those from the intertestamental period depicted in the extra canonical books of Maccabees (see especially 1 Macc 4:14–15, 20–22, 34; 5:22, 34 et al.) especially in the face of the terrors at the time Antiochus Epiphanes and his acolytes, are to be envisaged.[43]

v. 35 "Women received their dead again by resurrection. But others were tortured[44] refusing deliverance so that they may obtain a better resurrection." There are two occasions in the Old Testament when women had their dead

42. See Bruce, *Hebrews,* 336; Ellingworth, *Hebrews,* 117; Moffatt, *Hebrews,* 186n1.

43. Although the two books of Maccabees are not included in the biblical canon and are not used in the formulation of doctrine, the history of the events depicted is, for the most part, helpful. The individuals who are portrayed at the time, did make a tremendous difference in upholding the worship of Yahweh among the Jews in the land because of their acts portraying trust in him; see Moffatt, *Hebrews,* 186.

44 See the following note and Arndt & Gingrich, 837.

children raised from the dead. The first is the widow from Zarephath, whose son died (1 Kgs 17:18–23) but was raised up by Elijah and the second, the son of the Shunammite (2 Kgs 4:20, 32–36), raised to life by Elisha. The first was not even a Jew but the second certainly was. The construction of the Greek is such that resurrection is seen as the means of the miracle. There is no mention of faith on the part of the women, rather the faith of the prophets is what is involved and this is seen as the source of the resurrections.

All the text up to this point, has implied the positive outcomes of faith in the lives of the people mentioned but there is now a sudden change in the approach, which is very important. This is because if the next section were not included, the teaching would give the impression that unless the sorts of things mentioned here occur, it would indicate failure on the part of the believers in God who do not experience the kind of miracles included above. What the next verses show, is that the faith of the person who trusts in God, does not always mean that the outcome will automatically be what is usually regarded as the best and most successful, from mankind's perspective. This is an aspect often neglected in the teaching of those who major on what is called the "word of faith" doctrine which teaches that a failure to obtain a good outcome in the present, is an indication of a lack of faith (see the notes on "*The Word–Logos* . . ." 1:3).

But others were tortured in dreadful ways, in spite of their faith or rather, because of their faith; they accepted to submit themselves to this torture because of the hope they had. The Greek verb *tumpanizō* means to torture; a *tumpanon* is an instrument used to torture as in 2 Macc 6:19, 28 (where it is often translated "torment"). It is thought that this instrument was some sort of frame upon which the person was placed and stretched out before being beaten to death.[45] The reason given, is that they looked for a better resurrection than those who were raised by the faith of the prophets who prayed for them. If this is understood, it means that they awaited a better resurrection. This is obviously the resurrection at the return of Christ, resulting in eternal life and not just a prolonged and temporary stay upon the earthly scene. The word "better" here needs to be understood in terms of what was regarded as a more victorious resurrection.

v. 36 "*And others experienced mocking and flogging and even chains and prison.*" The others fall within the category of those who did not see the victorious deliverances of the first group listed. None of their names are given but they would have been people known to the readers and most

---

45. This instrument is mentioned by several authors of the day where its use is affiliated with beating someone to death after their torture. Aristophanes, *Plutus, 476*; Josephus, *Contra Apionem, i. 148*, quoting Berossus, *Aaborosoarchodos . . . hupo tōn philōn apetumpanisthē*: Arist. *Rhet.* ii. 5. 14, *hosper hoi apotumpanizomenoi*.

likely, those who lived within the period covered by the Maccabees including Eleazar and the seven brothers (see 2 Macc 6:18–31:7 the entire chapter
et al.). All these people faced death and torment with great faith in God and
faithfully held to the truth of their beliefs without hesitation. The author
focuses on the period relative to the history of Israel but it is without doubt
that the readers would also have been aware of those of their own time, who
qualified to fit in the same categories as those named here such as James the
brother of John (Acts 12:2).

vv. 37–38 "*They were stoned,*[46] *they were sawn in two. They died, killed
by the sword. They went about in skins of sheep and goats, destitute, afflicted,
mistreated (of whom the world was not worthy). They wandered over the deserts and mountains and in caves and holes in the ground.*" From the earliest
days of Israel's history, stoning was an established way of putting people to
death (see Achan in Josh 7:25). According to tradition, Jeremiah was stoned
to death by a band of Jewish rebels after he had been taken by them to Egypt
somewhere between 585 and 583 BC.[47] However, there is no absolute record of his death so it is not certain that this reference is to him. However,
Zechariah son of the priest Jehoiada was stoned to death at the word of king
Joash whom he opposed (2 Chron 24:20–21); he therefore, certainly fits this
description.

They were sawn in two. Although there is no biblical reference to Isaiah dying in this way, there is a strongly documented tradition to this in
extra canonical writings, which says that he was sawn in two at the order of
king Manasseh.[48] It is not possible to verify this from the Old Testament
canon. Untimely, violent death was prevalent among these people of faith.
They were killed by the sword as recorded in 1 Kings 19:10. This kind of
death was foretold by Daniel in 11:33. There are many who would have
experienced their end in a similar manner.

The next section highlights those who lived as outcasts from society,
in isolation and extreme poverty because of their adherence to the promises
of God. One such was Elijah (2 Kgs 1:8) and of course by the time of Jesus,

46. There is considerable disagreement between the Manuscripts at this point.
Even the final reading of the *Greek New Testament* (5th Ed. rev.) which omits the verb
epeiasthēsan (were tested or tried) indicates that their reading is highly questionable
{C} 743n4 on verse 37. The reading "*they were tested*"-*epeiasthēan* is included in 𝔓13
from the 3–4th C. A. Alexandrinus from the 5th C. and Aleph or Sinaiticus from the
4th C. in a different order. It is included in many translations but it is very general
under a category already covered in other verses so likely is a gloss.

47. Tertullian, *Scorpiace*, ch. viii; Jerome, *Adversus Jovinianum*, ii. 37.

48. *Babylonian Talmud, Yebamot*, 49b; *Sanhedrin* 103b; *Ascension of Isaiah*; *The
martyrdom of Isaiah*, 5.1b, 2, 11–12.

John the Baptist (Matt 3:1–4). These people preferred to live this way rather than forsake their communion with God and the love of his purposes. "*They went about in skins of sheep and goats, destitute, afflicted, mistreated.*" They may have been outcasts from man's perspective but from God's, the author says the world was not worthy of them. The main thought here is that they did not see the earth as their permanent home.

Society at enmity with God tends to reject anyone who holds to views contrary to those of the majority because their strong beliefs and witness tend to point to their own failures and highlight their own sins and injustice. Numbers of those who lived in this manner are described during the Maccabean period; they fled the cities to the mountains and the wilderness because they were zealous "for the law of God" (1 Macc 2:26, 28–29). In the canonical scriptures people like this are described in Ps 44:22. They were mistreated and put to death, mostly by the powerful and often even the religious hierarchy of the day. The wilderness often depicted a place of temporary demure, as with the forty years of wanderings of the people of Israel but it also was a place of safety, even if it was not a place of abundance. These individuals sought some kind of solace from the evil around them by cutting themselves off from those who opposed them and doing God's purposes. But the places where they went were in no manner preferable. The mountains, the deserts, caves and holes in the earth, provided them with some minimal security while they lived their earthly lives. The holes in the ground are considered to be smaller than caves. Some translations describe them as dens (ESV, MEV, TLB). These people knew that their time upon the earth was brief and not the place of their ultimate destiny.

v. 39 "*And all of these, having had witness borne to them by faith, did not receive what was promised.*" The following two verses conclude the record regarding all those who have been included in the chapter up to this point and who are men and women of faith. They had clung onto the hope and trust of God's promises, which make it very clear that what they hoped for was not going to be found during this age and not upon this earth. They may have been beneficiaries of temporal promises but they did not receive the ultimate promise because, as is declared in the next verse, there was a time in God's provision when that would happen and it was *not yet*. It is not stated here but the reason that it was not received was because Christ had not yet come and without his sacrifice it never would have been possible for the fulfilment of all that God had in mind. They all had witness borne to them by God himself as to their faithfulness and tenacity and that, in spite of the fact that the promise for which they sought was not yet received. The next verse explains the reason for that. If it were not so, it would appear that God had let them down and that he had not done what he said he would do, meaning that he could not really be relied upon. But that is far from being the reality of what occurred.

v. 40 "*God having foreseen something better for us, that without us they should not be made perfect.*" This final verse of the chapter explains exactly why the promise for which they awaited was not received during their time; that was the epoch of the Old Testament. God foresaw something better for "us" collectively. That means for all the saints of all time. The word foreseen (*problepsamenou*), indicates God's sovereign plan which was in place from the very beginning. It was a plan which looked to the future from the start. It bypassed the days of Israel, as God's sole instrument for salvation and looked to the coming of a new instrument: The Church. The thought is contained here within the pronoun "*us.*" The emphasis is upon something far broader than the previous instrument: Israel. However, essential to the formation of the "us," is the Church; this matter is developed further in 12:23 and described as "*an assembly and church of the firstborn.*" It is dependent upon the coming of the firstborn, the Messiah (Christ) who was the only one who could put this new body in place and thereby provide the way of salvation for all mankind.

The nature of everything that is underlined by what is "better," is reached here at every level for the follower of God, through Christ. The theme of superiority and what is better runs throughout the letter, as has already been seen from the earliest verses (1:4) so it is no wonder that it should be reinforced here. Earlier texts have spoken of a better hope (7:19), a better covenant (7:22; 8:6), better promises (8:6), better sacrifices (9:23), a better country/fatherland– *patrida*; see v.14–(11:16), a better resurrection (11:35) and now something better for "us," which means a better revelation based on Christ. The phrase that "*without us they should not be made perfect*" (*hina mē chōris hēmōn teleiōthōsin*), needs to be understood as has already been indicated, not merely in the sense of perfection but more in the sense of *completion*. In other words, God did not stop when it came to what was associated with Israel and the Law. That was all part of the earlier imperfect covenant, which has now been bettered in Christ and through his Church. All the readers of this letter, as it was intended, need to understand that even if they are Jews, they are indebted to Christ, who is their ultimate High Priest. Not only is he the way into the holy of holies for the Jew but for all who look to him, as the one who has put in place this new and better covenant, which opens its doors to all who trust in God through him.

Even for those who benefit from the arrival of the promise in and through Christ there is yet a sense in which what is perfect is *not yet come*. This is because the heavenly promises, which are the ultimate hope for all believers, await the return of the Christ. For this reason, the continuation to the next chapter handles the period of transition between what things are like now and what will be, in terms of what Paul describes as: the deliverance from the bondage of corruption and the freedom of the glory of the sons of God, with the full redemption of fallen life (Rom 8:21, 23).

The entire purpose of chapter eleven is to show that faith, as the author sees it, is a very practical matter of carrying out God's purposes consistently during the course of one's life. The outcomes however, are far from being ordinary because as the believer follows the direction of God, in what the next chapter describes as "running the race," God is at the helm. He is the one who determines what will transpire if we are faithful. The lesson is therefore that nothing is too menial nor too difficult if God remains at the center of all that is required of those who follow the Son; however, full engagement and strong conviction is essential on their part.

12.

There is a race to run 12:1–11

In this chapter there is a transition from gleaning truth and principles from the list of men and women of faith of the past, to looking to Jesus himself and his example. Consequently, as just mentioned, there is a race to be run, which indicates the necessity for discipline in the whole of one's life. This means there is no place for moral laxity or laxity of any nature. Once again, the past order is compared with the present. The new covenant has promises which exceed anything from the old and its rewards are everlasting because they are part of a kingdom that is immovable.

v. 1 "Therefore, since we are surrounded by such a cloud of witnesses, let us put aside every weight and the sin which entangles and let us run with endurance the race that is set before us." The Greek word which introduces the verse is *toigaroun*[1]–therefore or consequently. It is emphatic and in the New Testament is only found elsewhere in 1 Thessalonians 4:8. It links what has gone before with the application about to be made. The people in the list that was given in chapter 11, are those to whom witness was previously given by God himself (11:39). In the mind of the author and because of the way in which he has indicated the link between individuals and their backing by the Holy Spirit in previous chapters, it is possible to say that God has indeed born witness to the same people through the miracles and signs that took place in their lives (see notes on 2:4).[2] The passage now draws

---

1. This word is only found here and in 1 Thess 4:8 in canonical New Testament writings but is more common in the literature of the day such as in Philo, Josephus and 1 Clement 57:4, 6 and elsewhere. See Arndt & Gingrich, 828 where he renders *toigaroun*–τοιγαρουν as "for that very reason then, therefore."

2. For more on the link between God, the Holy Spirit and his inspiration of God's

attention to all who follow in the footsteps of those who have gone before. The author includes himself in the statement when he says that *"we are surrounded by such a cloud of witnesses."* Several scholars see the important matter here as what the present believers see in the lives of those who went before them, rather than in what the witnesses see in those who run the race at present. This is because those who are alive now are expected to follow their example.[3] Certainly, their example becomes an encouragement to those who are still engaged in their earthly contest. But there is no reason as to why both the aspect of present believers looking to the example of the saints of the former days, as well as those of former days looking on with equal interest in those of the present, are not important. This is because both are members of the same community of faith, all of whom make up the entirety of the general assembly of saints mentioned in 12:23. After all, the author has just said in 11:40 that without "us" they are not made perfect or complete.

The new emphasis is no longer that of the past but the present. It is as though those earlier men and women of faith look over the parapet of time to see how the present participants in this earthly race are running. They show great interest in what is taking place and wish to see the same kind of success in them that they experienced in terms of faith and trust in God during their time. The former are described here as *a cloud of witnesses*, who surround believers at the present. This brings the past and present into the same arena and shows how intricately linked are those of both epochs. The Greek word witness–*martus* (here in the plural–*marturōn*)–is not generally translated as "spectator" but in the context of those who have gone before and who now bear witness to those upon the earth, the imagery certainly fits the picture the author wishes to paint. Not only are they watching with great interest, but many of them have actually laid down their lives for their faith. The word "cloud" is likewise unusual but it shows the huge number of those who are involved. The use of the word *surrounded* (*perikeimenon*) gives a sense of their proximity and relationship, even if it is not a visible one from the perspective of those who are still on earth. It does appear to indicate that those who are in the heavenly sphere are aware of what is happening on the earth.

The next part of the verse focuses on the race in which the believer is involved. The Greek *agōna*[4] can be translated by *contest* or *race* but clearly has the sense of the latter here. This sort of imagery is common in Scripture,

---

followers see: 3:7; 6:4–6; 10:15–17 et al.

3. Moffatt, *Hebrews*, 193; Bruce, *Hebrews*, 346.

4. This is the word from which we get our English word *agony*.

especially in Pauline literature, where life is portrayed as a battle or contest (1 Cor 9:24; Gal 2:2; Phil 2:16; 1 Tim 6:11–12; 2 Tim 4:7) as well as in Jude v. 3. It is also found in the literature of the time. In IV Macc 17:11–15 the author writes of Eleazar being involved in a contest with spectators, in terms similar to those described here. In this particular race the follower of God is exhorted to put aside every weight (*onkon*–only found here in the NT), which in this sense, is equivalent to any sin. It is a weight because it is something extra to the purpose of the race which is being run and it is a sin because it works against God's purposes. The Greek *euperistatos–entangle,* which is another word only found here in the New Testament, can have several meanings but in this context appears to portray something, of an evil nature, which easily wraps itself around someone in order to ensnare and limit their progress.[5] For this reason, it is translated: entangles or ensnares, in this context and has to be deliberately set aside. The exhortation is *"let us run with endurance the race that is set before us."* The race is to be run with endurance and clear focus on its end and purpose. Endurance is already something that has been raised in the letter (10:36), together with its synonym patience (*makarothumias*) in 6:12. To participate in this context requires self-discipline on the part of the contestant over a prolonged period.

v. 2 *"Looking steadfastly to Jesus the founder and finisher of our faith, who against the joy that was set before him endured the cross, despising the shame and is seated at the right hand of the throne of God."* Verse one and two, form a single sentence in the original and ultimately focus on Jesus, about whom nothing at all has been said directly in the previous chapter. In the light of the running of the race from verse one, the phrase *"looking steadfastly to Jesus"* (*aphorōntes eis . . . Iēsous*) makes it very clear that if the end is to be achieved the runner is bound to keep his eye upon Jesus alone. The emphasis is upon the steadfastness of the gaze upon Jesus, who in this construction is the center of all that matters.[6] There is a very similar phrase found in the context of a passage from IV Macc 17:10, mentioned in the previous verse, where an aged priest Eleazar, together with his wife and their seven sons "looked steadfastly to God" when martyrdom was required of them. Here Jesus is designated as *"the author and perfector of our faith."* *"Our faith"* (*tēs pisteōs*) here speaks, not merely of "the faith" as exhibited in the previous chapter but the fullness of all that it means to be a Christian. It is the body of belief which encompasses all for which the believer stands (of course that includes the faith to trust in God as did those of the past).

---

5. See Moulton and Milligan, *Vocabulary,* 264; Arndt & Gingrich, 324. For a different view see Bruce, *Hebrews,* 349–50.

6. There is a very similar phrase found in IV Macc 17:10.

The Greek word "author" (*archēgos* see 2:10) has been translated here by "founder" because that is the sense that is central to the meaning in this instance. It means that he is the one who put the whole plan of salvation in place and it is upon him alone that the whole plan rests. The sentence is inclusive of all that Christ has done to provide salvation and all that is related to faith. He is the one who will, in the end, bring about its completion and it is in this way that "the finisher/perfecter" is to be understood. The plan is not yet at its end but until it is, the participants have to keep on keeping on. There is a day coming when Christ returns and when all who practice endurance and undergo suffering in his name will achieve their goal.

Some may ask: How could Jesus be the founder and finisher of the faith for those who lived during the time of the Old Testament? After all, chronologically he came after them. However, in the thinking of the author, he would accept that in his humanity, Jesus may have come after them but as the divine and eternal Spirit, who was introduced in 1:3 and as the maker of all things, who is the image of the Almighty, he always was and is. Therefore, he certainly is the founder and finisher for all, whether of the first covenant or the second. Because he is the founder and finisher of our faith, any attempt to side-line him by anyone, would automatically mean that Christ's work would be disregarded and become null and void as far as they are concerned.

The next part of the declaration appears to be out of place when it mentions "*the joy that was set before him.*" The joy was no joy in the submission of himself to the cross but in the knowledge of the outcome at the end of it all. The concept of joy in the New Testament is prominent throughout. In Jesus' words to his disciples, he talks of their sorrow turning to joy (John 16:20), indicating that the sorrow and despair of the crucifixion would turn to joy at the resurrection. The concept is similar here, where the agony and the pain of the cross provide the way of salvation and forgiveness for the perfection which will eventually follow all that was required in the sacrifice Christ provided. As James says: "*Count it all joy, my brothers, when you meet trials of various kinds*" (Jas 1:2). It was in the face of all this and the knowledge that eventually, what was necessary to bring the sinful race back into communion with God, was worth the trouble and pain required to apprehend it. Consequently, it was the realization of this future success that would bring about reconciliation between fallen mankind and a holy God that made it possible for Christ to endure the cross and despise the shame attached to it all. Perhaps it should be called pre-emptive, or anticipatory joy.

The author has already reminded the readers of the need for endurance. Here it is linked to the suffering of the cross. Christ was willing to endure the terrible agony of the cross, as well as its tremendous shame, in the light of the joy that would follow. The shame of the death of the cross for the one who was the nation's Messiah, should never be underestimated. To despise it, does not mean to ignore it but to count it of no importance comparatively, when it comes to the final reckoning of what the outcome will be. That is the ultimate victory of the entire plan and the completion of all that is necessary to restore God's creation to what he originally desired. The work is done and now Christ *is seated at the right hand of the throne of God*. The cross was and is, the only way to the throne at the right hand of God Almighty. The very same terms were stated at the very beginning of the letter (1:3 & 8:1) but here the designated way has been fully illustrated and its implications elaborated upon. The cross is not the end of the story but without it, the exhalation of Christ and the redemption of the creation would never be possible.

v. 3 *"For consider him who endured such hostility of sinners against himself so that you may not grow weary or fainthearted."* With the words of verse two still clear in one's mind: *"looking steadfastly at Jesus,"* it is necessary to consider him who endured such hostility of sinners against himself. The Greek word "to consider" (*analogizomai*), is found only here in the NT and is in the imperative, meaning that it is absolutely essential to consider and understand all that is involved relative to Jesus and all that took place in an attempt to prevent him from accomplishing the plan of God throughout his entire life and ministry. There was the opposition from the earliest by Herod, who wished to kill him as a baby, then constantly during his ministry the Jewish hierarchy attempted to kill him (John 5:18; 7:1, 30; 8:20; 11:49–53) because they saw him as a threat to their hold on religious power. In the light of what has just been written about him, and considering how he was treated throughout his life with disdain and hostility, how much more should those who are his followers now be willing to endure similar rejection and antagonism, without expecting any sort of exoneration? After all, that was exactly what Jesus said would happen to his own (John 15:20).

The author wishes to encourage his readers not to *"grow weary or fainthearted."* Once more endurance is required, which demands a mind fixed on the goal, in spite of any contrary circumstances. The right kind of mind set, is what is required of each runner in this race or combatant in the contest.

v. 4 *"You have not yet resisted to the point of shedding blood in your struggle against sin."* Having looked closely at what was required for Jesus in his endurance, the whole question of discipline and God's role in it, becomes central to the presentation. The metaphor shifts from the race track to that of wrestling or boxing where there is a fight going on for one's life.[7] If the list in chapter 11 is reviewed, many had to lay down their lives for their faith and certainly, Christ had to do the same in order to provide redemption. It is pointed out to his readers by the author, that at that time, none of them had been required to do the same. It is not the same situation today but it was then among this particular group.[8] It may have been true that some of them would have had to eventually submit to martyrdom but at that moment the author was willing them on in the contest and attempting to encourage them to understand that discipline and opposition was very much part of standing up for one's faith and for God. Sin is seen as the opponent against whom the struggle is carried out. The tense of the present participle (*antagōnizomenoi*–struggling/fighting/contesting) shows that the contest is ongoing and never ceases. The resistance which is called for, is the required action on the part of believers to stand firm in opposition to something. Here it is used first of all in the sense of resisting death but this goes on to the fighting or battling sin, head on. There is every evidence that resistance and not passivity is required in Christian life, as one stands against any and every form of evil. The enemy is seen as sin personified. That means any and all who stand against Christ and his purposes become the tool of sin. They are the dupes of Satan.

> vv. 5–6 "*And have you forgotten the exhortation that addresses you as sons?*
> '*My son, do not take lightly the discipline of the Lord,*
> *Nor lose heart when you are reproved by him.*
> *For the Lord disciplines those he loves,*
> *and chastises every son he receives.*'"

A rhetorical question is introduced by the author. He is showing the readers that either they have somehow believed that by following Christ they are suddenly exonerated from all of life's trials or they are unaware of the necessity to submit to the discipline of God which has the benefit of all God's lessons as each individual heads toward the ultimate goal. The former view would certainly fit many in certain evangelical circles today, where they believe that true men and women of faith never have to expect anything other than the best of everything. For them only those who live a second-class Christian experience will have to suffer the ups and downs of life. This is the teaching, as has been stated in part, of those who hold

---

7. Paul does this very same thing in 1 Cor 9:24–26.

8. It was estimated by Fowler "Christian Martyr Numbers," that there are approximately 90,000 Christians put to death each year by those hostile to the Christian message; Martin in an article "'70 Million Christians' martyred." quotes David B. Barrett who estimated that by 2014 that there had been 70 million martyrs since the time of Jesus.

to the so called *rhēma* doctrine of "positive confession" (see notes on: *The Word–Logos and Rhēma: What is the difference?* ch. 1:3).

The author gives his readers the benefit of the doubt when he asks them the question, which he quotes almost word for word from Proverbs 3:11, 12 in the Septuagint:[9] "*And have you forgotten the exhortation that addresses you as sons?*" The exhortation is meant to be both a challenge and an encouragement to the readers, not merely a rebuke. It appears that these readers somehow think that they have been abandoned by God because of the trials through which they are passing. Sons[10] are part of the family and fathers take much time and care to make sure that their sons are brought up in the right way as this upbringing is key to success in life as a whole. This procedure, known as *discipline* (*paideia*),[11] which at its root, has the concept of how children of young age, have to be taught how to behave in every area of life, was basic to nearly every people group at the time (see *Appendix G*). Fathers were willing to go out of their way to ensure that their children and especially their boys, were taught the basic lessons of life, respect, responsibility and self-control, in order that they would succeed later as adults. The motivation behind this discipline was love for the child and the desire to see it equipped for the future in the best way possible. If a father did not undertake this discipline and training, it would have been interpreted to mean that he had no real care for the child or that the child was considered to be illegitimate and unloved. This is how discipline should be understood here. Part of this disciplinary action is teaching a child how to perform what can be considered the ongoing acts of drudgery associated with life. Sometimes this means doing what is difficult, annoying and even painful over a prolonged period of time.

9. Moffatt, quoting from Conybeare's edition of Philo's *De Vita Contemplativa*, in *Hebrews*, 201, states that the word *paraklēsis* which is behind this exhortation is in "Alexandrian Judaism . . . 'the regular term of "an appeal" to an individual to rise to the high life of philosophy.'" 200.

10. The emphasis here is upon sons, as it would have been at that time in history and the cultural values which were held by many peoples, but this should not be considered to indicate a gender bias today. What is mentioned with regard to sons has the same application for daughters or children as a whole. This inclusion needs to be held throughout this section where "sons" are mentioned. So automatically think of "sons and daughters" or "family" when the word appears here.

11. The Greek word *paideia* as a noun can be translated as "upbringing" but is often rendered discipline, or training. It can be of an intellectual or moral nature. As a verb *paideuō,* in a context where God is the one administering the discipline, it can be giving guidance of any kind necessary to bring someone to the place that is required. So, it could be to chastise, punish, correct, or instruct, depending upon the context. Where human fathers or agents are the ones administering the discipline, it can also mean to chasten or scourge (Luke 23:16). See, Arndt & Gingrich, 608–9; Moulton & Milligan, *Vocabulary*, 474.

It means learning how to be tolerant and understanding of the predicaments in which, not only one finds oneself but of the relationship with others. Tolerance and endurance are vital.

These verses reinforce the fact that what happens to the individual during life is not by chance, since the Lord permits all to take place in order to bring his children to a place of maturity through the trials. These tests are not to be treated lightly, seen as insignificant, or despised. If the Lord rebukes or reproves his sons, it is for their own good and not because he has suddenly become their enemy. To regard these tests in that manner is to fail to understand who God really is and also an indication of a failure to grasp his purposes, which are the perfection of each one. The lessons must be learned and there needs to be change and growth. There must never be the thought that there is room to abandon faith in the face of discipline and hardship. Rather faith becomes the anchor which enables stability at times of storm.

God disciplines those he loves because of his long-term goals and what he wants to see as the finished product. God is the one who sets the agenda for each to follow. The second part of the couplet repeats the theme: "*He chastises every son he receives*." The language may appear harsh to the modern mind. To chastise means to beat and nowadays, that is considered by most in the West to be the equivalent of abuse and totally unacceptable.[12] But here is it not. It is guidance aimed at betterment and the inculcation of clear principles, foundational actions and correct thinking. This sort of thinking was, after all at the heart of Jewish family life and part of the teaching of their own scriptures (Prov 13:24; 19:18).

v. 7 "It is for the sake of discipline that you must endure. God is dealing with you as with sons. For what son is not disciplined by his father?" Discipline, sonship and endurance all go together. Here the sentence indicates that it is necessary to understand that the relationship with God as Father, is an ongoing one and therefore, he does not give up his care and best intentions for all his children. Parents do no stop loving and caring for their children because they want the best for them. If the individual understands the role of discipline, they will not balk at it but be thankful for what it accomplishes in them. Any child who does not receive the discipline that is required, from the scriptural perspective, has in fact been abandoned by the father and their chances of success are automatically reduced as a consequence. It is for this reason sonship and discipline go together, as do love

---

12. Physical discipline, including hitting someone with a cane, was common in many cultures until recent times, including during my own youth. In the United States there are still some States where similar forms of punishment are present and permitted even if it not the case everywhere.

and intervention. Fathers discipline, not just because it is part of their duty but because it is part of their heart's desire to see the betterment of the child and to save them the possibility of failure in the future. A father who fails to discipline his child, is in reality, not acting as a proper father should.

v. 8 "But if you are left without discipline, in which all share, then you are illegitimate children and not sons." It is assumed that all children will be disciplined. Any who are not, are regarded as not really belonging to the family and uncared for. The sons/children must acknowledge that belonging means acceptance of being a member of the family and discipline is very much part of that. Therefore, when these believers are called upon to suffer because of their testimony, it is a stamp of identity that they belong and God is permitting it to take place because they are family and not outsiders. Peter talks about the same sort of things happening when he writes about "a fiery trial" when it comes to test you not being seen as something strange but as an indicator of sharing in Christ's sufferings (1 Pet 4:12–13).

v. 9 "Moreover, we have had earthly fathers who corrected us and we respected them; should we not be much more subjected to the Father of [our][13] *spirits and live?"* The example of earthly fathers disciplining their children is then transferred to the Father of spirits. If those who are natural fathers seek the best for their children, how much more the Father of all life? There has been some discussion as to the sense of *"Father of* (our) *spirits,"* a term which is only found here in the New Testament.[14] In the context of comparison between natural and spiritual life, it is clearly indicating here, the fact that God is the Father of our very being and spiritual existence and as such has the ultimate word to speak over our present and future. If we submit to his discipline, we will live but the possibility of not being willing to submit also carries drastic consequences.

v. 10 "For they disciplined us for a short while according to what seemed good to them, but he for our good so that we may share his holiness." Human parents discipline their children according to their concept of what is right and wrong and according to cultural and human priorities based upon very limited and often faulty understanding. Again, their discipline is only in place for a short duration. Mostly only during childhood. God's intentions have eternal consequences and are based, not on human understanding but

13. If we note what Bruce has to say about the Greek construction: *tō patri tōn pneumatōn*, literally: "the Father of spirits," he makes it very clear that the phrase underlines the fact that the plural possessive *tōn* (of the) highlights the fact that God is the father of "our" spirits (*Hebrews,* 359n81); this makes him the one who has the ultimate authority over each one's existence.

14. See Hughes, *Hebrews,* 531; Spicq, *Hébreux,* II. 394; Moffatt, *Hebrews,* 203; Owen, *Hebrews,* 12:9.

on divine purpose and the fulness of his sovereign knowledge. His desire is to prepare each one for their eternal reward, which means being fitted into the eternal and perfect divine plan, where his holiness alone is the driving force. It is for the good or benefit, of the individual that this discipline is put in place and the outcome is that of sharing in God's holiness or divine life at the end of it all. The word used to depict holiness or sanctity (*hagiotētos* from *hagiotēs*) here, is only found once elsewhere in the New Testament in 2 Cor 1:12.[15] It depicts participating in the life that God alone attributes. Since God himself is holy, to share in this holiness, means to participate in the perfection of his permanent and eternal state, which only he is able to provide and which is obviously very different from that of the earthly.

v. 11 "*On the one hand all discipline now seems not to be joyful but painful but later on it yields the peaceful fruit of righteousness to those who have been trained by it.*" Discipline never is pleasant and those who are subject to it would normally attempt to avoid its implications by whatever means necessary in an attempt at natural self-defense. While it is in place and being experienced, discipline is painful and that cannot be denied. But the results of divine discipline have consequences which produce change in character and conformity to the holiness mentioned above. Here this is depicted as "*the peaceful fruit of righteousness.*" During the disciplining there is certainly no peace but this means that it is not endless. There will come a day when it will be over and the results will prove that the lessons were worthwhile. Jesus talks about the procedures behind the production of much fruit in his parable of the vine and in it he underlines the necessity of being pruned in order to produce more fruit (John 15:2). So too here discipline and the production of righteousness in permanence, which fits one for the ultimate state in God's presence, go together. It is only those who have learned the lessons of what the discipline has to teach, who will benefit from the outcomes that need to be in place to form one's character.

The recent emphasis in western culture to downplay the place of discipline of any kind has meant that it mostly has a negative connotation in today's societies. Perhaps that is why the concept is rejected and even despised. This means that Christians are not exempt from rejecting its teaching. However, in scripture it is expected and required in order to demonstrate the pathway to maturity and the means of attaining the complete fulfilment of an individual's potential. This passage demonstrates that it is the norm and a demonstration of God's care and love for his own.

---

15. It is found in literature of the time in 2 Macc 15:2 and *Testament of Levi* (a pseudepigraphal work originally in Aramaic), 3:4.

Determination in fulfilling God's requirements is an absolute 12:12–17

vv. 12–13 "*Therefore, lift your drooping hands and strengthen your weak knees and make straight paths for your feet so that what is lame may not be put out of joint but rather let it be healed*." Once more the author, depending upon what has just been said regarding the normality of discipline and using language applicable to the first verses of the chapter, is urging the readers to get on with the task at hand. It is necessary as with all athletes, to put one's all into what is required to succeed in the contest because it is not yet over; there is still much to accomplish. Most certainly there will be more trials to overcome and everyone needs to be ready to face them. The first part of the exhortation comes from Isaiah 35:3 while the second from Proverbs 4:26. Drooping hands and weak knees are indicators of being dispirited and inactive; this is due to the consequence of the loss of purpose in the individual's life. A similar turn of phrase is found in Job 4:3, as well as in the apocryphal book of *Ecclesiasticus* (*The Wisdom of Sirach*) 25:23, showing that the term was well known amongst Jews at the time. The opposite is being valiant and having strong hands (2 Sam 2:7). The author is making it evident that it is time to change one's attitudes and to get moving on the right course or along the right pathway laid down, so that the goal that is required will be attained. If there is a state of lameness, where knees are out of joint, walking along the right pathway is not going to be possible; not only will there be a halting along the way but others will be hindered as one gets in the way. The lame or the weak, are those who have the tendency to be turned aside (*ektrapē*) and give up. There needs to be a healing of the joints so that this failure will not take place. The "it" here before the "*be healed*," is not in the Greek text but understood and refers to whatever is lame and needs to be put back into correct order. This verse brings to an end the use of the athletic metaphors.

v. 14 "*Pursue peace with all men and holiness, without which no one will see God*." The application of the previous verses is now given. If a person is to achieve what is required, positive action needs to be undertaken. First, there needs to be a pursuit. Note that the construction of the sentence places the pursuit of both the peace and holiness together as one objective. The reader may want to separate them but here that is not possible. That means effort and planning need to go into the seeking after peace and holiness. Note that the word to *strive* or *follow after*, is a present imperative (*diōkete*), which means it is necessary to pursue and keep pursuing this peace endlessly. It is not enough to try for a time and give up because something does not work out quickly. This is a lifetime of striving after peace with all men, as well as the holiness indicated. The significance of the centrality of peace in the life of a Christ follower is, after all, completely in line with what Jesus taught his own disciples when he said, *"Blessed are the peacemakers for they shall be called the sons of God"* (Matt 5:9). If peace is to be pursued, it is likewise to be produced and effort needs to be exerted to ensure that it is achieved. It is a way of life and is directed at everyone, meaning all within one's personal sphere.

However, this is not peace at any price, as Paul points out in his Epistle to the Romans (Rom 12:18), since peace is based upon truth and righteousness. Here the peace which needs to be pursued is linked to holiness, meaning that it must fit within the criteria God has for peace. That means that there is no room for compromise in following after this peace as it has to reflect the person of God himself. So, both peace and holiness are seen as being the object of this pursuit as the follower of Christ lives with all of earth's encumbrances and also with all the other people who share the same time and space. That is the most difficult part. The return to the matter of holiness, which was raised earlier in this chapter at verse 10 is significant. It reflects all that has to do with purity, wholeness and God's character. It makes complete sense that without it, no one will see God, since it is one of God's primary attributes and for those who are part of his family there is the clear indication that they too should take on this likeness as his Spirit abides within them changing their very nature. There is no possibility of allowing sin of any shade to take root in the life of believers. It has to be eradicated immediately if this pursuit is to be successful. It also means that Christians have to be aware of the trends around them and not tolerate any form of laxity, moral or otherwise. Society and culture cannot ever set the standards a follower of Christ can accept.

The author declares unequivocally that without this holiness, together with the pursuit of peace, no one will see God. What does that mean? The phrase, to see something or not, is common in scripture and indicates not mere visible recognition but experience and participation in its fulness (Luke 3:6; 9:27; John 3:36). Here the verb *shall see* (*opsetai*), is a future tense which would indicate a future encounter with God in the fullest sense, in order to experience all that that means in terms of what he has in store as the fulfilment of all his promises (Matt 5:8). John uses the construction in a similar manner in 1 John 3:2 in connection with the return of Christ and the believer's meeting with him when he writes: *"when he shall appear, we shall be like him; for we shall see him as he is."* To not see God, means then that the individual would not enjoy the blessings of the future eternal state and as far as God is concerned, that person is not going to be included in any of his plans or promises. They are never going to enjoy any communion with him as they are automatically excluded. Obviously, therefore the sense here is that anyone who fails to pursue peace and holiness, deludes themselves if they think that the outcome of their claims to be followers of Christ are realistic and that their brand of belief is all that is required.[16] It should be added that not only is any future claim of hope for these people unrealistic, present thought of being recipients of God's favor would also be an illusion.

v. 15 *"See to it that no one falls from the grace of God; that no root of bitterness springs up and causes trouble, and by it many become defiled;"* The opening phrase, which is translated as *"see to it"* is a loose rendition of the verb which rather means "to take oversight of" (*episkopeō*) something and has the same root, from which the word bishop or superintendent comes. In 1 Thessalonians 5:14–15 Paul admonishes the believers to play an active and positive pastoral role in looking out for each other in the church and this is exactly what the author is doing here. In this instance there is the danger of falling from grace or failing to apprehend grace. Paul talks about the members of the church in Galatia as having fallen from grace (Gal 5:4) and this letter has already mentioned that mercy may be found through prayer as well as grace that helps at the time it is needed (4:16). Grace is the nature of all that individuals receive from God's hand throughout their lives and is the consequence of his mercy and love. Its purposes are not described here but grace is always given so that God's goals may be achieved and is not merely for the benefit of the receptor. Grace can therefore be abandoned or ignored because of the wrong attitude of the individual concerned. The thrust here is that it is up to those in a position to do so, to make sure as they keep an eye open for all those believers around them so that they do not become embittered and fall from this God given grace. The participle, "falls" or "is falling" (*husterōn*) is a present one, which shows that the falling is a process going on during the present. It is not something that happens suddenly and is then terminated. The process goes with the following part of the verse, which indicates that the cause of this *falling* and therefore *failing*, is a *root of bitterness which springs up*. Bitterness is something that appears and grows over time. Usually, it is the result of disappointment or unrealistic expectations and false perceptions. Here it is portrayed in terms of a plant that is growing or springing up. The background for the language is found in Deut 29:18 in the context of people being turned away from

---

16. This is an immediate warning for any, including the adherents of the so called *"Hypergrace* teaching" who maintain that once an individual has made claims to believe in Christ, there are no rules of any nature that need to be followed and that their futures are automatically and permanently guaranteed. The term *Hypergrace* needs to be understood in terms which go beyond any biblical understanding of how grace itself is to be understood in scripture.

God by the things around them and "a root sprouting poisonous and bitter growth" all given in detail as a warning against turning away from God and receiving his judgment and wrath, instead of his favor. Here the things are similar; the picture is one of the spreading growth of noxious and bitter results, which will eventually result in spiritual death. This bitterness results in defilement, an example of which is expanded upon in the next verse.

Once more, the fact that one may fall from grace means that it should never be assumed or taken for granted that a person's conduct and faith have no bearing on spiritual outcomes in their lives. It means that it is necessary to nurture faith and let grace bear its desired fruit through love and obedience to the will of God.

v. 16 "*that no sexually immoral or irreligious person like Esau, who for a single meal gave up his birthright.*" Defilement is a state of being that gives birth to evil works. It is the heart and mind of the individual who is at war with God and it results in actions which demonstrate what is the driving force within a person. It is the opposite of holiness and at variance with it. Here the author goes from the mention of defilement directly to immoral behavior. The Greek word (*pornos*) means a sexually immoral person or someone who is a sexual deviant. Here the defilement results in this kind of fruit and is also coupled with unholiness. It is not indicative of anything that represents God's person and is completely contrary to godliness and holiness. People who live in this sphere and practice its works, are defiled and the poison of the bitterness mentioned above, is slowly putting them to death spiritually. Esau was one such example of an unholy and irreligious person. In Jewish writings he is depicted as an immoral man who could only think about eating and sexual behavior.[17] It is true that the scriptures paint him as a crass and sensual man, driven by his appetites but there is no direct indication from scripture that he was a fornicator. However, the Greek construction would be best understood to mean that following the positioning of the two adjectives (*pornos*-immoral and *bebēlos*-irreligious) he was both.[18] It could mean that he was just irreligious but the combination and the inclusion of Esau's name here appears to uphold the thought that he was both.

---

17. Philo, *De Virtutibus*, 208; Kadari, "Esau, Wives of: Midrash and Aggadah," says that according to *Genesis Rabbati, Vayishlah*, 160, the names for Esau's wives attest that they were harlots and that in accord with those who lived at the time Esau took one wife to provide him with progeny and another for sexual pleasure. See also *Palestinian Targum* on Gen 25:29; *Genesis Rabbati*, 70d, 72a.

18. This view is in contradistinction to that of Bruce, *Hebrews*, 366–7; Owen, *Hebrews*, 12:16–17.

The surrender of his birthright is the subject at hand here. Esau was more interested in a one-off meal, than he was in the promises and privileges attached to all that went with the birthright (Gen 25:29–34). The Genesis record says that he actually despised his birthright. That means that as far as he was concerned at that moment, all he wanted was to satisfy his stomach and nothing else had any value. The implication here is that immorality and lack of religious focus, could have a similar outcome for the readers who ignore their heavenly birthright.

v. 17 *"For you know that later when he desired to inherit the blessing, he was rejected for he found no place to repent though he sought it with tears."* In the mind of the author, there is a clear link between the loss of the birthright and the loss of the blessing. The opening words here: *"For you know,"* suppose that the readers, as Jews who knew their scriptures, are aware of what took place between Esau and Jacob. Later Esau realized what had happened after his brother tricked his father Isaac into giving Jacob his blessings, just prior to Isaac's death (Gen. 27:34); in spite of his tears and the attempt to acquire what Esau saw as rightfully his, it was not forthcoming. Again, despite his crying and the desperate attempt to reverse what had happened, he never managed to change the consequences and the blessing was lost. Part of his crying and complaint was that, this was the second time he had been supplanted (Gen 27:36). This shows the fact that opportunities need to be seized while there is time.

According to the author, there are two important factors here. First, Esau was rejected and second, there was no place for repentance. The term translated *"was rejected"* (the aorist passive form of the verb *apodokimazō*) shows that he was no longer qualified; the reason had already been given in the previous verse and that was his godless nature. Therefore, the weeping did not indicate a true repentance. True repentance is much more than some visible and audible cry. It requires a real change of heart, which was obviously not part of what happened. True repentance is always possible when there is a truly penitent heart, so it appears that this must have been absent and he was more concerned with his status and earthly loss than of any spiritual standing. His was the sorrow of the world, which Paul says works out death rather than godly sorrow (2 Cor 7:10). What transpired here is an indicator of what has already been given in warnings elsewhere in the epistle. In 2:1 there is the warning to pay close warning to what has been heard and not let things drift away and in 6:4–6, the impossibility of being enlightened and then failing to be renewed by repentance afterwards. This appears to describe Esau's situation.

Two mountains: one earthly the other heavenly: Seek what is immovable 12:18–29

At the end of verse 17 there is a change in the way in which the presentation is made. The thought returns to what has been spelled out earlier in terms of the comparison between the old and the new systems, the imperfect and perfect, the earthly and the heavenly.[19] As in the previous verse, the author assumes that the readers will be aware of the circumstances relative to the giving of the Law at Sinai and although the name is not given, it is clear that Sinai is what is being referred to at the time of the giving of the Law of Moses. All that took place there is then compared with what is related to the heavenly city and mount Zion, which majors on the importance of the eternal and immovable.

vv. 18–19 "*For you have not come to what can be touched, a blazing fire, and darkness, and gloom and a tempest and the sound of a trumpet and a voice of words which made the ones hearing it beg that no further word be spoken to them.*" It is easy to understand why the alternative reading, "*For you have not come to the mount,*" which has added "*mount*" (*orei*) has been included in a number of the less important texts, accounting for its presence in the KJV.[20] The name of Sinai is not immediately present but it is most certainly intimated and understood and is mentioned as Sion at verse 22. The important factor, here, is that these believers have not come to the mountain and the place where this first covenant was given. To understand this, it is necessary to grasp the background of the next verses which were in mind when the author pens what is recorded here. The words recall the occasion of the giving of the Law on Sinai (Exod 19:12–24; 20:18–21). Strict orders were given to the people not to touch the mountain and the items listed here: blazing fire, which was in the original context a matter of fire, thunder and lightning, the darkness and gloom, were all integral to what took place (Exod 19:16, 18; 20:18; Deut 4:11–12; 5:4–5). In the narratives given in Exodus and Deuteronomy there are details such as "*the mountain was blazing up to the very heavens, shrouded in dark clouds*" (Deut 4:11 NRSV). On that occasion, together with the shaking of the mountain and accompaniment of the fire, darkness and gloom there was also the sounding of the trumpet, together with the sound or voice of words, which obviously indicated that God himself was speaking. This voice terrified the people so much that the people begged Moses, "*You speak to us and we will listen; but*

---

19. For the play on types the author uses see the notes below in verse 22.
20. D, K, L, P, Clementine Vulgate, Syriac, Armenian and other later MSS.

do not let God speak to us, or we will die" (Exod 20:19). They were afraid for good reason, as the next verse declares.

v. 20 "For they could not stand the command that was given, 'If even an animal touches the mountain, it shall be stoned.'" If even an animal touched the mountain it would die. It had to be either stoned or shot with arrows (Exod 19:12b–13.). The Exodus text includes the death of guilty individuals. In the light of this, how much more the people themselves had to take great care not to contravene God's commands. There was a mixture of awe and fear (see v.28) as they realized the nature of the moment and the distance between God and themselves in terms of being qualified to meet with his conditions and the holiness of his person. The entire system imposed by the Law, including that of the procedures relative to the holy of holies and the annual day of atonement, put distance between the ordinary man and woman and God himself. Here on Sinai, only Moses appeared to meet the requirements to be able to communicate with God, who answered him in thunder (Exod 19:19).[21]

v. 21 "Indeed so terrifying was the sight that Moses said, 'I am terrified and trembling'." The occasion was so terrifying that Moses acknowledges the uncertainty of the moment. It needs to be remembered that Moses had conversed with God on more than a few occasions yet here, the awesome nature of God was overpowering, even for him. There is no actual mention of this in any of the passages recording the event in Exodus or Deuteronomy but since Stephen describes Moses as trembling on the occasion of his encounter with God at the burning bush, it is not out of place (Acts 7:32 as compared with Exod 3:2–5). There is no clearly known written tradition of this nature, although a number of authors mention a possible Jewish haggadic record to this effect.[22]

The entire thrust of the verses from 18 to 21, is to show how under the covenant of the Law, the approach to God was not a simple matter and for the majority, any immediate communion with him seemed to be out of the question. God's awesome power and holiness compared to mankind's failing and sinfulness, kept them apart. This however, was all about to change, as is clear from the following verses.

v. 22 "But you have come to mount Zion, and the city of the Living God, to the heavenly Jerusalem and to innumerable angels in festal gathering."

21. Of course, Aaron accompanied him up the mountain (Exod 19:24) but he did not converse with God.

22. See Bruce, *Hebrews,* 372; Hughes, *Hebrews,* 543. The Haggadah is either a Jewish text which is recited at the Seer on the first two nights of the Jewish Passover and includes the story relative to the Exodus or a story used to illustrate a legal matter which is present in the Talmud.

There is a reminder to the readers of their status in this verse. It presents the situation for the follower of God through Christ now under the new covenant. The approach is no longer an earthly one with all its barriers and limitations. The opening of the verse assures the readers that the situation is very different for them. In spite of the previous warnings related to the possibilities of apostasy and indifference, the words are intended to spur them on to boldly embrace the eternal promises available for all Christ's followers. This mount Zion is not the earthly which has just been described in the previous verse but here stands for the residence of the Living God and his proximity. Therefore, all three additional qualifiers mentioned here: mount Zion, the Living God and the heavenly Jerusalem refer to the same thing. They underline the fact that this entity is very different from Sinai with its earthly covenant and unapproachable God.

When Paul presents his allegory to the Galatians in 4:24–31, he does so by using very similar types; he compares Sinai as Hagar, with her children in bondage, to Jerusalem above, which is free and the mother of all believers who are the fruit of promise. The parallels here, are far too close to be something unfamiliar to Jewish Christian readers at the time. The earthly, including the earthly mount and the heavenly are the points of focus; the earthly Jerusalem, with its temple and worship, includes all the shadows of things to come, while the heavenly Jerusalem speaks of the fulfilment of the actual realities of all that God had promised, including his tangible and actual presence. The latter replaces the former in totality here.

The believers have come to this heavenly city whose number of angels cannot be counted. The Greek word translated *innumerable* (*muriasin*), indicates a number that is so great that it is beyond human ability to fathom.[23] In the earliest chapters of the letter Christ was compared to the angels but now he has them serving him upon the throne, at the right hand of the majesty of God. The term translated "*in festal gathering*"[24] (*panēguris* here the dative–*panēgurei*)–is a word, showing the angelic host in joyful acclaim, worshiping and singing in the presence of God.[25] This fits the same

23. *Muriasin* is usually translated myriads or tens of thousands. This number is multiplied in Dan 7:10 and given as "thousand thousands . . . and ten thousand times ten thousand."

24. Note that this phrase is found in verse 22 in the *Greek New Testament* (5th ed. rev.) and not in v.23 as in some translations. But it could just as well be part of the following verse and incorporate "the assembly of the first born."

25. See Moffatt, *Hebrews*, 216. If the verse division is incorrect and the phrase "in festal gathering" qualifies both the innumerable angels as well as the church of the firstborn in the following sentence, then this would be inclusive of all the groups involved including both angels and those who are the redeemed now gathered together

picture given in Revelation 7:9–12 where unlimited acclamation and worship is given to God and the Lamb upon the throne and where the saints and the angels participate. The reader needs to recognize that this verse division which is in place here today, is out of place because the way in which the structure is presented the qualification of the *"festal gathering"* should not be limited to the innumerable angles alone but included *"the church of the firstborn enrolled in heaven"* etc. The actual place where the verse commences and which substantives are qualified by *"in festal gathering,"* is a matter of considerable debate among scholars.[26] Whatever the correct response should be, the most important fact is the way in which the details are put together here to highlight the realities that are presented relative to what exists in the heavenlies.

The simplest way of understanding the collective manner in which the question is to be handled, is to take the position that the conjunctions "and" *(kai)* link all the components involved. They qualify: first, *the city of the Living God*, which is *the heavenly Jerusalem;* second, the *innumerable angels;* third, the *church of those who are the firstborn enrolled in heaven;* fourth, *God the judge of all;* fifth, *the spirits of the righteous made perfect;* sixth, *Jesus the mediator of a better covenant;* seventh and finally, *the blood sprinkled which speaks better things than Abel's.* However, not only are these separate parts of the descriptor showing the nature of what this Mount Zion is all about, they also add to the confusion as to where the division(s) of the verse(s) should be and indicate why the translations vary so greatly.[27]

v. 23 "*And church of those who are the firstborn enrolled in heaven and God the judge of all and the spirits of the righteous made perfect.*" The main question here is: Who are these who are called *the church of the firstborn?* The word, church *(ekklēsia)* is rendered assembly, in some translations and this is certainly correct but it is also the same word Jesus used when he told Peter that he would build his church (Matt 16:18). Here however, it is the church or assembly of the firstborn *(ekklēsia prōtotokōn)*. The background here has to be understood against what took place at Sinai and the gathering together of God's people under Moses as the recipients of God's Law. The Septuagint presents that assembly as the *ekklēsia* or church (Deut 4:10; 9:10; 18:16).

---

in the heavenlies.

26. See Alford, *"Pros Ebraious,"* iv. 253–54 for the possibilities as well as Hughes, *Hebrews,* 552–555.

27. That all these components belong together in qualifying the nature of the angels and saints, is also the position held by Alford and others. *"Pros Ebraious,"* iv. 253.

Scripture shows that any firstborn son has a special favored position in God's sight and in a particular way, all were the property of God (Exod 13:2, 13; 22:29; 34:20), but also bore the role of responsibility and leadership. Israel, as a nation, was called God's firstborn (Exod 4:22), even though Jacob as an individual, claimed the right although it was not properly his by birth since in reality, it was Esau's. It is not by chance that the term is used here, considering that it is not long since Esau and his birthright (*prōtotokia*) were mentioned as the major issue (vv.16–17). In the Pauline literature, Jesus is exclusively the Firstborn (*prōtotokos*–see the notes on 1:5, 6), where the title does not touch on physical birth but of primacy of place. In this verse and in the context of Israel, where the title is applied in the plural, it refers collectively to all those who belong to Christ: The Firstborn.[28] That puts them all on the same level with each other and shows no preference but it also shows that they participate in the same privileges of the one who is "the Firstborn." The fact that they are all enrolled in heaven shows that, as in Revelation 21:27, they are legitimate members of God's people and nothing can change that fact. The recording of names (Luke 10:20) is something well understood in Scriptural terms to indicate recognized membership of God's heavenly family.

"*And to God the Judge of all*" or, as the word order may better reflect the idea: "*And to a Judge who is God of all*" (RSV). It is most likely the second order which best represents the thought of the author since the subject has already been mentioned as the Living God. Here he is the God who is also the Judge of all. The emphasis being upon the fact that he knows everything and that everyone will give account to him (4:13; 10:30). This matter is a consolation to those who are his own but it is a warning to those whose lives are not in order and who have not submitted to his demands.

The next clause: "*and to the spirits of the righteous made perfect,*" does not necessarily imply a group separate from the church of the firstborn, as some have suggested. The first school of interpretation, which does distinguish them, says that they are indicative of the Old Testament saints who awaited the inclusion of the promises made and without which they would not be perfected because Christ had not yet come (11:40).[29] Other scholars hold to a position similar to that of Spicq, who says that *pneumata* [spirits] "is a current designation of the souls of men separated from their bodies,

---

28. There are some like Spicq, *Hébreux*, II. 407, who judge that the term "firstborn" refers to the angels, since they were the first of God's creation, but the problem with that is that Scripture only records the names of the eligible among mankind as being recorded in any of God's lists and not angels.

29. This would include such scholars as Moffatt, *Hebrews*, 218, Bruce, *Hebrews*, 378.

prior to the resurrection."[my translation][30] In support of this he lists 1 Pet 3:19; Rev 6:9 and Enoch 12:3 et al. It is true that the concept fits passages such as Rev. 6:9–10 where those who were martyrs for their faith await Christ to avenge them but the context here is very different. As Hughes points out, the whole purpose of 11:40 is to show that the imperfection which existed prior to Christ's sacrifice, is no longer the issue.[31] Besides, if, as was suggested above (v.22), all these components, including these *spirits made perfect*, add to the entirety of the meaning of Mount Zion and what is now within the touchable realm for believers, the proposals do not fit. Rather, it is inclusive of believers from the beginning of time; it speaks of all who have run their race and are now in the presence of God awaiting, together with those upon the earth, the return of Christ for his own. This is the position held by a good number of scholars and fits best the emphasis of the text, since scripture does not categorize men and women of faith as being under different covenants.[32] All who are faithful are God's; Christ's work looks back as well as forward to all followers.[33]

v. 24 *"And to Jesus, the mediator of a new covenant and to the blood sprinkled which speaks better things than Abel's."* The last two things to which the readers have come (v.22) are now mentioned. The most important fact is that Jesus is the mediator of a new covenant. The implications of the old and new have already been seen. The fact that the old was inadequate, incomplete and obsolete and in need of replacement, has already been underlined throughout the epistle (7:22; 8:6–10, 13; 10:16). The most important matter here, is that this new covenant is Jesus' covenant. Everything about it depends totally upon him, his incarnation, his ministry, his sacrifice, and his resurrection, together with his conquest of death and the grave. He has already been shown to be a superior mediator of a new covenant (8:6–13; 9:15) but here it is to him that all come (v.22). It is new because it replaces everything from the past. Both Greek words, *neas* and *kainos,* mean *new.* In this phrase the first is used. It is indicative more of youth and something fresh[34] while the latter is used more widely to describe this new covenant. However, it is unlikely that the difference should be pressed too far because

30. Spicq, *Hébreux,* II. 408.

31. Hughes, *Hebrews,* 550.

32. Hughes, *Hebrews,* 550; Alford, *"Pros Ebraious,"* iv. 255; Owen, *Hebrews,* 12:23, 6(3).

33. It is obvious that those who live under the New Covenant benefit from the perfection and understanding of the person and work of Christ and the place of the Holy Spirit under the new regime but the teaching of dispensationalism goes too far as seeing those under the Law as being inferior to those under the dispensation of grace.

34. See Alford, *"Pros Ebraious,"* iv. 255; Spicq, *Hébreux,* II. 409.

the new covenant is described as a "*diathēkēs kainēs*" (new covenant) earlier in 9:15 when describing the very same covenant.

The blood of this covenant is Jesus'; it is different from Abel's blood which was the first blood spilled in sacrifice, whether that be the blood of the sacrifice of the animal he offered up to God or that of a life he gave in obedience to God, when he was killed by his brother. Since in Genesis 4:10, Abel's blood cries out to God from the ground for vengeance due to the wrong perpetrated against him, it is more likely that the latter is in mind here.[35] That same blood has already been mentioned in 11:4. The Greek construction of the sentence here does not mention blood at all. It merely says that Jesus' . . . "*blood sprinkled which speaks better things than Abel*" (*kreitton lalounti para ton Abel*). Nevertheless, since the comparative is with Jesus, the new covenant and the blood he sprinkled, it would make most sense that the blood of Abel is what is central to the comparison here. Certainly, the point is that it is the blood of Jesus which covers the sin of all evil doers who "come" and find in him their propitiatory offering, while Abel's blood speaks of vengeance and exclusion for the wicked. That was certainly the interpretation given to the passage in the pseudepigraphal book of I Enoch 22:7–8, generally considered to be written late in the second century BC.[36] It may seem strange that the blood of the covenant, sprinkled upon the people according to the word of Moses at Sinai (Exod 24:8), is not even mentioned in this text. It does not seem to warrant inclusion according to the author.

v. 25 "*Watch out that you do not refuse the one who is speaking. For if they did not escape when they refused him who warned them on earth, much less shall we escape when we turn away from him who warns us from heaven.*" This verse introduces the conclusion by highlighting the necessity to hear God who is speaking, since as he is described in verse 29, he is a consuming fire and there is no place for attempting to brush him aside. As already seen in verse 19, the Children of Israel refused to listen to the voice of God at Sinai because they were so afraid and wanted Moses to be the spokesman and intermediary but here the readers are warned that they are not to refuse to listen now. This must also be read in the light of the introduction to the letter, where it was made very clear that in the past it was the prophets who spoke for God (1:1) and that would include Moses, but now his spokesman

35. A similar call for justice for the martyrs is of course present in Revelation 6:9–10 calling out for God's vengeance against their persecutors.

36. In that passage Enoch inquires of an angel Raphael whose spirit is it that accuses and the response is: "This is the spirit of Abel who was slain by Cain his brother; and who will accuse that brother, until his seed be destroyed from the face of the earth; Until his seed perish from the seed of the human race." *1 Enoch (Ethiopic)* chapter xxii. 7.

is the Son (1:2). Not only has he spoken (*elalēsen* aor.) as a past action but he continues to speak (*ton lalounta*); the verb is a present active participle which shows that he does not stop speaking. This God is a God who continually communicates and therefore, cannot be accused of failing to make known his purposes to any who will listen. It is obvious that the author is referring to the occasion when those same people in Exodus 20:19 did not want to listen. The Greek verb *to refuse* or *to beg off* (*paraiteomai*)[37] is the same here as it was in verse 19. The thought is that when the message of the one who speaks is rejected, so too is the person himself. It was not merely on this one occasion at Sinai that the people refused to listen to the voice of God; it was a pattern that was followed throughout the forty years of wanderings. It was indicated by their frequent displays of rebellion and demonstrated their anarchic spirit as has already been seen (3:9–10). The purpose here is a reminder of the consequence of disobedience. If these readers continually fail to hear the voice of God and turn away, the results will be dire.

The main comparison here is between the warning on earth and the warning from heaven. Some scholars insist on there being two different speakers. They would say the first was Moses[38] as the earthly mediator and the second Christ, the heavenly. It is true that Moses was the spokesman but the message was nevertheless God's message. The difference is not in the speaker but rather in the context of the place where the words were spoken. The first was at Sinai where the first and inferior covenant was given, while the second is from heaven, the Mount Zion already mentioned in verse 22. The message from heaven is the message concerning all that pertains to Christ, his priesthood, his propitiation and entry into the very presence of the Almighty. Unlike the earthly and imperfect, the heavenly is the place of all that is final, perfect and enduring under the covenant of Jesus and this is made known through the gospel. If the warning which comes from there is rejected, in the same way it was by the Children of Israel at Sinai, then there is no hope at all of escape.

v. 26 "*At that time his voice shook the earth but now he has promised saying, 'Yet once more I will shake not only the earth but the heaven.'*" Accompanying the giving of the Law was the earthquake that occurred (Exod 19:18); it was something that left a lasting impression seared into the memory of the people of God. Together with the other manifestations

37. This verb can be translated several ways other than what has already been indicated in the text including: to decline, excuse oneself, reject, escape. See Arndt & Gingrich, 621–22; Moulton and Milligan, *Vocabulary*, 484. It has a strong negative sense of rejecting or turning away from something offered.

38. Moffatt holds strongly to this position. *Hebrews*, 219–20.

attributable to God's person, this particular aspect is recorded in the Psalm of David (Ps 68:8). In the Massoretic text of Isaiah 2:19, 21,[39] in a passage which refers to the Day of the Lord (Isa 2:12), once again the glory of the Lord will bring about terrible earthquakes. On that occasion not only is the earth to be shaken but the heavens as well (Isa 13:13);[40] it is time when God's anger is to be openly vented.

The last part of the verse here is a quotation from Haggai 2:6, where the same earthquake is again at the center. This passage refers to the same eschatological event when the climax of all things come to a head. The event coincides with the description given in Revelation 21:1, where the first heaven and the first earth pass away because everything will become new. The terminus of all that has been represented, as part of the age of rebellion, is then reached.

v. 27 *"Now the phrase, 'Yet once more,' speaks of the removal of the things that are shaken, that is created things, in order that the things that cannot be shaken may remain."* The author wishes to underline the significance of the words presented in the quotation from Haggai 2:6 in the previous verse. He interprets them here, *"Yet once more"* to reinforce the fact that this shaking was going to get rid of everything that has been made. What is significant here is to demonstrate that what was made, was not and is not permanent. It will pass away. The transient nature of this present creation has already been made known in Scripture, where the psalmist compares the enduring person of God with all that has been made. In Psalm 102:12, God is *"enthroned for ever"* but when it comes to the earth and the heavens, even if they are the work of God's hands, *"They will perish, but you endure; they will all wear out like a garment . . . but you are the same and your years have no end"* (Ps 102:25–26 NRSV; see the notes in 1:10–12).

In this new order, the old and shakable has no place because they are temporary, while the unshakeable lasts forever. The author is linking the old order and the present creation with what is passing, even if at the present it does not appear to be that way. The first series of shaking in this verse, includes all the systems which have been under review in the letter, relative to the shadows and types, as well as all the inadequacies of previous covenants. The nature of what is unshakeable, is not elaborated upon. The only thing about it that is absolute, is that it lasts forever. In addition, it is central to everything relative to the eternal future. The whole purpose of the

39. The Greek text of the LXX does not use the same verb but speaks of breaking the earth.

40. In this instance the LXX does use the future of a verb (*seisthēsetai* shall be shaken) from which the English seismic, has its origins.

shaking for destruction and removal, is to highlight what will remain. What is shaken is equivalent in Revelation 21:1b, to what passes away, so that what remains is the same as the new heaven and the new earth; this latter is also called: the holy city and *"the new Jerusalem coming out of heaven from God"* in the same context (Rev 21:1, 2). At least one scholar suggested that this last shaking of the unshakeable is coincidental with the return of Christ at his Second Coming.[41] It will certainly commence at his return.

v. 28 *"Therefore, as we are receiving a kingdom which cannot be shaken, let us have grace through which we may serve/worship God in a pleasing manner, with reverence and awe."* Immediately, the author turns from the unshakeable to the reception of a kingdom, which indicates the equivalent value of what has been mentioned previously. First, he states that he, together with the readers, are all receiving this kingdom. The time of the verb (*paralambanō* here as a present participle) indicates that the reception is not complete but ongoing. It is a process which needs to be pursued throughout one's life. Just as in the previous verse, the nature of what was unshakeable was not developed, so too here neither is the nature of this kingdom. However, the two are clearly linked in terms of necessary events that have to take place. This means that the kingdom is everlasting and since all that is imperfect and transient will have already been removed (shaken), this kingdom will be perfect and complete. Those who receive it must also be fitted for its perfection and meet with all the criteria required. Since all the members are integrated, it must also speak of the new community which in verses 22, 23 was called *"heavenly Jerusalem"* and the *"assembly of the firstborn"*; these places include all the other components described in that context. Even if the fulness of this kingdom is not yet realized in totality, its reality is in place. This is because Christ is already on the throne and the believers are moving toward what will be the final fulfilment of it when Christ returns to complete his work and when all the shaking will finally be over.

In the light of the assurance of this kingdom and the perfection to come, all worship which incorporates service (in the subjunctive of the Greek verb *leitourgeō*) by God's followers during this present time, has to be carried out with grace and in the right manner.[42] The phrase *"let us have grace,"* is a likewise in the subjunctive (*echōmen charin*) with the sense of the necessity of showing grace in multiple ways, including in the giving of thanks, as well as in actions that are the fruit of grace. For this reason, the

---

41. Gregory of Nizianzus, *Oration*, xxi. 25.

42. Worship is a major theme throughout the letter but often is viewed as part of a system or procedure carried out in the temple when as has been seen above, this is not all that worship and service mean; see particularly notes on 9:2 & n14; 10:19–20.

translation given here, expresses more of a literal rendition of the Greek, which underlines the significance of all that the reception of grace involves. However, it is admittedly, a difficult construction in Greek and for that reason, is rendered variously in the translations (let us be grateful ESV, RSV; let us give thanks NRSV; let us be thankful NIV; let's show gratitude NASB; let us have grace KJV).

Grace affords privileges, including worship, which as has already been seen, is far more than expressions of praise at special times and in particular contexts associated with verbal praise, whether prayer or song. Many Christians limit worship to what happens in the prayer closet or in the church building at special times when gatherings occur, especially on Sundays. It is far more than that. Worship is better understood as a complete life-style and incorporates all actions as well as the words of the follower of God. Certainly, words of thanksgiving are part of that but reverence and awe have to be far more than what transpires at praise times, if worship is a life dedicated to the service of God; this is because of all that is implied in what worship and service of God means.

The author makes it clear that this service/worship has to be given in a pleasing manner. This means that worship is never mechanical or merely correct because it meets with certain visual and audible expectations. Jesus told the Samaritan woman that worship did not have anything to do with perspectives related to places but the worship of God in Spirit and truth (John 4:23–24). In that same passage the implication is that a right understanding is also necessary while it is implemented. This means the worshipper has to have a correct understanding of who God is and what it is that he requires; rituals alone never suffice. In Deuteronomy 6:5, repeated in Matthew 22:37, the emphasis is on a deep and complete love for God, as well as total involvement with him at every level of life. Outward acts will never satisfy the requirements of God. In addition to this heart of love and dedication, there has to be reverence and awe. That means recognition of the majesty and might of God. There is no place for frivolity and pretense. Awe is a mixture of the deepest respect and godly fear towards God. The reason for this is given in the last verse. God is wonderful, he is powerful, he is merciful, forgiving, and enabling. But as the next verse says there is another factor which is central.

v. 29 "*For our God is a consuming fire.*" When Moses addressed the nation of Israel before they crossed over the Jordan, he gave them a solemn warning. He told them that because of God's anger against him, following the disobedience of the people, he was not going to enter the promised land. They had to do what was right and there was no room for any idols in their lives (Deut 4:23). Then, in order to drive home the severity of any disobedience or rejection of God's person and plans, he added the words which our author repeats here: *"For our God is a consuming fire"* (see the notes on 10:27). The thrust is that the nature and purity of God does not make room for anything outside his holiness (see the notes above in verses 1 & 14). As was seen at the beginning of the epistle, this descriptor of God's nature is also closely linked to his glory (see notes on 1:3). God will destroy any and all who oppose him and engage in sin, especially the sin of idolatry. In the context of this letter, any attempt to reject God's message of hope through Christ, falls into this category and any who fail to embrace his grace and offer of forgiveness, must not expect to escape his ultimate judgement and wrath. For any and all who wish to partake in the fulness of this unshakeable kingdom with God and Jesus at the center, then God needs to be approached with reverence and awe.

13.

Conclusion: Practical advice and prayer 13:1–25

Up until this point in the letter, the content has been taken up with the danger of people falling away from Christ and the purpose of preserving them from the possibilities of apostasy. It has not looked so much like a letter as a theological treatise. However, now there is a radical change as the last chapter is reached. There are a good number of very down to earth and practical issues that are broached in this last chapter. In fact, so different is the approach that there are numbers of scholars who would like to attribute the chapter to someone other than the author of the rest of the letter.[1] However, there is no manuscript evidence which would substantiate such a proposal. In addition, even if there is a change in the way the material is presented, there are certainly links with what has gone before. These would include matters such as imitating the faith and life of those who have gone before (v.7 where this applies to their leaders), with the list of all those heroes of chapter eleven, the mention of Jesus sacrifice[2] (7:27; 9:14 et al. compared with 13:10–13), the continuing city (v.14), which has been seen in in 11:16 and is also spoken of in terms of the unshakeable kingdom in 12:28, Jesus' everlasting priesthood which is guaranteed by his unchanging person (13:8) and the nature of true worship and praise (13:15). All these and more, go together with the true nature of service and sacrifice which is doing God's will (10:7–10 compared with 13:21).

1. On the discussion see Williams, "A word-study of Hebrews XIII," 129–136; also, Jones, "The Authorship of Hebrews XIII," 129–136. For an overview of different opinions see Guthrie, *Hebrews,* 268n22.

2. See Spicq, *Hébreux,* II. 415; also, on the section Spicq, «L'authenticité du chapître XIII » 226–36.

In addition to these links, it needs to be understood that sound doctrine, as is generally recognized,[3] has to be the precursor to all moral conduct of a biblical nature. Although some see this as the sole chapter dealing with such matters, that is not completely correct. There are a number of texts in the preceding doctrinal section, which give more than a hint relative to moral and practical behavior: identification with those in prison (10:34); the running of the race with focus and purpose (12:1); Esau and his moral laxity (12:16); the purity of life is also hinted at in terms of hearts and consciences being sprinkled (10:22). Love and good works are part of what have already been encouraged in 10:24 and fit into the practical exhortations of 13:1–3, 16. Besides, if Hebrews is recognized as a letter, it is only reasonable that what is found in the last chapter should leave room for what may otherwise appear out of order with the rest of the material. Certainly, the earlier chapters are more planned and logical in terms of the way the arguments are presented. For example: The subject matters appear disjointed when in verse 7 there is an exhortation to remember the place of leaders followed by declarations related to Jesus, warnings not to follow strange doctrines and numerous other matters before a return in verse 7 to the place of leaders and the need to obey them.

v. 1 "Let brotherly love continue." This is an exhortation and as an imperative (*menetō*), an order to continue to display what the Early Church considered as an absolute essential characteristic of Christian faith. The fact of belonging to the same Father and the same Lord meant that all believers were considered family; as such they are all members of one another. This exhortation does not indicate that brotherly love was absent in any way. This kind of love reminds the participants of their heritage and immediately links them because of Christ. Earthly backgrounds, ethnicity and race meant nothing in this family. This expression of brotherly love was one of the things that attracted outsiders to the message of the Gospel since its practical expression spoke louder than words. In addition, this was the command of Christ to his disciples (John 13:34; 15:12) and fits well with the exhortations of Paul, Peter and John in their letters (Rom 12:10; Eph 4:2; 1 Thess 4:9; 1 Pet 1:22; 3:8; 1 John 3:11, 23 et al.).

For brotherly love to be part of the Christian community it requires getting involved in the lives of those who are fellow believers. In today's church this is not simple because often we hardly know each other. As mentioned elsewhere in this work many of us live far from the centers where we gather, sing, praise, and listen to exhortations. It is true to say that most do not find it practical to exhibit what this scripture demands of us. This must

---

3. See Pink, *John and Hebrews*, ch. 13:1.

become a priority of today's churches and effort must be made to see how it can become a reality.

v. 2 "Do not forget hospitality for through this some have entertained angels unawares." Hospitality is and always has been, considered important for believers (Rom 12:13; 1 Tim 3:2; Tit 1:8; 1 Pet 4:9). The Greek word for hospitality is a combination of two words: *philo* and *exenia,* meaning to love guests or strangers.[4] At the time this letter was written, it was not just Christians who were taught to show hospitality.[5] For Christians, it was considered as an extension of brotherly love and expressed the need to take care of one another. Here, it is evident that Abraham was in mind, since it was he who, while he was in the oaks of Mamre, had received three visitors who turned out to be angels (Gen 18:2–8). They are clearly the angels of whom the author writes as having been entertained unawares; when Abraham invited them to eat and drink with him, he had no idea of their identity.

It needs to be remembered that at the time of the New Testament, for anyone travelling, it was not a simple matter to find somewhere to spend the night. The local inns were not only places of ill repute because of prostitution and filth but they were also dangerous because of the class of people who often frequented them; even the innkeepers were known to threaten and rob those who passed their way. Some inns did not provide food or even bedding.[6] For that reason, local churches often provided lodging and hospitality to fellow believers. This practice of giving help to strangers was perpetuated throughout the period of the first centuries but as *The Teaching of the Twelve Apostles*[7] indicates, there were some who abused this hospitality and took advantage of the believers by pretending to be travelling preachers who then outstayed their welcome.[8] This sort of practice is still a difficulty in some majority world nations today, where so-called apostles and prophets leech off churches and make excessive claims upon them in

---

4. Paul makes hospitality one of the qualifications for anyone who wanted to be involved in church oversight (1 Tim.3:2).

5.. This was taught in *The Odyssey,* 1.141–156 where Homer writes of Telemachus unknowingly showing Athena hospitality. Other references to hospitality in the same writing include King Nestor entertaining Athena disguised as Mentor 3.394 and later again in 3.404–20. In the Greek culture the though was that the gods visit people disguised as strangers, so you had better entertain them properly. Further references to the proper treatment of strangers are found in the Odyssey 7.245–46.

6. For more on the nature of the inns and roadside accommodation at that time see Firebaugh, *Inns of Greece & Rome,* 108–125.

7. Also known as "*The Didache.*"

8. *Didache* 11:4–6; 12:1–5.

the name of their supposed gifts. Nevertheless, the presence of abuse gives no excuse for the neglect of hospitality.

v. 3 "*Remember those who are prisoners as though in prison with them, and those who are mistreated as you are also in the body.*" The matter of prisoners has already been raised in 10:34. The practice of brotherly love is to be extended to them, as their circumstances are even more difficult than those of any traveler. Because of the Christian family, the concept of the need to identify with all who are Christ's, is to be real and practical. This care is to be carried out to the extent that when someone is in prison and unable to have even the basics of life, their Christian family is to take care of them. At that time many who were in prison, were there because of their faithful testimony to Christ. They would have been seen as a threat to the Roman State and treated extremely harshly by the authorities. Many as already noted, would have only been fed only when some benefactor or friend brought them food. As already indicated, there are still many nations in today's world where similar procedures are followed and prisoners are not fed by the state. Paul writes about Onesiphorus, who from what he says, must have brought him help on more than a few occasions while he was in prison; he clearly went to considerable lengths to find Paul in prison and come to his aid. He was not at all afraid of identifying with Paul even though his actions could have meant that he would also have become a target of suspicion. The authorities would have wanted to know why he associated with this man who was considered an enemy of Rome. Scripture shows us that Onesiphorus was involved with Paul over a considerable time and in a good number of different places (2 Tim. 1:16–18).

Not only are the prisoners to be given help but all who are mistreated. The context is still that of fellow believers but the indignities are of all sorts because these individuals have stood for the truth. The phrase, "*as you are also in the body,*" seems strange but it means nothing more than that while we are still alive upon the earth. This is similar to what Paul writes in 2 Corinthians 5: 6 when he says "*while we are at home in the body, we are absent from the Lord.*" While life carried on and we are still part of this present world, each person has clear and ever-present needs of food and clothing in order to be able to keep body and soul together. When circumstances are such that one is not able to meet those needs, then they realize how important it is that others provide for them in order to keep alive. So, the message here is that fellow believers are to realize the importance of looking out for each other and especially for those who do not appear to have a voice to be able to cry for help because of their circumstances. This phrase does not mean, as some scholars in the past have suggested, that being in the body means being in the Body of Christ or the Church.[9] Being in the Church certainly means that we should be even more aware of our responsibilities but that is not what the author has in mind here.

v. 4 "Let marriage be honorable among all and let the marriage bed be undefiled, for God will judge the sexually immoral and adulterous." The New Testament teaching on marriage and sexual purity is very clear. The undefiled marriage bed means that couples keep true and faithful to each other and that there is no room at all for any kind of extra marital sexual behavior. God intended each man to have his own wife and each wife her own husband (1 Cor 7:2). Only death can rupture that association (Rom 7:2). All other sexual relationships are deviant. During the period of the New Testament, great laxity existed in matters of sexual mores in what was then the Roman Empire. Immorality of all sorts was not only tolerated but indulged in and considered normal. However, Christians were expected to cling to biblical ethical standards of behavior in all areas of their lives; that meant their sexual morality had to be exemplary in every way. There was absolutely no place for adultery or what the Bible includes under the word fornication (*porneia*) which is actually any deviant form of sexual behavior. Adultery was any kind of sexual conduct outside marriage. Misbehavior in these areas were considered the equivalent of a denial of all that was expected of them as followers of Christ. Likewise, fornication or any kind of sexually deviant conduct is also out of the question.[10] This kind of moral expectation was completely foreign to the thinking of the day, just as it is today in many parts of the western world. It is for this reason that throughout the New Testament, there is so much stated in favor of a morality which pleases God and which is required by him.

The declaration that marriage should be honorable and the marriage bed undefiled is meant to underline the need to continue this moral example within Christian marriage. Purity in the marriage relationship is mandatory. The sexually immoral and adulterers will be judged by God. The severity of failure needs to be understood by all. Moral failure has severe repercussions. In Paul's letter to the Galatians, together with a list of other matters which he calls the works of the flesh, he states categorically that those who do the things spoken against, will not inherit the Kingdom of God. That means exclusion from God's eternal reward will be the judgment rendered (Gal 5:19, 21). Followers of Christ can never afford to let down

9. See Calvin, *Hebrews*, 13:3.

10. Today's list of what is incorporated under *porneia* would be a very long list including: bestiality, homosexuality, pedophilia, any kind of sexual activity outside recognized marriage; this also means any kind of sexual activity within marriage other than with one's own wife or husband.

their guard with regard to sexual matters, as to do so results in abandonment of the principles of all those who have been redeemed. All who follow the standards of godless society, will suffer the judgement which results in what the author of this epistle calls being shaken, or destroyed and passing away (12:27).

v. 5 *"Let your life be free from the love of money, being satisfied with what you have for he has said. 'I will never leave you nor by any means forsake you."* Again, the New Testament has much to say about the dangers associated with the love of money (1 Tim 3:3, 8; Tit 1:7b.) and the need to be content with what you have (Phil 4:11; 1 Tim 6:8). The love of money is what has to be avoided since that is what causes many of the difficulties individuals experience during their lifetime. Money itself is not intrinsically evil but when it becomes the driving force behind every action it brings about the downfall of morality as the right treatment and concern for others becomes secondary in the pursuit of one's own ends. When money becomes one's God, greed becomes central to every decision; relationships are then ruined. Basically, this love of money it is a matter of covetousness, which means that a person is never content with what they have, no matter how much it may be. It is certainly a form of idolatry.

The phrase which states that it is necessary to be satisfied with what one has, is well explained in Jesus' words in the Sermon on the Mount when he talks about having to choose to serve God or money/things (Matt 6:24–31). In that same context he points out that God takes care of his own and provides for them; to worry about food and clothing is not what counts; seeking the Kingdom of God has to be the priority (Matt 6:31, 33–34). That background goes well with the last part of this verse, which otherwise would appear not to fit the context. However, it is central to the whole declaration. Riches are not the abundance of the things of this world one may possess (Luke 12:15) but the knowledge that one is totally safe in the hands of God. This needs to be understood in the light of the so called "prosperity" gospel, which states that God wants everyone to have all the money they desire and even more.

The quotation in this verse could be slight modification from either Deuteronomy 31:6 or Joshua 1:5 (see a similar assurance in Gen 28:15; Isa 41:17). The Greek construction of the sentence contains five particles of a negative nature (*ou, mē, oud', ou, mē*), This would give a literal translation of the sentence, as cumbersome as it is, something like: "I will not, not ever, leave you nor ever, ever, forsake you." The idea is to reinforce the fact that God will never ever, leave nor forsake his own. In English, negatives cancel each other out but in Greek they reinforce the action described. The fact here then underlines the fact that the follower of God does not have to be concerned and worried about money, food and clothing or any of life's basic necessities, as God is looking on and he is well aware of all the details of a person's life including all their needs. He is not going to leave them without his help. This does not mean that he will give them all that they desire but he will certainly provide what is necessary in terms of a person's "daily bread" (Matt 6:11) and whatever he sees fit to grant them by his grace. This exhortation, together with what follows in the next verse, shows that what is required to be the motivating force of anyone's life, is God alone. He must be at the center, and is the source of all provision.

v. 6 "So that we can say with confidence:[11]

'The Lord is my helper;

I will not fear;

What can man do to me?'"

This verse is a slight variation of Psalm 118:6 and is most significant in this context. First, it shows that the follower of Christ can take the word of God in the Old Testament and apply it to him or herself because that is what the author is doing here. Second, it can be said that this verse is a summary of all that this messianic Psalm (see Ps 118:22) maintains in terms of God: his enduring love for his people (Ps 118:1–4), the fact that he is on the side of all who call upon him (Ps 118:5–6), he is their refuge against all who are their enemies (Ps 118:8–9), their helper (Ps 118:7a, 13), their strength and salvation (Ps 118:14) and so much more. It encapsulates the message of this portion showing that there is no place at all for fretting and worrying about money, provision, safety or anything else. All that matters is the placing of one's complete confidence in God. This confidence is an expression of the inner man, as it trusts in God as Savior of the whole person. Again, this confidence is to be active in the present, for the future and for the entirety of one's existence. If this lesson is understood, then the faith taught in chapter 11, is very much part of all that is involved here too.

It is necessary to examine the quotation in detail. "The Lord is my helper." It is only here in the New Testament that the Lord has this direct title. The inference is that, in looking at the Lord alone, as the one who is deeply involved in every aspect of one's life, it will be recognized that any help that is necessary will have its source in him. Consequently, "I will not fear"; there is no place for fear. That is because confidence and boldness go together. Finally, "what can man do to me?" Mankind may threaten and may even take one's physical life but they cannot remove anyone from God's hand. The trust in God, as one's helper, recognizes that every step taken is

11. *Tharrountas* is the present participle of the verb *tharreō* which has the force of being confident, bold or of good courage.

according to his plan because, as Psalm 37:23 declares, *"The steps of a man are established by the Lord, when he delights in his way;"* (ESV). This means that God will not allow anything outside his plan to side-track any follower of Christ, provided that the individual keeps his or her heart fixed on God.

v. 7 "Remember your leaders; those who spoke the word of God to you. Consider[12] *the result of their conduct and imitate their faith."* The author of the letter is not the only author in the New Testament to remind believers that they are to remember their leaders. Paul does likewise in his first letter to the Thessalonians (5:12–13). But the verb here, *remember* (*mnēmoneuete*) needs to be understood as a present imperative, which means that they must remember and keep on remembering continually. The remembrance here is not just a matter of mental assent. It is a matter of remembering and then acting accordingly. Remember what they said, and remember the example they gave to back up their words. There are two groups of leaders mentioned. The first includes those in this verse and the second those in verse 17. The first group, mentioned in this verse, are the first to have influenced them; this is evident from the tense of the qualifying verb, *those who spoke* (an aorist or complete action) *the word of God to you*; it is apparent that the author is referring to those in the past who shared God's word with them but are no longer doing so. Most scholars interpret this to mean that they were the ones who were the first to bring them the word of God or were those who were their past teachers and instructors.[13] This is not the place to get into a deep discussion relative to the meaning of leadership but it does show that leadership is important and needs to be fully grasped; the teaching and the role of leaders is vital to the welfare of believers (and the church).

If the model of exemplary lives, given in chapter 11 is considered, then we have a similar example here with their leaders who have gone before. That list of people given in chapter 11 together with their activities are certainly to be followed; so too here, the more recent and intimate links these Hebrews had with their leaders is to be viewed with equal importance. The author exhorts them to remember what they taught, as well as what they did. It is not at all clear who those leaders were and it is not known what they taught in any detail but from the fact that these readers are regarded as followers of Christ, they must have preached and taught the truth of the word of God to these people. The author not only draws attention to what

12. The verb *anatheōreō* is to look very carefully at something and is similar to *analogizomai*–to consider–in 12:3.

13. See Kendrick, *Hebrews*, 182; Guthrie, *Hebrews*, 271–72; Hughes, *Hebrews*, 569; Bruce, *Hebrews*, 395; Alford, *"Pros Ebraious,"* iv. 263–64.; Spicq, *Hébreux*, II. 421.

they said but to their lifestyle and faith as something to be imitated; this means that their lives must have been helpful and clear examples to follow. There are some like Moffatt who believe that these leaders must have "sealed their testimony with their . . . blood."[14] However, there is nothing in the text to show that this is what happened and if 12:4 is read in context, it means that this did not happen.

v. 8 "Jesus Christ is the same yesterday, and today and forever." It is important to note the immediate introduction of Jesus Christ after the emphasis being placed upon God the Father. This link is not a problem for the author so neither should it be for the reader. The statement made by the author here may, at first sight, appear to be out of place. It seems to be abrupt and unnecessary. However, in the previous verse the closing emphasis is upon the imitation of the faith and conduct of their former leaders. There is a link here with the force of the statement above because the example of these leaders lives on, even if they are no longer there to be consulted; now that they are no longer present does not mean these followers of God have been abandoned to their own resources. Jesus Christ who was with the earlier leaders, is now with them in the same way as he was always with those who have made him their master. They have his continued presence and oversight, as they did in the past, do in the present and will have in the future. Their faith in Jesus, just as the faith of their mentors, guarantees that his unchangeable High Priestly office and ministry (to use the language of earlier chapters: see 9:11), continues forever. Therefore, the confidence mentioned in verse 6, is as assured as it ever could be, by means of this declaration. Christ's unchanging nature has already been asserted in 1:12 (see also 7:24). He is the one who is their everlasting mediator, interceding on their behalf (7:25). He laid down his life as the sacrifice for all in the past (our yesterdays), he continues his work in the present (our today) and the future (our forever or eternity) is also in his hands; all these characteristics substantiate the words of this verse. If Christ is to be considered, then he is the supreme example to be followed. Not just relative to faith but everything.

v. 9 "Do not be carried away by various and strange teachings, for it is good that the heart be established[15] *by grace, not by* [rules concerning] *foods, which those following them were not benefited."* In contrast to the steadfast and unchanging character of Jesus Christ, accompanied by all that belongs to his Kingdom and his purposes, are the various and strange teachings which mankind loves to concoct. It is immediately evident that there were

14. Moffatt, *Hebrews*, 230.

15. The verb *bebaioō* has the meaning of establishing, confirming or strengthening something or someone.

teachings circulating within the sphere of these readers, which were liable to immediately oppose Christ and his will for his followers. The inference is that the foundation which was laid in the past, is all that is necessary to keep a believer on the right pathway. The teachings which are likely to carry the readers off on a tangent, are described as being "various and strange." The variety is compounded by their strange content. Something that is strange, when it is related to biblical teaching, is immediately something that attempts to upset orthodox or correct teaching. Anything that is additional to the truth laid down by God and not clearly aimed at biblical morality is included within what is called strange because, what is not essential to truth, is automatically identifiable being inappropriate. It could indeed be described as heretical. Faith rests in the person of Christ, in his love and provision, all of which are based upon God's grace. The fact and place of grace was introduced early in the letter (2:9; 4:16), indicating the vital role of God's mercy toward his own. It is only when the nature of grace is misunderstood that anyone can think that by means of their own efforts and the keeping of human rules that it is possible to please God. The satisfaction that God looks for in the individual is the heart which rests in God's work alone. It does not always have to be looking for ways to add to the work that God has freely and fully provided through Christ.

Because of the next part of the verse, it is assumed that the various and strange teachings which have or are aimed at bringing disruption into the lives of these recipients of the letter, are related to rules about food. The futility of rules related to food, drinks, and washings have already been highlighted in 9:10. They are external matters, which in the long run, have no real influence upon the inner man. The words translated "those following them" (*hoi periopatountes*), literally mean, "those that walk." They convey the sense that those who were constantly keeping these food rules, were given hope that they were somehow going to profit from keeping them. The expression may seem strange but in the light of the similar usage by other New Testament authors, its presence indicates a certain lifestyle. It seems a fairly common way to demonstrate something that was habitual (Gal 5:16; Eph 2:2, 10; Col 4:5; 1 Pet 4:3; 1 John 1:6, 7; Jude v. 17 et al.). The author says that the opposite was in fact true; there was no benefit from adhering to these food rules. Today we can say that the only justification for following such rules would be due to dietary reasons and nothing more.

Paul, in his letter to the Corinthians, pointed out to them that food was not a factor in gaining God's favor; eating something or not eating something was never the issue (1 Cor 8:8). Elsewhere he tells Timothy that in the "*latter times*" there would be those who, among other false teachings would tell people to abstain from foods which God made to be received with thanksgiving (1 Tim 4:1–5). He added that those teachings had their source in seductive spirits and demons. In the context of the former verse which highlights Jesus, these instructions make it evident that to rely on food laws like these, would tend to minimize his person and work by placing the emphasis upon mankind's own efforts.

v. 10 "*We have an altar from which those who served the tent*[16] *have no authority to eat.*" The question of food leads to the matter of the altar and sacred meals. The altar has already been introduced in 7:13. It seems that some had been telling the Jewish believers that their form of faith was deficient because it had no altar. For the Jews, as with those of other religions, it was and is necessary to have visible objects such as altars, sacrifices, and temples. The Romans required statues and forms, without which, in their thinking, worship of the gods was not possible. That was why they accused the Christians of being atheists;[17] they thought that because they had no visible forms or sacrifices, that they had no God.

For the author of this letter, the physical altar and the tent seen in chapters 9—10 only stood as representations of the heavenly. The way in which the word "altar" is used here appears to encompass everything that includes the entirety of the new priesthood made possible by Christ. Bruce says that "The word 'altar' is used by metonymy for 'sacrifice.'"[18] However, it would appear that it is far more than representative of sacrifice, since it includes more than the work of Christ on the cross; all the consequences of the cross with the opening of the way into the holy of holies in the heavens are part of this altar. Certainly, the cross, as the altar on earth, where Jesus offered up himself as the once for all sacrifice, is a vital part of the whole (Heb 10:19) but it leads to the holy of holies in the heavens, which is the true and permanent tent where God is eternally present with the Son: the Great High Priest of the New Covenant. The cross is depicted by the altar in the tent or tabernacle of the Old Covenant.

It has already been seen that the real tent, is in the heavenlies (8:2; 9:11); therefore, so too is the holy of holies with the real altar (8:2; 9:12, 24). By the sacrifice of Christ, the eternal covenant has been set in place and it is from this that all followers of the Son now benefit. There is no longer any necessity to return to the types of the old covenant which are limited to forms, buildings, and religious procedures. The benefits of this sacrifice of Christ and this altar are available on an everlasting basis for all

16. The tent here is the tent or tabernacle of the Old Testament.

17. Athenagoras, *Plea for the Christians*, chs. 3—4.

18. Bruce, *Hebrews*, 399; for more on the nature of the altar see Hughes, *Hebrews*, 577–78 and n32.

who are believers in the Son. Therefore, Christians have a sacrifice and an altar which is far better than anything made possible in types in the physical objects provided under the old order. This order has no need of a physical altar in the present because what happened at the cross makes available something spiritual and real; it is the substance itself (see notes on *hypostasis* in 1:3; 3:14; 11:1) and opens the door to the very throne room in the heavenlies with the Father and the Son.

What does it mean then that those who served or worshipped (*latreuones* pres. part. of *latreuō*; see comments on 9:1 and note.) at the tent have no authority to eat at this altar? Even the priests, under the rules of the Law, had to obey regulations which applied to the eating of meat from the offerings which were made at the altar in the tent. They could eat the meat of animals offered in thanksgiving but not that of the sin offerings (Lev 6:30). Here the context appears to be linked to the matter of the offering made on the Day of Atonement, when the annual sacrifice for the sins of the people was made (Lev 16). The priests could not eat anything offered as a sin offering. The bodies of the animals were burned outside the camp. The author is saying that those who continue to carry out the practices related to the Old Covenant, have not yet entered into any relationship with Christ; they do not therefore benefit from his sacrifice on their behalf. They remain ignorant of his provision and are therefore left out of his promises. This is because they have made the worship of the symbols and types the emphasis, rather than the reality to which they pointed. They cannot therefore enjoy the privileges flowing from the altar that Christians now have. However, Christians have access to this altar and the sacrifice of Christ in an unlimited way; in a spiritual sense they have access to all the benefits of that altar and its system because they have embraced Christ's person, his sacrifice, and all he represents. Anyone who drew back from following Christ would, like those Jews who reject his sacrifice, also abdicate any rights to all those benefits.

This would have been an ideal time for the author to link Christ's offering to the Eucharist but the striking fact is that there is absolutely no mention made of it anywhere in the letter. Therefore, any attempt to force such identification here only demonstrates that such types which scholars make here are forced. It can be maintained unequivocally, that no sacramental celebration was present in the mind of the author when he penned this verse. The reference here relative to food and eating, indicate that what was associated with the first altar was of a physical nature but here what Christians partake of is spiritual. The way in which eating is depicted here is similar to the language Jesus used to describe himself as the bread of life when he told his audience that if they would eat the bread which spoke of him, they would live forever (John 6:48, 51–56). Clearly, he was not talking about eating physically; the failure to understand what he really meant, was what offended the Jews (John 6:52). In fact, he had made it clear in an earlier verse (John 6:35) that belief in him was the way in which this action of "eating" was to be understood.[19]

vv. 11–12 "*For the bodies of those animals whose blood is brought into the holy place by the high priest as a sin offering are burned outside the camp. For that reason, Jesus also suffered outside the gate in order to sanctify the people by his own blood.*" This verse is intended to show how it is impossible for the worshippers or servers at the altar under the old regime to eat of the sacrifices that were offered on the Day of Atonement. In Leviticus 16:27 it was specifically the bull and the goat of the sin offering whose blood had been shed for the atonement, to which reference is made. After their blood was sprinkled, the remains of the animal were taken outside the camp and burned. With Christ there was no burning of his body but certainly the fact of Jesus' suffering outside the gates of Jerusalem after making atonement by his own blood, is the important fact in the parallelism and symbolism here. Once more the superior nature of the sacrifice being that of Jesus' own blood, shed once for all for all the people. That means specifically for all the people who accept him as their redeemer. It is also significant that whereas the offering on the Day of Atonement had to be made in the holy place, here it is made outside and yet its power is without question and results in all those who identify with Christ being set apart or sanctified by means of what was done. This means that no longer do Christians rely on holy places for the efficacy of their worship.

v. 13 "*Therefore, let us go to him outside the camp bearing his reproach.*" The significance of the above verses relative to the role of Jesus and the altar which Christians have, is brought home here. The Greek word *toinun*–therefore–is only found four times in the New Testament and has the sense of inferring something as a consequence of what has gone before. Here, because of what has been explained above, it is time to make a clear and open declaration, "*let us go to him outside the camp*" (*exerchōmetha pros auton exō tēs parembolēs*) which shows that the individual has to be willing to sever links with the past that depended upon the shadows that were associated with the Old Covenant sacrifices and all the Jewish protocols. The camp is associated with the gathering of the people of Israel while they made their journeys in the wilderness (Exod 33:7).

Up until that time, many appeared to cling onto the past and were reticent to let go. There has to be a clear break with the system of old and a

---

19. See also Hughes, *Hebrews*, 576 on this question.

willingness to be misunderstood and cut off from the procedures previously viewed as essential to the service of God. Now was the time to forsake the Old for the New and bear any reproach which may be part of serving Jesus; his sacrifice and his blood are the only things that will provide the necessary atonement to allow entry to the real holy of holies. There also needs to be a recognition and a willingness to accept that being separated from the past and the system which it upheld, would very likely have repercussions leading to antagonism and persecution. Orthodox Jews would not be happy to see these people leaving the fold. The actions of the Jews in the book of Acts against converts to Christ demonstrate what happened to many who had been formerly faithful followers of the legal codes (Acts 5:18; 7:58–59; 21:31; 23:12). After all, it was the Jewish religious hierarchy which had been responsible for the crucifixion of Christ. Here the exhortation is to bear his reproach or insults. That means when identification with Christ is made, the same kind of reproach will fall upon them. According to 11:26 this is what Moses did when he rejected the treasures of Egypt for the reproaches of Christ (see notes on 11:26). Nevertheless, in the letting go and in the willingness to go outside the camp, the object of faith and hope was Jesus, so the realization of what that would mean should have spurred them on.

v. 14 "For we do not have a continuing city here, but we seek one that is to come." All who held to the old system with its earthly foundations needed to understand that all that belongs to this earth is transitory. There is a lot about a city in this letter. Abraham looked for a city "which had foundations of which God was the architect and builder" (11:10) because he knew that he was a sojourner on earth and knew that all that belonged to this earth was going to be shaken. Those men of faith in chapter 11 knew that God had prepared a city for them (11:16) and the readers have previously been told that they have not come to an untouchable mountain but to Mount Zion and the city of the living God which is the heavenly Jerusalem. Therefore, the background to what he is saying has been well established. Any earthly city, whether it be Jerusalem or any other, can never be the center of focus, as it belongs to the earth and will be shaken. The only city which will never pass away is an entirely new heavenly one. The city of Jerusalem, represented a community of the people who were supposed to be followers of God but their track record was anything but exemplary. The new city will be everlasting and representative of a new community, not made up of the physical sons of Abraham but of all who have gone outside the camp to identify with Christ. The nature of this new city, is nowhere described in the letter but, as already mentioned elsewhere (see notes on 9:15; 12:27), is most certainly identified as the New Jerusalem in Revelation 21:2. That city is made up of all who are, in that context, described as a "bride" and

God's "people" (Rev 21:2, 3). The author wishes to indicate to his readers the futility of pinning one's hopes on anything that belongs to this present world and its systems.

v. 15 "Therefore, though him let us always offer up a sacrifice of praise to God, that is, the fruit of lips confessing his name." The sacrifice for sin had now been taken care of, once for all, by Christ. There would be no need for anything that attempted to resemble it ever again. What this verse is saying is that there is nevertheless, still a place for sacrifice and on a continual basis: "*always offer up a sacrifice of praise to God.*" This sacrifice has nothing to do with the spilling of animals' blood or anything that in the past would have been associated with the earthly altar. It was to be a sacrifice of praise (and service). This is the new and continual sacrifice to be offered up to God by all who are followers of Christ and servants of God. This sacrifice it to be offered to God through Christ, who is the mediator at the right hand of the Majesty on High (1:3). In the past there had been of course, sacrifices of thanksgiving (Lev 7:12; 22:29; Ps 50:14, 23; Jonah 2:9 et al.) but nearly all of them were associated with the earthly sanctuary.

Here there is no need of any such sanctuary or tent and the nature of the sacrifice is to be one expressed verbally or as the author declares: as "*the fruit of lips confessing his name*"; that is, in the name of Christ and addressed to God. In reality, the fruit of lips are the fruit of the heart verbalized. The words are the innermost feelings of an individual addressed to God in thanksgiving and praise. If they are mechanical and mere utterances of the lips, as already seen, they will never meet the criteria necessary to qualify as any sort of sacrifice. They will then be only noise.[20] There is a danger that prayers learned by heart may become such. Prayers of a sacrificial nature and of real praise have to be from the heart. This is the sort of sacrifice God now seeks. This is therefore, the greatest shift in the nature of sacrifice because Christ has provided everything else that needed to be done in order to reconcile man and God. The thought is not mentioned by the author here but Peter in 1 Peter 2:5, makes it very clear that each believer is part of a new royal priesthood, which means that it is not only as individuals but also collectively that all are more than qualified to offer up this praise.

v. 16 "But do not be forgetful to do good and to share [what you have] *for God is pleased with sacrifices of that nature."* The nature of sacrifice is broadened in this context to include ongoing good works. For this reason, the author underlines the importance of what has already been introduced

---

20. In some parts of the world and especially in Africa, unless there is a lot of noise during worship with the preachers shouting as well as the members of the congregation, the worship is not considered to be acceptable nor adequate. However, it is not the volume that counts but the heart from which the praise flows.

in verses 1–3, in terms of behavior which sees the importance of looking after other people. Some evangelicals wrestle over what they see as the priority of verbalizing the message of the Gospel over against the significance of what is often called a social gospel. Both are essential and the one is part of the other. Words alone are not enough. Certainly, the significance of the proclamation of the message of Christ and his provision of salvation is essential; however, this priority is meaningless if the practical aspects of what it means to be a follower of the Savior are not evident in works of love and care for the people Christ came to change. The works highlight the loving and caring nature of the God/Man who died to give each a life that is very different from the lives of those who do not know him. Peter's sermon to those of the house of Cornelius in Acts 10:38, describes Jesus as the one who *"went about doing good and healing all who were oppressed by the devil"* (ESV); therefore, it is no wonder that the author of the letter makes it very clear that the acts which indicate the "doing good" and the "sharing" are also to be regarded as sacrificial. This means that the motives behind the actions need to be as "unto God."

v. 17 "*Obey those who lead you and submit to them for they watch over your souls,*[21]*as those who will give an account, in order that they may do this with joy and not groaning for that would not be advantageous to you.*" The earlier mention relative to leaders was the importance of remembering their teaching and the imitation of their lifestyle (v.7). Here the question at hand, is one of the need to obey (*peithesthe* a present imperative of *peithō*) and submit (*hupeikete* a present imperative of *hupeikō*) them. Nothing direct is known as to the identity of these leaders, since, as was noted in the introduction, the exact destination of the letter is unknown. The only thing that we can assume is that the author had confidence in these leaders and was consequently able to tell his readers that they needed to obey them and submit to them on an ongoing basis. The reason for this order was that they were constantly watching over (*agrupneō*) their souls. The verb has the sense of watching often, even spending sleepless nights, to make sure that all was well. Souls here can mean their spiritual wellbeing but it is more likely that it means the people and their lives as a whole, including their spiritual status. In other words, the leaders were greatly concerned with the lifestyle of these believers and wanted only the best for them.

The second reason why they should both obey and submit to them is that on the day of accountability, they would have to answer to the Lord who gave them their pastoral gifts concerning the way in which they had

---

21. *Psuchē* is usually translated soul but it has a variety of nuances and can mean the heart or inner being of a person or merely their life. It could be the latter here.

exercised their responsibilities. The fact that everyone will have to give an account for what they have done is nothing new (Rom 14:12; 1 Pet 4:5); Paul makes it very clear that everyone's work will be revealed for what it really is worth (1 Cor 3:13–15). Here the thought is that when the account is given, it is hoped that it will be such that it will result in joy, both for those who had the oversight and responsibility for them, as well as for the believers themselves. No one wanted the outcome to be full of disappointment and groaning (*stenazō* has the idea of inward groaning and lamentation) because of a negative outcome due to the fact that the leaders' counsel had been ignored and their work had been apparently, in vain. The desired outcome would be a victorious and joyous one for all, in the courts of heaven.

v. 18 "*Pray for us for we are certain that we have a good conscience desiring to behave well in all respects.*" It is most likely that the plural "us" is a stylistic matter because in the following verse the author immediately changes back to the singular.[22]Nevertheless, some believe that the author may have had an official responsibility. Certainly, at that time in the governance of the Early Church, plurality of eldership and team work meant individuals did not act independently. They would have had colleagues and associates as part of any oversight or group.[23] Even Paul had close associates in all he undertook, whether he was on a journey or based in a single locality such as Antioch. If the latter view is correct, when the author says: "Pray for us" he is asking for prayer, not just for himself but also for all who collaborated with him in the work of God. The question is not simple to resolve but it does not change the fact that the author requests prayer from his readers. This would indicate that, in spite of any doubts in earlier sections of the letter, with regard to their standing before God and the indications that some were tottering on the brink of apostasy, it had not happened yet.

The author does not give exact details as to what it is that he wants his readers to pray about on his behalf until the next verse, other than that his conscience and behavior in everything may be correct. There is a similar request for prayer made by Paul when he writes to the Corinthians asking that the nature of his ministry and conduct, especially that which is directed toward them, be full of God's grace (2 Cor 1:11, 12). Here, by acknowledging the need for prayer and God's hand upon his life, the author indicates a mutual dependency of trust and care for each other. It also demonstrates that the author is no autocratic or dictatorial individual who sees himself as more than able in all of life's vicissitudes. The way he writes with strength and direction, shows that he cares deeply about these people but that at the

22. Bruce, *Hebrews*, 409 and n107; Moffatt, *Hebrews*, 241; Owen, *Hebrews*, 3:18.
23. Guthrie, *Hebrews*, 278; Spence, "Hebrews," 13:18.

same time he recognizes the need of God's guidance and empowerment. This desire of his, is particularly focused on the areas of his conscience and thoughts, as well as the activities to which he gives himself. Both the mind/conscience and the activities have to be good; in this context that means to be correct in the eyes of God. If individuals are not motivated correctly, they will not be able to achieve what God requires: actions motivated by the Spirit of God and coming from the heart.

v. 19 "*I urge you all the more strongly to do this so that I may be restored to you sooner.*" This verse underlines the fact that the author has it in his heart to be among these believers once more. This verse indicates without any question that he was known to this group of people, even if his name is not present anywhere. The Greek verb *apokathistēmi,* has the sense of restoring or bringing someone back, who was previously in place. This likely means that he was at one time part of their group. So, he is no unfeeling or unknown outsider giving them orders from a distance. His actual circumstances remain unknown and any suggestions, including his possible imprisonment or some illness, have to be seen as mere conjecture.

vv. 20–21 "*But now the God of peace who brought again from the dead our Lord Jesus, the great shepherd of the sheep, through the blood of the eternal covenant, equip you with every good thing in order that you should do his will, working in us*[24] *what is pleasing in his sight through Jesus Christ, to whom be the glory for ever and ever. Amen.*" This doxology is the conclusion of the letter in real terms, with the following verses appearing to be a postscript added afterward.

God is here called the God of peace. He is the God whose nature is that of peace and he grants peace to all associated with him. This designation is similar to the title used by Paul in Romans 15:33 and 16:20. The question may be asked whether or not the presence of this title is aimed here at any specific circumstance present among the readers of the letter. Certainly, they needed to understand that in the midst of the world's conflicts and antagonism aimed at believers, God is the one who can bring about the peace they seek. On the other hand, is its insertion a hint that there was some sort of friction between them because of their various preferences and doctrines? It is not possible to be certain. All that can be said here is that God is a God of peace and this peace can only become a reality individually when people are reconciled with him by means of the sacrificial work of Christ. Since this latter fact is important, it is most likely that this is the way in which it is meant to be read. Any other applications would be secondary, even if true.

---

24. Some manuscripts have "you."

The next important matter here is that this is this same God who raised up Jesus Christ from the dead. It may seem strange that it is necessary to wait for the doxology before this fact of the resurrection is spelled out so clearly, as although it has been assumed since chapter 1:3, the resurrection has not been mentioned previously. In Romans 1:4 Paul says that Jesus was *"designated the Son of God in power according to the Spirit of holiness by his resurrection from the death."* Here the resurrection is attributed to God the Father. Nevertheless, there is no conflict whatever, because both the Spirit and the Father were involved in enacting this resurrection. The fact is, that by it, God justified the life and ministry of Jesus. It was God's way of declaring that Jesus' offering of himself had been accepted. He was raised to life again as proof of this. Without this resurrection there would be no salvation at all. Jesus is called "our Lord," meaning that he is our Master but if the contexts are examined in the Greek Old Testament, where Lord (*kurios*) is the translation of the Hebrew *yhwh* (יהוה), then he is also the believer's Yahweh.

The next significant factor is that Jesus is called "*the Great Shepherd of the sheep.*" Several scholars see here a reference to Moses in Isaiah 63:11, where he was instrumental in saving God's people from the Red Sea in the Exodus from Egypt. In this case however, it is not from the Red Sea that Jesus saves his people to be their Shepherd but from the dead, to give them life eternal.[25] Certainly, there are other shepherds in Israel but they are never seen to be laying down their lives for the sheep, which is something that is introduced in a unique manner in the New Testament by Jesus himself. He described himself as the Good Shepherd who lays down his life for the sheep (John 10:11). In the Old Testament the leaders are often described as shepherds (Jer 23:2; Ezek 34:2, 7, 8 et al.; Zech 10:3) but up until now, in this epistle, Jesus has been identified with the Great High Priest, not with just any shepherd. Anyway, he is the Great Shepherd of the sheep. It is a picture of leadership and intimacy. It needs to be remembered that the task of the shepherd was to take care of the sheep, never to abuse them. The sheep are clearly the people of God and he is their great leader, just as he said he would be in John 10:15–16. In that text he said there would be one flock under his leadership indicating the unifying factor of his person and work in bringing all followers, whether Jew or otherwise, under his authority. That particular aspect of his work is not highlighted in Hebrews other than that he has made all one (2:11).

The blood of the eternal covenant is Jesus' own blood. This sacrifice has already been alluded to earlier in the epistle (9:26, 28; 10:12, 14) and it is now highlighted as the eternal covenant; it is the new which supersedes

---

25. Kendrick, *Hebrews*, 187; Alford, *"Pros Ebraious,"* iv. 271; Bruce, *Hebrews*, 410–11.

any previous covenant or covenants. This covenant demonstrates no need for any other offerings ever again. The covenant is Jesus' covenant. It is dependent upon him in every way. His resurrection validates it in perpetuity.

The prayer here is that the provision of this eternal covenant may equip the readers in every good thing. The word equip is the rendition of an interesting Greek word *katartisai,* which in the literature of the day has the sense of setting something in place so that is it suitable for a specific task. It is translated variously in the New Testament by: perfecting, preparing, constructing, furnishing, repairing, equipping etc. It is the desire of the author here, to see the readers overcome the difficulties they have been experiencing and to do away with doubts and indifference, in order to become active agents in the work of God. For this reason, equip is used here to indicate that there is work in which these people are to be engaged for which they need to be prepared. The provision in this equipping does not depend upon the individual but God alone. Consequently, the reason to be prepared *"in order that you should do his will."* Ultimately, the only thing that really counts in God's economy is the doing of his will because it is perfect and inclusive of all that he envisages. This equipping has its source in the eternal covenant and enables the recipients, those who here are incorporated in the pronoun "us," to do what is directly pleasing to God. Again, finally all of this work and provision is through Jesus Christ. He is the Great Shepherd who is also the Great High Priest; the one bringing harmony between mankind as the creature and his Creator God, is re-established.

It is not absolutely clear whether the words: *"to whom be glory for ever and ever. Amen"* refer to God the Father who is grammatically the subject of the sentence or to Christ who is the immediate and preceding subject. Both would be correct, not only grammatically but also theologically. Most likely, it is better to see it as applying to the entire doxology and therefore, to God the Father. Bruce believes that since it has already been stated that all offering of praise is to be given to God though Christ, in verse 15, that this would tend to confirm that God is the object of this final attribution of glory.[26]

v. 22 "*But I urge you brethren, endure my word of exhortation for I have written to you briefly.*" The author urges his readers to take his word of encouragement seriously. That means the word of encouragement is in fact, the entire letter which he has written to them. There is some debate as to the exact sense of the Greek *paraklēseōs,* which is translated "exhortation" here. It is an encouragement for those who are inclined to accept the teachings it promotes but it could be seen as a rebuke for those who wanted to cling to any legalistic and old covenant position. Perhaps, that is why the

---

26. Bruce, *Hebrews,* 412.

author encourages his readers to endure patiently (*anechesthe* is the present imperative of *anechomai*) when it comes to what he has written. Some will not find it easy to rethink their whole way of worship as well as the theological implications of all that has been presented. He wants them to do so and not just brush aside anything that may appear unpalatable because it seems difficult for them; they have to consider it carefully and continuously as the *enduring* is a present continuous imperative.

In the author's mind this is not a long letter. He says that he has written briefly. It is not as long as some of the other New Testament letters like Romans. Moffatt states that the Greek expression *dia bracheōn epesteila*–"I wrote in a few words," is a common phrase used frequently by authors of the time.[27] Considering the content and the material covered the material is not nearly as long as it could have been. There are sections where it is stated that more could have been said (5:11; 9:5).[28] Anyway, the entire letter needs careful and ongoing reflection.

v. 23 "Know that our brother Timothy has been released, with whom I shall see you if he comes soon." It is because of the mention of Timothy that some have made links between this letter and Paul but this is no automatic indication that this thought is justifiable (see the Introduction on this matter). There is nevertheless an indication that there may be some kind of intersection between Timothy, this author and Paul, as this Timothy must be the same man to whom the letters to Timothy were addressed. He was someone who was well known among the churches and must have been known this this group of believers. There is sufficient evidence from other New Testament literature that Timothy travelled widely so would have been known by many in the churches (Acts 18:5; 19:22; 20:4; 1 Cor 4:17; 16:10; Phil 2:19; 1 Thess 3:2). There is no information with regard to the immediate context of Timothy's imprisonment here. All we know is that he has been released from incarceration. One thing that is evident from the New Testament letters and the book of Acts is that Christian leaders were among the first to suffer imprisonment during the epoch under review. The author was planning to visit those to whom the letter was addressed and was wanting to have Timothy accompany him. The way Timothy's name is included and he is called *"our brother"* indicates that he was known to these people and that the author must have been in communication with him.

27. Moffatt, *Hebrews*, 244.

28 I have read the entire letter aloud in 45 minutes so it can be read in one session at a regular church gathering; Bruce, *Hebrews*, 413, concurs with the timing when he states that the entire letter can be read in less than an hour.

v. 24 "*Greet all those who lead you and all the saints. Those from Italy greet you.*" In a manner typical of that followed by the biblical literature of the day, the letter requests that his greetings be conveyed to the leaders of this group as well as to all the believers, who are within the wider Christian community of which they are a part. There is no evidence as to how they relate to the wider group included within the author's desire to share his greeting. The mention of those from Italy has led to much discussion. It actually denotes nothing more than a group of people from Italy. It does not prove that they are presently either in Italy or not. It could merely mean "the Italians" greet you. If they were Italians in Italy, it would mean that the letter originated in Italy and that these Jewish believers came from Italy and went somewhere else. If they were Italians outside Italy then is the group to which the letter addressed a group of Jews living in Italy? It could be that these Jews were part of a community of Jews elsewhere which had a number of Italian members. Nothing can be proven from this statement with regard to its provenance or its destination other than there is some kind of connection with people who are Italians.

v. 25 "*Grace be with you all.*" In a manner resembling many of the Christian letters of the day this letter ends with the emphasis upon God's grace, the source of all God's help and strength (Rom 16:20; 1 Cor 16:23; 2 Cor 13:13; Eph 6:24 et al.). It is sought here for all without exception. The *Amen* which is found in the KJV, is not substantiated by the best manuscripts. The only legitimate place for any Amen is at the end of verse 21.

Appendix A

Christ's Substitutionary death

The subject of Christ's substitutionary death is a matter of considerable debate and has been since the earliest days of the Christian era. The contribution here is not intended to be a thorough treatment of the subject but a brief outline which deals with the subject from the perspective of biblical exegesis and not from the perspective of systematic theology, although the two are and should be closely related.

In Hebrews 2:9 the subject of the substitution springs from the fact that Jesus *"might taste death for everyone."*

The breadth of the substitution

In the clearest of terms, the text speaks of Jesus dying for everyone. There is no place here to discuss in detail the efficacy of the substitution but in the overall thrust of the teaching of the epistle to the Hebrews (which is in accord with the same teaching in other New Testament writings), for any substitution to be applied, it has to be embraced. That means that the individual has to accept the conditions which are necessary to its application. The teaching of the entire epistle is such that it declares that failure to believe in Christ and his sacrificial work, automatically excludes anyone from participating in the promises which follow this substitution. Therefore, even if theoretically and in terms of possibilities, this substitution is without limit, in terms of its application it is not. Its offer is universal but its acceptance is not. It is necessary to underline this because even if Christ tasted death for everyone, not everyone has taken up the offer or accepted the conditions. The result of its provision could have been universal but it is not; therefore, the teaching that maintains all will be saved because of Christ's work is not something that the New Testament teaches.

The necessity of the substitution

Mankind's sin, inherited from his first ancestor Adam (Rom 5:12, 14–19), has created a permanent barrier between himself and a holy God. This can never be removed by anything that he can do because his entire nature has been perverted and any work on his own part will never be able to satisfy the demands of God. God is therefore, the only one in a position to be able to find a satisfactory solution to this problem. The solution, and the only solution, was for Jesus to take on human form through the incarnation, live a sinless life in its entirety and then take on mankind's punishment by suffering the death that all mankind was appointed to experience as a consequence of that same sin. However, because of Christ's sinless life, he takes on the role of the representative human being who overcame death and now lives forever. All who then accept him as their own representative also benefit from the victory he won as a man who experienced all the same sorts of temptations as every human.

The identification with Christ results in God the Father seeing each person who believes in Jesus, as being pardoned by his sacrifice; thereby they have their sin covered by the blood and death of Christ who took their place. That is what substitution is all about. This means that Christ, his life, his death and his resurrection is embraced by those who believe in him. The outcome of his victory over death is then acquired by all who identify with him.

Any question regarding the person to whom the substitution is paid is never the matter at hand. In fact, it is not paid to anyone. It is the demand of what it right and required according to God's attributes and nature. God's person requires what is right and nothing less. That is why Paul writes about Christ being the means of propitiation through faith in his blood and that his righteousness justifies those that believe in him (Rom 3:25, 26). Christ did what was right and yet he had to die because of the sin of mankind. So, all of the members of this sinful creation who submit to his lordship are then, according to God's plan, exonerated from the automatic consequences of sin, which is death. Death is much more than the cessation of physical life. It is being cut off from all good and from God, eternally. Death also means bearing the results of the actions perpetrated against a holy God during one's lifetime; it includes experiencing God's displeasure which is spoken of in Pauline terms as his wrath (Rom 1:18). Wrath is aimed at redressing unrighteousness's consequences. Substitution covers the entire matter of mankind's sin and rebellion because of Christ.

Any attempts, modern or otherwise, to do away with the necessity of the substitutionary atonement of Christ, do damage to the reading of

Scripture and in the end the need for the life and death of Christ. It must be remembered that as the author to the Hebrews writes *"without the shedding of blood there is no forgiveness of sin"* (Heb 9:22).

There are a good number of helpful articles and books on the subject.[1]

---

1. Morris "Atonement," 54–57; Godfrey, "Atonement," 57; Hilario, "Substitutionary Atonement."

Appendix B

Chapter 4:9 The Sabbath rest in Hebrews

The Sabbath rest is based initially upon the fact that God rested from his creative work on the seventh day and subsequently, especially from the time of the Exodus from Egypt, the Sabbath became a special day when work was forbidden (Exod 16:23–29; 20:8, 10–11 et al.). The prophets extoled the place of the Sabbath and warned the Sabbath breakers of the consequences of their conduct (Isa 56:4; Jer 17:21–22; Eek.20:16) and yet there were also indications that the heart of the people was what God was looking for rather than the mere keeping of days (Hos 2:11).

In Hebrews, rest is far more than the Sabbath under the Old Covenant. In chapter 4 the *rest* is based initially on getting the people of God to the Promised Land. However, it goes on to speak of an eternal rest or an eternal Sabbath. In that state God is at the center of everything that takes place and fully controls the existence of all those who participate in this new existence in the heavenly Kingdom. This Sabbath is far more than human effort to keep a set of rules about a specific day which is the emphasis that the Seventh Day Adventists claim to be the most important thing required of followers of God. The author to the Hebrews declares that the requirement for entering this promised rest is simply a matter of belief alone (Heb 3:19). If people do not enter into it, the cause is unbelief. Obviously, belief must be accompanied by actions which indicate submission and obedience to God (Heb 3:16–19) but it is far more than keeping one day out of seven, separate from the other six. When this Sabbath is put in place every day and every moment will belong fully to God. In Hebrews the Sabbath is the eternal age of rest in the presence of God for all who are the true followers of God.

Appendix C

Apostasy: chapter 6:6 and 10:26

In chapter 6:6 the author tells his readers that those who have been enlightened, shared in the Holy Spirit's work and participated in the power of
the age to come, cannot expect to be renewed if they fall away. He declares
dogmatically that such a renewal would be impossible. Is he saying that
these Hebrew Christians have actually arrived at the place where they have
committed the unpardonable sin or is he merely warning them that if they
do then there is no hope for the future? Has the point of becoming an apostate been reached? It would appear that although the author has these stern
words for them, that in his mind, they are at the point of going one way or
the other but it is not yet too late. If they pursue their present track, they
will be at the point of no return but if they do an about face, and that very
promptly, then they will avoid disaster.

The Old Covenant was clear that intentional and blatant sin was without pardon (Num 15:30–31). Therefore, it cannot be expected that under
the New Covenant the situation would be more lenient. This has to be considered as the background to the statement in Heb 10:26 that willful sin has
no sacrifice which will deal with its consequences. The behavior indicates
apostasy is followed by a terrible judgment (Heb 10:27).

The Early Church really struggled with the whole question of apostasy
and sin, as is evident from writings such as those in *The Shepherd of Hermas*[1]
where one of the main questions is related to how many times a person can
repent. Baptism was seen as the major step of repentance and some questioned whether if you sinned after having been baptized you could indeed
repent and be forgiven. Much ink was spilled over such matters. Certainly,
the teaching against sin was important but it appears that much was left up to
the ability of the individual and little to the grace of God in the discussions.[2]

---

1. See as in the section: Command iv, 18 & 22–28.
2. See Bruce's discussion of this matter. *Hebrews*, 260–62.

When it comes to the matter of who is lost and who is not and what constitutes the unforgivable sin, the teaching of John Calvin and Jacobus Arminius come to the fore. Those on one side of the argument will not bend to consider those on the other; therefore, the matter goes on *ad infinitum*. Rather than opt for a systematic approach it is best to attempt a biblical one.

An example of how to proceed would be to look at how Paul writes about the whole question of salvation. In a variety of contexts, he writes about individuals who have been saved, others who are being saved and again, of others who eventually attain permanent salvation. The significance of the action involved, which is relative in each case to salvation, is indicated by the tense of the verbs. To highlight the timing of salvific action on the part of God in saving mankind, the importance of the three tenses associated with the final outcome salvation are what need to be noted in each case. They indicate that there are a series of steps, all of which are necessary, to arrive at the final and complete state when it is possible to call a person "fully saved." These steps are demonstrated by Paul although it needs to noted that his treatment is not carried out in any systematic manner in the original contexts where the statements are recorded. The examples appear in Romans and 1 Corinthians:

1. We "are saved" by hope. This salvation takes place at the moment the individual makes a decision to follow Christ (Rom 8:24 ἐσώθημεν–*esōthēmen*–"we were saved." 1st person pl. aorist 1 indicative passive). This moment of faith and hope, indicates the initial entry into the plan of God. It is the equivalent of the Johannine being "born again" or the Pauline "conversion." The entrance is complete as the aorist tense shows.

2. We are "being saved" each and every day. It is a process that continues. The preaching of the message of the cross conveys the power of God to the believer to help them to have the ability to grow and progress once they become Christ's followers (1 Cor 1:18 σωζομένοις–*sōzomenois*–"being saved." dative pl. masculine present passive participle). The passive participle in the present indicates that this action is something that continues and the one who is doing the saving is other than the person themselves: God. It underlines the fact that salvation is an ongoing process. This action lasts from the moment of accepting Christ (as in the above) until the very end of one's physical life. Here the growth is in the area of obtaining God's power and help through the message of the Gospel. If the process is cut short by unbelief or disobedience, then the next and final stage is not reached; this would mean that there would be the equivalent of an aborted life. This does

not mean that every time a person makes a mistake, or sins through ignorance that they are sent back to the beginning to start all over again. But if they abandon their hope and trust in Christ and live in a state of sin, as the normal way of life, rather than walking in the Spirit, then the outcome is very different. They distance themselves from God who is the means of salvation; their own disobedience means that they are no longer being saved because their behavior becomes indicative of a blatant rejection of God's offer of forgiveness.

3. Finally, we "shall be saved" from the wrath of God on the last day because of the justification which Christ makes possible by his sacrifice and the shedding of his blood. This means that when the judgment of the world takes place at the end of time, when the final accounts are made, all believers arrive at the terminus and are counted righteous in Christ (Rom 5:9, 10 σωθησομεθα–sōthēsometha–"we shall be saved." 1 p. pl. fut. ind. pass.). This juncture has not yet been reached because it is, as the verb indicates, in the future. It is passive because the one who brings about the final salvation and grants it to the individual is God himself. Once all the former stages (1 and 2) have been completed, this final point becomes a reality. It affirms the entirety of all for which the word salvation stands; it demonstrates that the first two steps were successful so that the entire journey is now complete and the race has been completed.

The first two steps indicate that each of them can be accomplished without the finality that is required by arriving at the last. Therefore, without the tenacity which the author to the Hebrews insists upon in the face of all of life's trials, it is possible for someone to become an apostate who was once a Christian.

Since apostasy is the immediate subject of concern, it means that when it occurs, there is an interruption in the procedure. The steps are not completed and the provision of salvation after the initial decision to believe is never achieved. Somewhere during the second continuous process of "being saved," there is a cessation that interrupts the desired outcome. This is not, in any way, due to God but to the individual's blatant turning away from Christ. This is not merely due to indifference but a clear choice to stop believing. It will also be accompanied by an attitude of antagonism toward God as well as an open rejection of all that Christ offers to the sinner.

The signs of this rejection are evident in deliberate sin and a return to a lifestyle which is indicative of a life that is not submitted to Christ. It means denying Christ and his sacrifice and is often visible when the person becomes, not just indifferent to Christians and their message but their open enemy. Often it results in the persecution of Christians by those who previously called themselves followers of Christ. The author of Hebrews in 6:4–6, describes them as having been enlightened and benefited from the heavenly gift but then having fallen away. The latter shows that the rupture is complete for them. They will not and cannot, according to these verses, be restored once this point has been reached. Further, the author of Hebrews states dogmatically in 10:26, that when people sin blatantly, meaning knowingly, the sacrifice of Christ is no longer applicable. The result is then the same as in the previous description in chapter 6:4–6. They are "destroyed" (Hebrews 10:39) as apostates. The author to the Hebrews is dogmatic that apostates cannot be restored.

It is not the purpose of this appendix to examine apostasy in depth but to raise the issue and clarify what is involved in its presence. False teachings of any kind, which turn believers away from truth and subsequently from Christ, may be behind any apostasy, as they become a tool of Satan. This is because wrong thinking leads to wrong behavior. It is for this reason that any wrong teaching with regard to the person of the Father, the Son or the Holy Spirit can lead to apostasy. Any mindset of man, which causes someone who follows Christ, to turn from his teaching so that there is disobedience and the withdrawal of allegiance to the Savior, will result in eternal damnation. Apostasy is the condition which leads to the lost state in permeance, of any individual who at one time claimed to be a believer in Jesus Christ. The author of the Epistle to the Hebrews, as well as other writers of the New Testament (1 Tim 4:1; 2 Pet 3:17), warn of the danger of this condition, so that correct action may be taken to avoid the consequences of apostasy before it is too late.

It should be noted that if someone is concerned about their spiritual state, after being indifferent or even after what may be considered committing a sin of great significance, it probably means that they are not apostate. The reason for this is that their concern alone becomes an indicator that the Spirit of God is bringing them to a place of conviction so that they may repent and be forgiven.

Appendix D

The nature of perfection or completeness (teleiōsis)

Chapter 7:11 highlights the importance of God's desire for perfection. It needs to be understood just what this means in his overall plan. Perfection in Scripture is often linked to the person of God and his holiness. Here, it is not the fact that individuals become perfect in any moral way during their lifetime. That concept goes together more with the teaching of Pauline sanctification, which is not an emphasis in this letter. In the letter to the Hebrews perfection (*teleiōsis*) is more a state of completeness, which indicates that what is partial or incomplete, needs to be is fulfilled in its ultimate form. This form or completeness, is therefore, unlike anything that preceded it and may at the time have been regarded as being perfect.

The letter presents those earlier former states as shadows or types, like the forms present in the book of Leviticus. The author to the Hebrews highlights the fact that they were only visible and tangible symbols, indicative of the actual things which exist already in the heavenly or permanent sphere. This means that the physical objects which were in place and even the procedures for worship which had to be followed, were never to be regarded as perfect, even if the imagery was understood as equal to perfection by the people who lived in the epoch of the Old Testament. That was when the physical forms such as the tent, the altar, including the holy place and the cherubim with all the objects used for the service and worship on the Day of Atonement, were all part of the system which was required to be adhered to under the first incomplete covenant.

In Hebrews, perfection and completion all belong to the reality which Christ brings about under the second and complete covenant. His sacrifice, his atonement and his presence as the Great High Priest, speak of the fulfilment or completion of all the types. In the end the perfection only comes about when Christ comes again, but this is not always something which is presented in such clear terms in the letter even if it is hinted at.

In chapter 7:27 (see notes on the passage) there is a list of adjectives describing the perfection of Christ. All of them indicate the purity and complete image of God's person (holiness, innocence, purity, separated from sinners). The fact that Christ lived among other men and women and retained this perfection shows that all of those attributes have nothing to do with physical contact but a state of being. In the case of mankind, they are only going to be changed by a person's heart and mind. If the mind is in sync with God and his will, then these acts which demonstrate perfection and completeness will be the consequence. They are what is known as the consequence of sanctification or the taking on of divine characteristics. Even the phrase "separate from sinners" does not speak of physical distancing but a lifestyle which is not influenced by people who are sinful. This shows that the concept of some of the early saints and monastics who hid themselves away from the crowd in deserts, caves and secluded sites is far from being what is required, if perfection or completeness is sought after.

Appendix E

Diathēkē–διαθήκη–Covenant or Will in Hebrews 9:16–18

This will or covenant–*diathēkē,* is the result of God alone, who has laid down the conditions for any inheritance (just mentioned in 9:15). They include obedience, a subject concerning which much has already been stated elsewhere in the epistle (2:2, 3; 3:7 et al.). God alone established the conditions, as he announces in Genesis "*I will make my covenant between me and you*" (Gen 17:2–8) but he also tells Abraham what his part is in it (Gen 17:9–14). In the majority of cases in this letter a covenant–*diathēkē*–is used in the traditional Hebrew manner to show, as the notes in the body of the work on Hebrews 9:16 indicate, an agreement made by God, who has overall authority and power, which is imposed upon his people Israel. The covenant is put in place with the shedding of blood of an animal or animals (Exod 24:5–8). It can only be changed by the one who sets it in place and never by those upon whom it is imposed. That means that only God is in a position to bring about any changes to it.

However, when it comes to Hebrews 9:16–17 (see the notes in this chapter) the word *diathēkē* is suddenly used in a very different sense. It no longer has the sense of a covenant but of a will or testament.[1] If this switch in sense is not grasped the interpreter will immediately find himself in difficulty. Greek speakers would not have had this difficulty because, for them, *diathēkē* would immediately mean a will. That was the most natural sense of the word for them and was part of normal usage in everyday life when someone needed to draw up a will. Indeed, for Greek speakers the aspect of the covenant would not have been part of their reckoning. It would have been difficult for them to grasp in the sense of a covenant as it was not practiced widely by peoples during that period.[2] It would have been Jews

---

1. For more on this subject and the way in which *diathēkē* is used in non-biblical literature see Morris, *Apostolic Preaching,* 87–90.

2. The practice of making covenants with the shedding of blood at that time

who were aware of the word having different meanings and that would be because of its presence as the Greek translation (the LXX) of the Hebrew term: *carath berith* (כָּרַת בְּרִית) or "to cut a covenant" in the Exodus narrative concerning the granting of the covenant at Sinai. So Greek speaking Jews would have learned to distinguish between what was recognized as a will and what was a covenant. The context would make that clear. This is therefore what needs to be done here in Hebrews 9:16–18 in order to eliminate any confusion.

---

appears to be very limited and was practiced by the Jews as well as the Hittites but at a much earlier time than that of the Greek or Roman dominance. See McCarthy, *Treaty and Covenant*, 7, 141–53; Mendenhall, "Oriental and Biblical Law," 26–46 and "Covenant Forms," 50–76; Kitchen, *Ancient Orient*, 90–102.

Appendix F

The Question of the tithe

There are those today who claim that since tithing is an Old Testament teaching and that we are no longer in the Old Testament and under the dispensation of the Law, that Christians do not have to tithe. If the payment of the tithe by Abraham is examined closely, it demonstrates that the tithe was given to Melchizedek prior to the coming of the Law and the teaching given to the people of Israel that they needed to tithe under the Levitical system came later. This tenth that Abraham gave to Melchizedek was not ordered. It was given freely and spontaneously, as a thank offering to God for the way he had delivered Abraham's enemies into his hand and in fact enriched him at the same time. This means that the principle of the giving of the tithe precedes the Law and stands on its own, even though the Law has been replaced by the principle of grace. Further, the fact that Christ died to redeem each believer means that not only does the believer belong to Christ so does all his or her life and all that belongs to them (1 Cor 6:19–29). In reality, all our finances, time, and effort, are due to God and his service but the principle of the tithe lays down the fact that God asks for the tithe to continue to be the minimum that the believer owes to their God.

Tithing should not be seen on its own as the New Testament has much to say about giving from a thankful heart. Jesus spoke of the woman who gave from the little that she had in terms of her true sacrifice and giving to God from her poverty as compared to the rich who gave from their abundance (Mark 12:41–44). Jesus was indeed magnifying her person and example. This shows that it is not the sum that is given but the heart behind the gift that counts. Paul talks about sowing and reaping and that the person should not sow sparingly but that at the same time the giving needs to be from the heart and that those who give of themselves abundantly would receive an appropriate reward because God looks at the heart and loves cheerful givers (2 Cor 9:6–7).

Jesus blamed the Pharisees who were bent on tithing and being very exact in doing so. They exaggerated the necessity to give from the smallest things they gained, like spices but did not have any love or mercy for the people around them in great need. These were the things that God really was concerned about from his people, together with giving flowing from a love of God and for his service and people as a whole (Matt 23:23). This shows that tithing, giving, serving, and showing a rounded life in all that one does, is what God requires. It is not merely keeping rules about how much one has to give that meets God's criteria. If the heart is not right in any giving and the motives are wrong, the gift is not going to make a lot of difference in God's sight.

So, to conclude the matter of the tithe and Abraham's gift to Melchizedek, it is evident that he gave it with a heart full of praise and thankfulness to God and it was received by the Most-High, because of the way in which it is recorded and remembered so clearly, in both the Old and New Testaments.

Appendix G

Discipline in Chapter 12:5, 6

Discipline,[1] which included physical punishment, used to be very ridged and was regarded as a normal and required part of upbringing for all children until some fifty to sixty years ago, even in western cultures. That was when abuse and exaggerated extremes in its administration led to what has now become, almost the complete absence of any physical discipline or punishment in many nations and families.[2] The consequences have been that for many, strict parental guidance and even discipline of any kind is often lacking in western society. This has resulted in free expression on the part of children and the assumption on the part of many adults in the generations that have followed, that discipline, which includes any physical prohibitions and punishment, is the equivalent of child abuse. This is not how ancient cultures viewed discipline; any critique of the subject here in the context of the teaching of discipline in Hebrews, has to be done, not in the light of modern concepts but of the views at the time at which the literature was recorded. It is not the purpose of this presentation to critique either ancient or modern views of discipline. It is nevertheless, necessary to understand that Jewish culture, like most others at that time, was insistent on the necessity of discipline including physical punishment.

1. Discipline as a verb is viewed as the procedure employed to inculcate what are viewed as good, consistent and necessary forms of behaviour in any individual to enable them to handle all the vicissitudes of life. They will include physical, emotional, rational and spiritual elements. They are normally commenced from a young age and continue in both a formal and informal way, into adulthood and even beyond. It is not to be understood here in the sense of an academic discipline or area of study leading to professional competency. For the sense of the Greek words as a noun and verb see the footnote on *paideia* in the notes on Hebrews 12:5, 6.

2. In a number of western nations any form of physical punishment has become illegal. Not even spanking is permitted.

Apart from its mention in Hebrews 12, The physical nature of discipline and punishment is especially evident in the book of Proverbs. See Prov 13:24 where it is stated clearly that the one who spares the rod from his son, hates him; chastening is a demonstration of love. Other texts referring to its practice include Proverbs 22:15; 23:13, 14 and 29:15 which all continue in the same vein of thought. The emphasis throughout these references is that physical pain instils discipline of a lasting nature, which will bring correction and result in conduct that is of the kind that is desired and beneficial. The rod is the instrument of this disciple but needs to be distinguished from the rod of God's anger. The motivation for the administration of the discipline is what makes the difference.

Bibliography

I Enoch, Ethiopic Parallel Translations, (R.H. Charles' revision. Oxford: Clarendon Press, 1913, of Richard Laurence's original English translation in 1883), http://qbible.com/enoch/22.html.

Aland. Barbara, et al. eds. *The Greek New Testament,* 5th rev. ed. (Stuttgart: Deutsche Bibelgeselleschaft, 2014).

Alford, Henry. "*Pros Ebraious,*" *The Epistle to the Hebrews.* In *The Greek New Testament.* IV, Chicago, Ill: Moody, 1958 ed. 1968. 1–273.

The Apocalypse of Baruch. http://www.pseudepigrapha.com/pseudepigrapha/2Baruch.html.

Aristophanes. *Plutus.* 476; Josephus, c. Apionem, i. 148, quoting Berossus, *Aaborosoarchodos . . . hupo tōn philōn apetumpanisthē: Arist . Rhet .* ii. 5. 14.

Arndt, William F., and Wilbur F. Gingrich. *A Greek-English Lexicon of the New Testament, and Other Early Christian Literature.* Chicago: University of Chicago Press, 1957.

Athenagoras. *A Plea for the Christians,* chapters 3—4. https://www.newadvent.org/fathers/ 0205.htm.

Athanasius. *Orationes contra Arianos.*

Augustine, *De Civitate Dei.* https://www.documentacatholicaomnia.eu/03d/0354 -0430,_Augustinus,_De_Civitate_Dei_Contra_Paganos,_EN.pdf.

Aust, Jerold., and Scott Ashely. "Jericho: does the Evidence Disprove or Prove the Bible?" April 24, 2002; https://www.ucg.org/the-good-news/jericho-does-the-evidence-disprove-or-prove-the-bible

Babota, Vasile. "The High Priesthood of Simon (142–140)." In *The Institution of the Hasmonean High Priesthood.* Supplements to the *Journal for the Study of Judaism,* vol. 165, Leiden, Netherlands: Brill, 2013, 225–267.

Bannon, M. Jeff. "'The Heavenlies' in Ephesians, A Lexical, Exegetical, and Conceptual Analysis," PhD diss., in New Testament and Christian Origins, University of Edinburgh, 2010.

Barclay, William. *The Letter to the Hebrews,* The Saint Andrew Press, Edinburgh: 2nd ed. 1957.

Bengel, J.A. *Gnomon Novi Testamenti,* Stuttgart: J.F. Steinkopf, 1860.

Brown, Raymond. *The Message of Hebrews: Christ above all.* The Bible Speaks Today Nottingham: Inter-Varsity Press, 1982.

Bruce, F. F. *The Epistle to the Hebrews,* London: Marshall, Morgan & Scott, 1964.

———. *New Testament History,* London: Oliphants, rev. ed. 1971.

Calvin, John. *The Epistle to the Hebrews*. Original translation by Clement Cotton, 1605, ed. J.O. Thrussington, 1853. https://www.studylight.org/commentaries/eng/cal/hebrews.html.

Carson, D.A. et al. "Hebrews." In *An Introduction to the New Testament*. Leicester, UK.: Apollos, 1992, 391–407.

Chrysostom, John. *Ad Hebraeos*; https://www.documentacatholicaomnia.eu/03d/0345-0407,_Iohannes_Chrysostomus,_In_epistulam_ad_Hebraeos_[Schaff],_EN.pdf.

Clement of Alexandria. *Hypotyposes*, cited in Eusebius, *Hist. Eccl.* vi. 14. 2.

Clement of Rome. *1 Clement to the Corinthians*, Translated by J.B. Lightfoot. https://www.earlychristianwritings.com/text/1clement-lightfoot.html.

Docherty, Susan E. *The Use of Old Testament in Hebrews: A Case Study in Early Jewish Bible Interpretation*, Tübingen: Mohr Siebeck, 2009.

Dodd, Charles H. *The Epistle of Paul to the Romans*. London: Collins/Fontana, 1959.

Dyer, Bryan R. "The Epistle to the Hebrews in Recent Research Studies on the Author's Identity, His Use of the Old Testament, and Theology." In *JGRChJ* 9 (2013) 104–31 https://www.academia.edu/4963939/The_Epistle_to_the_Hebrews_in_Recent_Research_Studies_on_the_Authors_Identity_His_Use_of_the_Old_Testament_and_Theology

Daube, David. *The New Testament and Rabbinic Judaism*, London: Athlone, 1956.

The Didache: The Teaching of the Twelve Apostles, Copyright 2013, 2016 Legacy Icons Zeeland: Michigan. USA.

Delitzch, Franz. *Commentary on the Epistle to the Hebrews*, Translated by Thomas L. Kinsbury, London: Vol. 1, T & T. Clark 1871. ed. Klock & Klock, Minneapolis, MINN: 1978.

Ellingworth, Paul. *The Epistle to the Hebrews*, (Epworth Commentaries), London: Epworth, 1991.

Eusebius, Pamphilus. *Historia Ecclesisastica (or Historia Ecclesiae)* For a translation in English see: *Eusebius' Ecclesiastical History*. Translated by Arthur Cushman McGiffert, n. pl., Adansonia Publishing, 2018.

Feinberg, Charles L. *Jeremiah: A Commentary*, Grand Rapids, Michigan, Zondervan, 1982.

Field, Fridericus. *Origenis Hexapla quae supersunt*. Oxford: Oxford University Press, 1875, reprinted, Hildesheim Georg Olms, 1964.

Firebaugh, W.C. *The Inns of Greece & Rome, and History of Hospitality from the Dawn of time to the Middle Ages*, Chicago: Pascal Covici, 1928, chapter VIII, 108–125.

Fowler, Megan. "Christian Martyr Numbers Down by Half in a Decade. Or are they?" *Christianity Today*, February 17, 2020 https://www.christianitytoday.com/ct/2020/march/christian-martyrs-numbers-down-by-half-in-decade-or-are-the.html.

Garnet, Paul. "Atonement Constructions in the Old Testament and the Qumran Scrolls," *The Evangelical Quarterly*, 46, 1974, 131–163.

Garrard, David J. *Paul's Epistle to the Galatians*, Preston, England: CAM International, 2017.

———. *The Epistle of Paul to the Ephesians*, Eugene, Wipf and Stock, 2023.

Godfrey, W. Robert. "Atonement, Extent of." In *New Dictionary of Theology*, Edited by Sinclair B. Ferguson and David F. Wright. Leicester: Inter-Varsity Press, 1988, 57.

Gregory of Nizianzus. *Oration* xxi. 25 (*In Praise of the Great Athanasius*). [https://people.ucalgary.ca/~vandersp/Courses/texts/cappadoc/gnazor21. html].

Grudem, Wayne. *The Gift of Prophecy in the New Testament and Today*, Wheaton, Ill: Crossway Books, ed. 2000.

Guthrie, Donald. *Hebrews: An Introduction and Commentary*, Nottingham: Inter-Varsity Press, 1983.

Hilario, Conrad. "The Christian Doctrine of Substitutionary Atonement." Christian Fellowship, Columbus, OH: DWELL community Church https://dwellcc.org/learning/essays/christian-doctrine-substitutionary-atonement

Homer. *The Odyssey*. London: Harper Press, ed. 2011.

Hughes, Philip Edgecumbe. *A Commentary on the Epistle to the Hebrews*, Grand Rapids: Eerdmans, 1977.

Javet, Jean-Samuel. *Dieu vous parle: commentaire sur l'Epître aux Hébreux*, Paris: Delachaux et Niestlé, 1945.

Jerome. *Adversus Jovinianum.*

———. *Liber quaestionum hebraicarum in Genesim Opera.*

Jones, Edmund D. "The Authorship of Hebrews XIII," *The Expository Times*, XLVI, Sept. (1935) 129–136.

Josephus, Flavius. *Antiquities of the Jews*. Translated by William Whiston. https://www.gutenberg.org/files/2848/2848-h/2848-h.htm

———. *Contra Apionem.*

———. *The Wars of the Jews*. Translated by William Whiston, London: 1737; https://www.pdfdrive.com/flavius-josephus-the-antiquities-of-the-jews-index-e7866672.html.

Justin Martyr. *First Apology.*

Kadari, Tamar. "Esau, Wives of: Midrash and Aggadah." In *The Encyclopedia of Jewish Women*, https://jwa.org/encyclopedia/article/esau-wives-of-midrash-and-aggadah

Käsemann, Ernst. *Das wandernde Gottesvolk*. Göttingen: Vandenhoeck & Ruprecht, 1961 [1938].

Kendrick, A.C. *Commentary on the Epistle to the Hebrews*. In *An American Commentary on the New Testament*, edited by Alvah Hovey, 6:1–207. Valley Forge, PA: The Judson Press, 1889.

Kitchen, Kenneth A. *Ancient Orient and the Old Testament*, London: Tyndale, 1966, 90–102.

Kittel, Gerhard., and Gerhard Friedrich, et al. eds. *Theological Dictionary of the New Testament*, Translated by Geoffrey W. Bromiley, Grand Rapids: Eerdmans, 1964–76.

Manson, William. *The Epistle to the Hebrews: An Historical and Theological Reconsideration*. (The Baird Lecture 1949), London: Hodder and Stoughton, 1951.

Manson, Thomas W. *Studies in the Gospels and Epistles*. Edited by Matthew Black, Manchester: Manchester University Press, 1962.

Martin, Cath. "'70 Million Christians' martyred for their faith since Jesus walked the earth." In *Christianity Today*, 25 June 2014. https://www.christiantoday.com/article/70.million.christians.martyred.faith.since.jesus.walked.earth/38403.htm

Martin, Ralph P. "Sonship." In *New Dictionary of Theology*, edited by Sinclair B. Ferguson and David F. Wright. Leicester: Inter-Varsity Press, 1988. 651–653.

McCarthy, Denis J. *Treaty and Covenant: A Study in Form in the Ancient Oriental Documents and in the Old Testament*. In series *Analecta Biblica*, 21, Rome: Pontifical Biblical Institute, 1963,

Mendenhall, George E. "Ancient Oriental and Biblical Law." In *The Biblical Archaeologist*, 17. 2, 1954, 26–46.

———. "Covenant Forms in Israelite Tradition." In *The Biblical Archaeologist*, 17.3, 1954; 50–76.

Montefiore, Hugh W. *A Commentary on the Epistle to the Hebrews*, London: Adam & Charles Black, 1964.

Moo, Douglas. *The Epistle to the Romans*. Grand Rapids: Eerdmans, 1966.

Moffatt, James. *A Critical and Exegetical Commentary on the Epistle to the Hebrews*, ICC, Edinburgh: T. & T. Clark, 1924.

Morris, Leon. *The Apostolic Preaching of the Cross*. (3rd ed.), London: The Tyndale Press, 1965.

———. "Atonement." In *New Dictionary of Theology*, In *New Dictionary of Theology*, edited by Sinclair B. Ferguson and David F. Wright, Leicester: Inter-Varsity Press, 1988, 54–57.

Moulton, James Hope., and George Milligan. *The Vocabulary of the Greek Testament: Illustrated from the Papyri and Other Non-Literary Sources*, London: Hodder and Stoughton, 1914, 1929.

Nacht, Jacob. "The Symbolism of the Shoe with Special Reference to Jewish Sources." In *The Jewish Quarterly Review*, New Series, 6,1 (Jul., 1915), University of Pennsylvania Press. 1–22.

Nairne, Alexander. *The Epistle to the Hebrews with Introduction and Notes*. Cambridge Greek Testament for Schools and Colleges, Cambridge: Cambridge University Press, 1922.

———. *The Epistle of Priesthood: Studies in the Epistle to the Hebrews*. Edinburgh: T. & T. Clark, 1913.

Origen. *Homilies on Genesis and Exodus*. Translated by Ronald E. Heine. In *The Fathers of the Church: A New Translation*. Washington, DC: The Catholic University of America Press, 1981.

Owen, John. *Exercitations on the Epistle to the Hebrews*. Edinburgh: Johnstone Hunter, 1855. https://www.studylight.org/commentaries/eng/joc/hebrews-12.html.

Pfann, Stephen J. "The Essene yearly Renewal Ceremony and the Baptism of Repentance." https://www.uhl.ac/wp-content/uploads/2016/06/Baptism.pdf.

Philo. *De Agricultura*.

———. *De sacrificiis Abelis et Caini*.

———. *De Virtutibus*. Translated by F.H. Colson and G.H. Whitaker, *On the Virtues,* in

———. *De Vita Contemplativa*.

———. *Legum allegoriae*.

———. VIII, Loeb Classical Library, Cambridge MASS: Harvard University Press, 1939, 1999.

———. *Who is the Heir of Divine Things?* xlvi, xlvii https://www.loebclassics.com/view/philo_judaeus-who_heir_divine_things/ 1932/pb_LCL261.277.xml.

Pink, Arthur W. *Commentary on John and Hebrews*. https://www.studylight.org/commentaries/eng/awp/ hebrews-13.html.

Quell, P., and J. Behm. "διαθήκη."[*Diathēkē*] In *TDNT*, II , eds Kittel, *et al.*, Eerdmans, 1965, 106–134.

Rohr. I. *Der Hebräerbrief, The heilige Schrift zum Neuen Testament*, 14, Bonn, 1932.

Salmon, George. *Introduction to the New Testament*. London: John Murray, 1892.

Shrenk, G. *TDNT*, II, 446 n.4.

Spence, Hendry Donald Maurice. "Hebrews." In *Pulpit Commentary*, 13:18 https://biblehub.com/commentaries/pulpit/Hebrews/ 13.htm.

Spicq, Ceslas. *L'Epître aux Hébreux*, (2 Volumes). Paris: Gabalda, 1952, 1953.

———. «L'authenticité du *chapître* XIII de l'Epître aux Hébreux, » *Conjectanea neotestimentica* XI (1948), Upsala, 226–36.

Swetnam, James. "*Diathēkē*in the Septuagint Account of Sinai: A Suggestion." In *Biblica*. 47, 3, 1966, 438–444. https://www.jstor.org/stable/43595179?read-now=1&seq=1#page_scan_ tab_contents

Turner, Cuthbert H. *Novum Testmentum Sancti Irenaei Lugdunensis*. Edited by Sandy, W., and C.H. Turner, Oxford: Clarendon, 1923.

Tertullian. *Scorpiace*.

van der Woude, A. S. "Melchisedek als himmlische Erlösergestalt in de neugefunden eschatologischen Midraschim aus Qunmran Höhle XI." *Oudetestamentische Studiën* 14 (1965) 354–373, pl. 1; 11Q13 Melchizedek 1207–1209, 11QMelchiz edek.pdf (marquette.edu).

von Harnack, Adolf. "Probabilia über die Adresse und den Verfasser des Hebräerbriefs," In *ZNTWT*, 1, 1900, 16–41.

———. *What is Christianity? Lectures delivered in the University of Berlin during the Winter term 1888-1900*. Translated by Thomas Bailey Saunders, London: Williams and Norgate, 1908 2nd ed. rev., Lecture IX, https://www.ccel.org/ccel/h/harnack/christianity/cache/ christianity.pdf.

Welch, Adam. "The Authorship of Hebrews." In *The Authorship of the Epistle to the Hebrews and other papers*, Edinburgh: Oliphants, 1898, 1–33.

Westcott, Brooke F. *The Epistle to the Hebrews*. London: McMillan & Co., 1892.

Williams, Clarence R. "A word-study of Hebrews XIII." In *The Journal of Biblical Literature*, 30, 1911, 129–136.

Windisch, Hans. *Der Hebräerbrief, HNT*, 14, Tübingen: J.C.B. Mohr, 1931.

Windle, Bryan. "Biblical Sites: Three Discoveries at Jericho," 25/5/2019; https://biblearchaeologyreport.com/2019/05/25/biblical-sites-three-discoveries-at-jericho/

Weiss, Bernard. *Handbuch über den Brief an der Hebräer*. Meyer Komentar, Göttingen: Vancenhoeck und Ruprect, 1888.

Wood, Bryant. "The Walls of Jericho." *Creation*, 21, 2, March 1999, 36–40.

Wright, Tom. *Hebrews for Everyone*, London: SPCK, 2003, 2004.